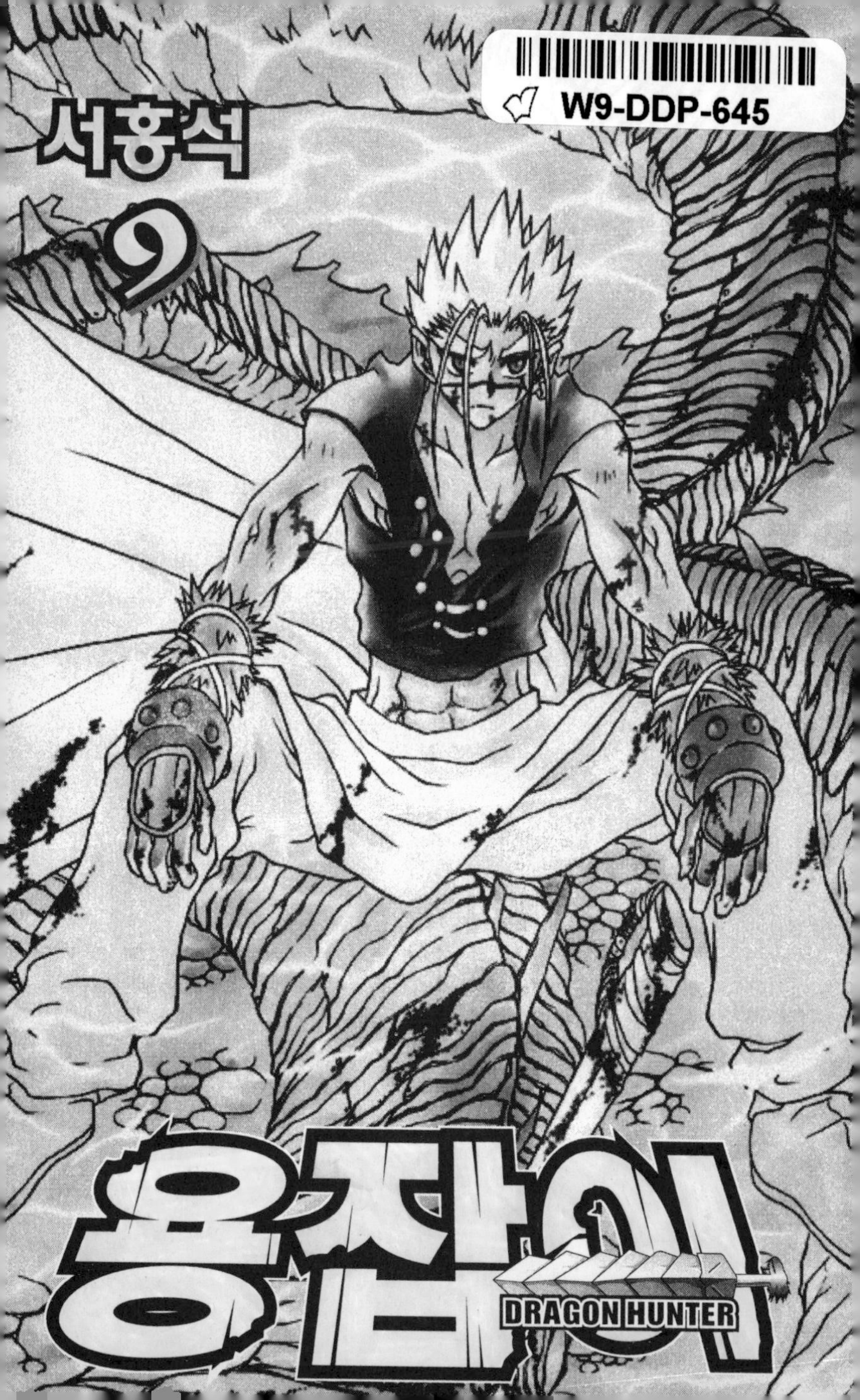
서홍석
9
용잡이
DRAGON HUNTER

Dragon Hunter Vol. 9
Created by Hong Seock Seo with Studio Redstone

Translation - Hye-Young Im
English Adaptation - J. Torres
Associate Editor - Troy Lewter
Retouch and Lettering - JUNEMOON Studios
Production Artist - John Lo
Cover Layout - Patrick Hook

Editor - Rob Tokar
Digital Imaging Manager - Chris Buford
Pre-Press Manager - Antonio DePietro
Production Managers - Jennifer Miller and Mutsumi Miyazaki
Art Director - Matt Alford
Managing Editor - Jill Freshney
VP of Production - Ron Klamert
President and C.O.O. - John Parker
Publisher and C.E.O. - Stuart Levy

A  Manga

TOKYOPOP Inc.
5900 Wilshire Blvd. Suite 2000
Los Angeles, CA 90036

E-mail: info@TOKYOPOP.com
Come visit us online at www.TOKYOPOP.com

ISBN: 1-59182-439-7

First TOKYOPOP printing: November 2004
10 9 8 7 6 5 4 3 2 1
Printed in the USA

DRAGON HUNTER™

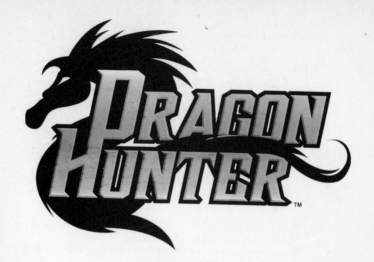

VOLUME 9
BY
HONG SEOCK SEO
WITH
STUDIO REDSTONE

TOKYOPOP®

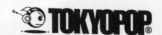

HAMBURG // LONDON // LOS ANGELES // TOKYO

WHO'S WHO IN DRAGON HUNTER

SEUR-CHONG:

There's only one thing Seur-Chong loves more than hunting dragons, and that's getting paid for doing it. He's infected with the Dragon's Curse, a condition that gives him incredible strength and stamina, but is slowly killing him. Despite his greedy nature, he has a heart almost as big as his enormous sword.

As far back as he can remember, Seur-Chong was part of the gang of assassins known as the Yong-Chun. He doesn't recall when he started working for them or why...only that his life was forfeit if he didn't. The closest thing Seur-Chong had to a father figure was his master, the Captain of the Fight Instructors. Seur-Chong's master also mentored Kok-Jung, despite worries about the young man's innate brutality. Seur-Chong and Kok-Jung were like brothers...until the master defected from the Yong-Chun.

Unfortunately, quitting the Yong-Chun is considered betrayal, and betrayal is punishable by death. The Yong-Chun offered the Captain of the Fight Instructors' job as a reward for whomever killed him. Seur-Chong could never kill his own master... but Kok-Jung had no such qualms. That day, Seur-Chong decided to leave the Yong-Chun and, soon after, the politically troubled country splintered into many new kingdoms. Many members of the Yong-Chun were absorbed into the Chunjoo, a group that has already tried to kill Seur-Chong and his associates.

Recently, Seur-Chong embarked on a quest to rescue his mother frozen in ice atop Mount Bak-Do, home to the powerful Blue Dragon. In the subsequent battle with the Blue Dragon, Seur-Chong's mother sacrificed herself to save him and his friends. He was also shocked to learn that the Daechang-Nim of the Chunjoo was his father.

In the context of this book, Mi-Ru-Me is Seur-Chong's title and means "The best of all dragon hunters." In Korean, Mi-Ru (mee-roo) is an old word for dragon and "me" (meh) means mountain peak. Together, the two terms mean "best" or "highest".

MYUNG-HO:

A rare male shaman born with exceptional gifts (most shamen are female), Myung-Ho can cast spells that confuse or control the minds of most dragons. Myung-Ho lost his right eye during a dragon hunt that went awry. In an uncharacteristic moment of sympathy, Seur-Chong helped Myung-Ho in his moment of need, and the two young men became business partners.

Recently, during a particularly difficult dragon hunt, Seur-Chong and Myung-Ho were betrayed by the Chunjoo, a mysterious and powerful dragon-hunting gang that doesn't tolerate competition. The Chunjoo planned to kill Myung-Ho and, with him, the control spell Myung-Ho was casting. With the spell gone, Seur-Chong would have been no match for the dragon. In the ensuing melee, Myung-Ho was mortally wounded.

Seeing only one way to save Myung-Ho's life, Seur-Chong gave his dying friend a drink of dragon's blood. The young shaman's strength was restored, but now Myung-Ho must endure the dreaded dragon's curse: power that will eventually cost him his life. Myung-Ho has already manifested an incredible "second sight"...seen through a monstrous third eye in the middle of his forehead!

In their latest battle with the Blue Dragon, Myung-Ho's sister sacrificed herself to save him. He has since blamed himself for her death and carries a heavy conscience.

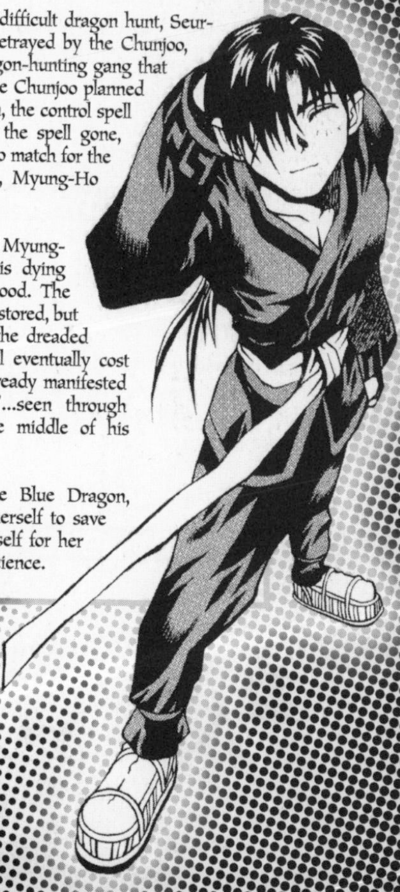

MONG-YEUN:

A shaman with a soft spot for dragons, she was in So-Chun's service until she stole a dragon from her master. Now she's joined with Seur-Chong and Myung-Ho, but she finds the mercenary lifestyle not to her liking.

ARANSEUR:

Myung-Ho's little sister, Aranseur died saving her brother's life.

CHUNJOO

A shadowy clan of professional dragon hunters originally from Bal-Hae. Over the years, their numbers grew as they forced independent dragon hunters to join them...or die. Now, the clan is huge and powerful and still just as determined to wipe out their competition as they are to kill dragons.

DAECHANG-NIM / SEUR-CHUN:

Leader of the Invisible Shadow Killer Clan of the Chunjoo. Like Seur-Chong, he, too has the Dragon's Curse. He recently revealed that Yeun-Wha (Seur-Chong's mother) is his wife, and that Seur-Chong is in fact his son.

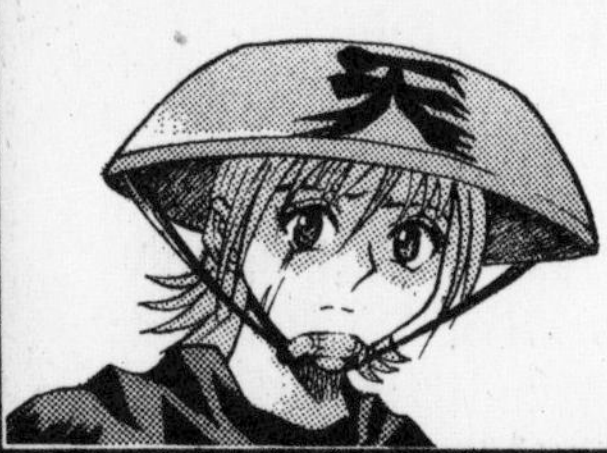

天

RU-AHN

Daechang-Nim's right-hand woman. Daechang-Nim assassinated her father, so she is biding her time as his assistant until she can avenge her father's death.

TAE-RANG / KOK-JUNG

A former colleague turned rival of Seur-Chong, formerly known as Kok-Jung (which means "worry" in Korean).

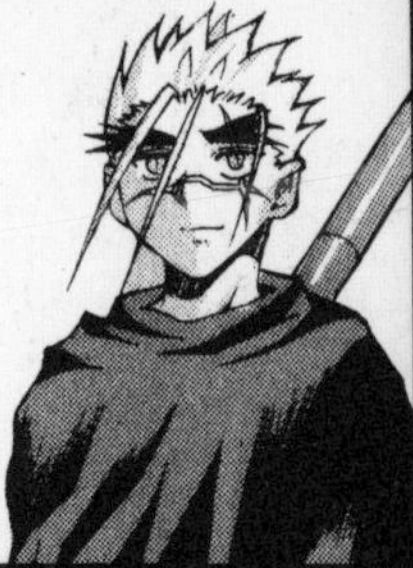

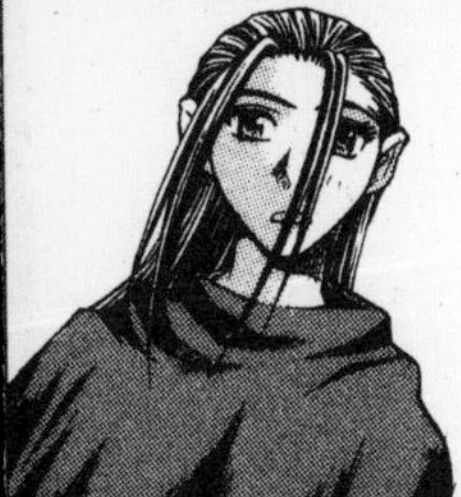

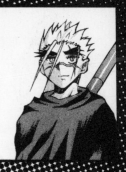

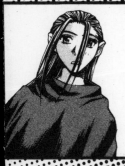

BEUL-HEE

A sometimes mean and stuck-up shaman, Beul-Hee trained at the same time and place as Mong-Yuen...though Mong-Yuen's abilities far outshined Beul-Hee's. When her training had been completed, Beul-Hee's first assignment was to a rough, unglamorous area near the Chinese border.

SO-CHUN

A powerful shaman, she's also the feudal lord of the Kaya Province. She served as a shaman's apprentice under Yeun-Wha.

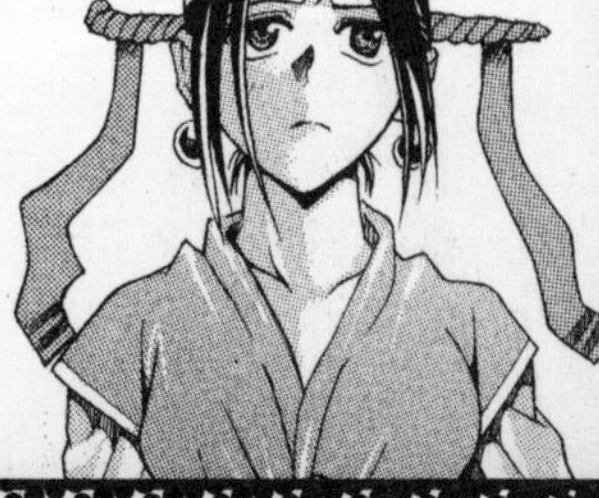

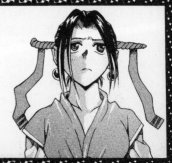

THE STORY THUS FAR

SEUR-CHONG IS AN ELITE (AND CASH-OBSESSED) DRAGON HUNTER WHO, DUE TO AN INVOLUNTARY INFUSION OF DRAGON'S BLOOD, POSSESSES INCREDIBLE STRENGTH AND DURABILITY...ALONG WITH A SUBSTANTIALLY SHORTENED LIFESPAN. SEUR-CHONG'S PARTNER, MYUNG-HO, IS A SHAMAN WHO CAN USE MAGIC TO CONTROL DRAGONS--AND THUS MAKE THEM EASIER TO KILL.

NOT LONG AGO, DURING A PARTICULARLY DIFFICULT DRAGON HUNT, THE CHUNJOO--A MYSTERIOUS AND POWERFUL DRAGON-HUNTING GANG THAT DOESN'T TOLERATE COMPETITION--INTERFERED, AND MORTALLY WOUNDED MYUNG-HO.

SEEING ONLY ONE WAY TO SAVE MYUNG-HO'S LIFE, SEUR-CHONG GAVE HIS DYING FRIEND A DRINK OF DRAGON'S BLOOD. THE YOUNG SHAMAN'S STRENGTH WAS RESTORED, BUT NOW MYUNG-HO MUST ENDURE THE DREADED DRAGON'S CURSE: POWER THAT WILL EVENTUALLY COST HIM HIS LIFE. MYUNG-HO HAS ALREADY MANIFESTED AN INCREDIBLE "SECOND SIGHT"...SEEN THROUGH A MONSTROUS THIRD EYE IN THE MIDDLE OF HIS FOREHEAD!

RECENTLY, SEUR-CHONG AND COMPANY LEFT THE KAYA PROVINCE FOR SHI-LA. THEIR QUEST: TO END THE DRAGON'S CURSE ON THE TWO MEN BY SLAYING THE DRAGON GOD. OF COURSE, NOBODY GETS TO THE DRAGON GOD WITHOUT FIRST DEALING WITH DRAGON GOD'S GUARDIAN...AND THE DRAGON GOD'S GUARDIAN HAS NEVER BEEN DEFEATED.

SEUR-CHONG COULDN'T HELP BUT NOTICE AN UNSETTLING CONNECTION BETWEEN HIMSELF AND THE DAECHANG-NIM OF THE CHUNJOO. UPON REACHING SHI-LA, MYUNG-HO DISCOVERED THAT SEUR-CHONG HAD BILLIONS HORDED AWAY IN A PERSONAL SAVINGS ACCOUNT...AND THAT THE MONEY WAS SLATED TO EQUIP A MISSION TO RESCUE SEUR-CHONG'S MOTHER, YEUN-WHA, WHO HAD BEEN FROZEN IN SUSPENDED ANIMATION WITHIN THE ICE ATOP MOUNT BAK-DO (SPIRIT MOUNTAIN) FOR 15 YEARS.

WITH THE HELP OF MYUNG-HO'S SISTER ARANSEUR, AS WELL AS DRAGON HUNTER GOON-CHUN AND SHAMAN MONG-YEUN, SEUR-CHONG AND HIS COMRADES JOURNEYED TO MOUNT BAK-DO. ALSO LEADING EXPEDITIONS TO SLAY THE BLUE DRAGON WERE THE CHUNJOO AND THE DAEMACKLEEJEE (PRIME MINISTER) OF KO-GU-RYO. HOWEVER, EVEN THOUGH THEY SHARED THE SAME MISSION, THEY WERE NOT NECESSARILY ALLIES.

WHEN SEUR-CHONG'S PARTY ARRIVED AT MOUNT BAK DO, THEY WERE CONFRONTED BY THE CHUNJOO AND DAECHANG-NIM. DAECHANG-NIM WARNED SEUR-CHONG TO STAY AWAY FROM THE MOUNTAIN, AND LATER, EN ROUTE TO RETRIEVE YEUN-WHA AND BRING HER BACK TO THE BLUE DRAGON'S REALM, REVEALED TO HIS APPRENTICE RU-AHN THAT YEUN-WHA IS HIS WIFE.

DESPITE DAECHANG-NIM'S WARNING, SEUR-CHONG LED HIS PARTY TO FACE THE BLUE DRAGON. UNFORTUNATELY, THE ALREADY DAUNTING MISSION BECAME EVEN MORE DIFFICULT WITH ATTACKS FROM CHINESE DRAGON HUNTERS, THE CHINESE ARMY AND ONE OF SEUR-CHONG'S OWN HIRED FIGHTERS.

WHILE FRANTICALLY TRYING TO ESCAPE THE BLUE DRAGON'S CAVE, ARANSEUR SACRIFICED HER LIFE TO SAVE MYUNG-HO, WHILE DAECHANG-NIM CAME TO AID THEM IN ESCAPING THE BLUE DRAGON. AFTER ESCAPING, SEUR-CHONG WAS REUNITED ONE LAST TIME WITH HIS MOTHER BEFORE SHE DIED. DAECHANG-NIM ALSO REVEALED TO SEUR-CHONG THAT HE IS SEUR-CHUN--SEUR-CHONG'S FATHER--BEFORE GOING TO FACE DOWN THE PURSUING BLUE DRAGON.

AFTER A FEROCIOUS BATTLE, RU-AHN TOOK THE SEVERELY INJURED DAECHANG-NIM TO SAFETY. THOUGH RU-AHN RECALLED THAT DAECHANG-NIM ASSASSINATED HER FATHER, THE YOUNG WOMAN PASSED UP THE EASY OPPORTUNITY FOR VENGEANCE.

WHAT LIES IN STORE FOR OUR TWO MOURNING HEROES? WILL TIME HEAL THEIR PAIN, OR TEAR THEM FURTHER APART?

DRAGON HUNTER

About Dragon Hunter, Part 9

Hey, guys! Welcome to volume 9! Finally, the Western dragons are here! However, it won't be until volume ten that you find out more about these creatures. Nonetheless, a dragon is a dragon, despite how differently they are depicted in Asia versus the West.

Allow me to briefly explain: unlike Asian dragons, the Western dragon has wings to fly with, as well as being able to stand on its feet. I borrowed the design and even the history of this dragon from the legend of Siegfried. Siegfried is not the name of the dragon, but rather a character from a German folk tale. It's the story of a knight named Siegfried who saved a princess from an evil dragon who was once a prince. So, I use the name Siegfried because this story has a dragon that fights a heroic knight.

Of course, *Dragon Hunter* and this folk tale are set in different eras, but I simply combined the stories without worrying about the time period. Another special thing in this *Dragon Hunter* story is that King Arthur and his wizard Merlin make a guest appearance. There'll be more on this in volume ten.

Meanwhile, I hope you enjoy the story!

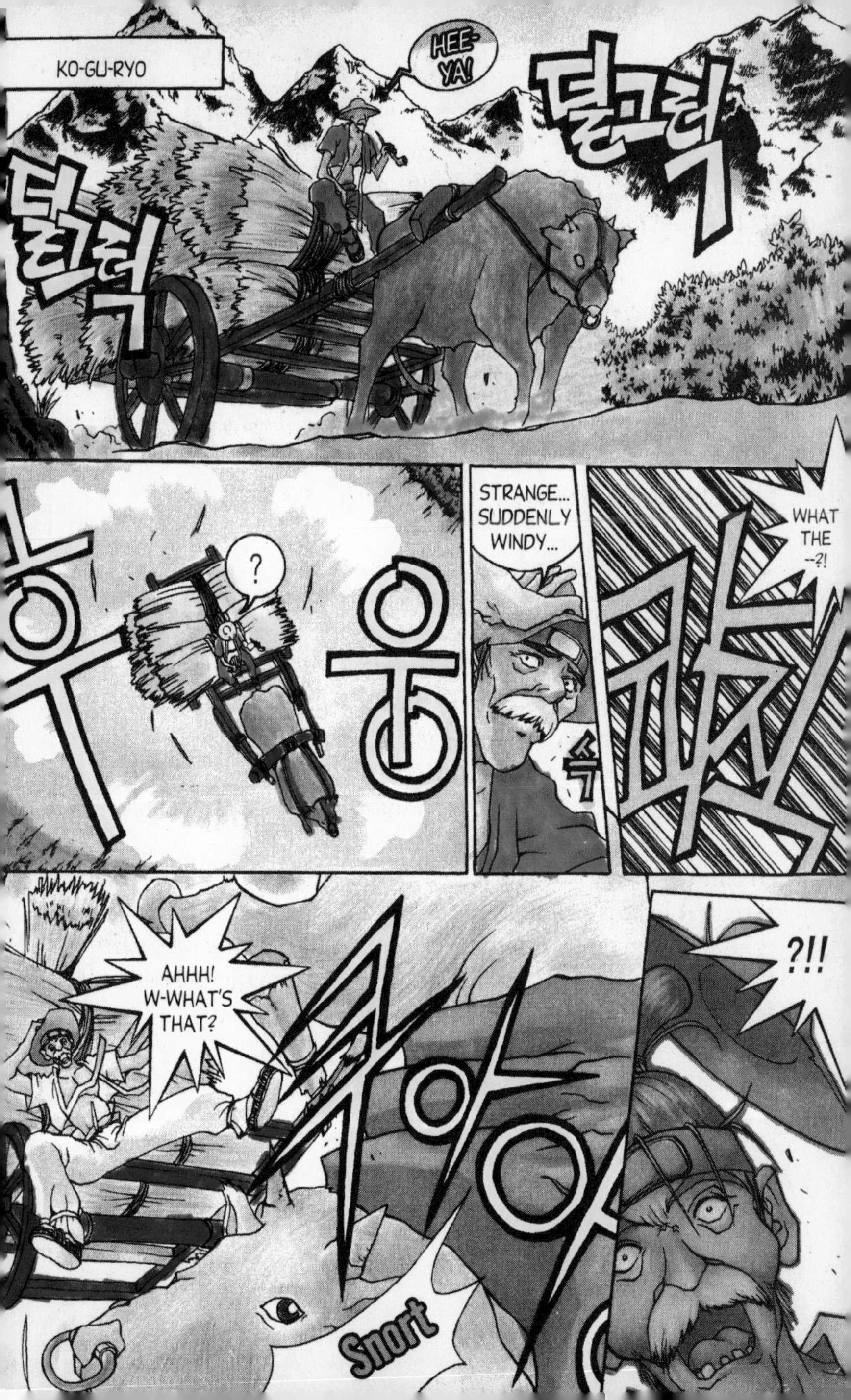
KO-GU-RYO
HEE-YA!
덜그럭
덜그럭
?
STRANGE... SUDDENLY WINDY...
WHAT THE --?!
AHHH! W-WHAT'S THAT?
Snort
?!!

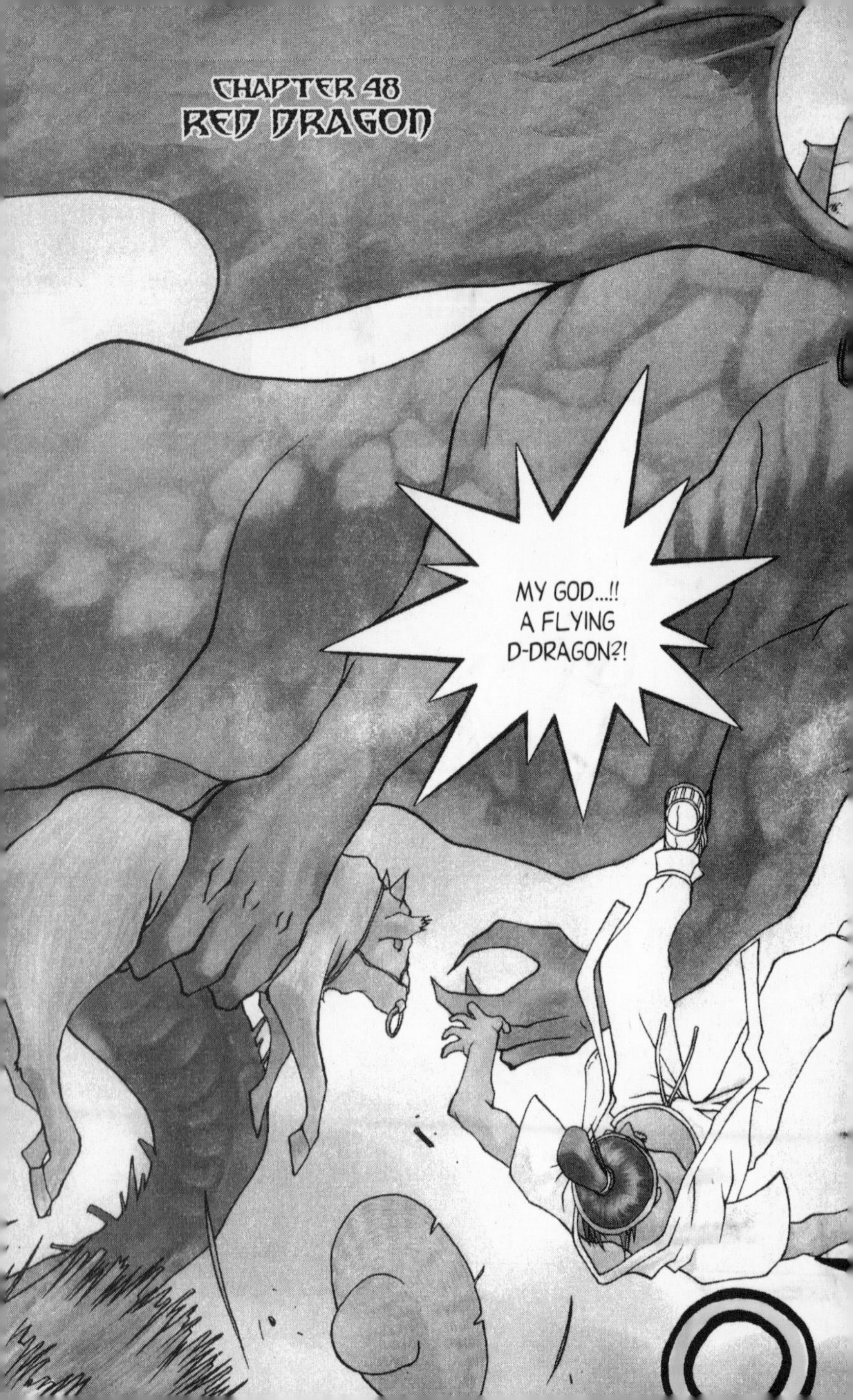
CHAPTER 48
RED DRAGON
MY GOD...!! A FLYING D-DRAGON?!

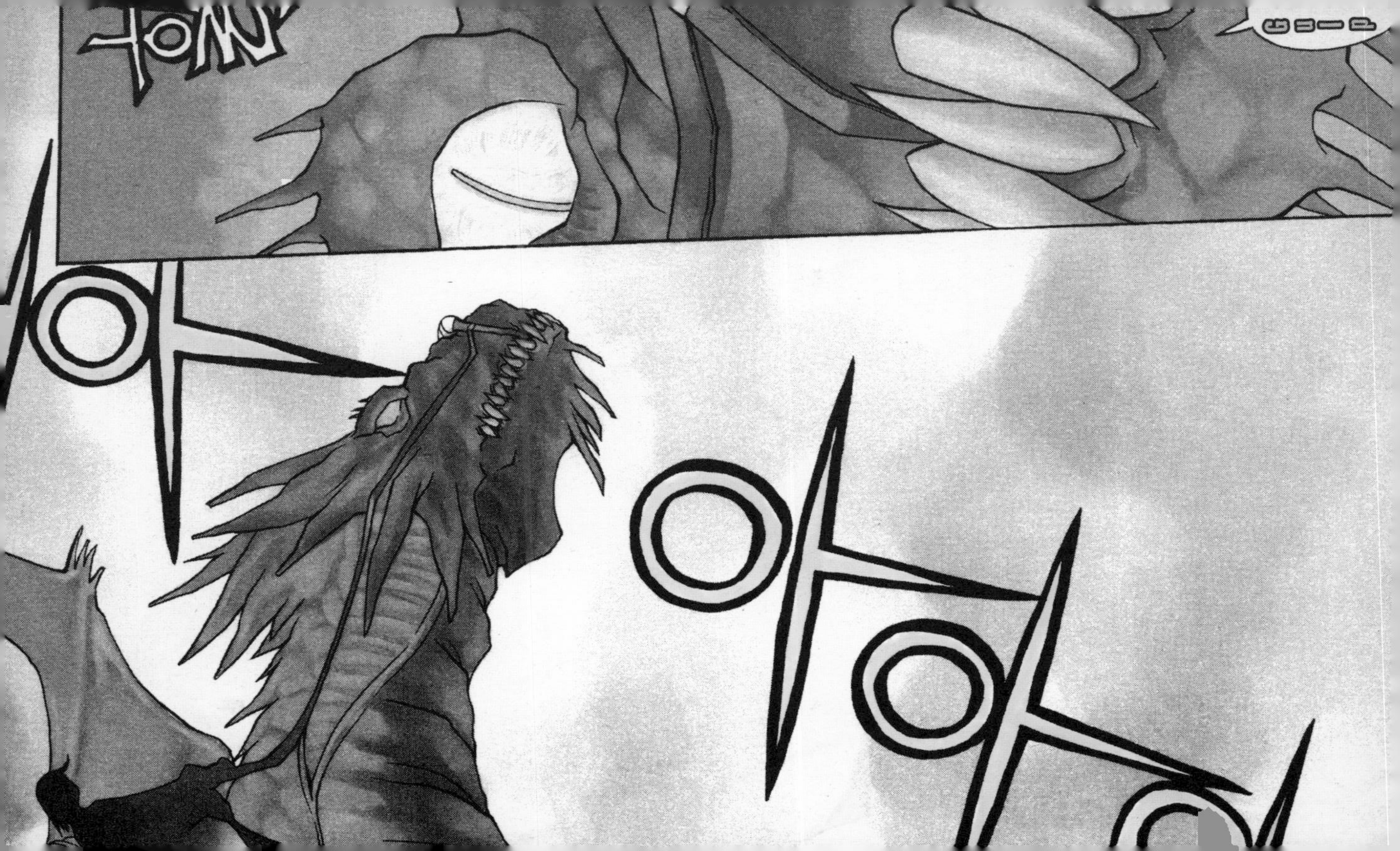
GULP

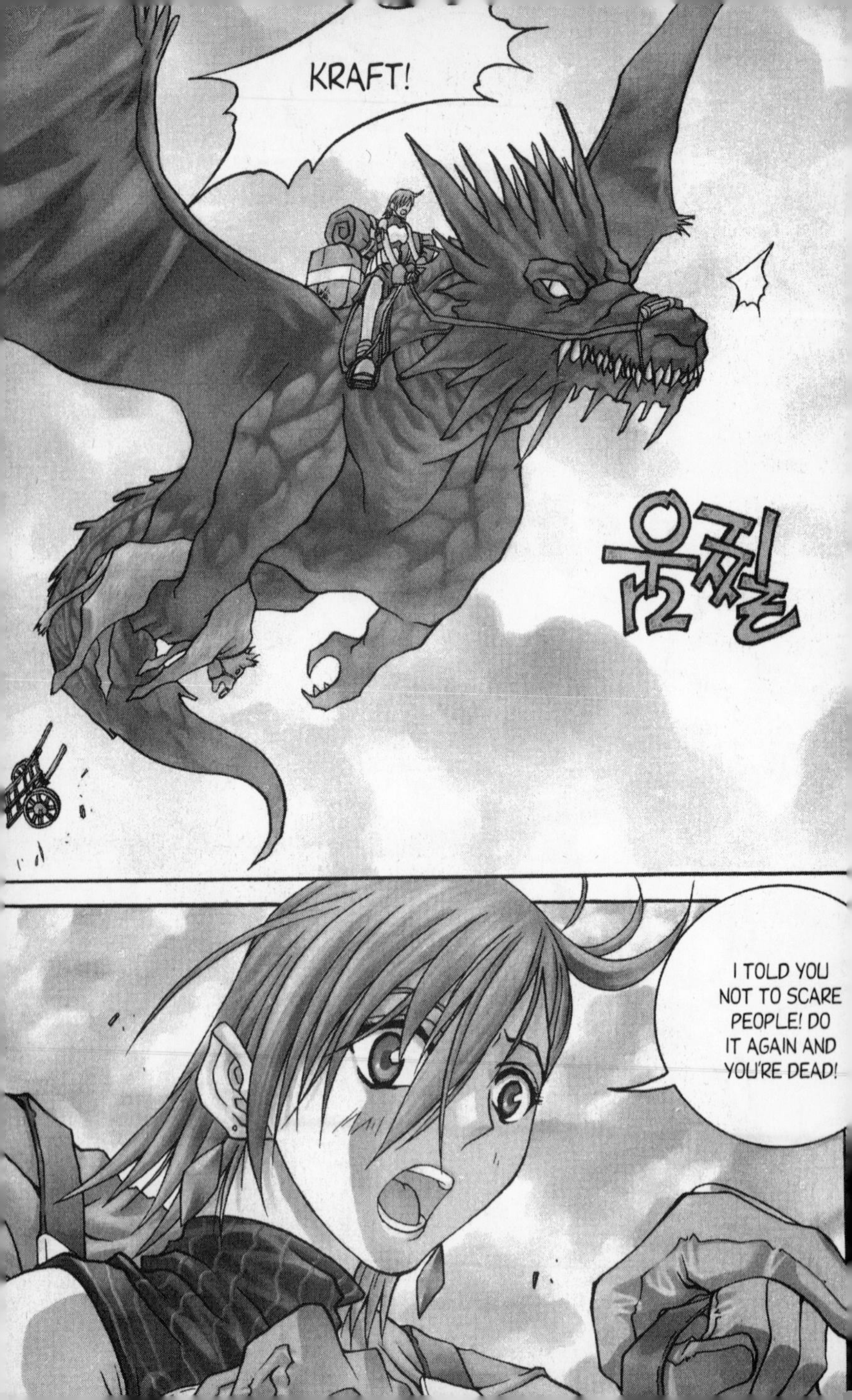
KRAFT!
I TOLD YOU NOT TO SCARE PEOPLE! DO IT AGAIN AND YOU'RE DEAD!

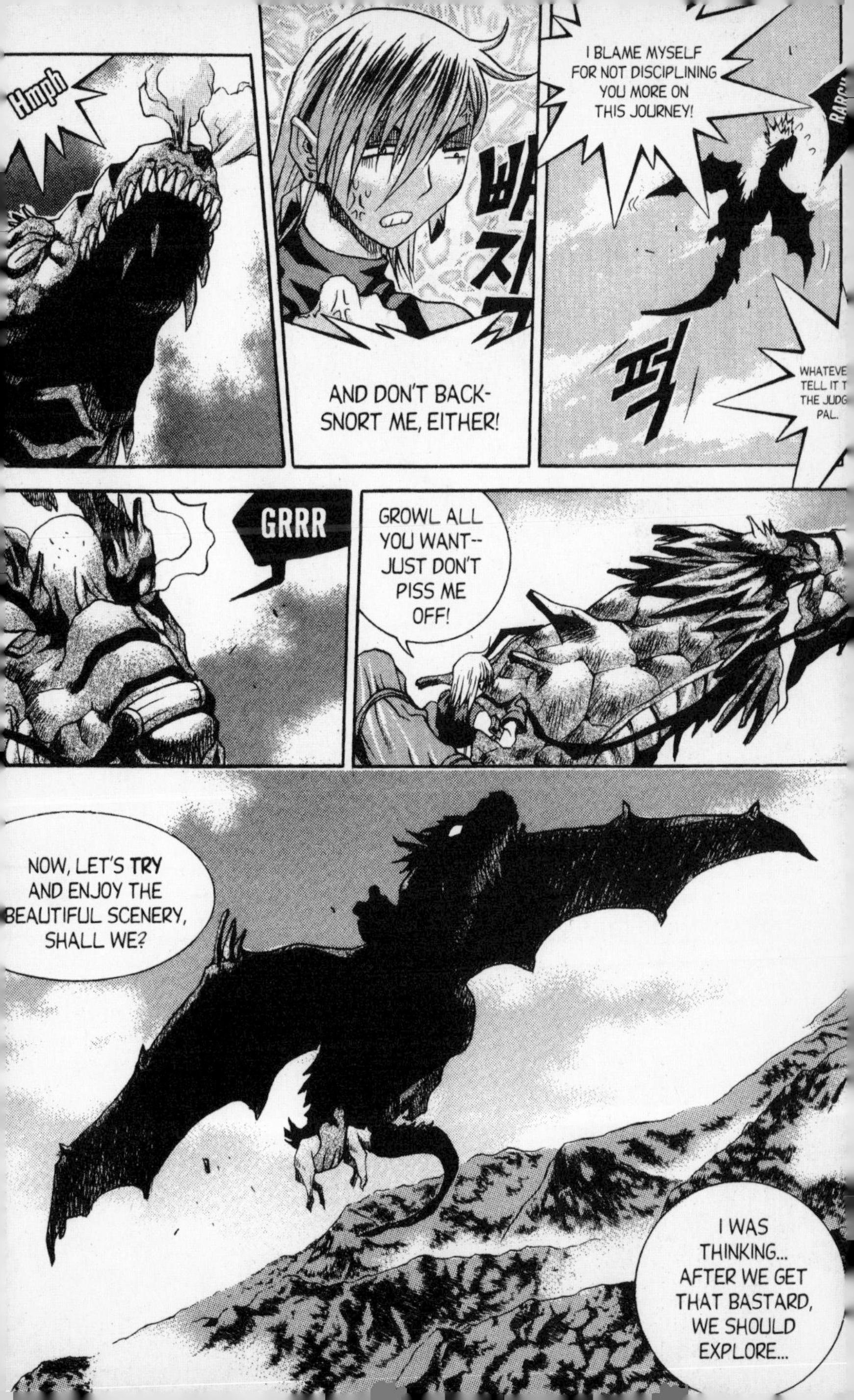
Hmph
AND DON'T BACK-SNORT ME, EITHER!
I BLAME MYSELF FOR NOT DISCIPLINING YOU MORE ON THIS JOURNEY!
퍽
GRRR
GROWL ALL YOU WANT-- JUST DON'T PISS ME OFF!
NOW, LET'S **TRY** AND ENJOY THE BEAUTIFUL SCENERY, SHALL WE?
I WAS THINKING... AFTER WE GET THAT BASTARD, WE SHOULD EXPLORE...

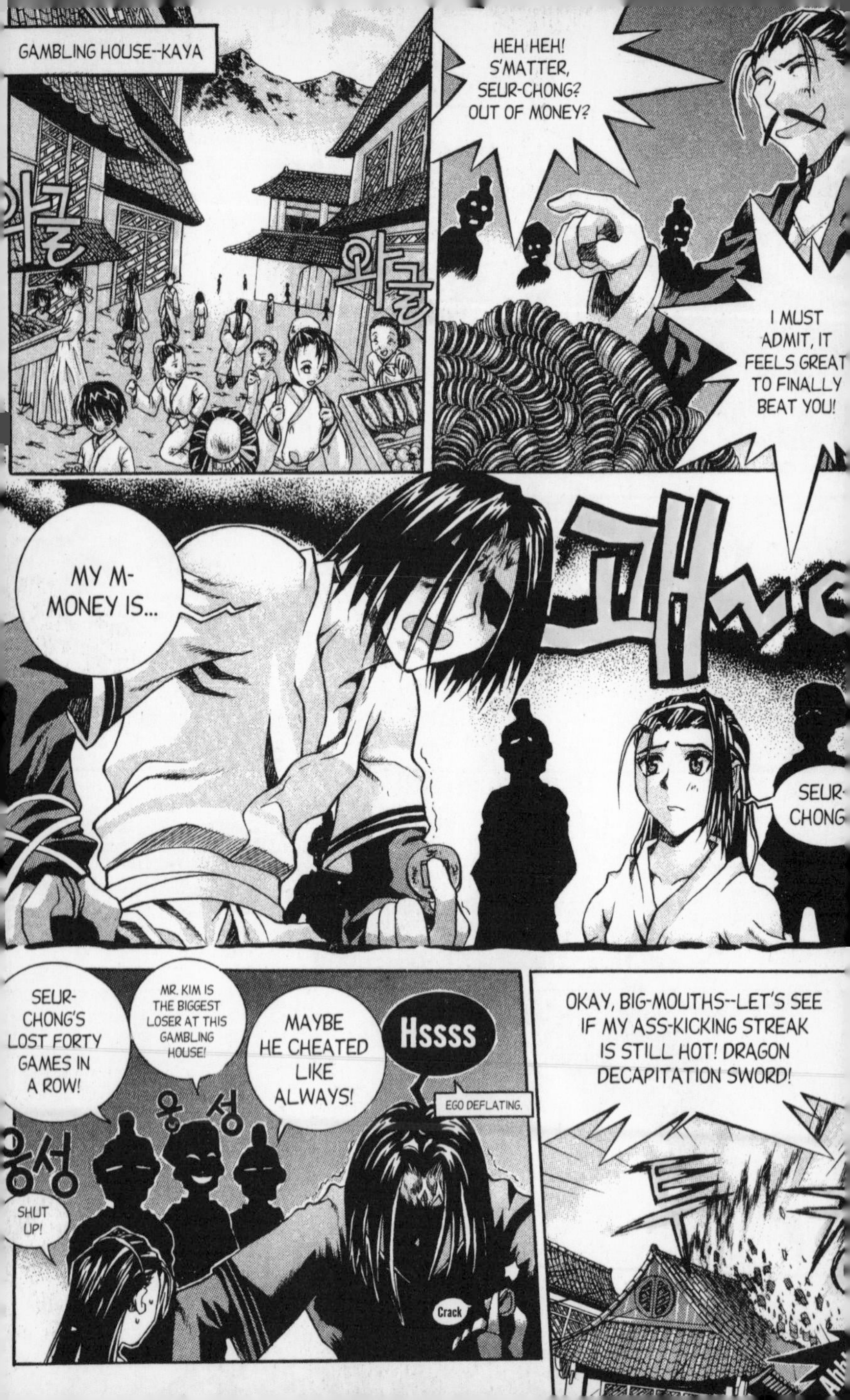
GAMBLING HOUSE--KAYA
와글
와글
HEH HEH! S'MATTER, SEUR-CHONG? OUT OF MONEY?
I MUST ADMIT, IT FEELS GREAT TO FINALLY BEAT YOU!
MY M-MONEY IS...
SEUR-CHONG
SEUR-CHONG'S LOST FORTY GAMES IN A ROW!
MR. KIM IS THE BIGGEST LOSER AT THIS GAMBLING HOUSE!
MAYBE HE CHEATED LIKE ALWAYS!
Hssss
EGO DEFLATING.
웅성
웅성
SHUT UP!
Crack
OKAY, BIG-MOUTHS--LET'S SEE IF MY ASS-KICKING STREAK IS STILL HOT! DRAGON DECAPITATION SWORD!

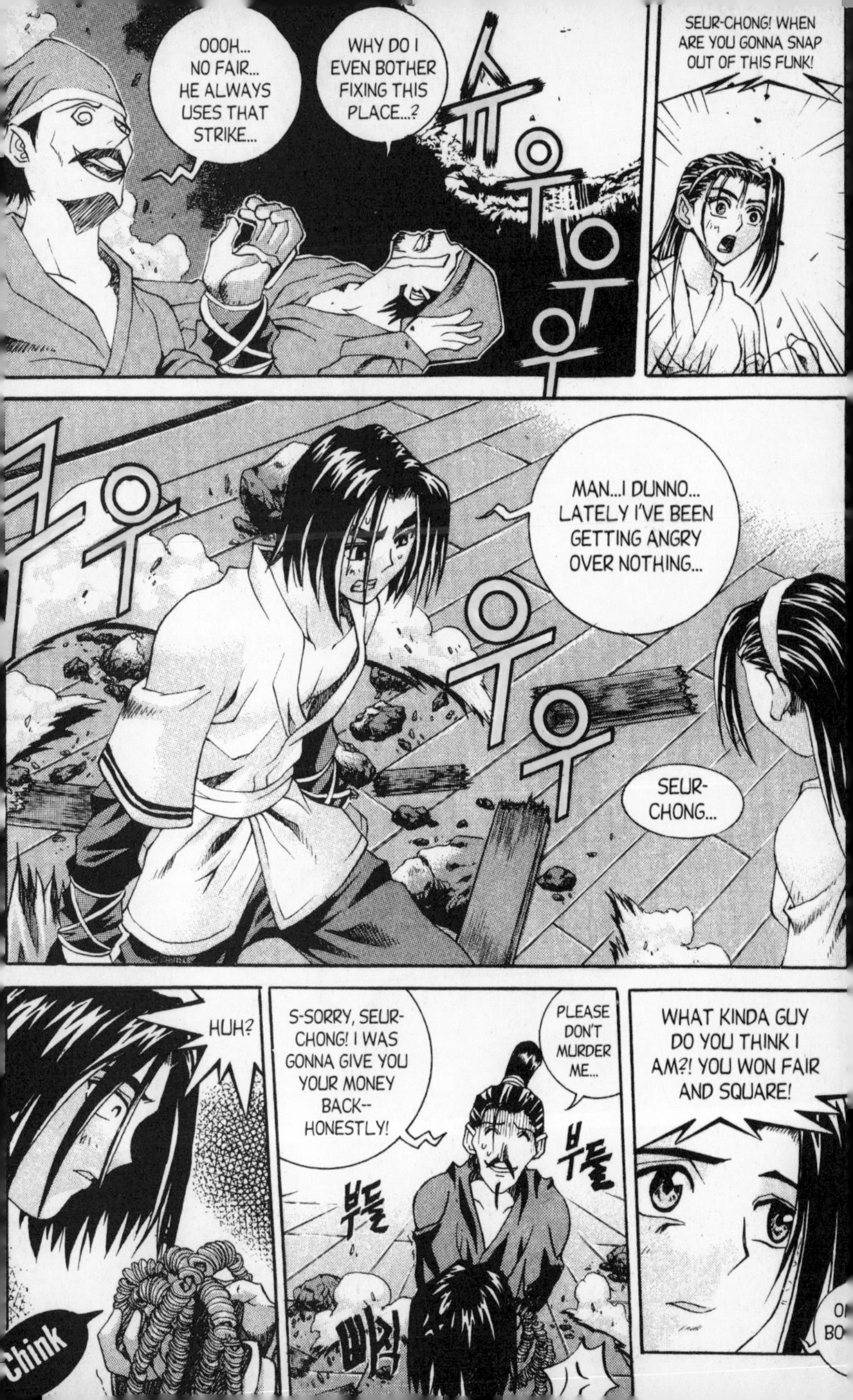
OOOH... NO FAIR... HE ALWAYS USES THAT STRIKE...
WHY DO I EVEN BOTHER FIXING THIS PLACE...?
SEUR-CHONG! WHEN ARE YOU GONNA SNAP OUT OF THIS FUNK!
MAN...I DUNNO... LATELY I'VE BEEN GETTING ANGRY OVER NOTHING...
SEUR-CHONG...
HUH?
Chink
S-SORRY, SEUR-CHONG! I WAS GONNA GIVE YOU YOUR MONEY BACK--HONESTLY!
PLEASE DON'T MURDER ME...
부들
부들
WHAT KINDA GUY DO YOU THINK I AM?! YOU WON FAIR AND SQUARE!

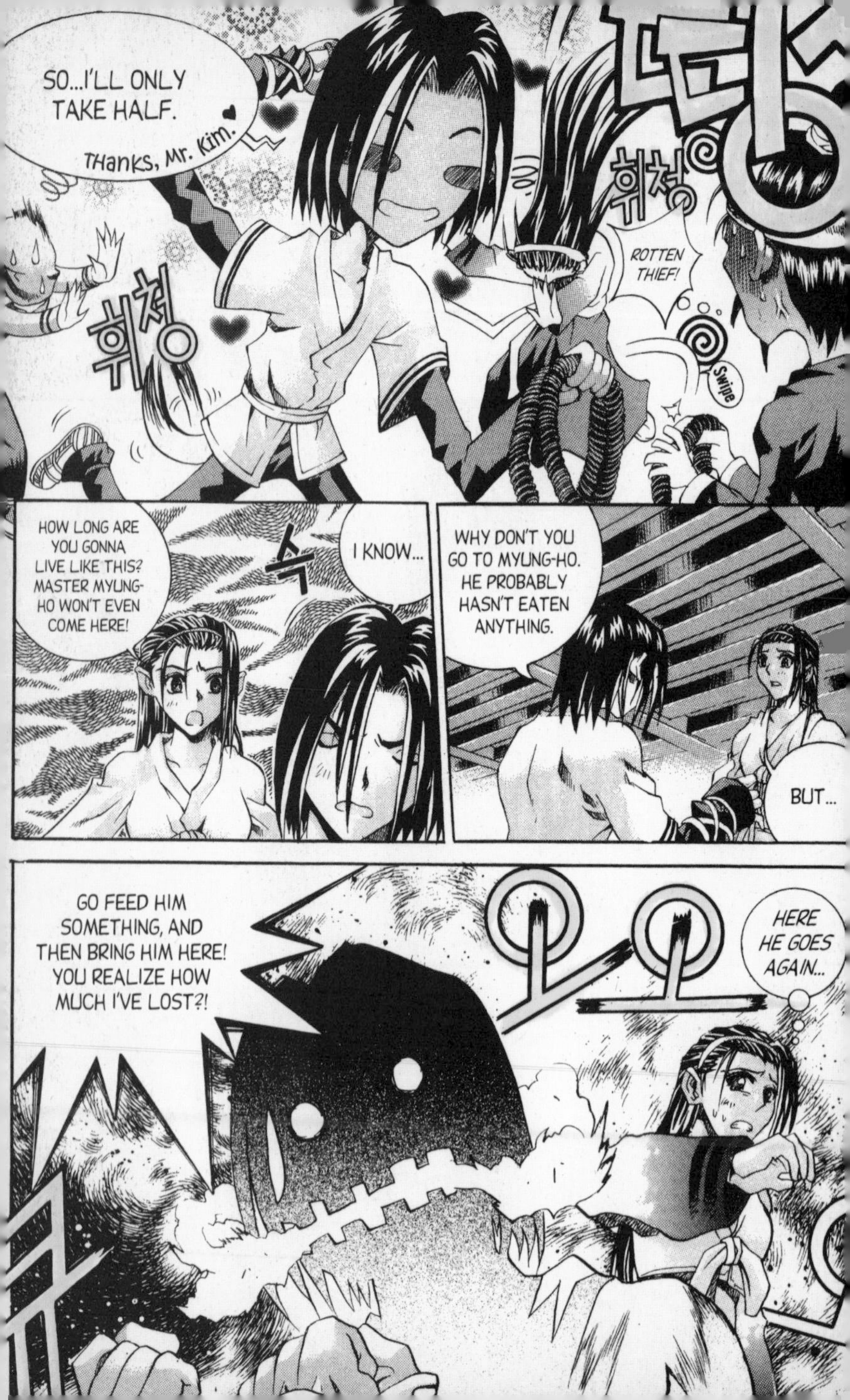
SO...I'LL ONLY TAKE HALF.
Thanks, Mr. Kim.
휘청
휘청
ROTTEN THIEF!
Swipe
HOW LONG ARE YOU GONNA LIVE LIKE THIS? MASTER MYUNG-HO WON'T EVEN COME HERE!
I KNOW...
WHY DON'T YOU GO TO MYUNG-HO. HE PROBABLY HASN'T EATEN ANYTHING.
BUT...
GO FEED HIM SOMETHING, AND THEN BRING HIM HERE! YOU REALIZE HOW MUCH I'VE LOST?!
HERE HE GOES AGAIN...

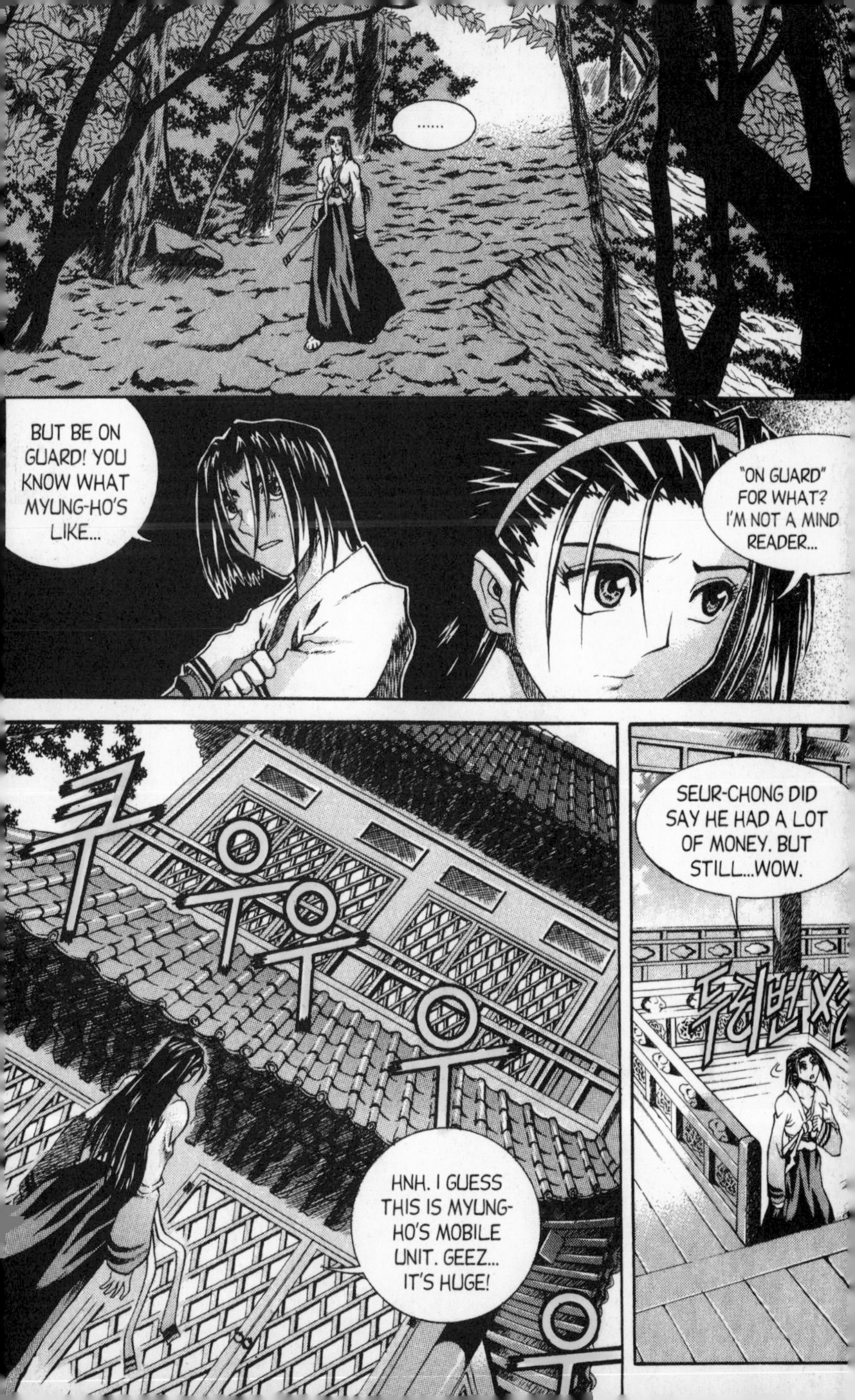
......
BUT BE ON GUARD! YOU KNOW WHAT MYUNG-HO'S LIKE...
"ON GUARD" FOR WHAT? I'M NOT A MIND READER...
HNH. I GUESS THIS IS MYUNG-HO'S MOBILE UNIT. GEEZ... IT'S HUGE!
SEUR-CHONG DID SAY HE HAD A LOT OF MONEY. BUT STILL...WOW.

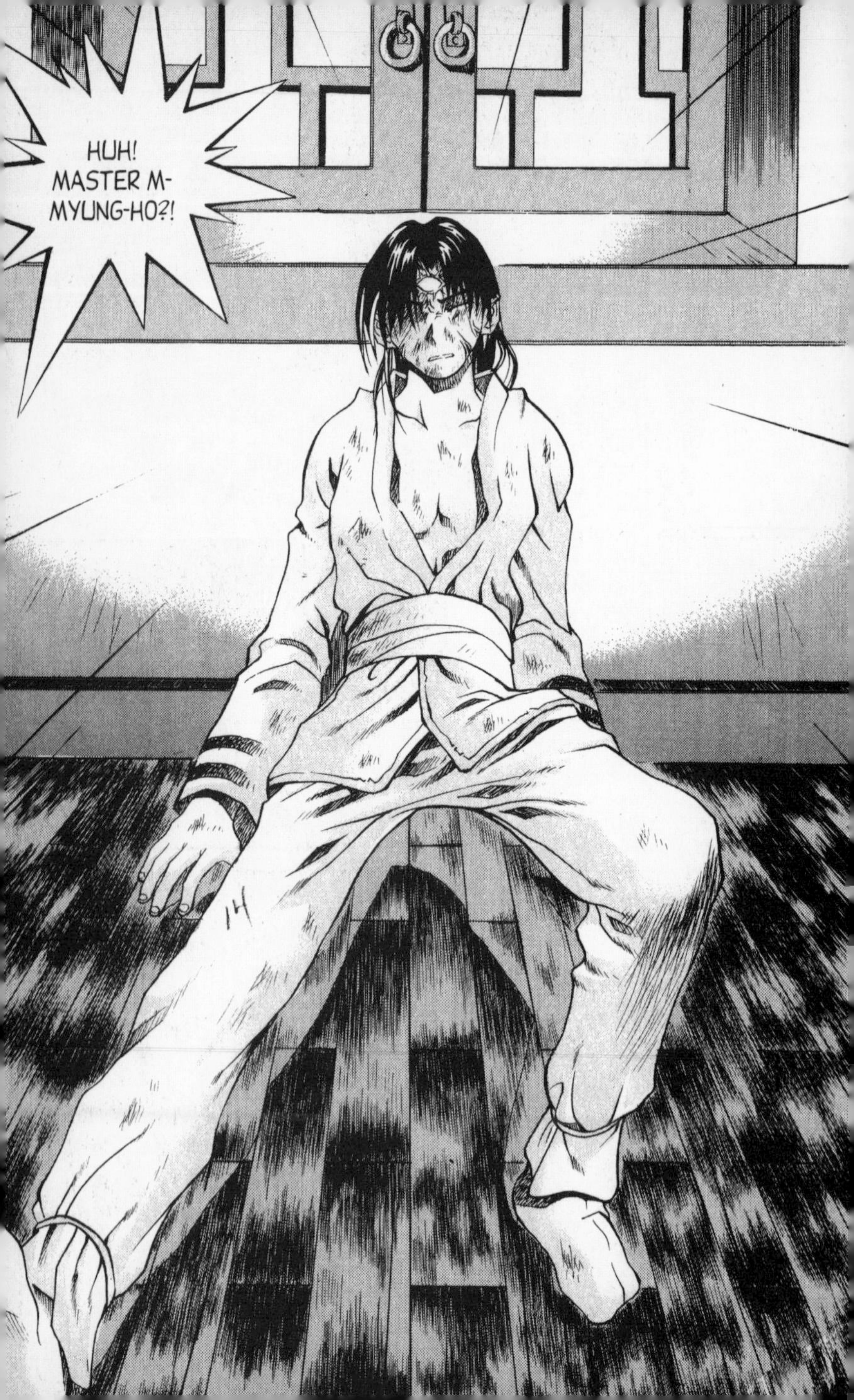
HUH! MASTER M-MYUNG-HO?!

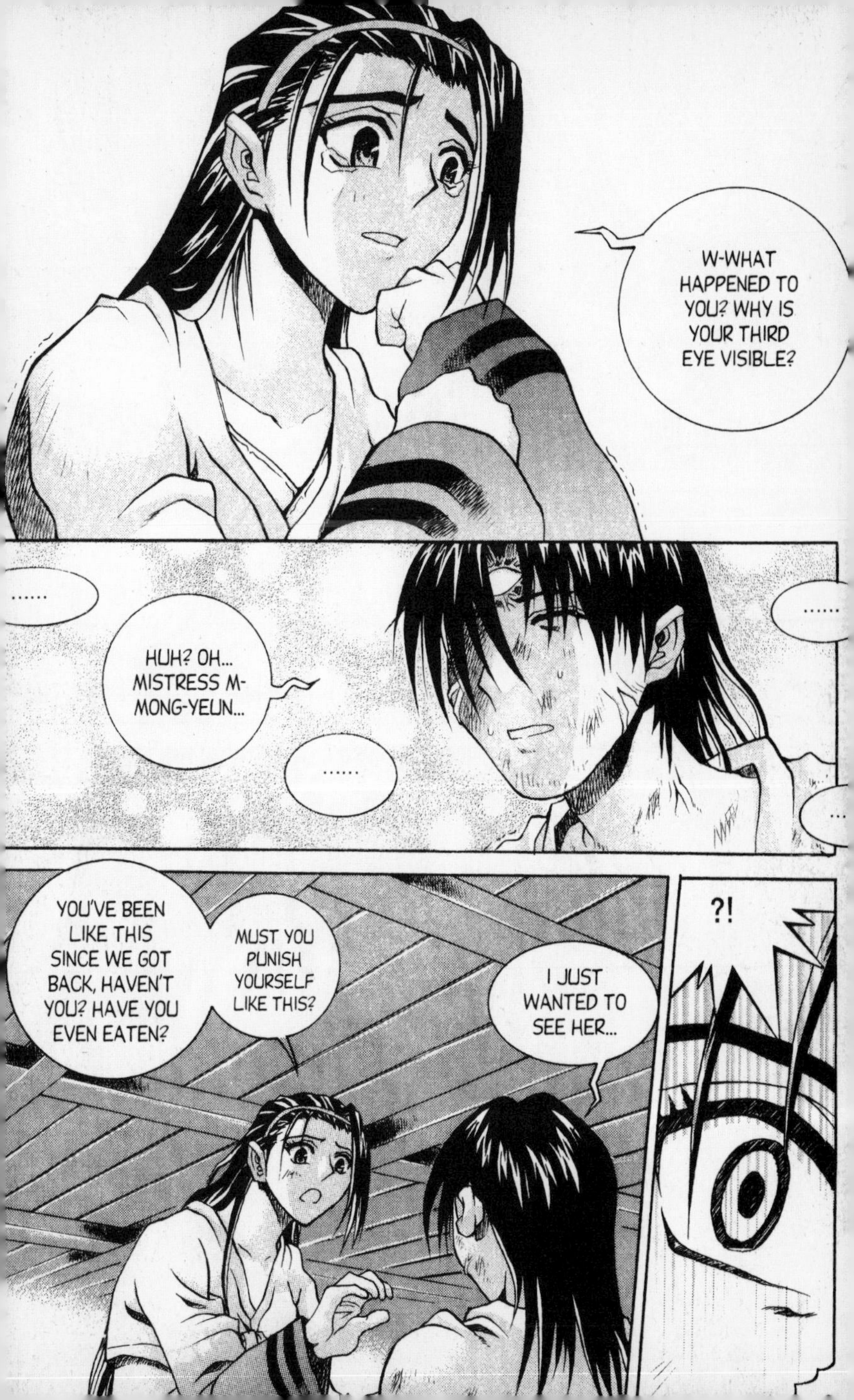
W-WHAT HAPPENED TO YOU? WHY IS YOUR THIRD EYE VISIBLE?
......
HUH? OH... MISTRESS M-MONG-YEUN...
......
......
...
YOU'VE BEEN LIKE THIS SINCE WE GOT BACK, HAVEN'T YOU? HAVE YOU EVEN EATEN?
MUST YOU PUNISH YOURSELF LIKE THIS?
I JUST WANTED TO SEE HER...
?!

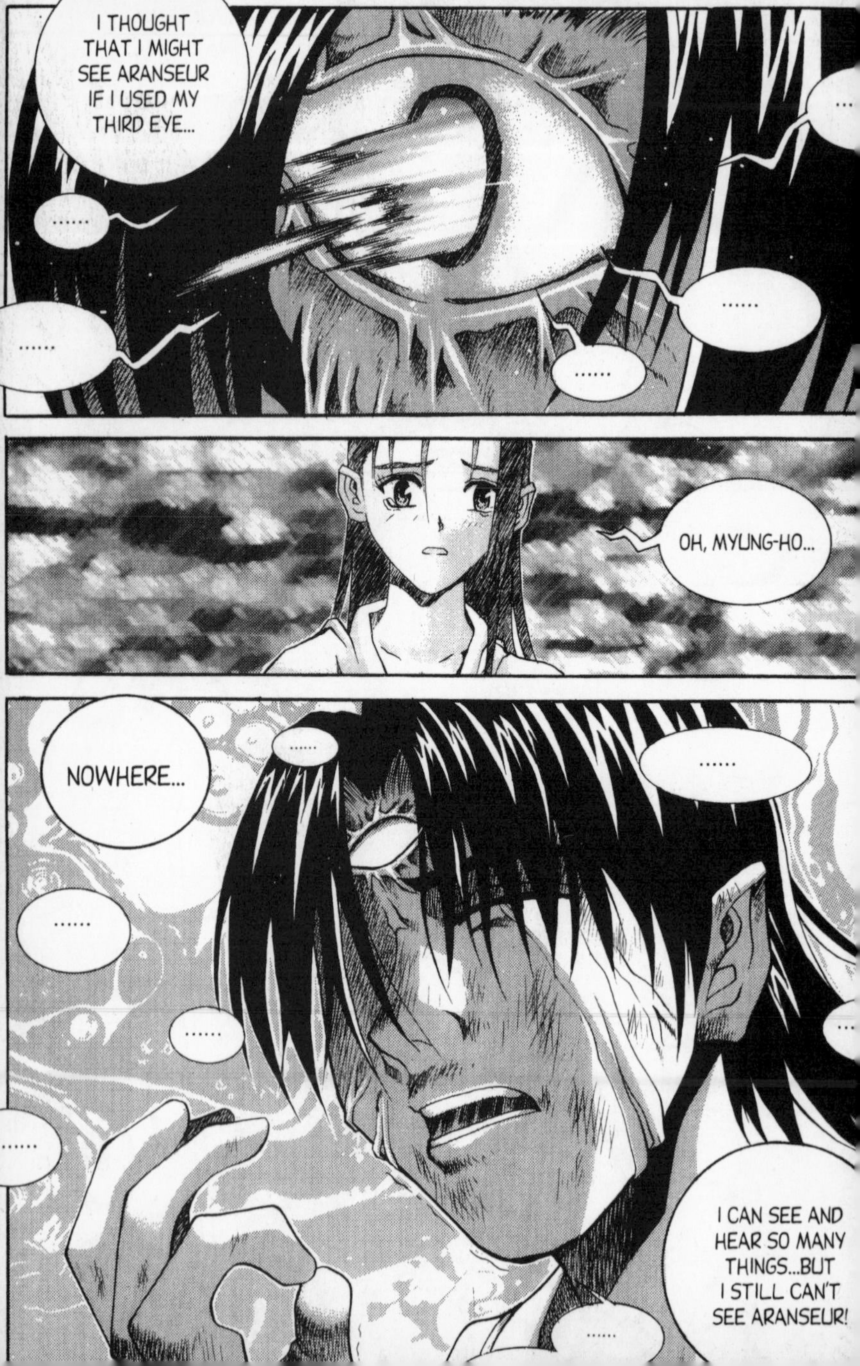
I THOUGHT THAT I MIGHT SEE ARANSEUR IF I USED MY THIRD EYE...
......
......
......
......
OH, MYUNG-HO...
NOWHERE...
......
......
......
......
......
I CAN SEE AND HEAR SO MANY THINGS...BUT I STILL CAN'T SEE ARANSEUR!
......

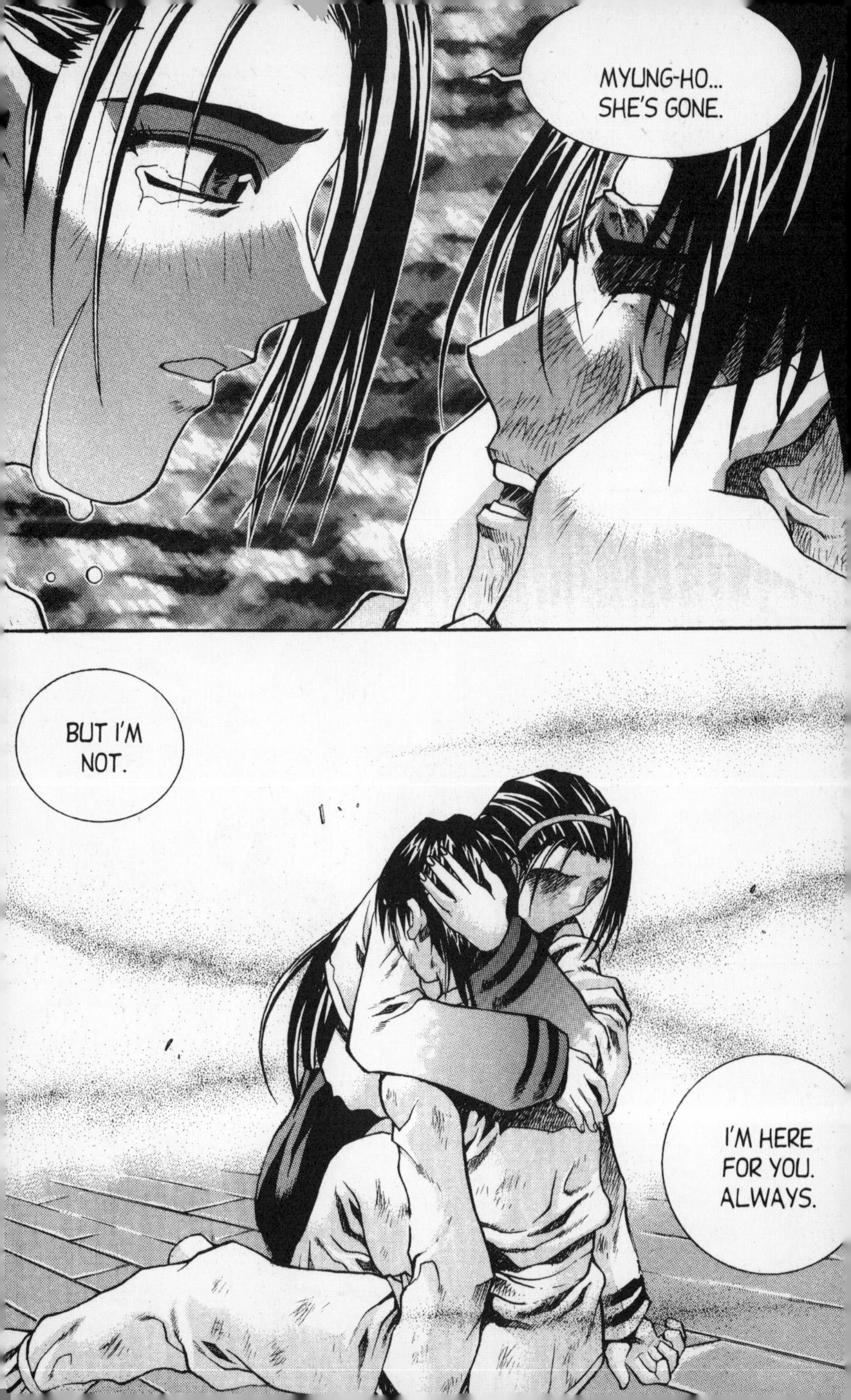
MYUNG-HO... SHE'S GONE.
BUT I'M NOT.
I'M HERE FOR YOU. ALWAYS.

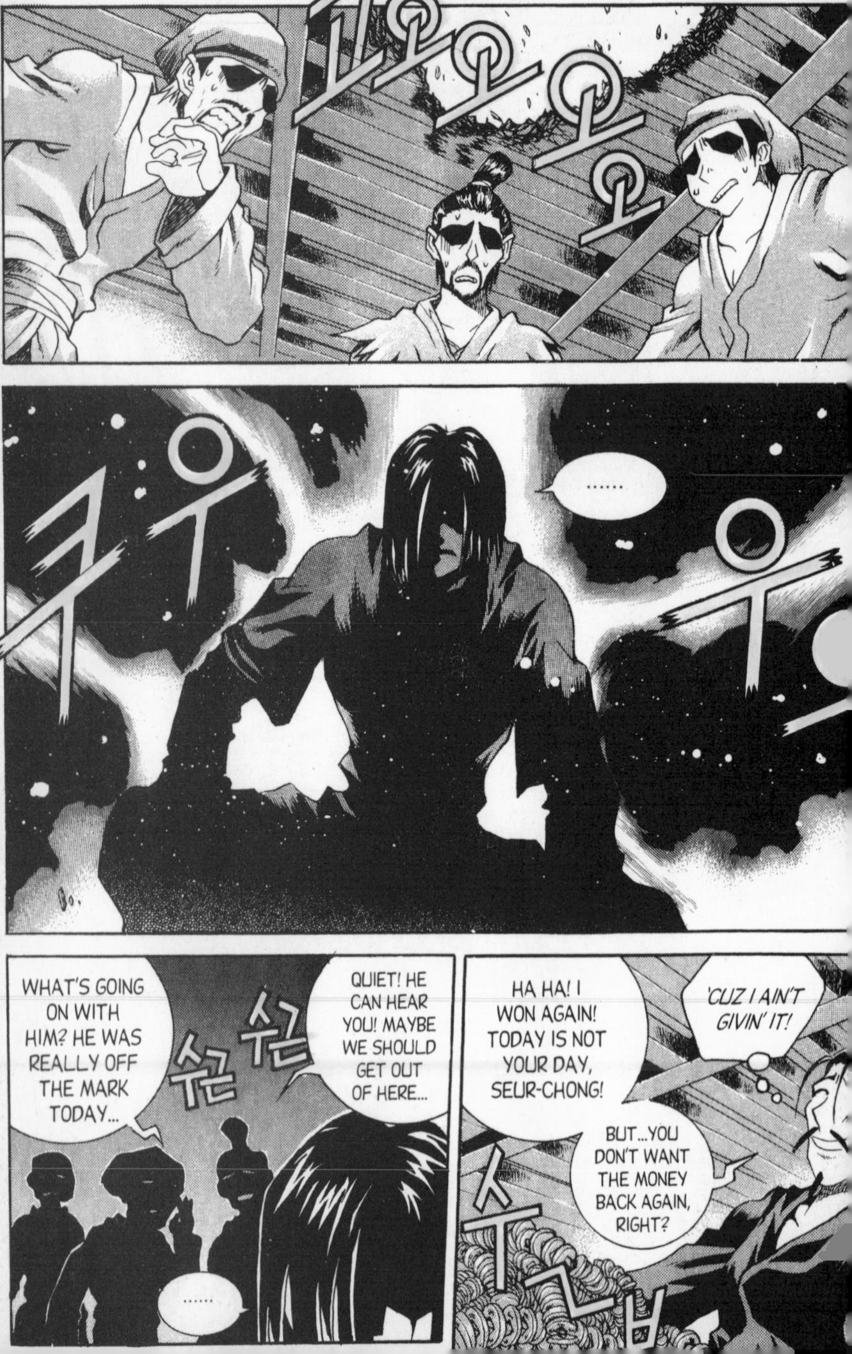
......
WHAT'S GOING ON WITH HIM? HE WAS REALLY OFF THE MARK TODAY...
수근 수근
QUIET! HE CAN HEAR YOU! MAYBE WE SHOULD GET OUT OF HERE...
......
HA HA! I WON AGAIN! TODAY IS NOT YOUR DAY, SEUR-CHONG!
'CUZ I AIN'T GIVIN' IT!
BUT...YOU DON'T WANT THE MONEY BACK AGAIN, RIGHT?

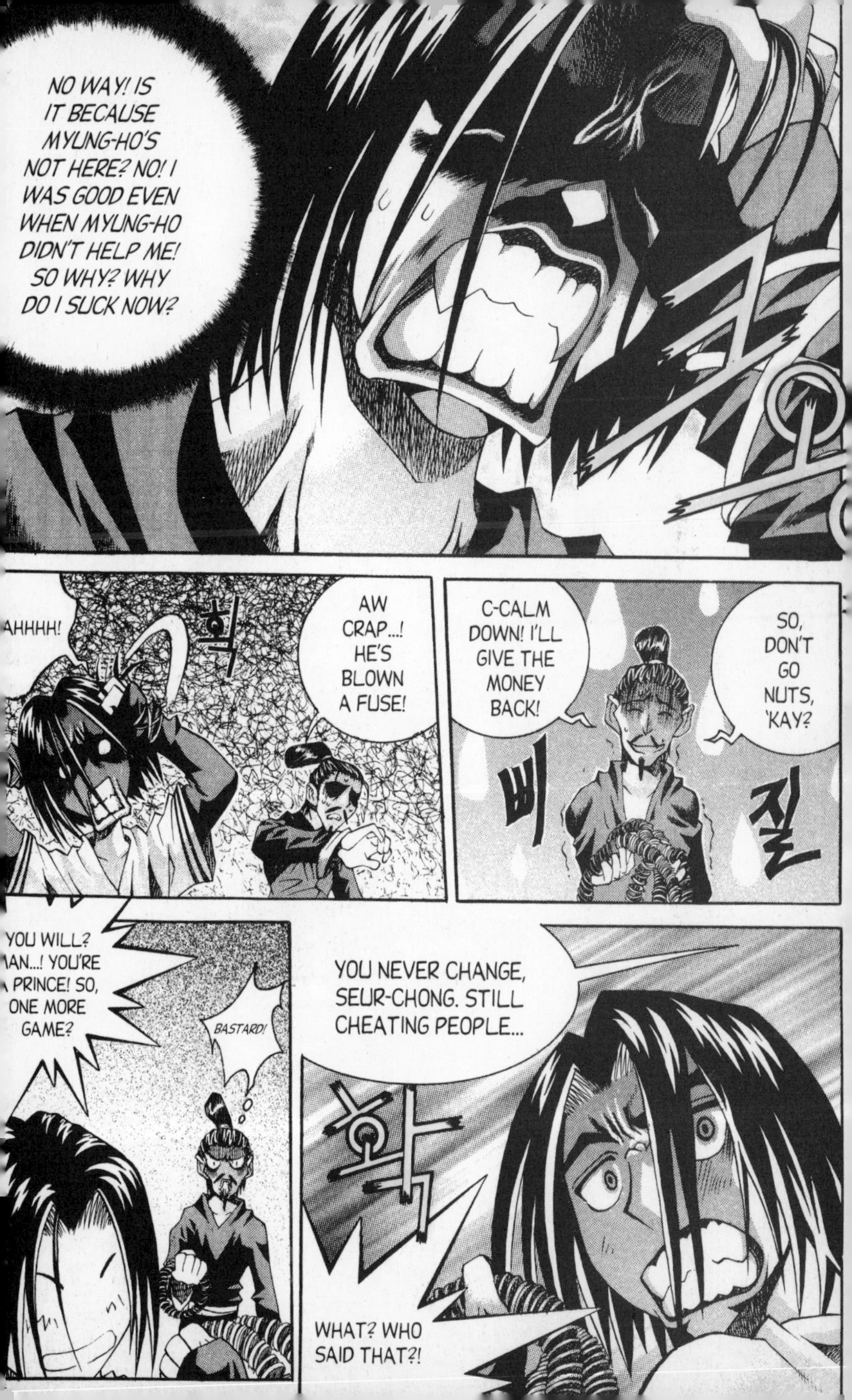
NO WAY! IS IT BECAUSE MYUNG-HO'S NOT HERE? NO! I WAS GOOD EVEN WHEN MYUNG-HO DIDN'T HELP ME! SO WHY? WHY DO I SUCK NOW?
AHHHH!
AW CRAP...! HE'S BLOWN A FUSE!
C-CALM DOWN! I'LL GIVE THE MONEY BACK!
SO, DON'T GO NUTS, 'KAY?
삐질
YOU WILL? AN...! YOU'RE PRINCE! SO, ONE MORE GAME?
BASTARD!
YOU NEVER CHANGE, SEUR-CHONG. STILL CHEATING PEOPLE...
WHAT? WHO SAID THAT?!

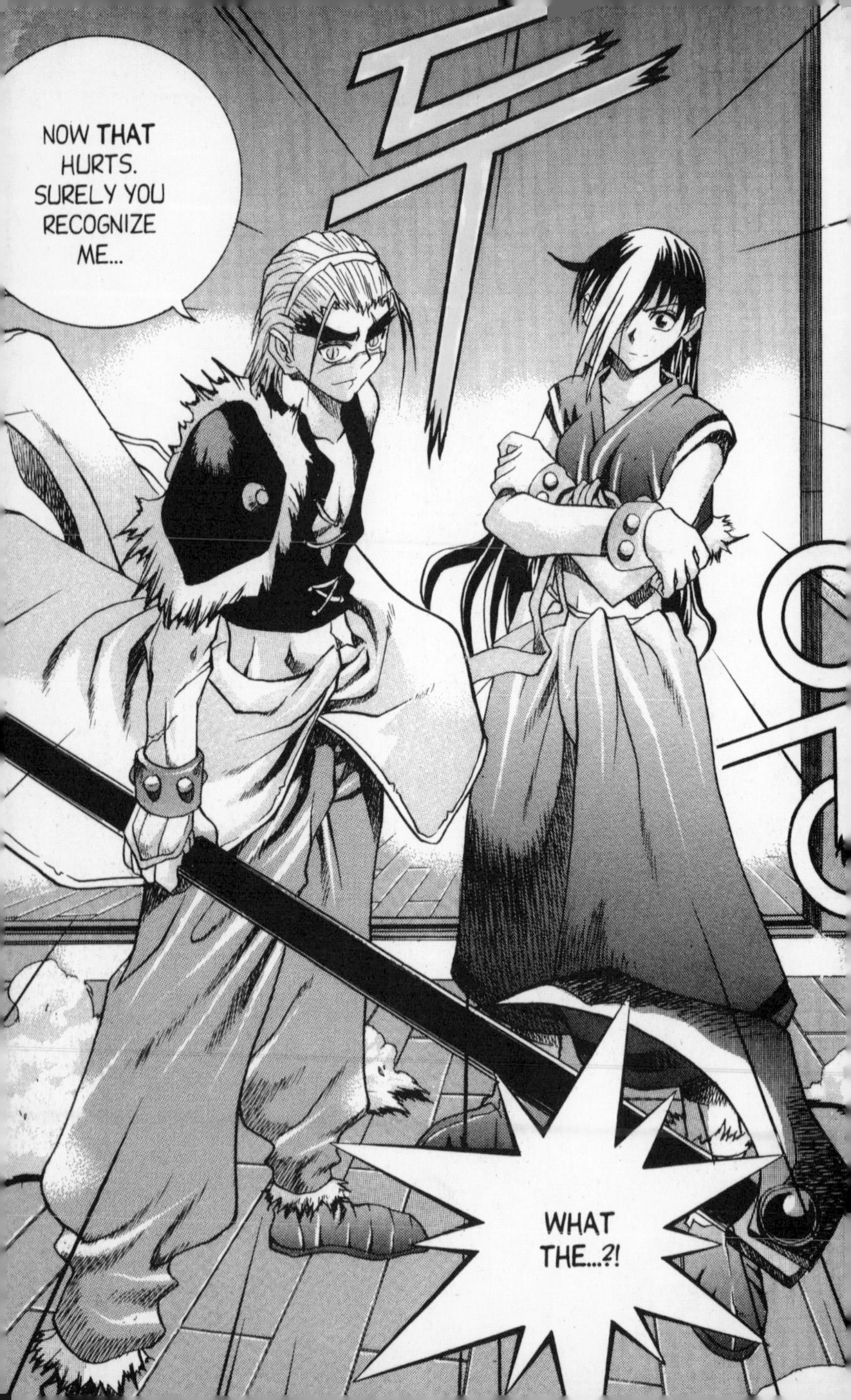
NOW THAT HURTS. SURELY YOU RECOGNIZE ME...
WHAT THE...?!

CHAPTER 49
TAE-RANG...NO, KOK-JUNG?

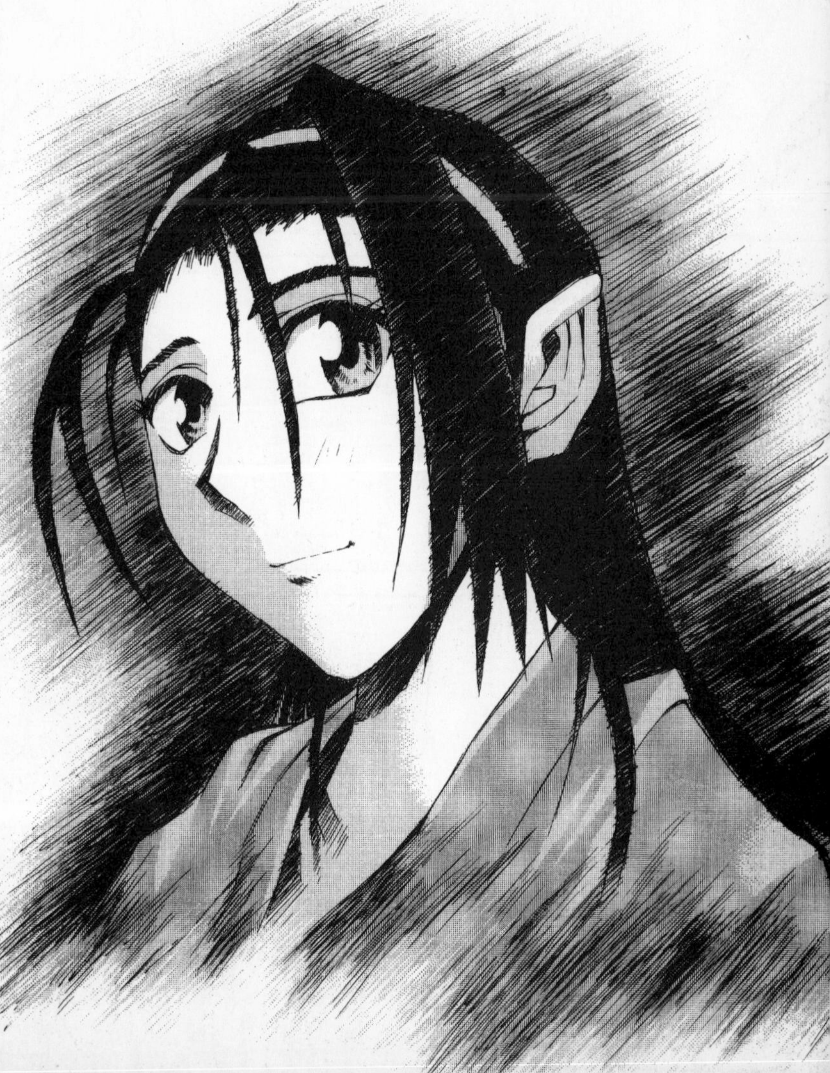

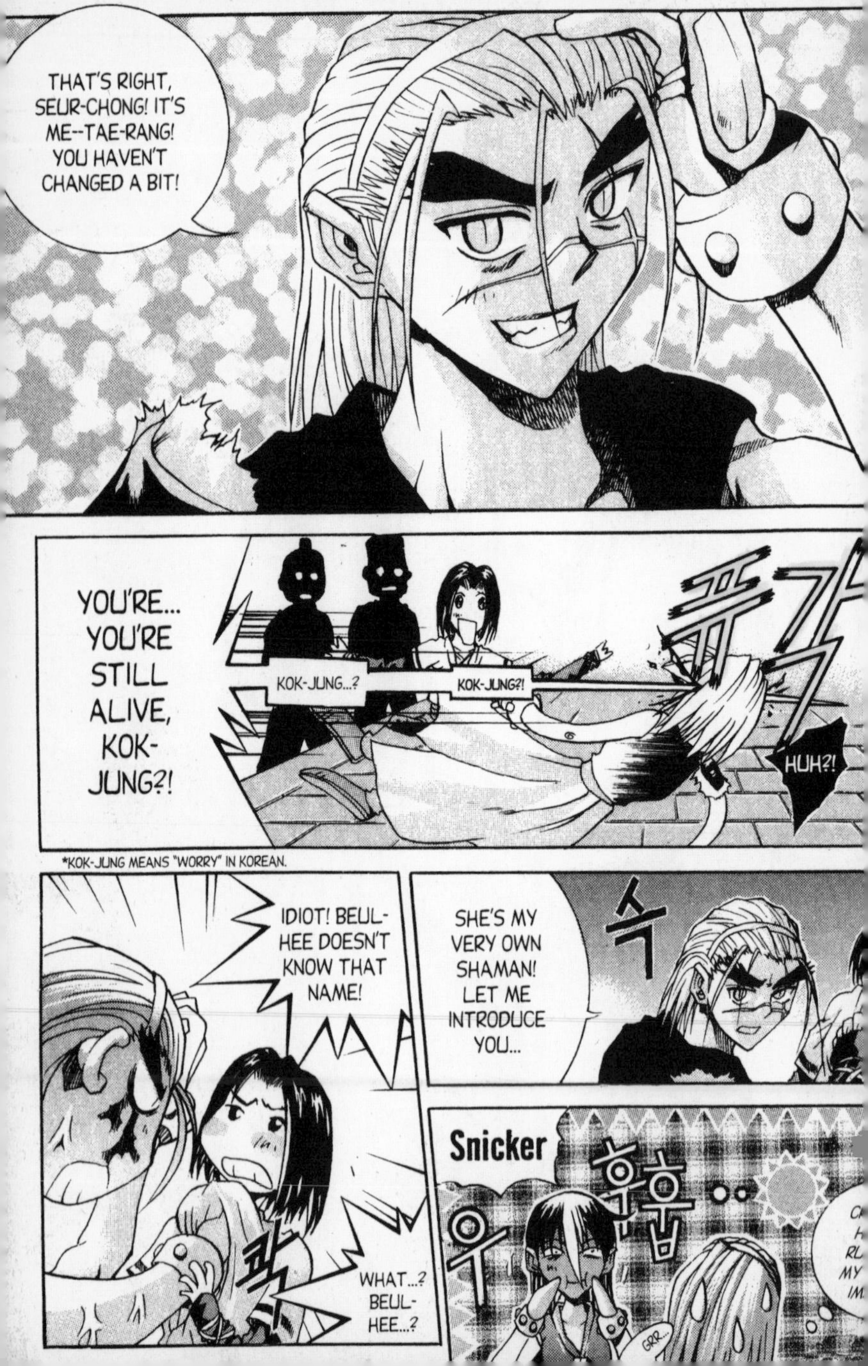
THAT'S RIGHT, SEUR-CHONG! IT'S ME--TAE-RANG! YOU HAVEN'T CHANGED A BIT!
YOU'RE... YOU'RE STILL ALIVE, KOK-JUNG?!
KOK-JUNG...?
KOK-JUNG?!
HUH?!
IDIOT! BEUL-HEE DOESN'T KNOW THAT NAME!
팍
WHAT...? BEUL-HEE...?
SHE'S MY VERY OWN SHAMAN! LET ME INTRODUCE YOU...
슥
Snicker
GRR...
*KOK-JUNG MEANS "WORRY" IN KOREAN.

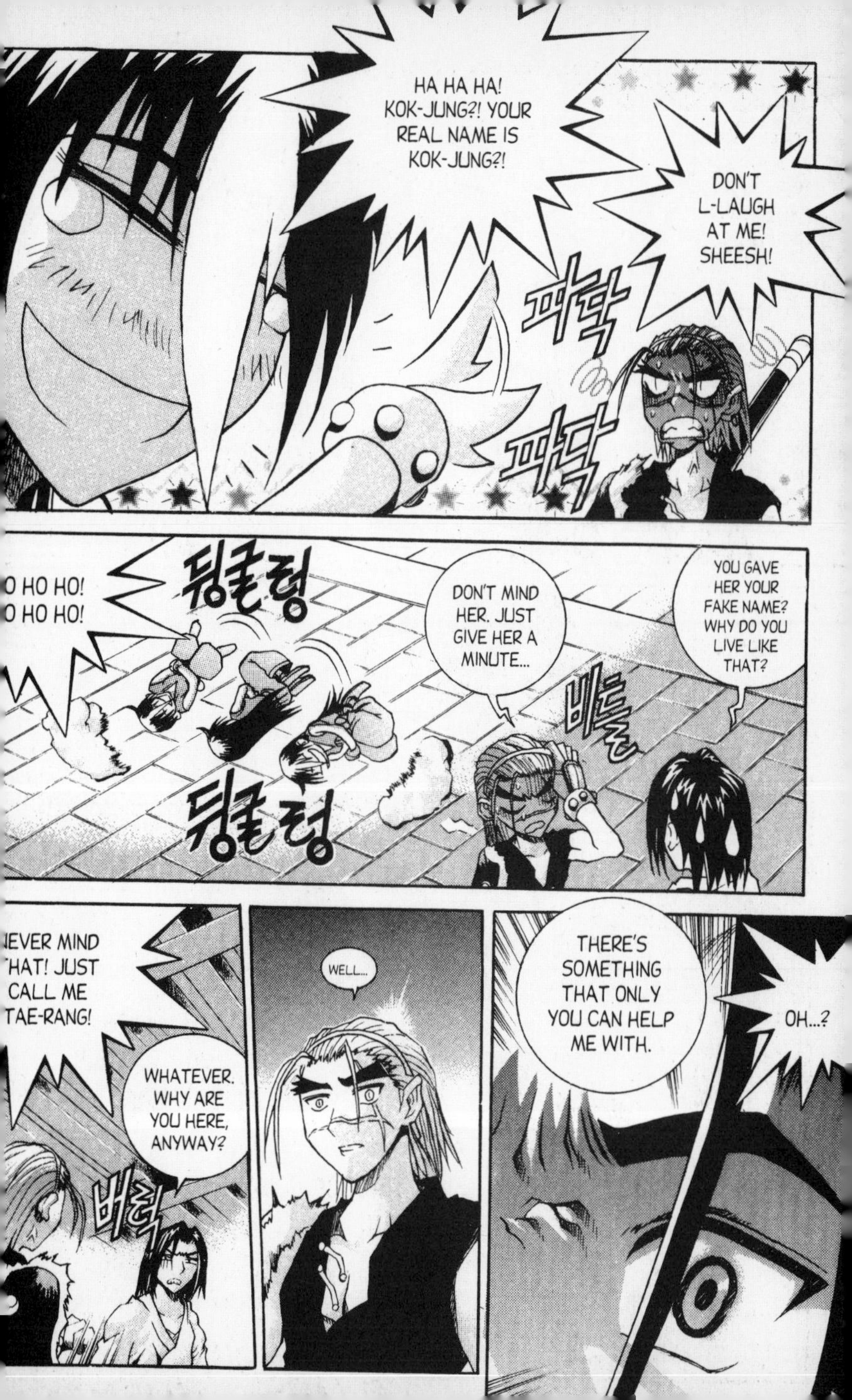
HA HA HA! KOK-JUNG?! YOUR REAL NAME IS KOK-JUNG?!
DON'T L-LAUGH AT ME! SHEESH!
파닥
파닥
O HO HO! O HO HO!
뒹굴렁
뒹굴렁
DON'T MIND HER. JUST GIVE HER A MINUTE...
YOU GAVE HER YOUR FAKE NAME? WHY DO YOU LIVE LIKE THAT?
NEVER MIND THAT! JUST CALL ME TAE-RANG!
WHATEVER. WHY ARE YOU HERE, ANYWAY?
WELL...
THERE'S SOMETHING THAT ONLY YOU CAN HELP ME WITH.
OH...?

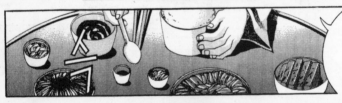

PLEASE--HELP YOURSELF. YOU KNOW...I WAS THINKING OF ASKING SEUR-CHONG TO MOVE IN.

......

YOU C-CAN GO NOW, MISTRESS MONG-YEUN. I W-WILL EAT, SO DON'T W-WORRY...

HMM... HAVING TROUBLE WITH YOUR THIRD EYE?

I HAVEN'T BEEN ABLE TO CONTROL IT SINCE THE BATTLE WITH THE BLUE DRAGON.

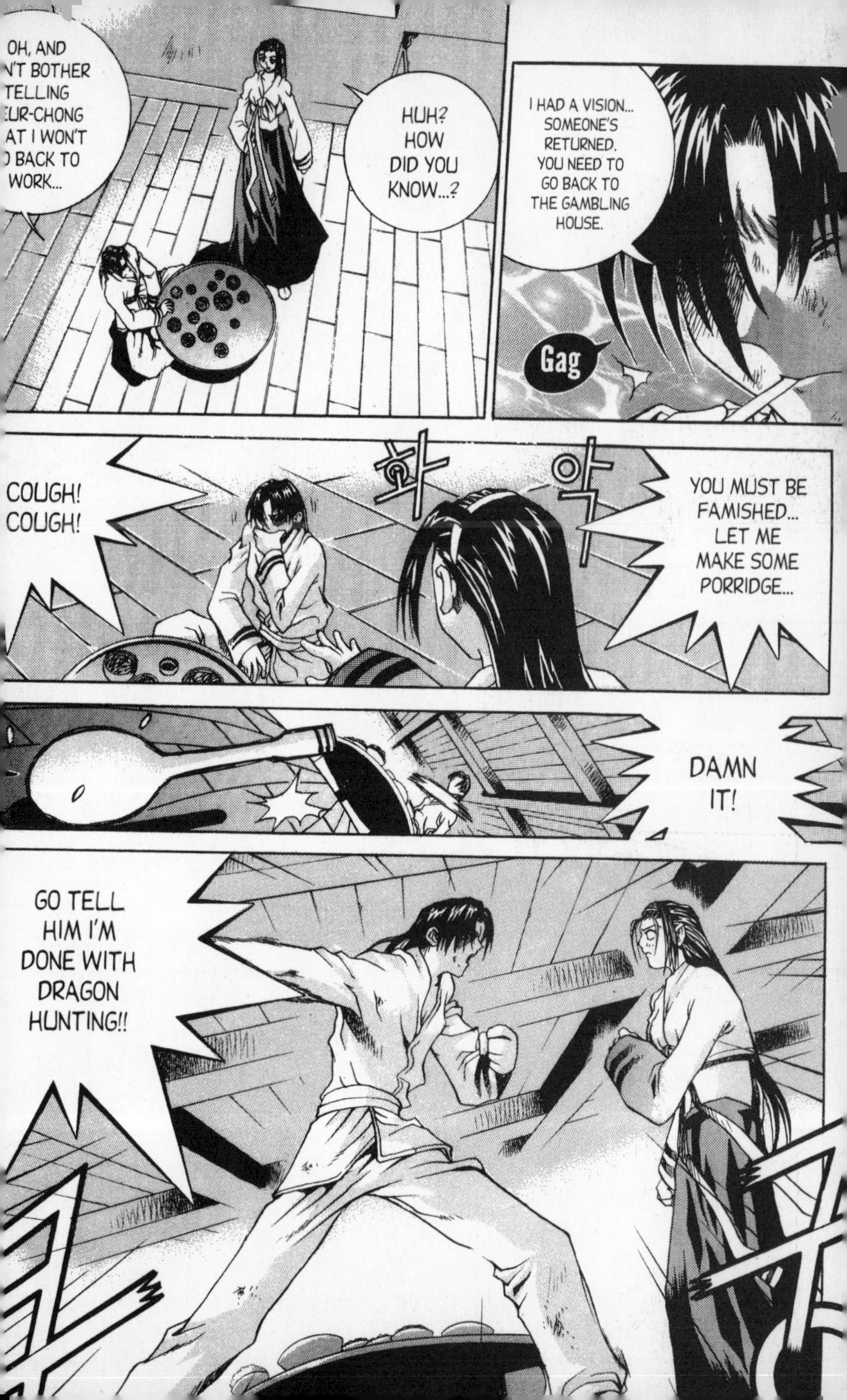
OH, AND N'T BOTHER TELLING EUR-CHONG AT I WON'T BACK TO WORK...
HUH? HOW DID YOU KNOW...?
I HAD A VISION... SOMEONE'S RETURNED. YOU NEED TO GO BACK TO THE GAMBLING HOUSE.
Gag
COUGH! COUGH!
화악
YOU MUST BE FAMISHED... LET ME MAKE SOME PORRIDGE...
DAMN IT!
GO TELL HIM I'M DONE WITH DRAGON HUNTING!!

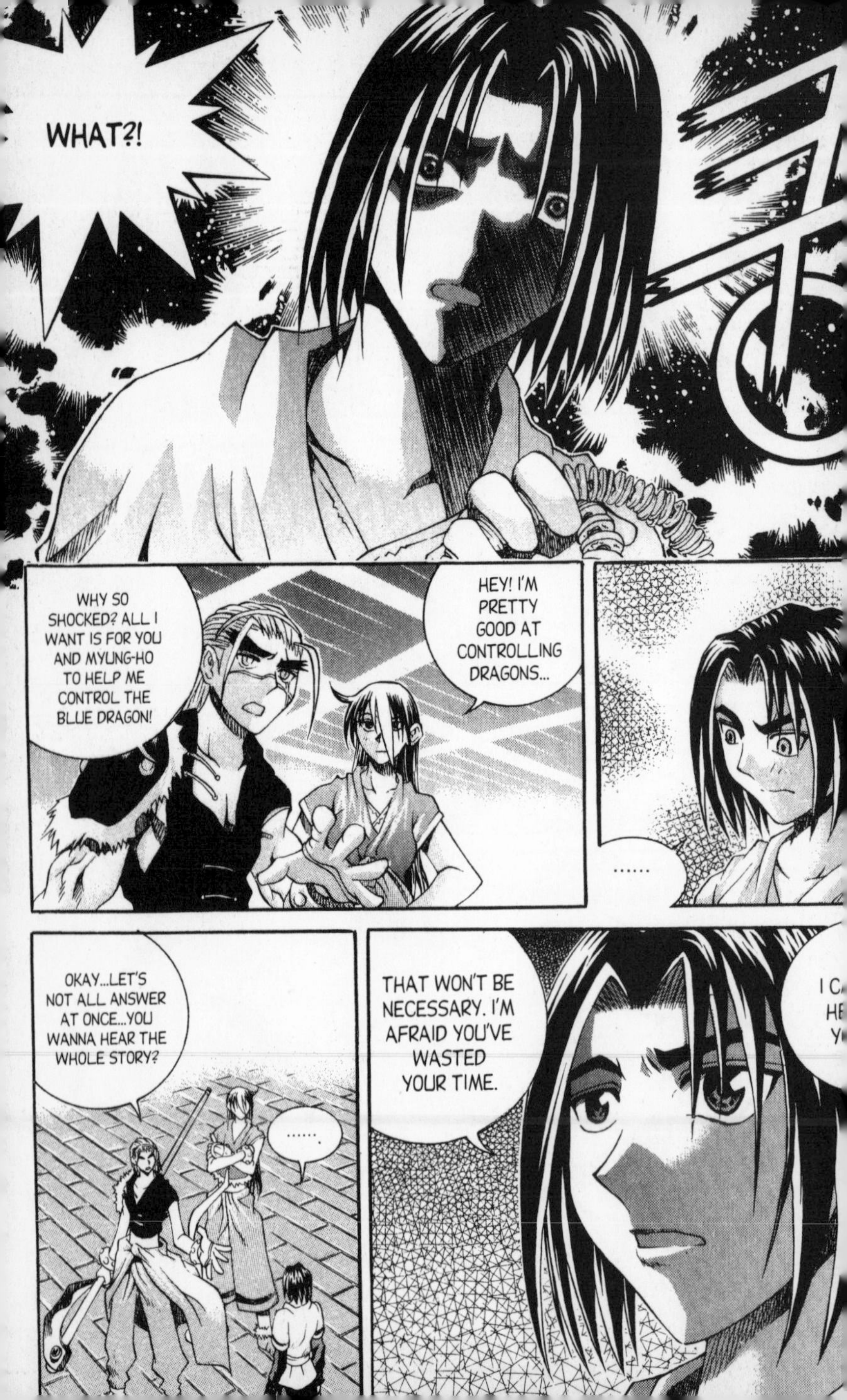
WHAT?!
WHY SO SHOCKED? ALL I WANT IS FOR YOU AND MYUNG-HO TO HELP ME CONTROL THE BLUE DRAGON!
HEY! I'M PRETTY GOOD AT CONTROLLING DRAGONS...
......
OKAY...LET'S NOT ALL ANSWER AT ONCE...YOU WANNA HEAR THE WHOLE STORY?
....
THAT WON'T BE NECESSARY. I'M AFRAID YOU'VE WASTED YOUR TIME.

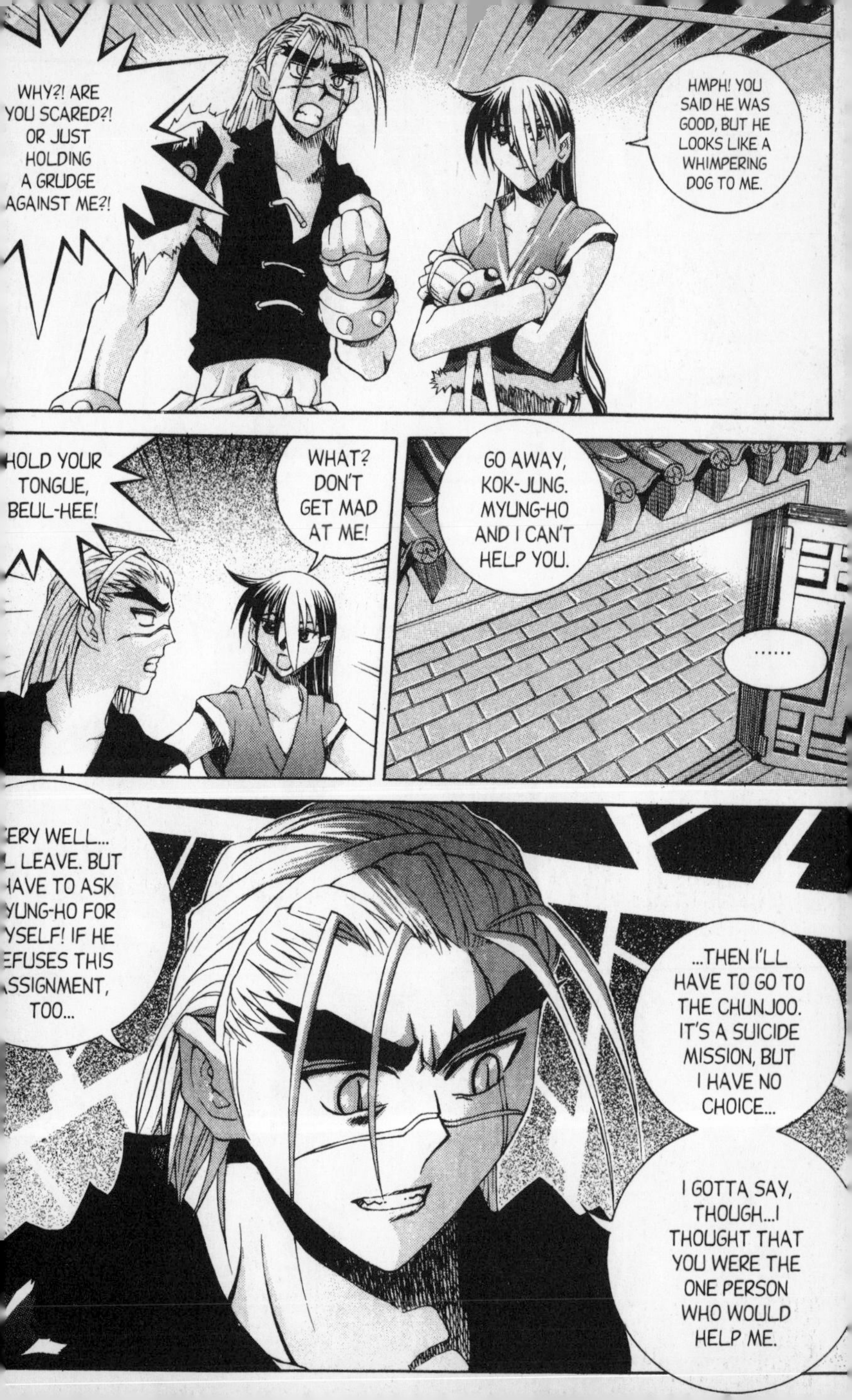
WHY?! ARE YOU SCARED?! OR JUST HOLDING A GRUDGE AGAINST ME?!
HMPH! YOU SAID HE WAS GOOD, BUT HE LOOKS LIKE A WHIMPERING DOG TO ME.
HOLD YOUR TONGUE, BEUL-HEE!
WHAT? DON'T GET MAD AT ME!
GO AWAY, KOK-JUNG. MYUNG-HO AND I CAN'T HELP YOU.
......
ERY WELL... L LEAVE. BUT HAVE TO ASK YUNG-HO FOR YSELF! IF HE EFUSES THIS SSIGNMENT, TOO...
...THEN I'LL HAVE TO GO TO THE CHUNJOO. IT'S A SUICIDE MISSION, BUT I HAVE NO CHOICE...
I GOTTA SAY, THOUGH...I THOUGHT THAT YOU WERE THE ONE PERSON WHO WOULD HELP ME.

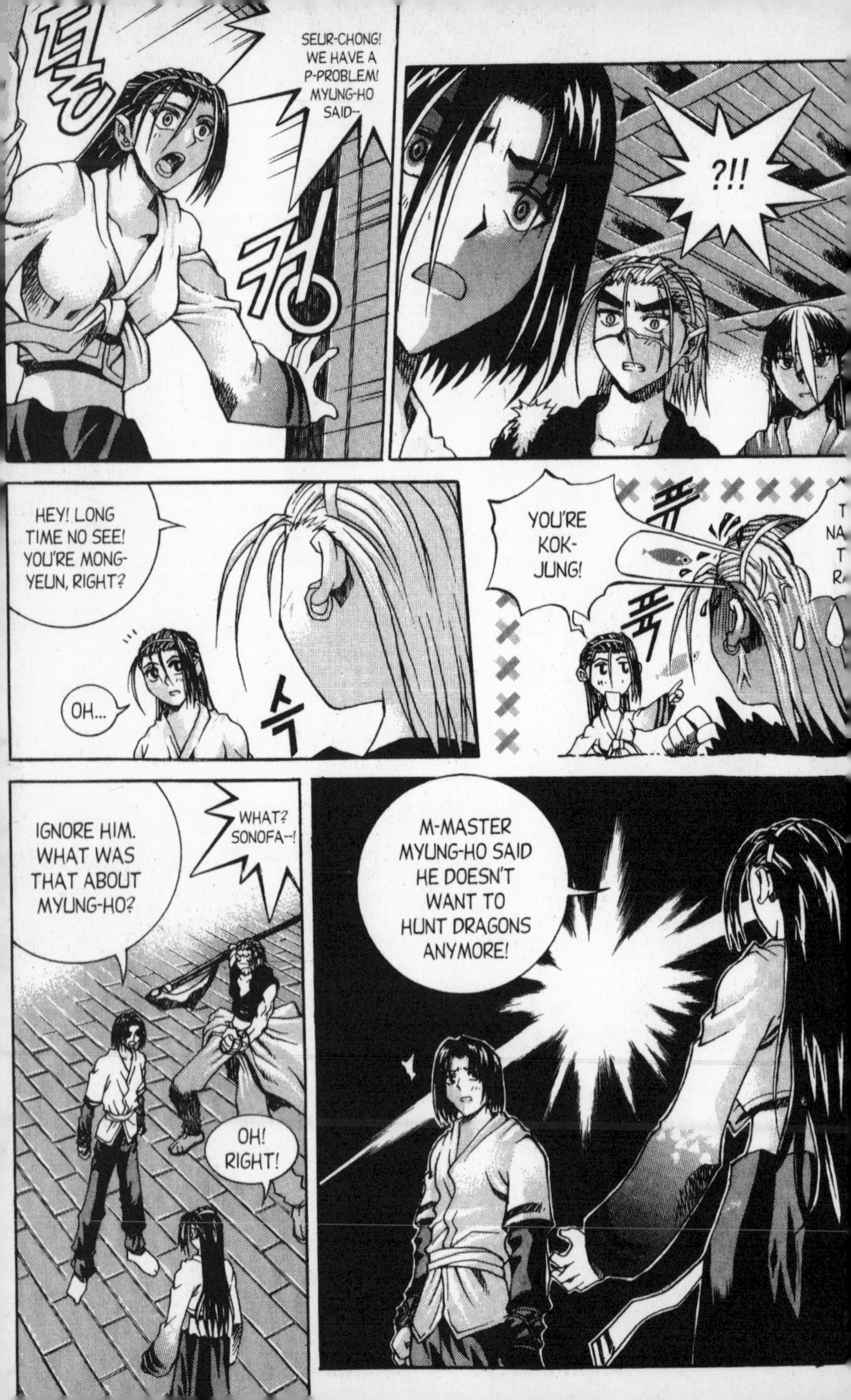
SEUR-CHONG! WE HAVE A P-PROBLEM! MYUNG-HO SAID--
?!!
HEY! LONG TIME NO SEE! YOU'RE MONG-YEUN, RIGHT?
OH...
YOU'RE KOK-JUNG!
IGNORE HIM. WHAT WAS THAT ABOUT MYUNG-HO?
WHAT? SONOFA--!
OH! RIGHT!
M-MASTER MYUNG-HO SAID HE DOESN'T WANT TO HUNT DRAGONS ANYMORE!

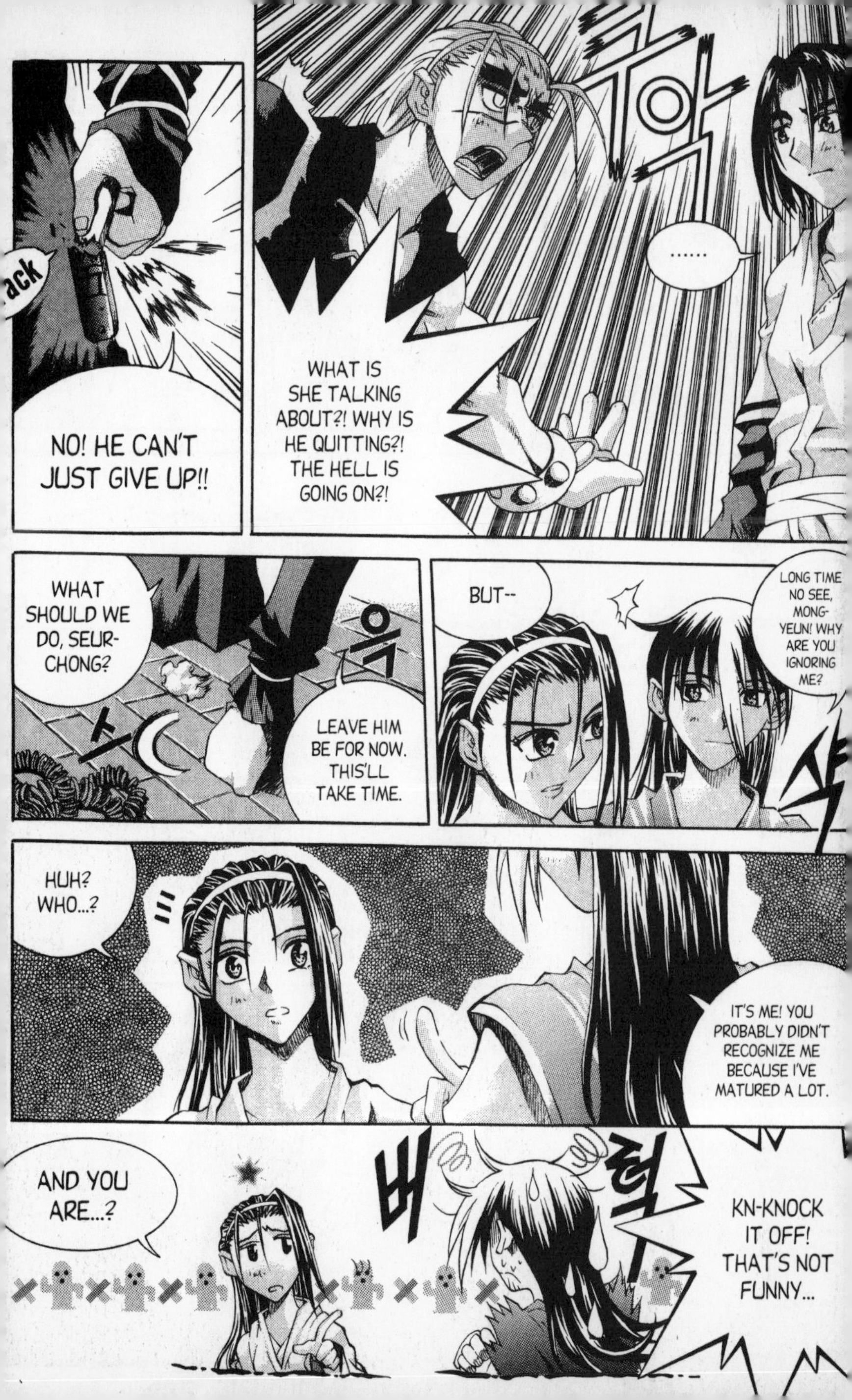
ack
NO! HE CAN'T JUST GIVE UP!!
WHAT IS SHE TALKING ABOUT?! WHY IS HE QUITTING?! THE HELL IS GOING ON?!
......
WHAT SHOULD WE DO, SEUR-CHONG?
LEAVE HIM BE FOR NOW. THIS'LL TAKE TIME.
BUT--
LONG TIME NO SEE, MONG-YEUN! WHY ARE YOU IGNORING ME?
HUH? WHO...?
IT'S ME! YOU PROBABLY DIDN'T RECOGNIZE ME BECAUSE I'VE MATURED A LOT.
AND YOU ARE...?
KN-KNOCK IT OFF! THAT'S NOT FUNNY...

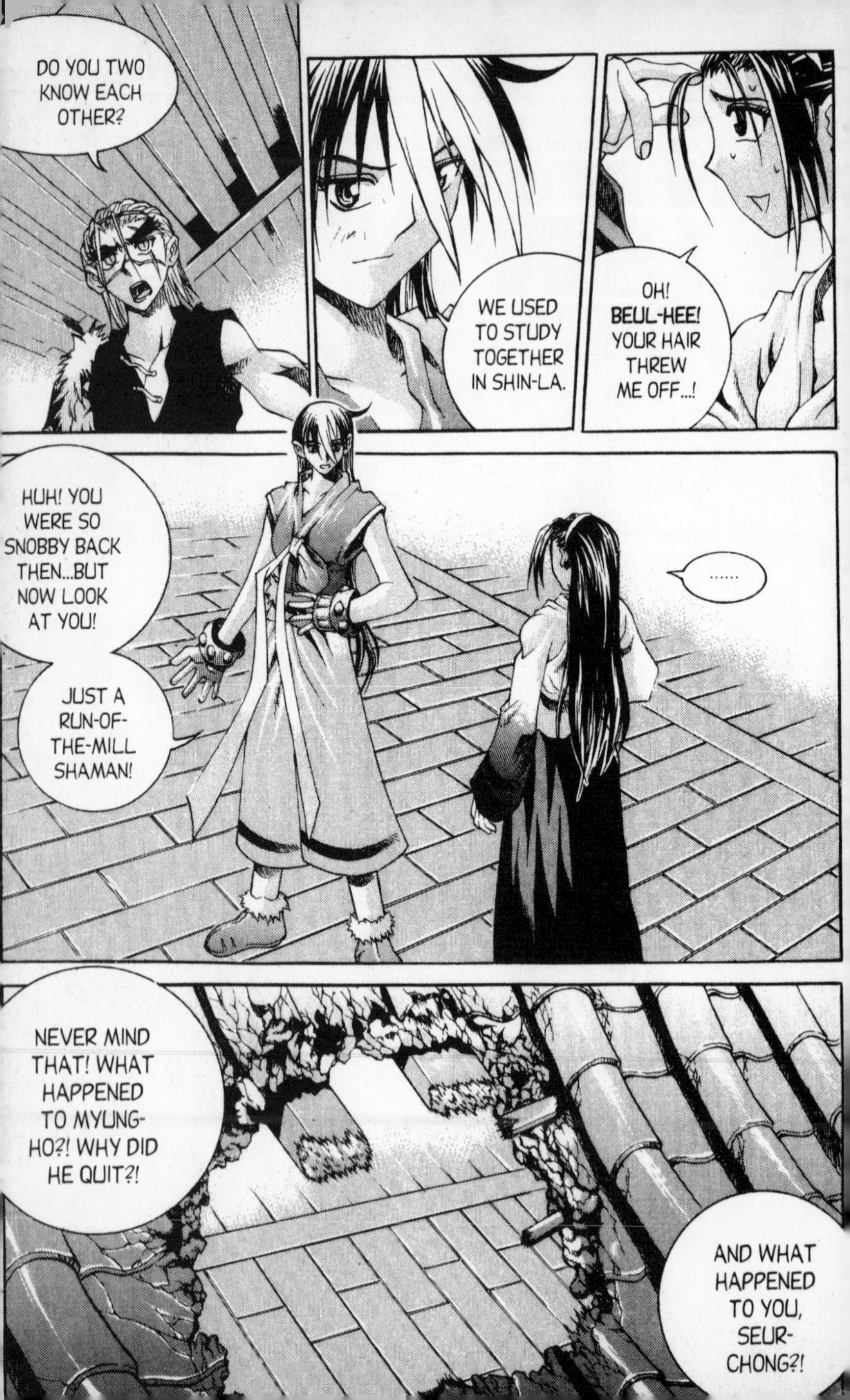
DO YOU TWO KNOW EACH OTHER?
WE USED TO STUDY TOGETHER IN SHIN-LA.
OH! BEUL-HEE! YOUR HAIR THREW ME OFF...!
HUH! YOU WERE SO SNOBBY BACK THEN...BUT NOW LOOK AT YOU!
JUST A RUN-OF-THE-MILL SHAMAN!
......
NEVER MIND THAT! WHAT HAPPENED TO MYUNG-HO?! WHY DID HE QUIT?!
AND WHAT HAPPENED TO YOU, SEUR-CHONG?!

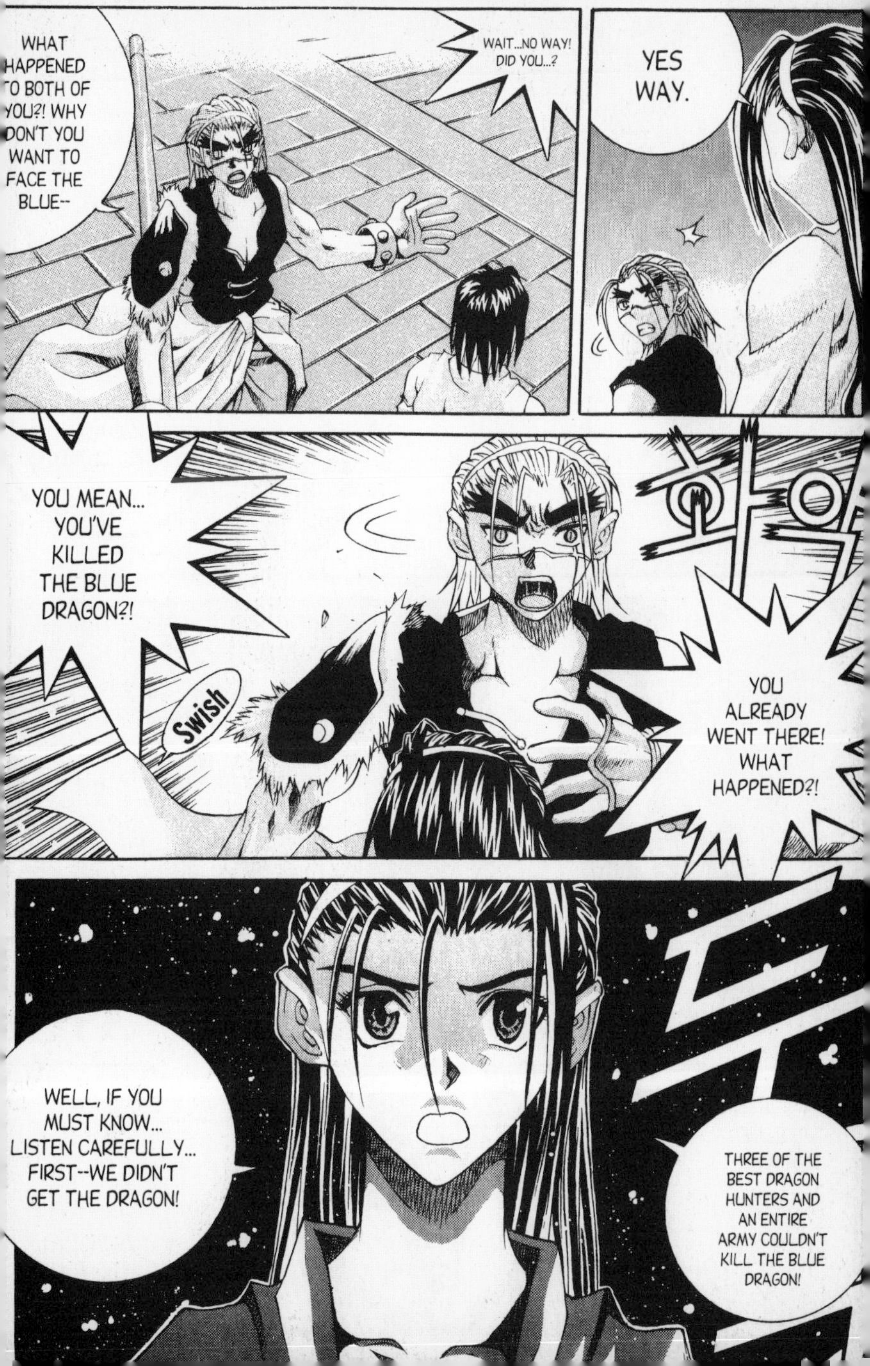
WHAT HAPPENED TO BOTH OF YOU?! WHY DON'T YOU WANT TO FACE THE BLUE--
WAIT...NO WAY! DID YOU...?
YES WAY.
YOU MEAN... YOU'VE KILLED THE BLUE DRAGON?!
Swish
YOU ALREADY WENT THERE! WHAT HAPPENED?!
WELL, IF YOU MUST KNOW... LISTEN CAREFULLY... FIRST--WE DIDN'T GET THE DRAGON!
THREE OF THE BEST DRAGON HUNTERS AND AN ENTIRE ARMY COULDN'T KILL THE BLUE DRAGON!

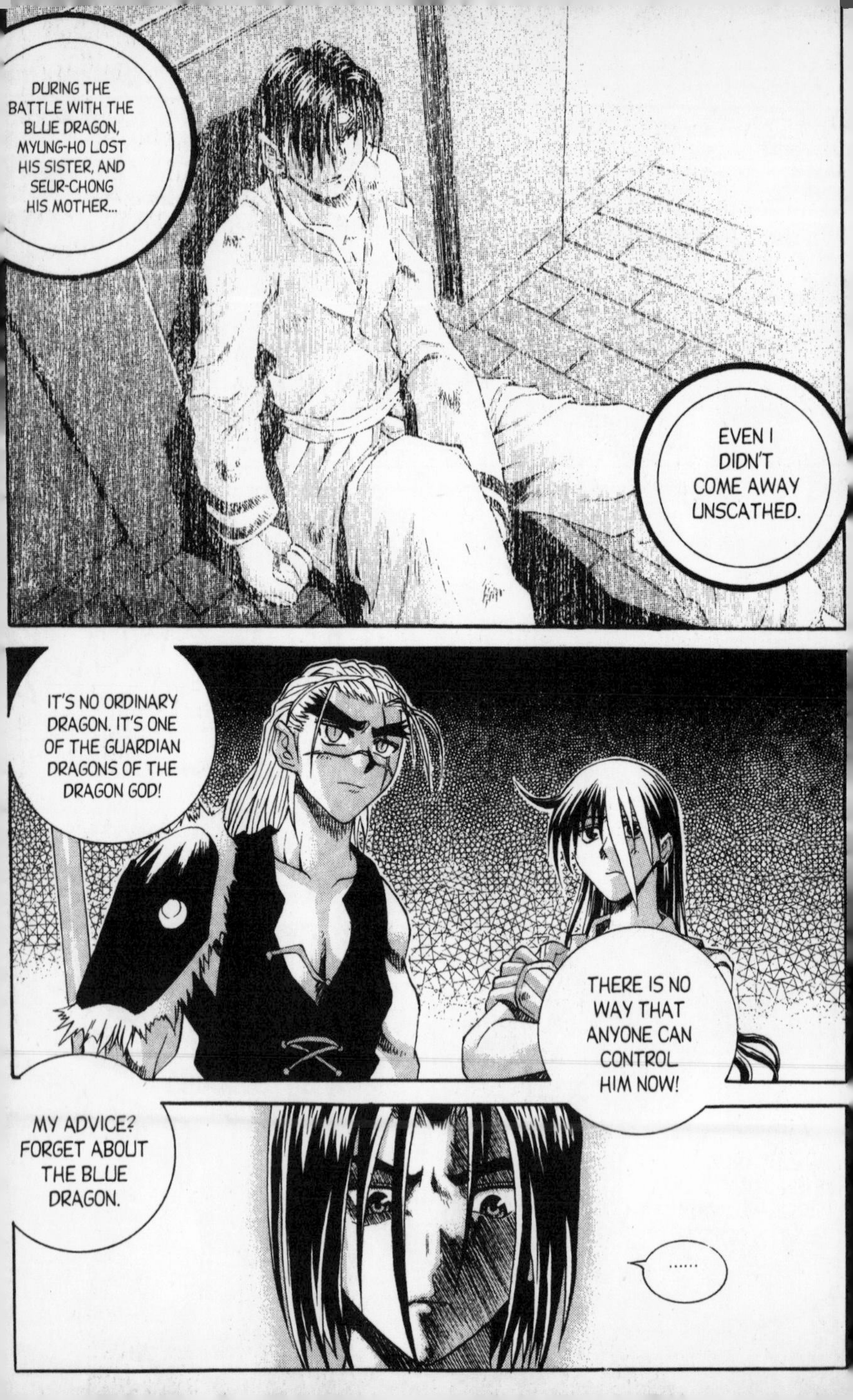
DURING THE BATTLE WITH THE BLUE DRAGON, MYUNG-HO LOST HIS SISTER, AND SEUR-CHONG HIS MOTHER...
EVEN I DIDN'T COME AWAY UNSCATHED.
IT'S NO ORDINARY DRAGON. IT'S ONE OF THE GUARDIAN DRAGONS OF THE DRAGON GOD!
THERE IS NO WAY THAT ANYONE CAN CONTROL HIM NOW!
MY ADVICE? FORGET ABOUT THE BLUE DRAGON.
......

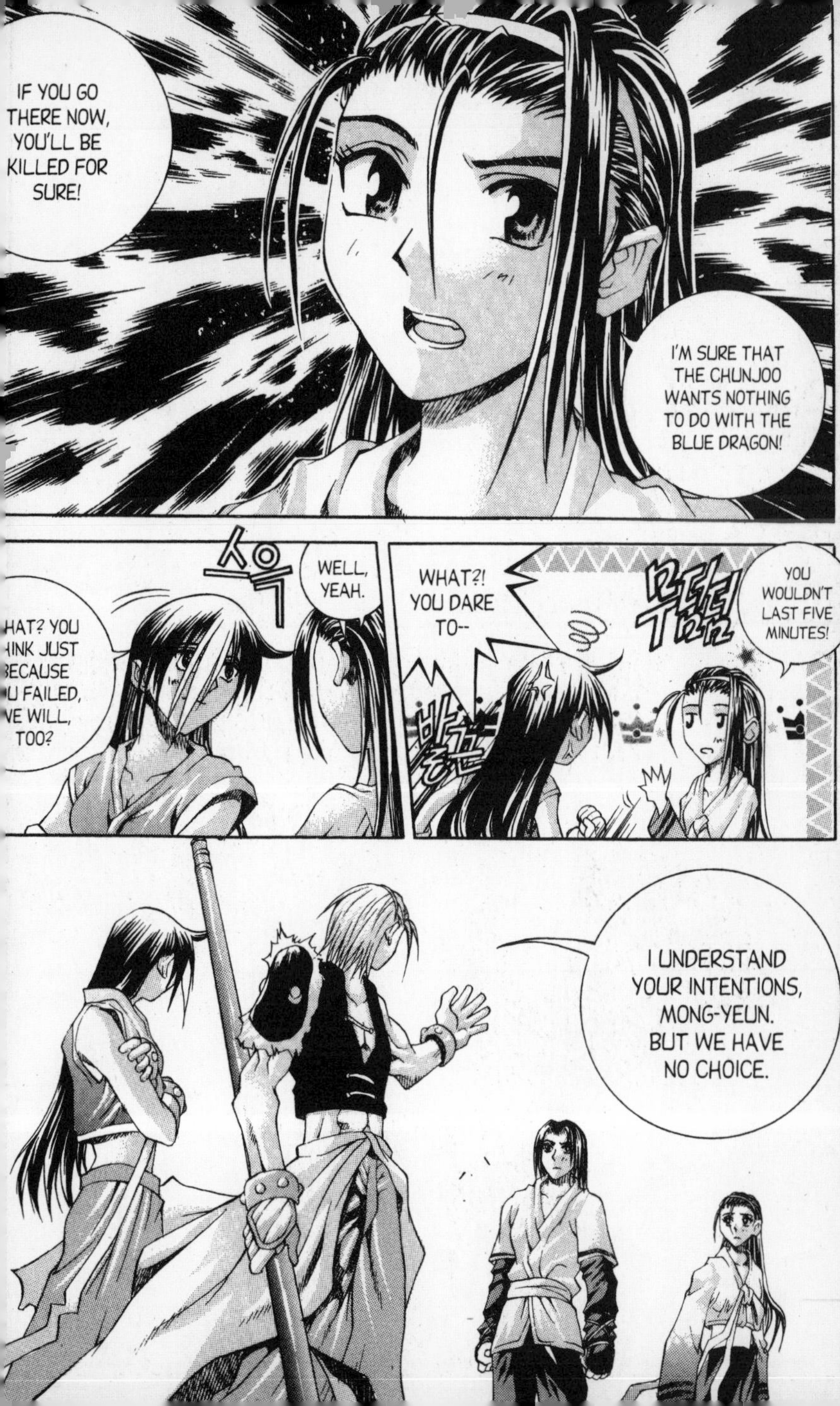
IF YOU GO THERE NOW, YOU'LL BE KILLED FOR SURE!
I'M SURE THAT THE CHUNJOO WANTS NOTHING TO DO WITH THE BLUE DRAGON!
HAT? YOU HINK JUST ECAUSE U FAILED, VE WILL, TOO?
WELL, YEAH.
WHAT?! YOU DARE TO--
YOU WOULDN'T LAST FIVE MINUTES!
I UNDERSTAND YOUR INTENTIONS, MONG-YEUN. BUT WE HAVE NO CHOICE.

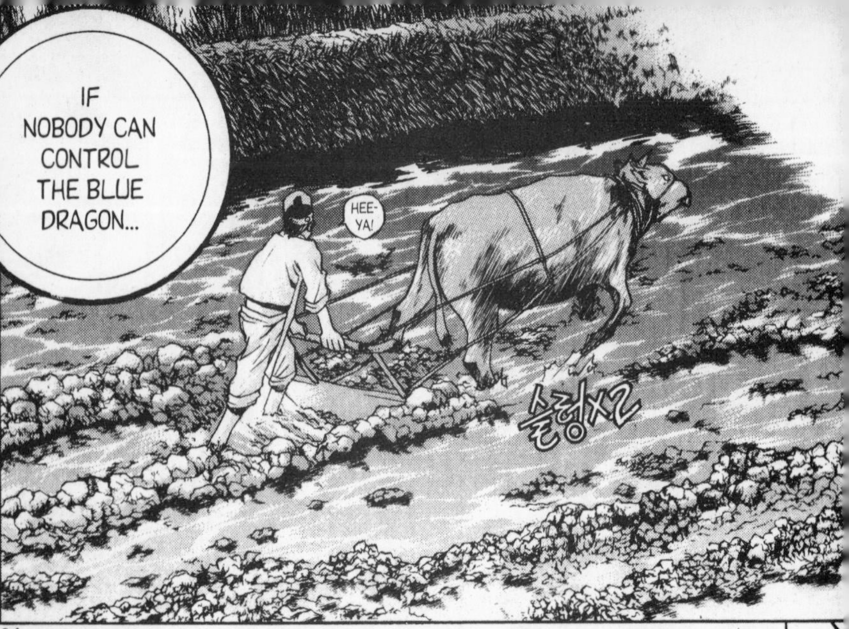
IF NOBODY CAN CONTROL THE BLUE DRAGON...
HEE-YA!
슬렁x2

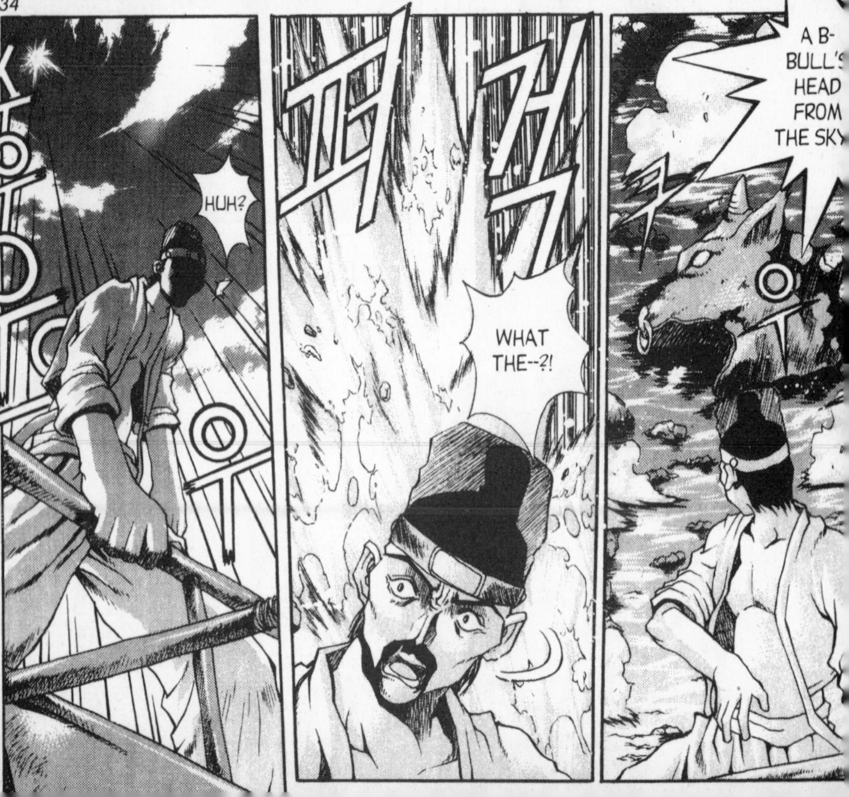
HUH?
WHAT THE--?!
A B-BULL'S HEAD FROM THE SKY

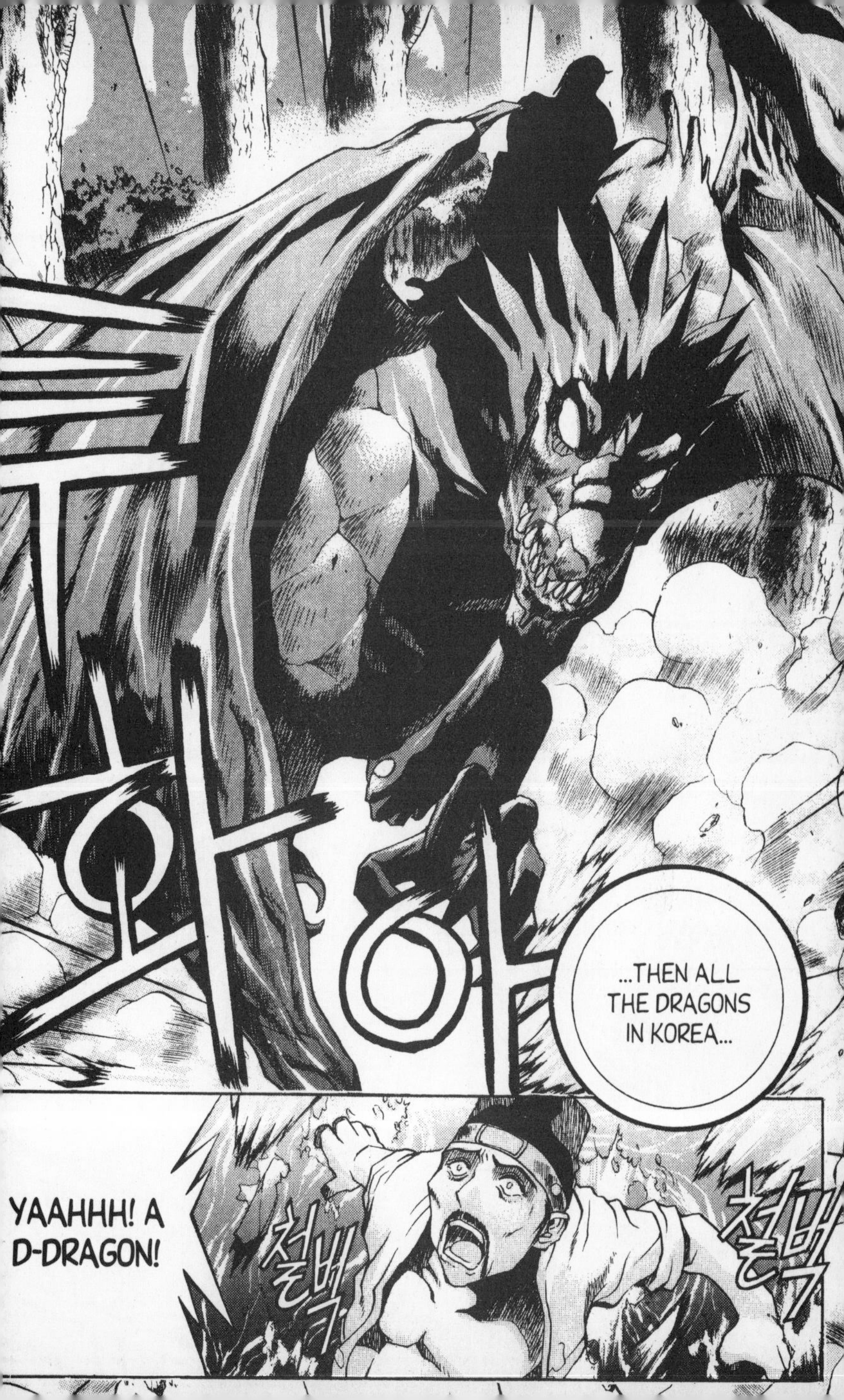
...THEN ALL THE DRAGONS IN KOREA...
YAAHHH! A D-DRAGON!

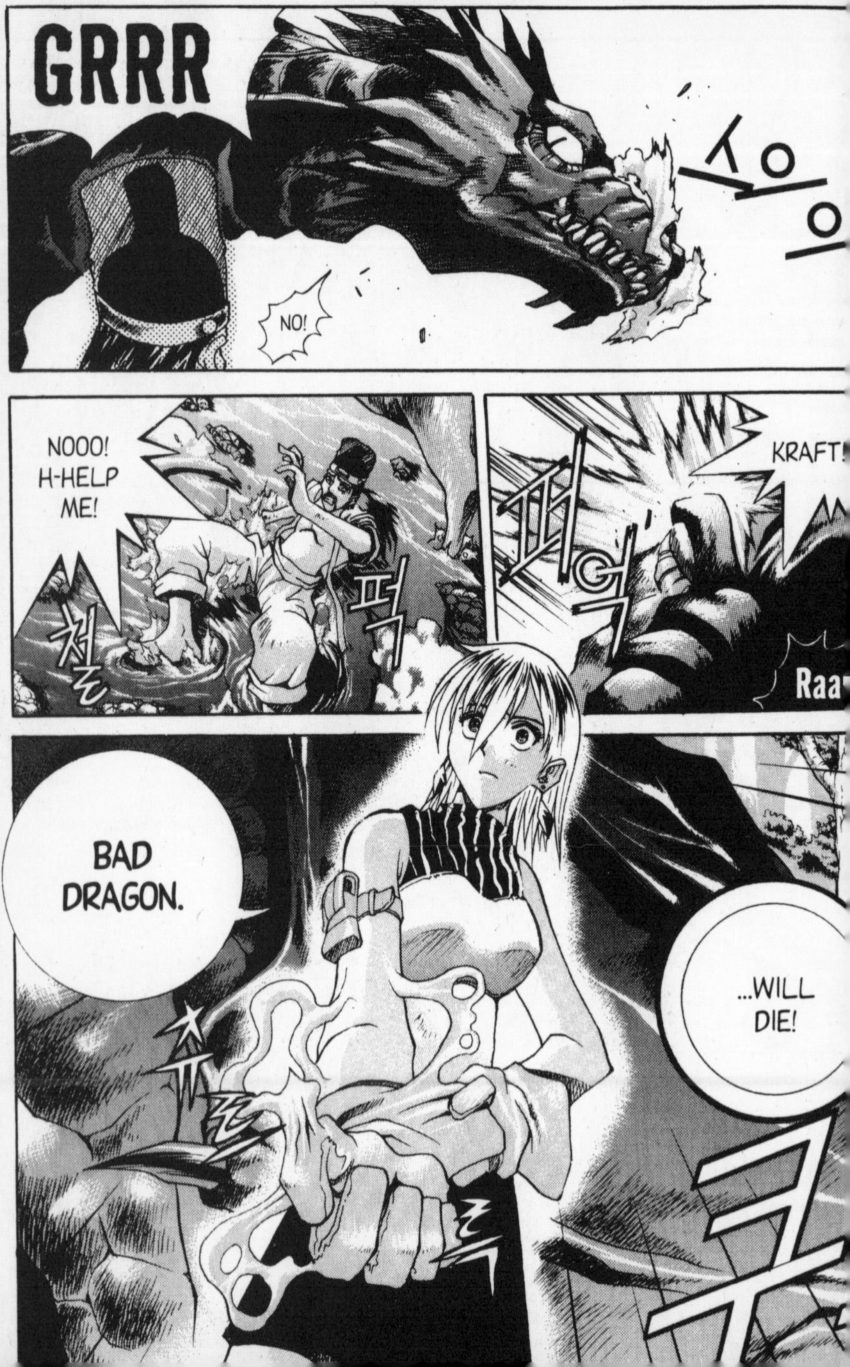
GRRR
NO!
NOOO! H-HELP ME!
KRAFT!
BAD DRAGON.
...WILL DIE!

CHAPTER 50
AN ORDER OF KNIGHTS

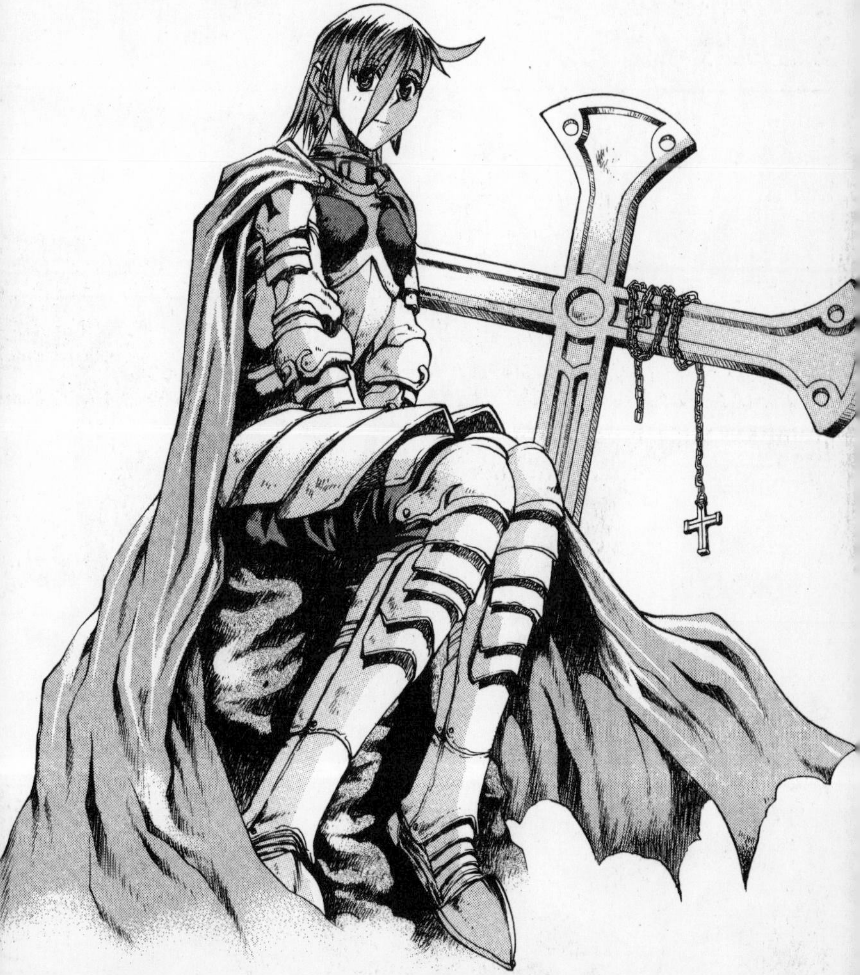

KRAFT--HIDE SOMEWHERE UNTIL I COME BACK! DON'T SHOW YOURSELF TO ANYONE!

I'LL BE BACK SOON. BEHAVE YOURSELF, 'KAY?

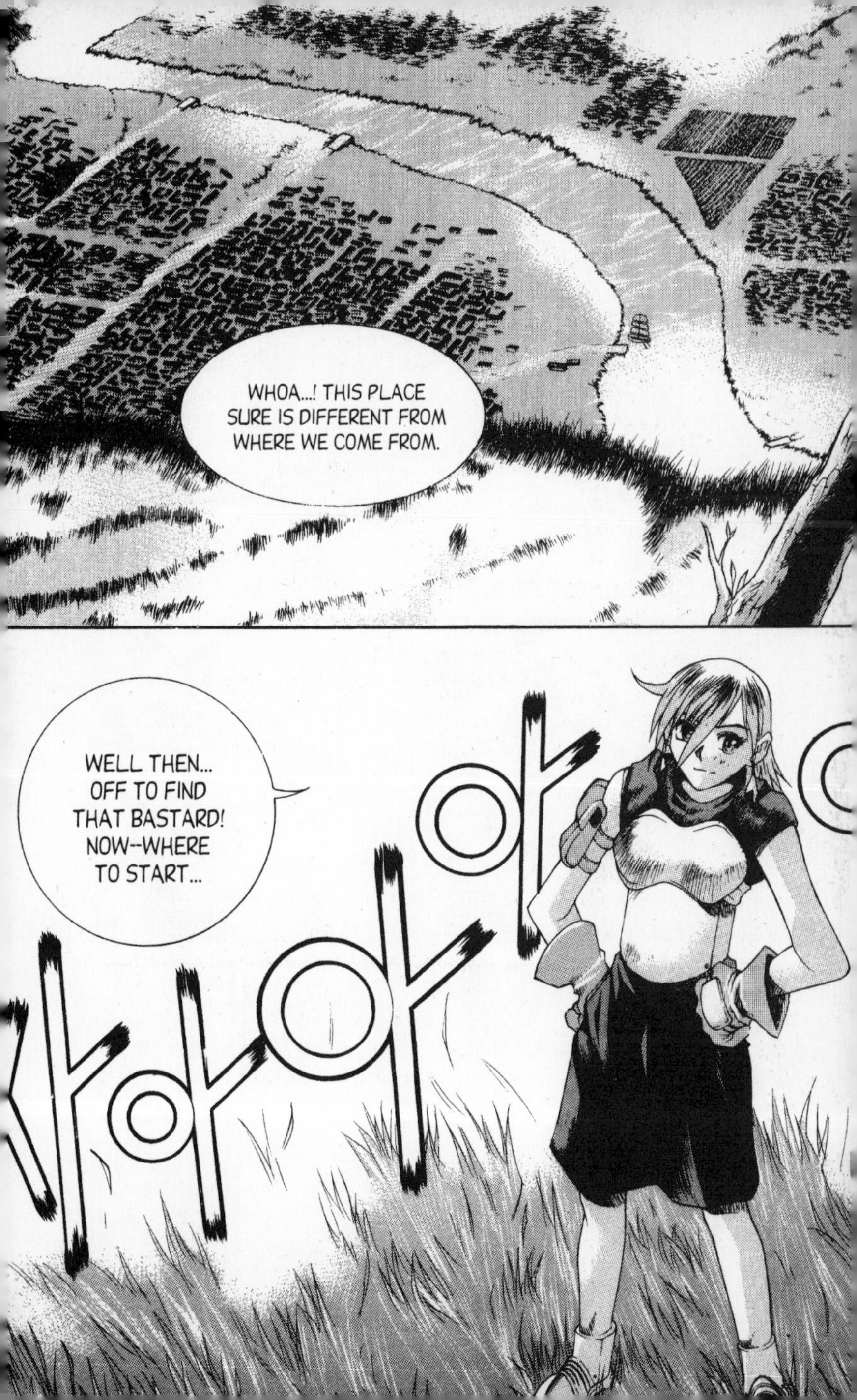
WHOA...! THIS PLACE SURE IS DIFFERENT FROM WHERE WE COME FROM.
WELL THEN... OFF TO FIND THAT BASTARD! NOW--WHERE TO START...

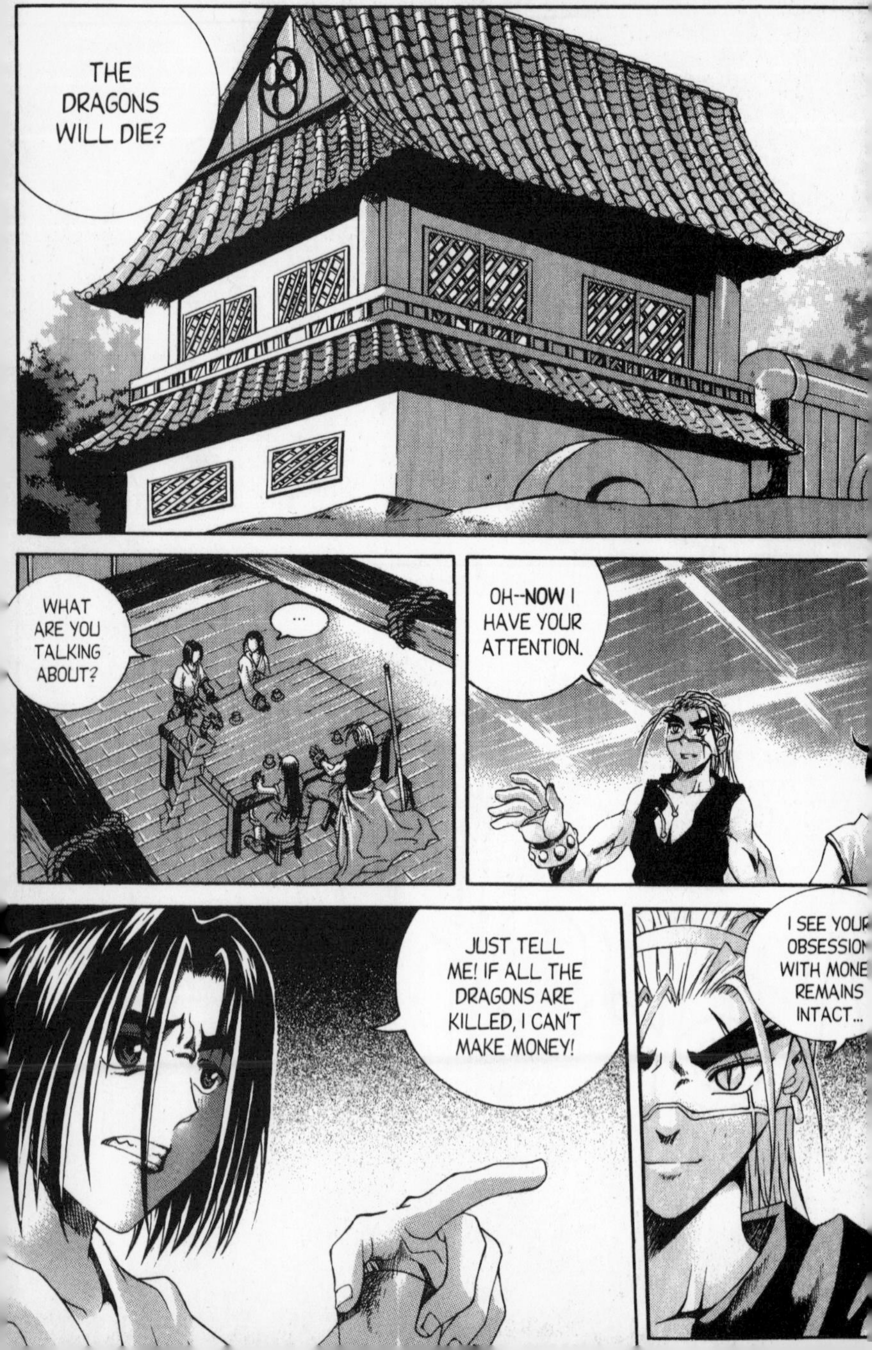
THE DRAGONS WILL DIE?
WHAT ARE YOU TALKING ABOUT?
...
OH--**NOW** I HAVE YOUR ATTENTION.
JUST TELL ME! IF ALL THE DRAGONS ARE KILLED, I CAN'T MAKE MONEY!
I SEE YOUR OBSESSION WITH MONE REMAINS INTACT...

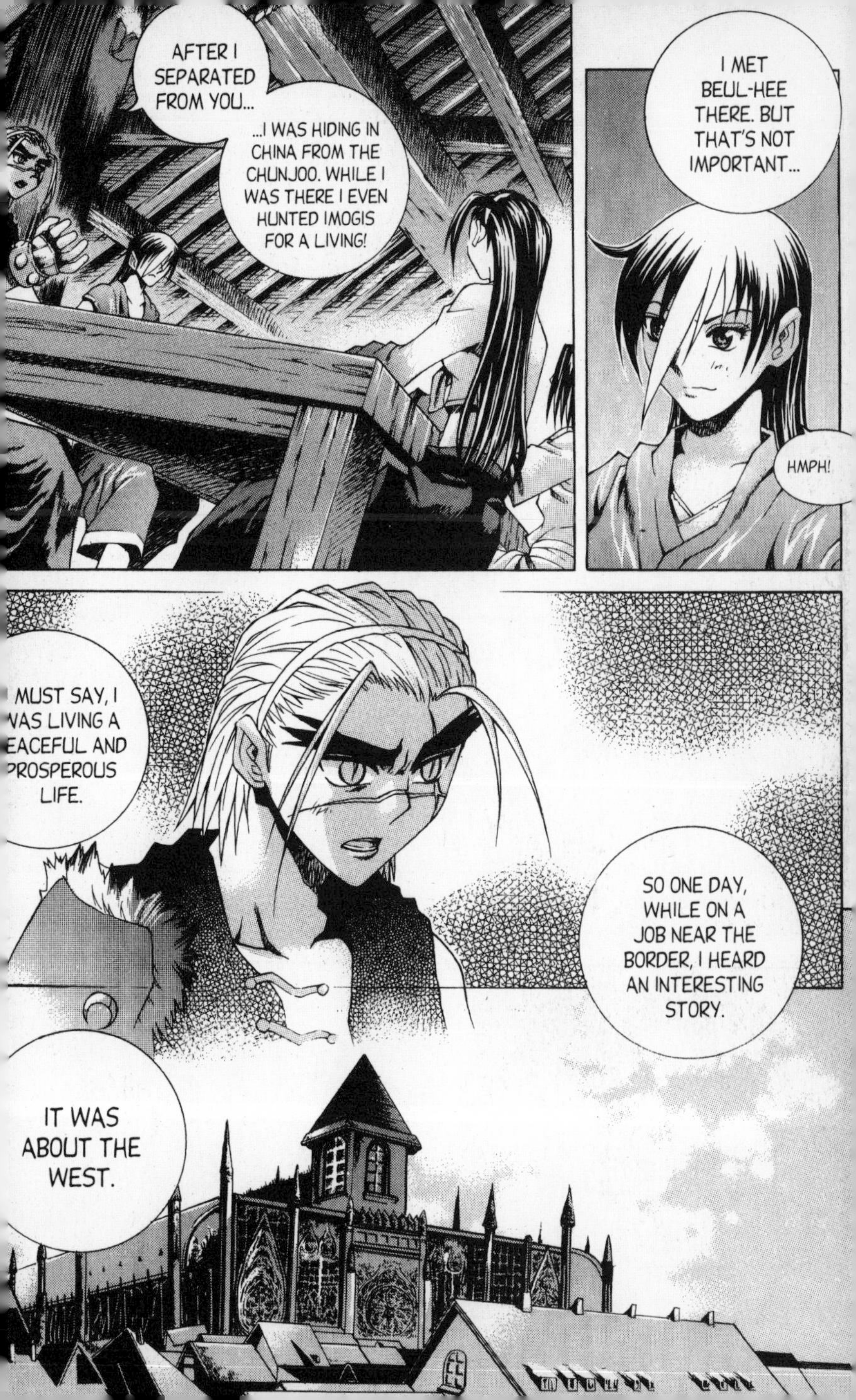
AFTER I SEPARATED FROM YOU...
...I WAS HIDING IN CHINA FROM THE CHUNJOO. WHILE I WAS THERE I EVEN HUNTED IMOGIS FOR A LIVING!
I MET BEUL-HEE THERE. BUT THAT'S NOT IMPORTANT...
HMPH!
MUST SAY, I WAS LIVING A EACEFUL AND PROSPEROUS LIFE.
SO ONE DAY, WHILE ON A JOB NEAR THE BORDER, I HEARD AN INTERESTING STORY.
IT WAS ABOUT THE WEST.

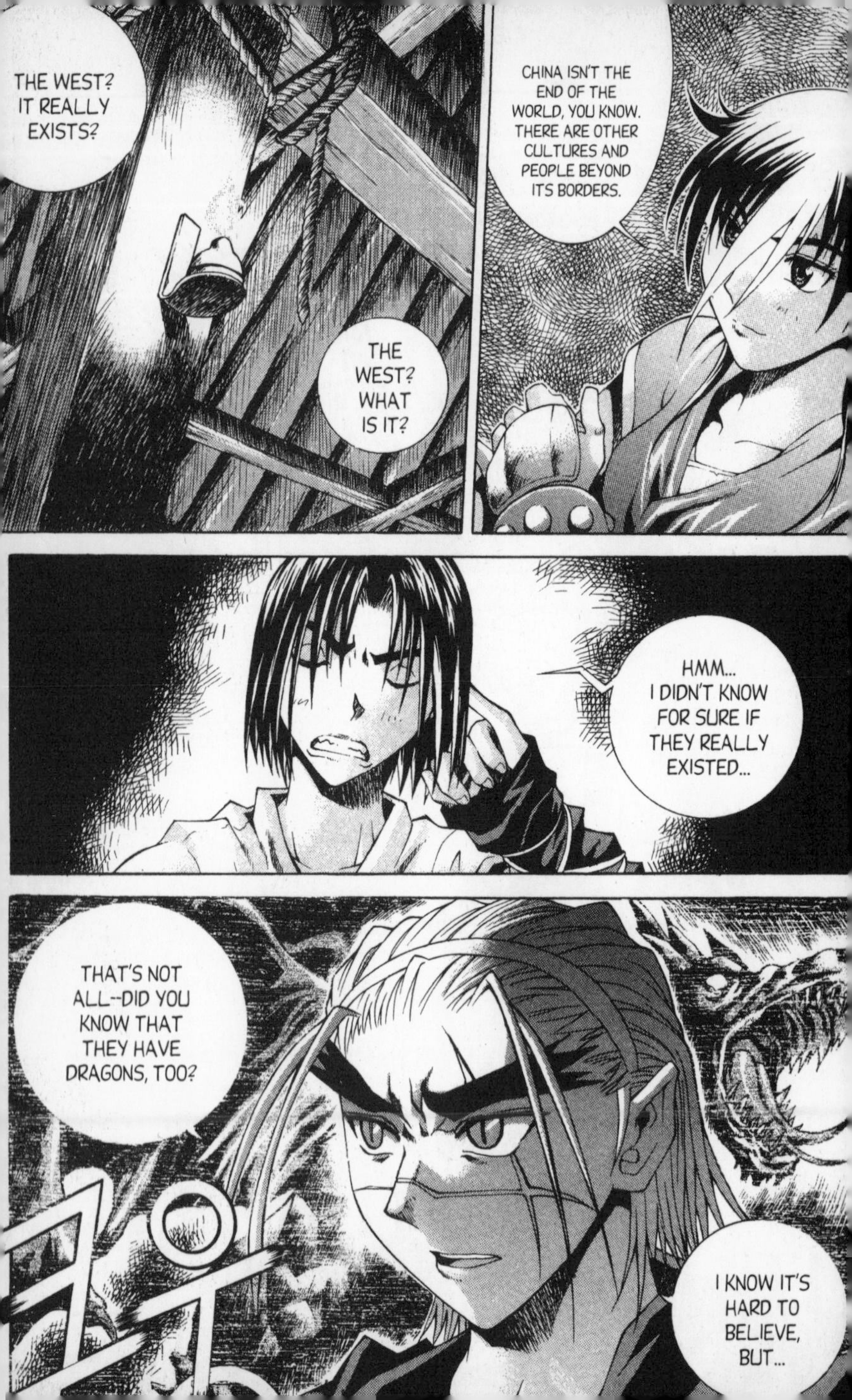
THE WEST? IT REALLY EXISTS?
THE WEST? WHAT IS IT?
CHINA ISN'T THE END OF THE WORLD, YOU KNOW. THERE ARE OTHER CULTURES AND PEOPLE BEYOND ITS BORDERS.
HMM... I DIDN'T KNOW FOR SURE IF THEY REALLY EXISTED...
THAT'S NOT ALL--DID YOU KNOW THAT THEY HAVE DRAGONS, TOO?
I KNOW IT'S HARD TO BELIEVE, BUT...

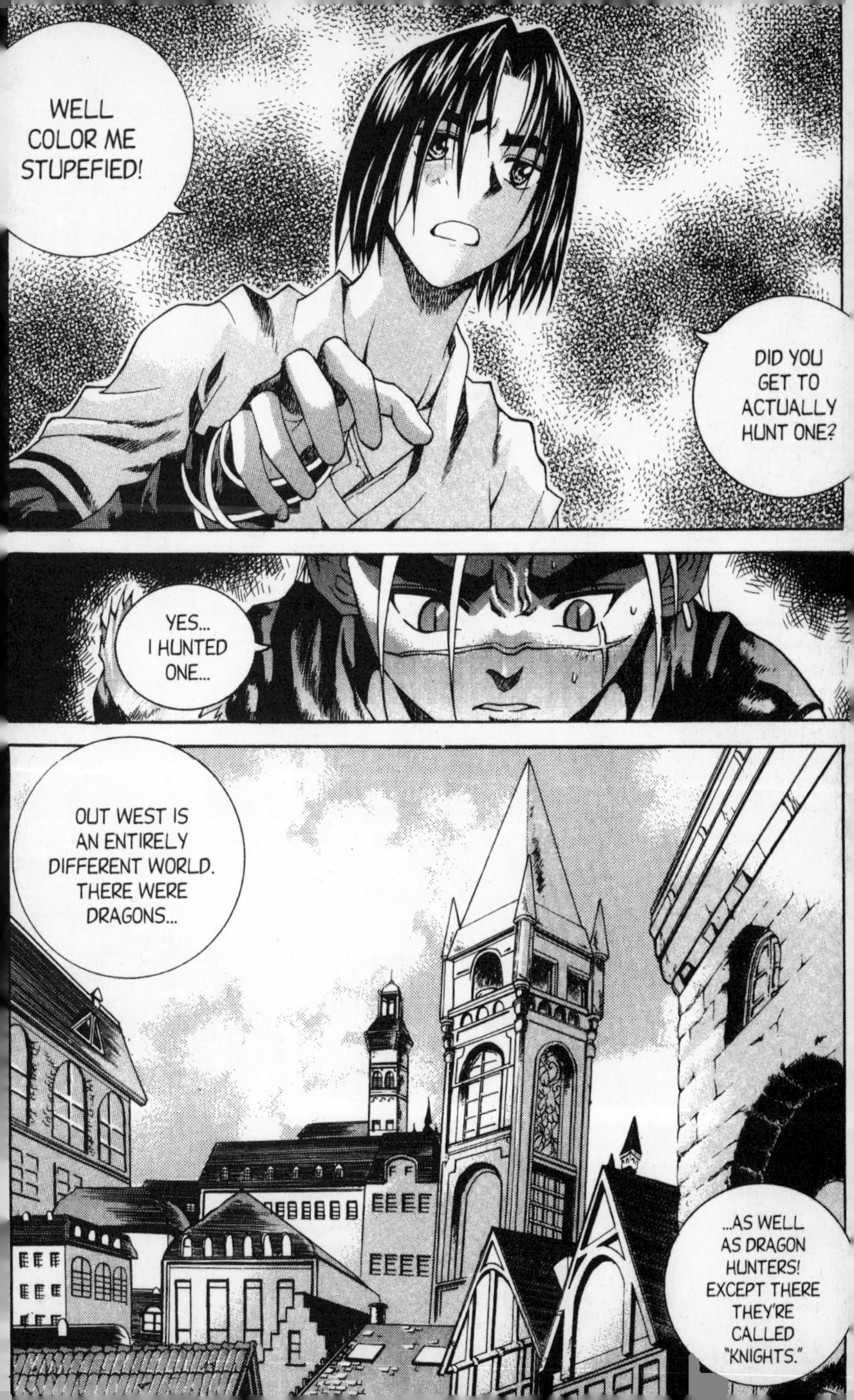
WELL COLOR ME STUPEFIED!
DID YOU GET TO ACTUALLY HUNT ONE?
YES... I HUNTED ONE...
OUT WEST IS AN ENTIRELY DIFFERENT WORLD. THERE WERE DRAGONS...
...AS WELL AS DRAGON HUNTERS! EXCEPT THERE THEY'RE CALLED "KNIGHTS."

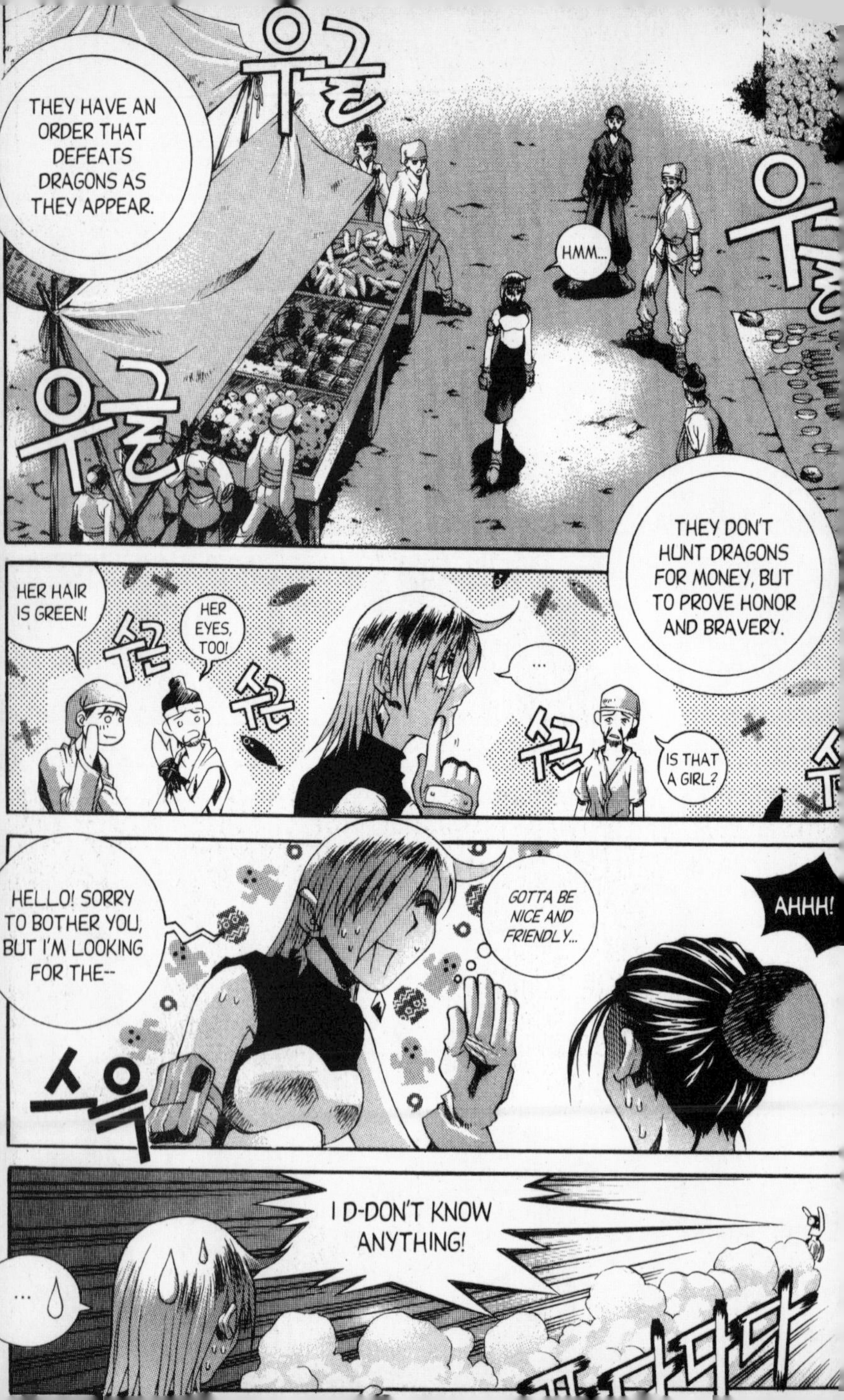

THEY HAVE AN ORDER THAT DEFEATS DRAGONS AS THEY APPEAR.
우글
우글
HMM...
우글
THEY DON'T HUNT DRAGONS FOR MONEY, BUT TO PROVE HONOR AND BRAVERY.
HER HAIR IS GREEN!
수군
HER EYES, TOO!
수군
...
수군
IS THAT A GIRL?
HELLO! SORRY TO BOTHER YOU, BUT I'M LOOKING FOR THE--
스윽
GOTTA BE NICE AND FRIENDLY...
AHHH!
...
I D-DON'T KNOW ANYTHING!

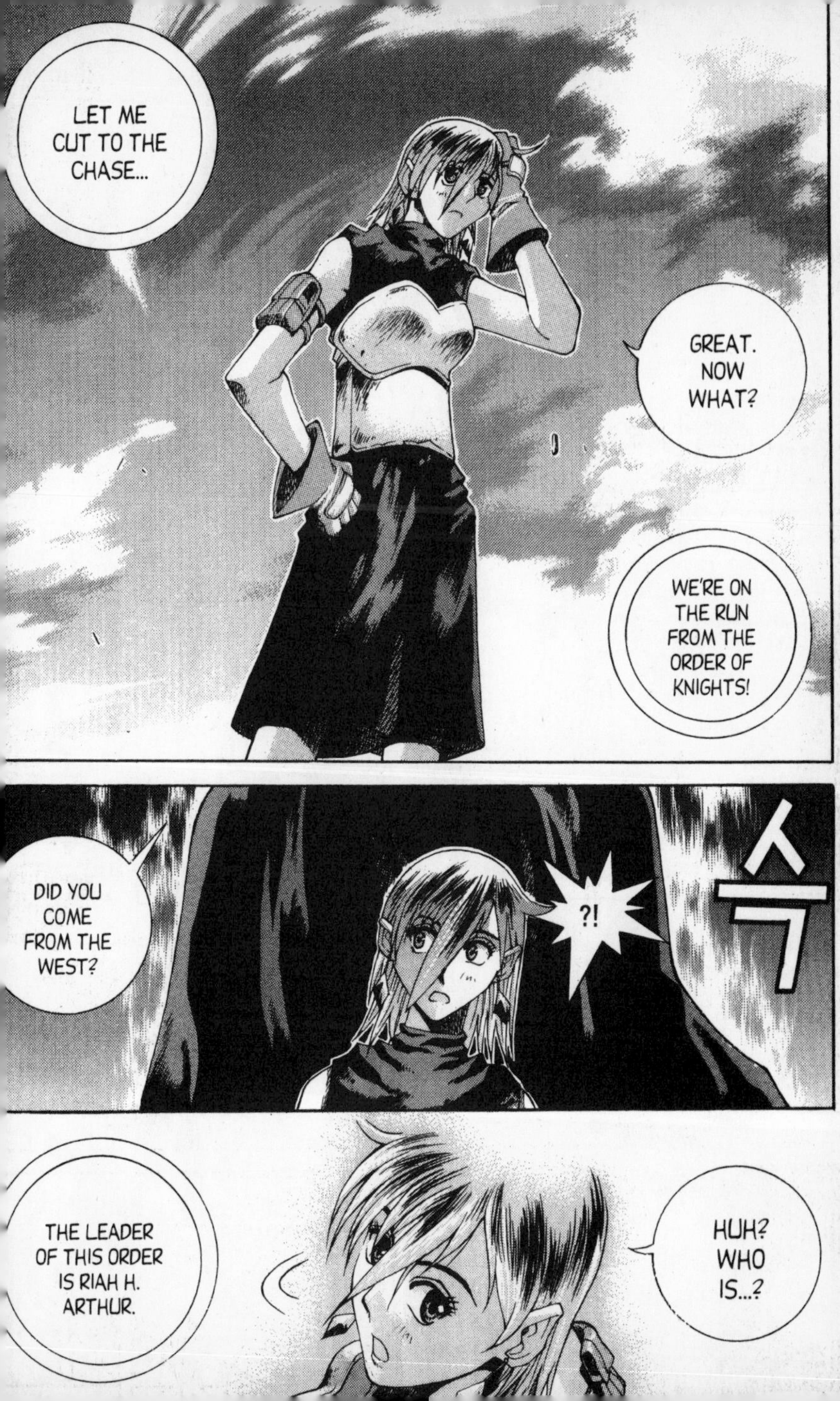
LET ME CUT TO THE CHASE...
GREAT. NOW WHAT?
WE'RE ON THE RUN FROM THE ORDER OF KNIGHTS!
DID YOU COME FROM THE WEST?
?!
THE LEADER OF THIS ORDER IS RIAH H. ARTHUR.
HUH? WHO IS...?

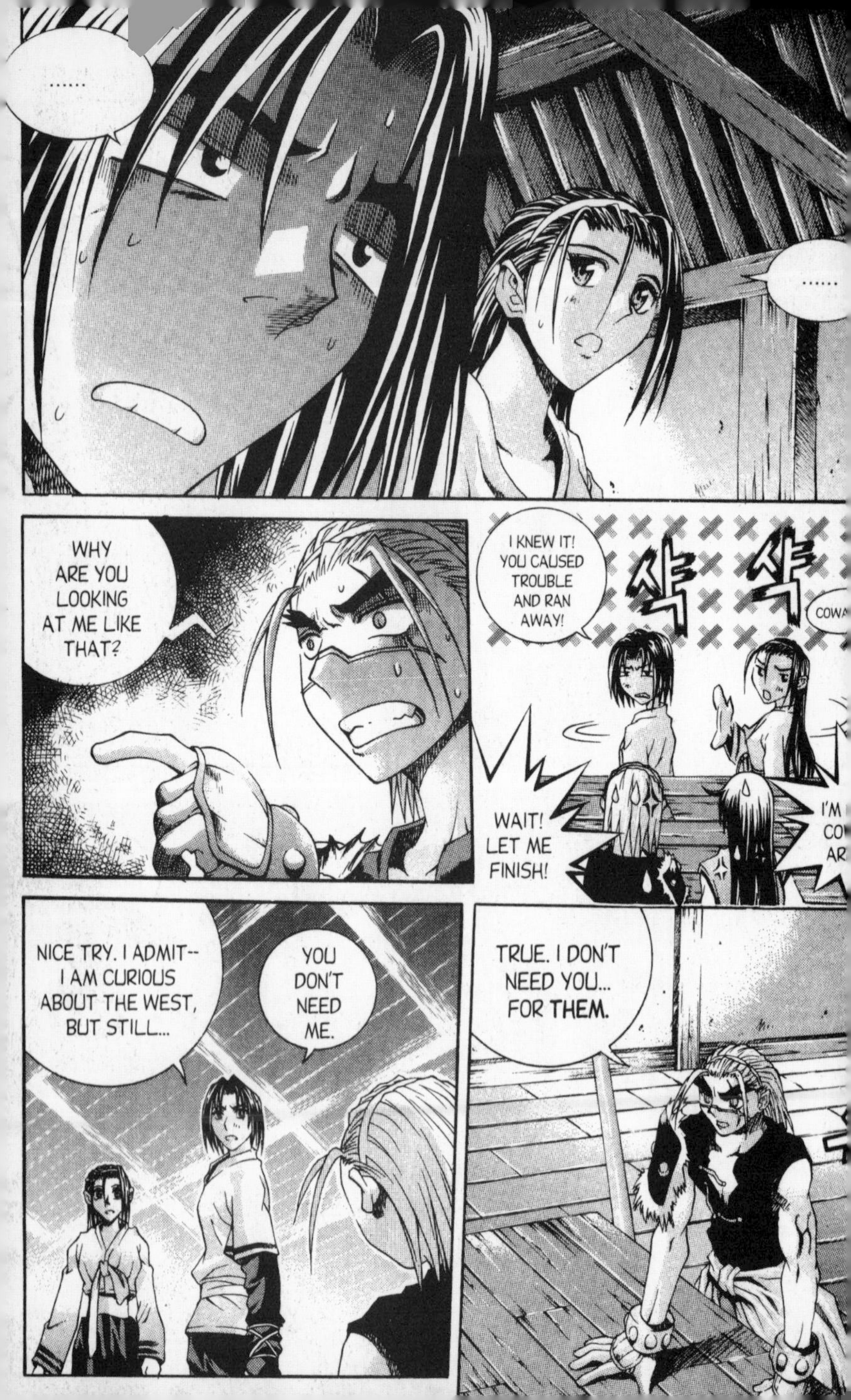
......
......
WHY ARE YOU LOOKING AT ME LIKE THAT?
I KNEW IT! YOU CAUSED TROUBLE AND RAN AWAY!
샥 샥
WAIT! LET ME FINISH!
NICE TRY. I ADMIT-- I AM CURIOUS ABOUT THE WEST, BUT STILL...
YOU DON'T NEED ME.
TRUE. I DON'T NEED YOU... FOR THEM.

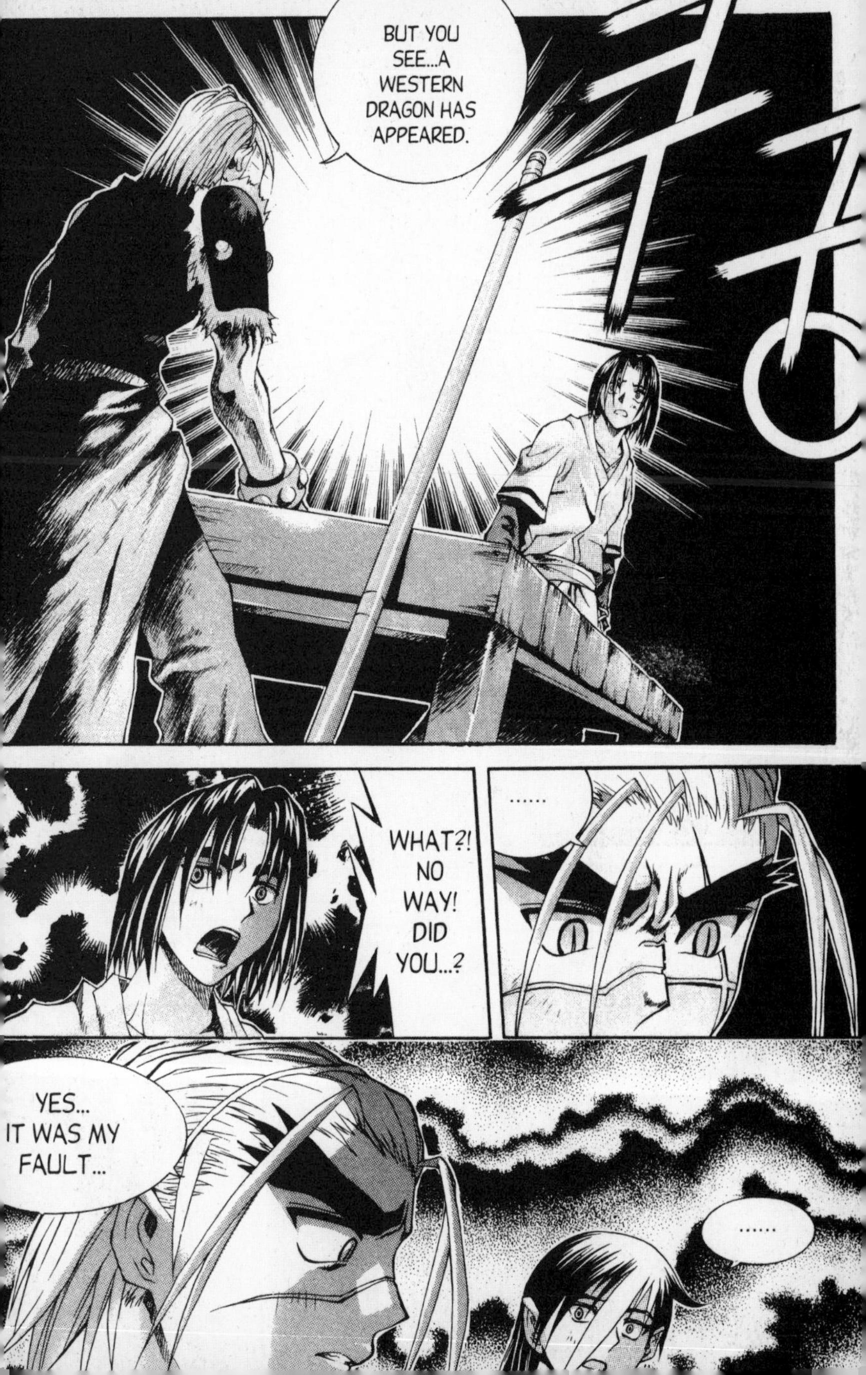
BUT YOU SEE...A WESTERN DRAGON HAS APPEARED.
WHAT?! NO WAY! DID YOU...?
......
YES... IT WAS MY FAULT...
......

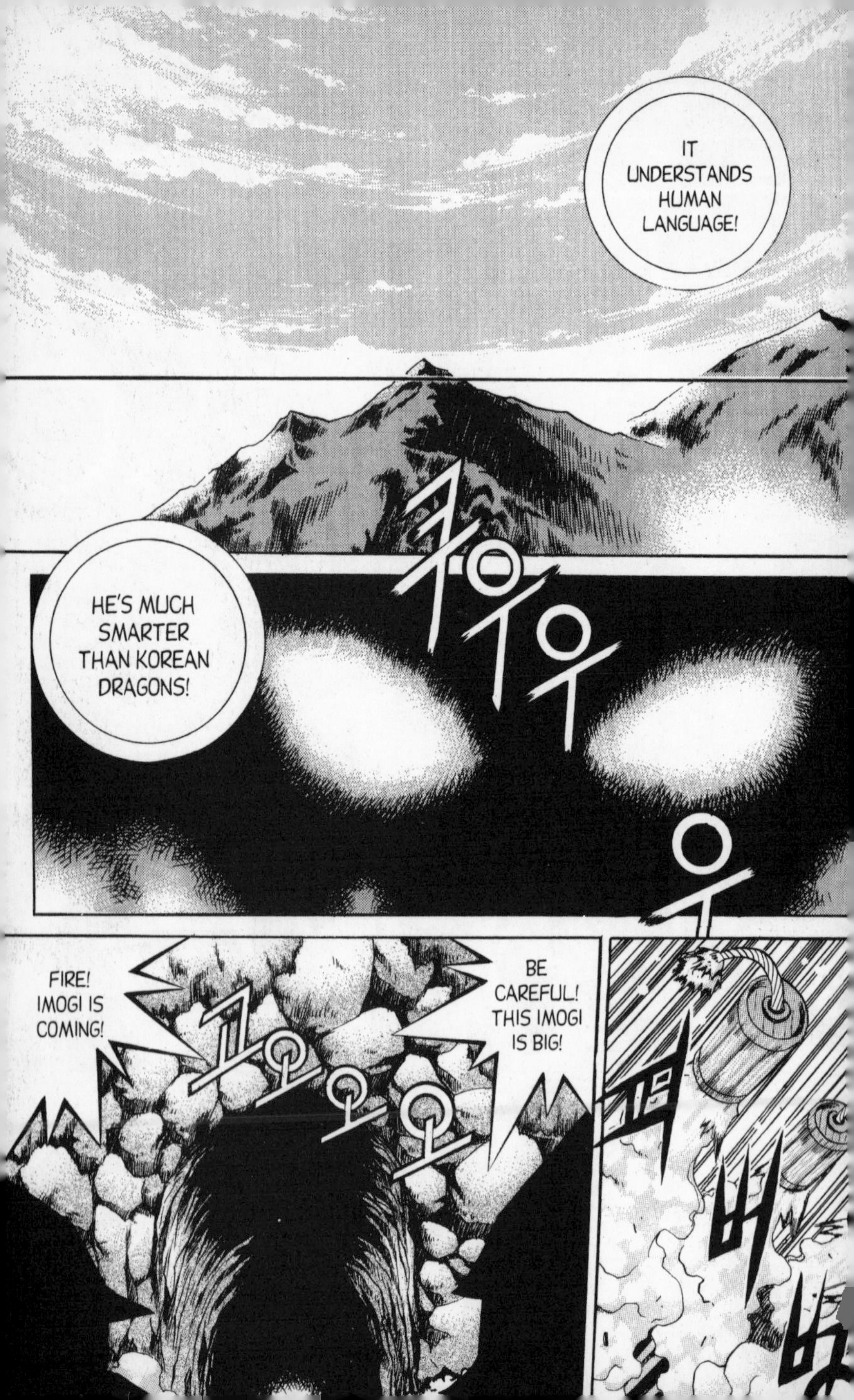
IT UNDERSTANDS HUMAN LANGUAGE!
HE'S MUCH SMARTER THAN KOREAN DRAGONS!
FIRE! IMOGI IS COMING!
BE CAREFUL! THIS IMOGI IS BIG!

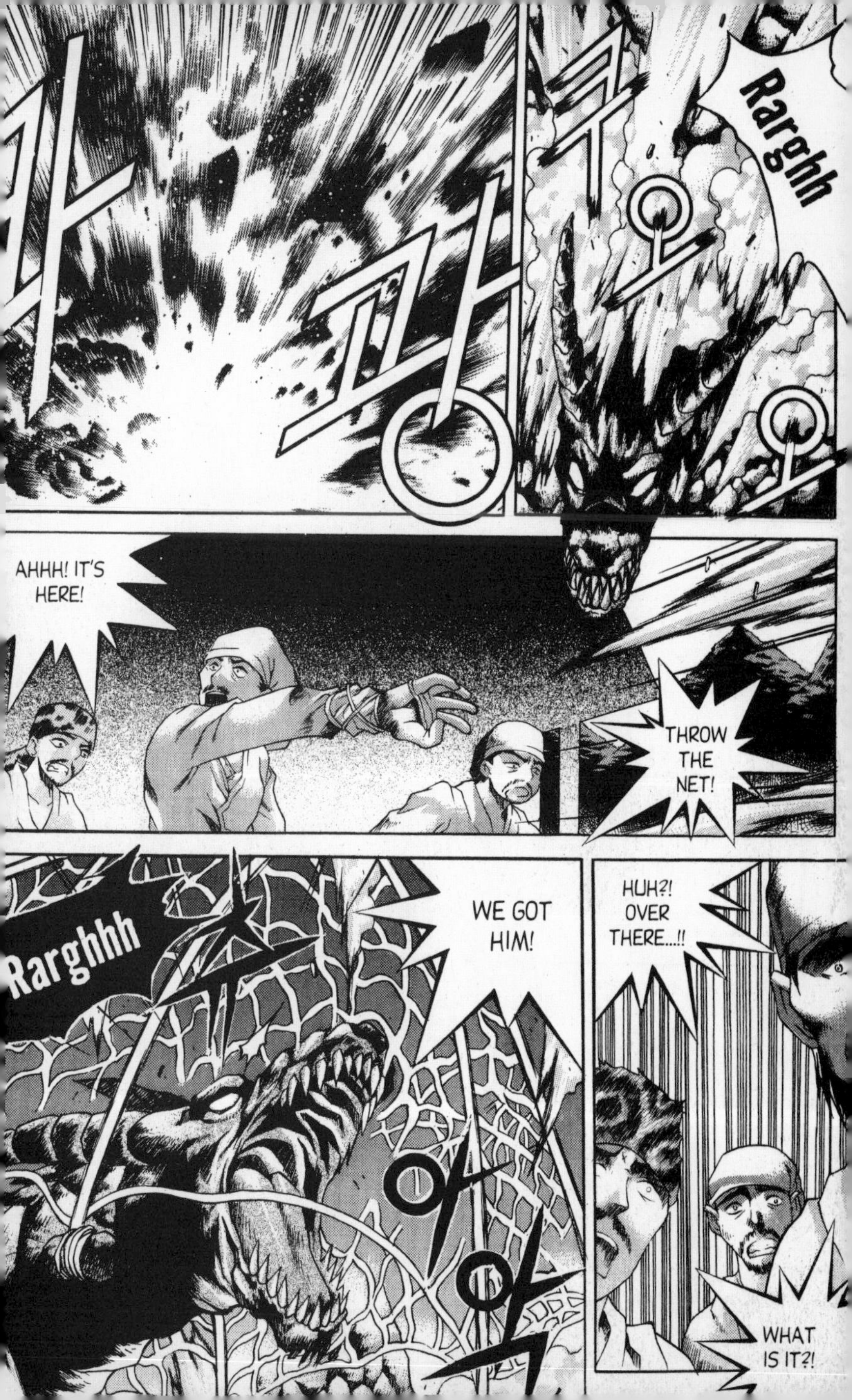
Rarghh
AHHH! IT'S HERE!
THROW THE NET!
Rarghhh
WE GOT HIM!
HUH?! OVER THERE...!!
WHAT IS IT?!

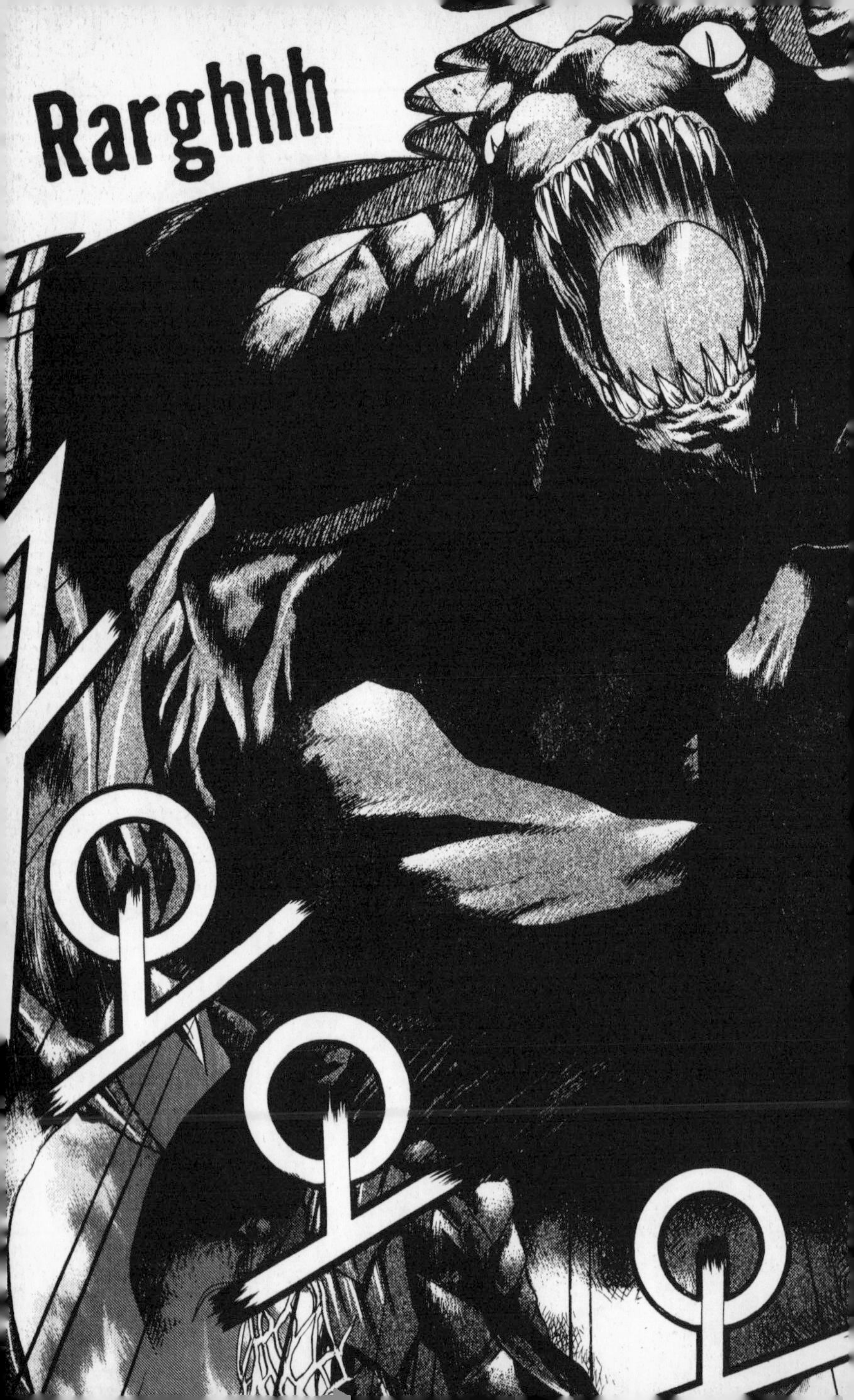
Rarghhh

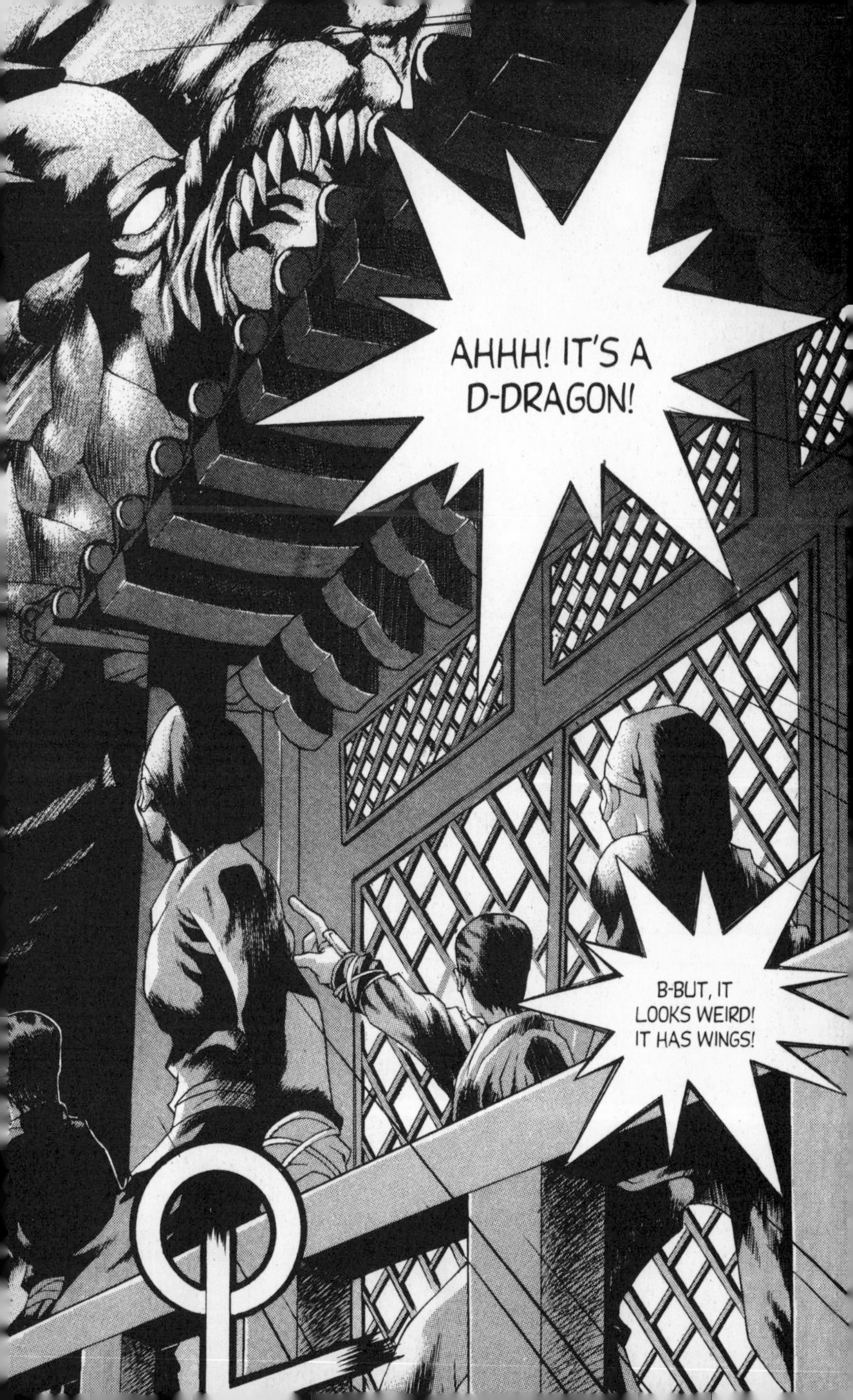
AHHH! IT'S A D-DRAGON!
B-BUT, IT LOOKS WEIRD! IT HAS WINGS!

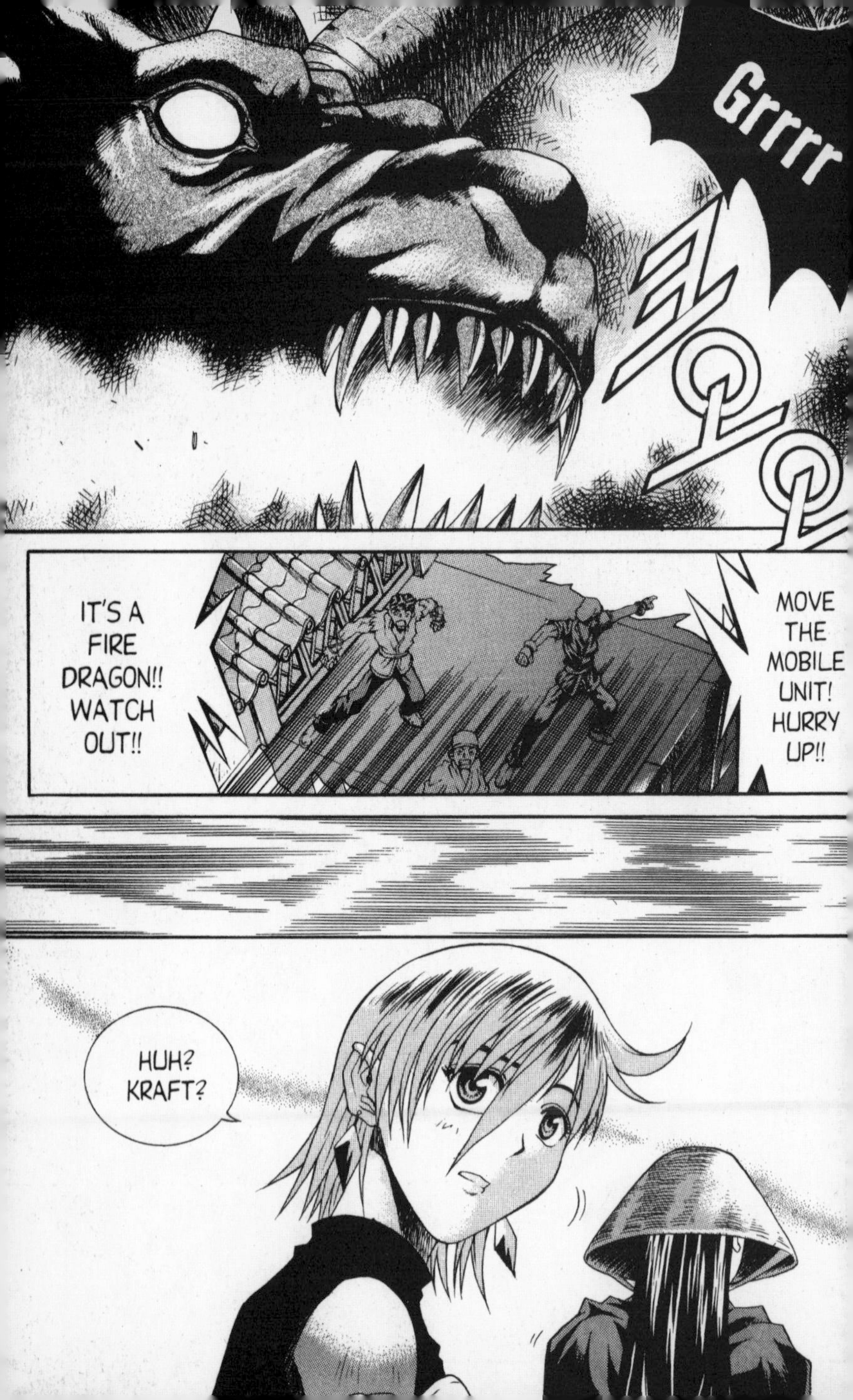
Grrrr
ZIGGY
IT'S A FIRE DRAGON!! WATCH OUT!!
MOVE THE MOBILE UNIT! HURRY UP!!
HUH? KRAFT?

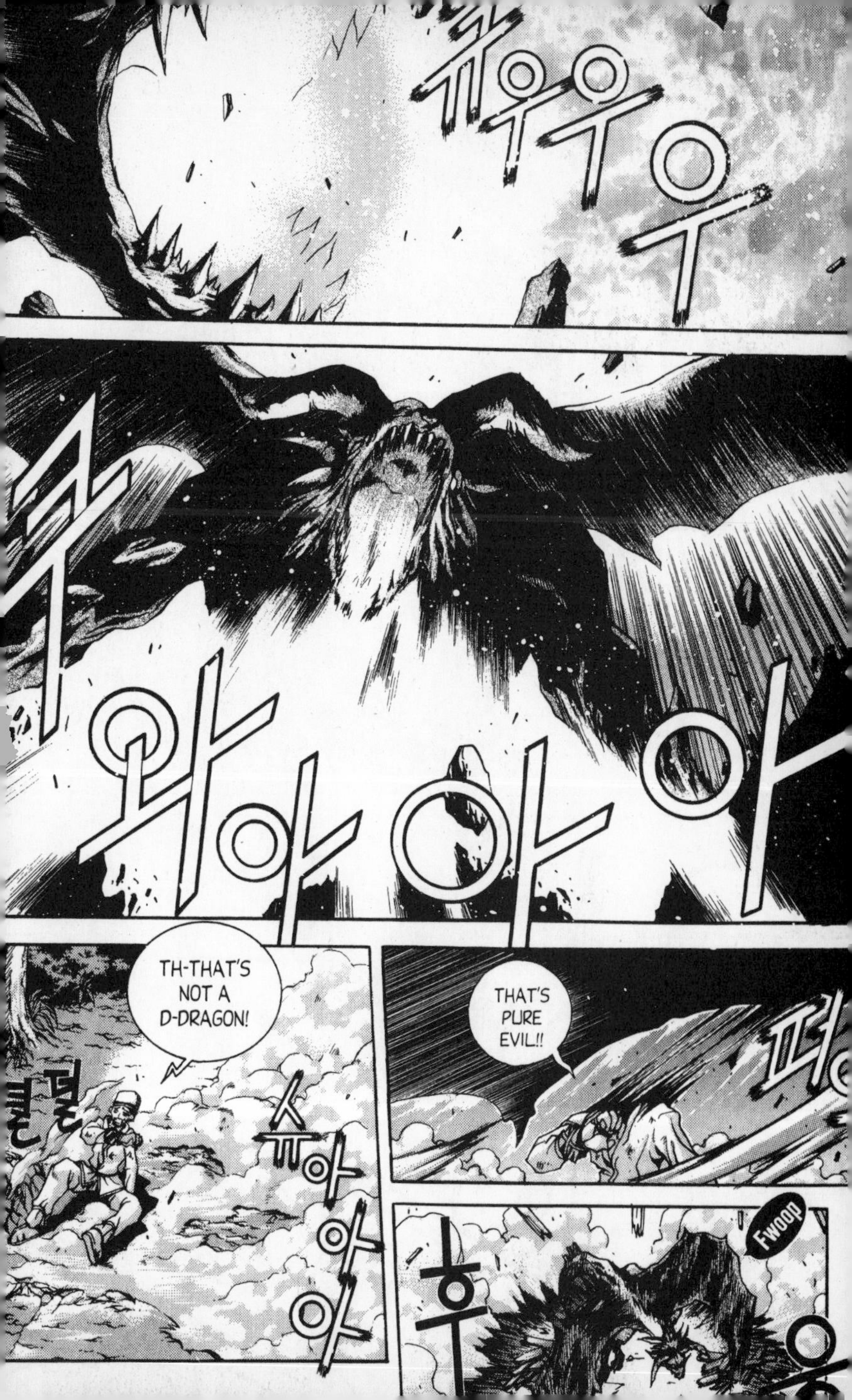
TH-THAT'S NOT A D-DRAGON!
THAT'S PURE EVIL!!
Fwoop

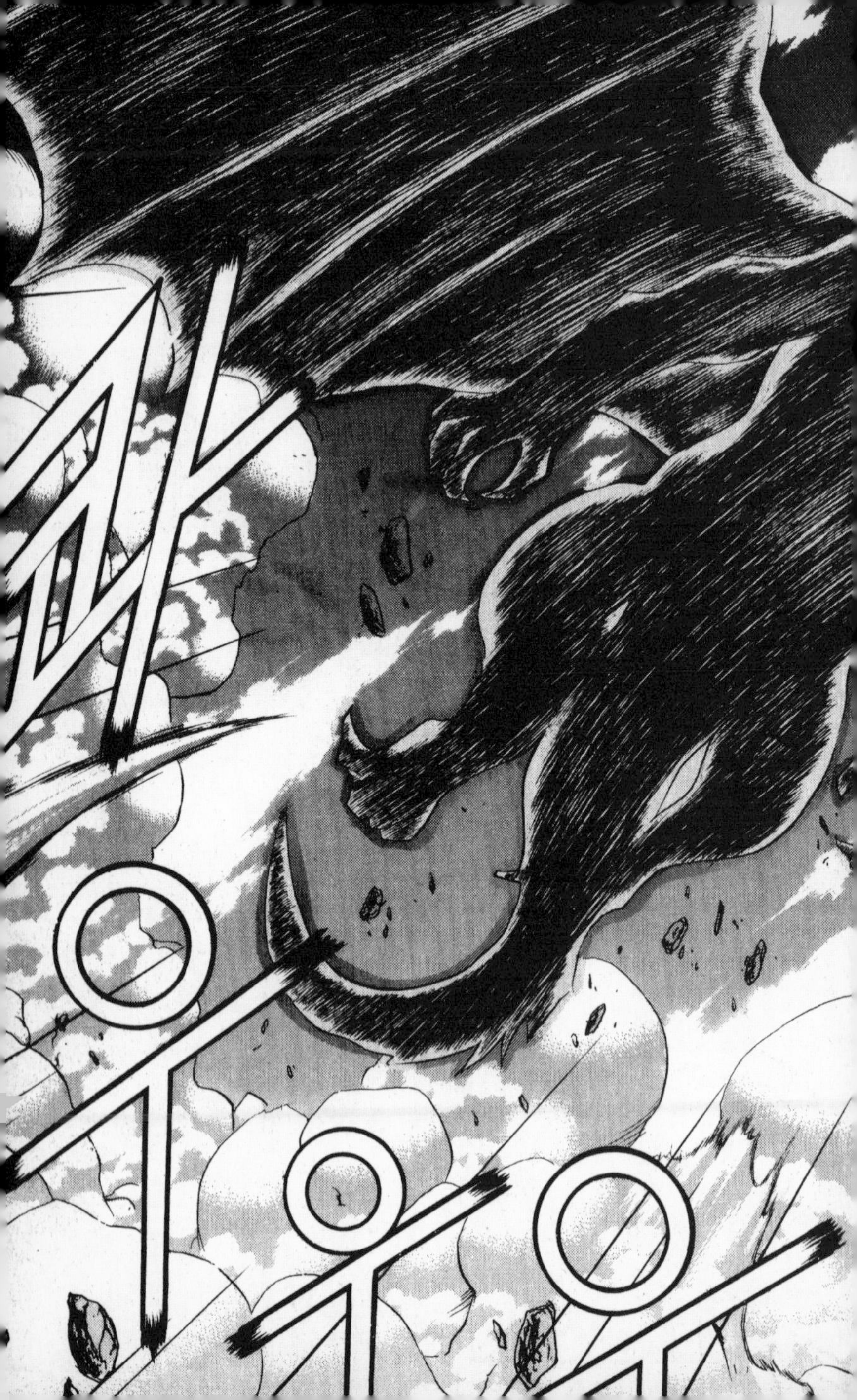

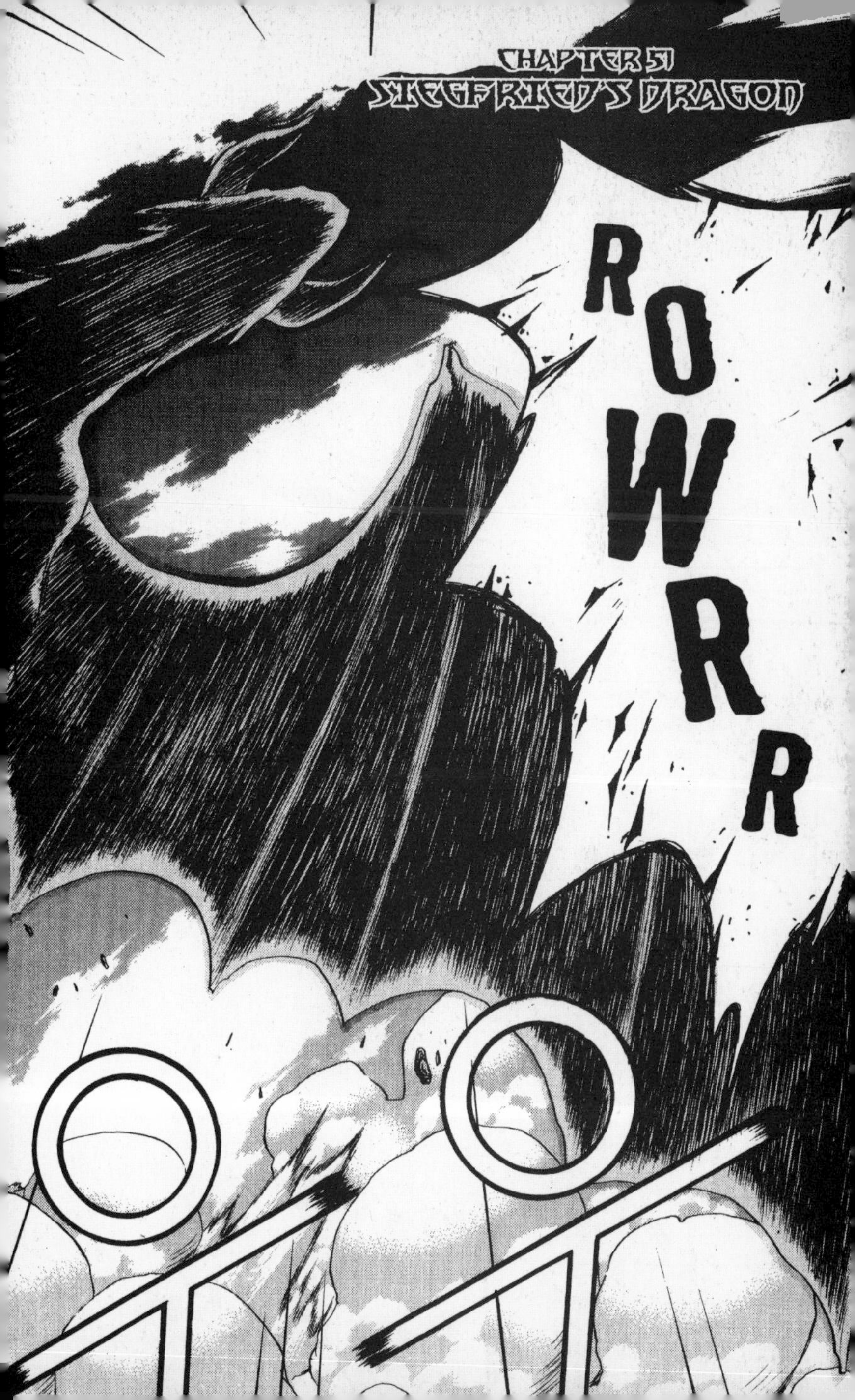
CHAPTER 51
SIEGFRIED'S DRAGON
ROWRRR

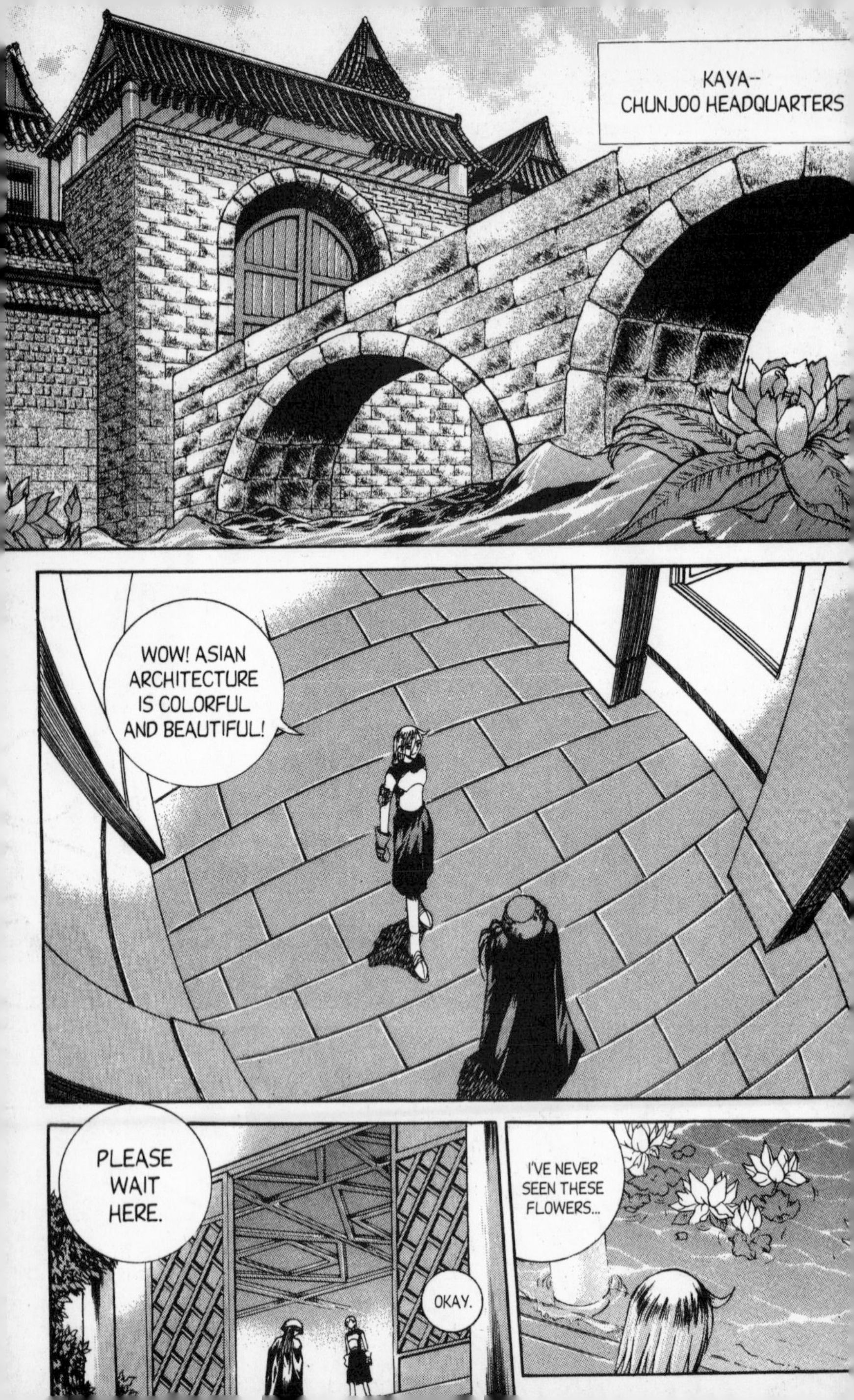
KAYA--
CHUNJOO HEADQUARTERS
WOW! ASIAN ARCHITECTURE IS COLORFUL AND BEAUTIFUL!
PLEASE WAIT HERE.
OKAY.
I'VE NEVER SEEN THESE FLOWERS...

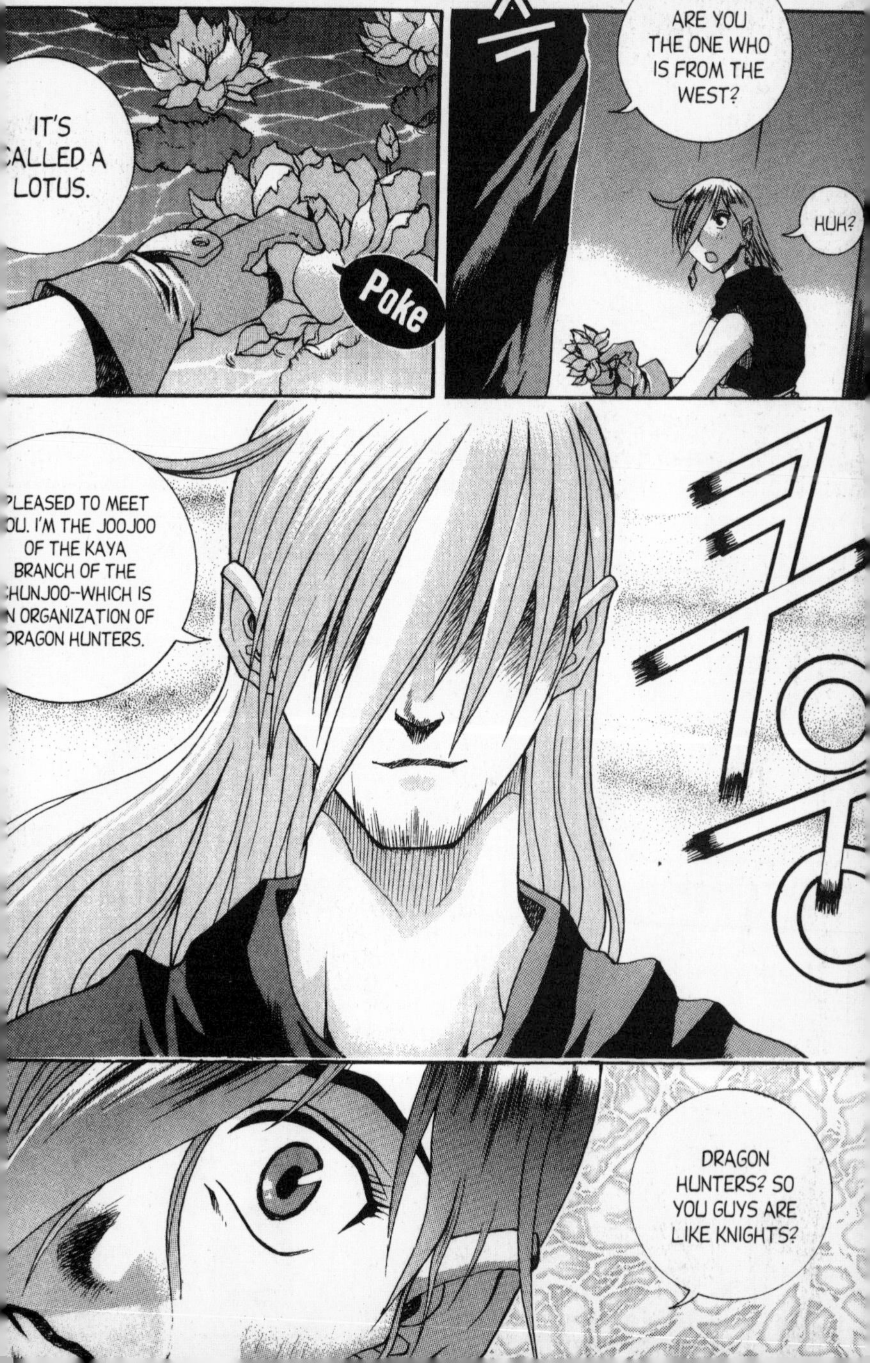
IT'S ALLED A LOTUS.
Poke
ARE YOU THE ONE WHO IS FROM THE WEST?
HUH?
LEASED TO MEET OU. I'M THE JOOJOO OF THE KAYA BRANCH OF THE HUNJOO--WHICH IS N ORGANIZATION OF RAGON HUNTERS.
DRAGON HUNTERS? SO YOU GUYS ARE LIKE KNIGHTS?

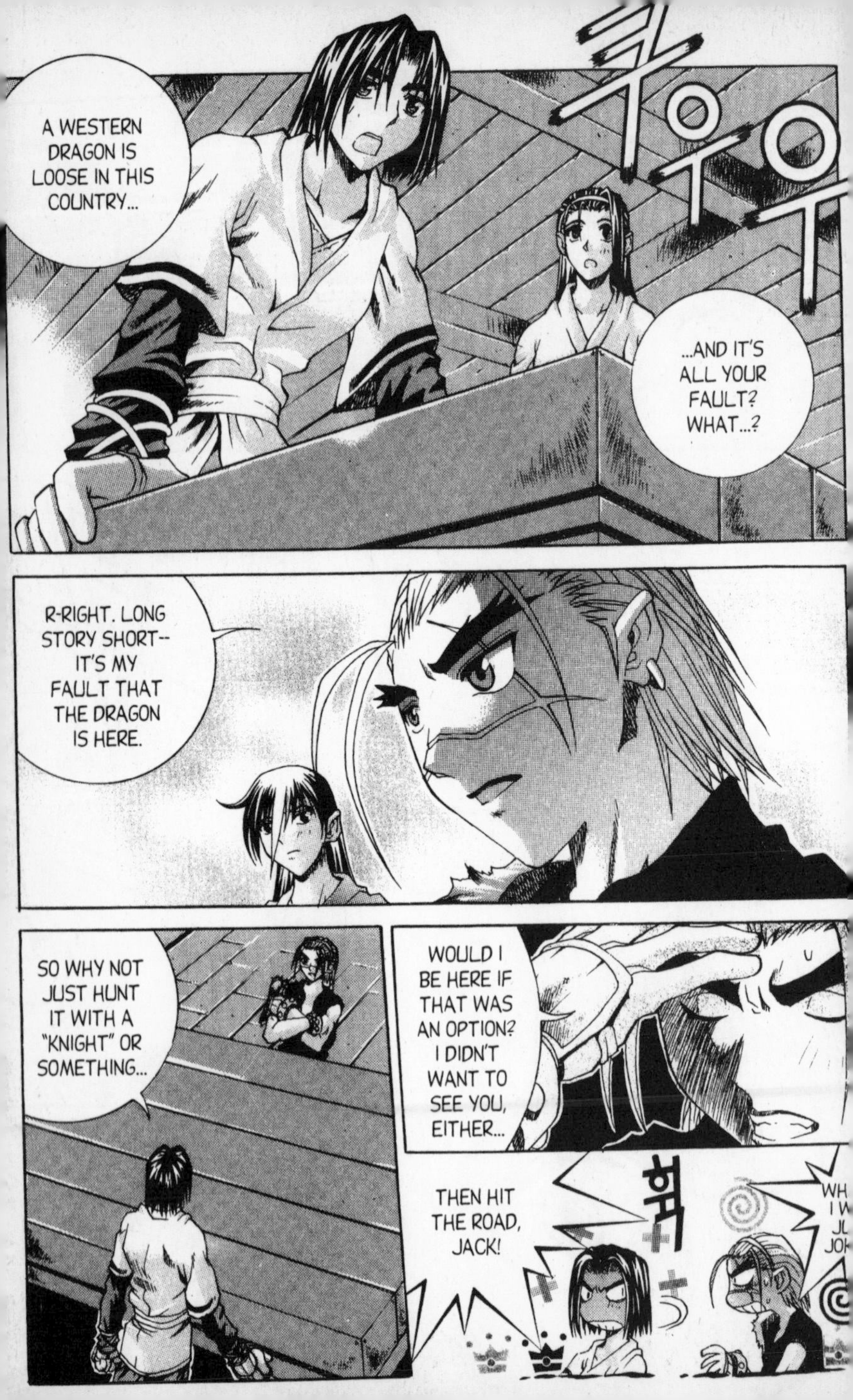
A WESTERN DRAGON IS LOOSE IN THIS COUNTRY...
쿠우우
...AND IT'S ALL YOUR FAULT? WHAT...?
R-RIGHT. LONG STORY SHORT-- IT'S MY FAULT THAT THE DRAGON IS HERE.
SO WHY NOT JUST HUNT IT WITH A "KNIGHT" OR SOMETHING...
WOULD I BE HERE IF THAT WAS AN OPTION? I DIDN'T WANT TO SEE YOU, EITHER...
THEN HIT THE ROAD, JACK!
홱

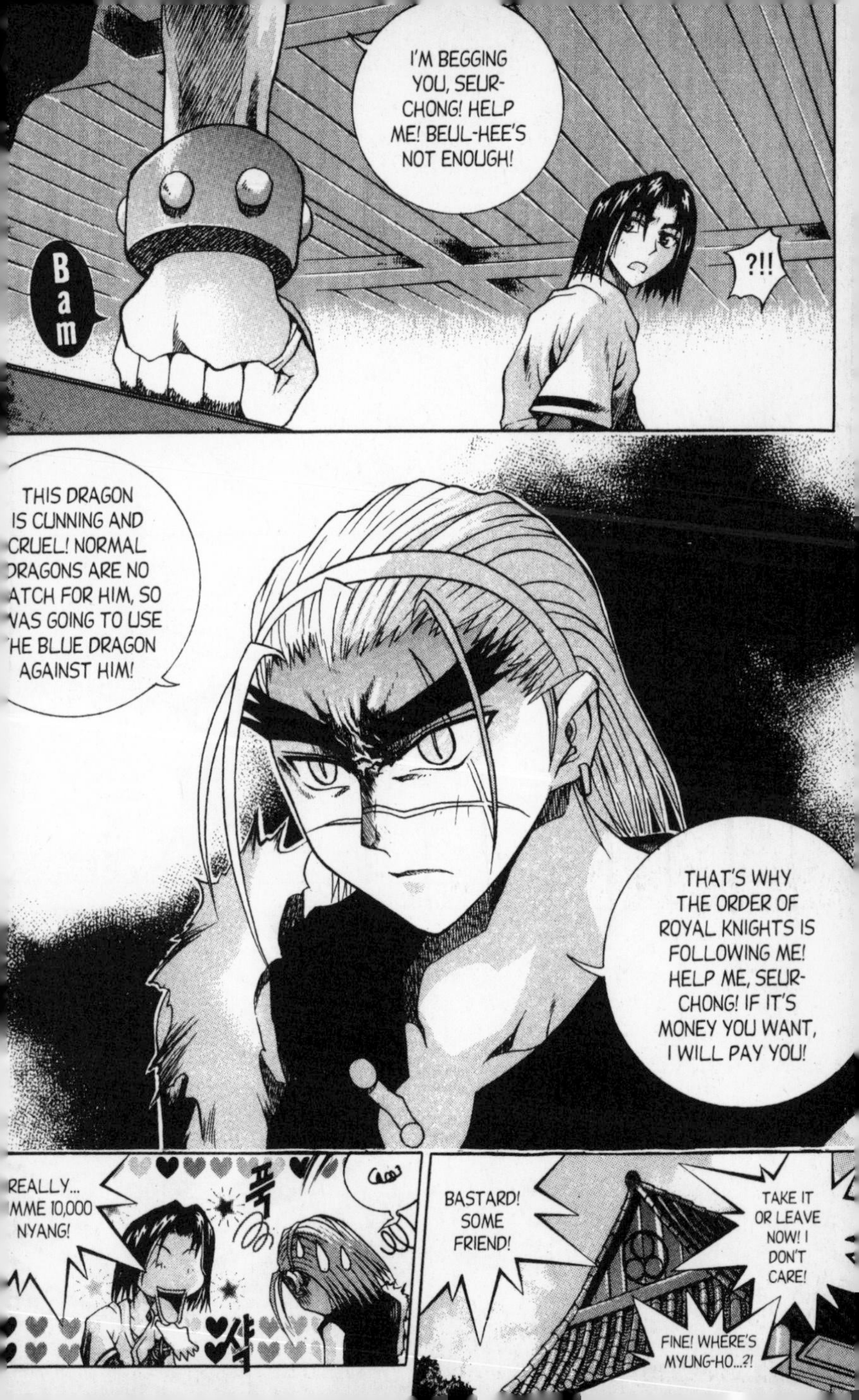
I'M BEGGING YOU, SEUR-CHONG! HELP ME! BEUL-HEE'S NOT ENOUGH!
Bam
?!!
THIS DRAGON IS CUNNING AND CRUEL! NORMAL DRAGONS ARE NO ATCH FOR HIM, SO VAS GOING TO USE HE BLUE DRAGON AGAINST HIM!
THAT'S WHY THE ORDER OF ROYAL KNIGHTS IS FOLLOWING ME! HELP ME, SEUR-CHONG! IF IT'S MONEY YOU WANT, I WILL PAY YOU!
REALLY... MME 10,000 NYANG!
푹
샥
BASTARD! SOME FRIEND!
TAKE IT OR LEAVE NOW! I DON'T CARE!
FINE! WHERE'S MYUNG-HO...?!

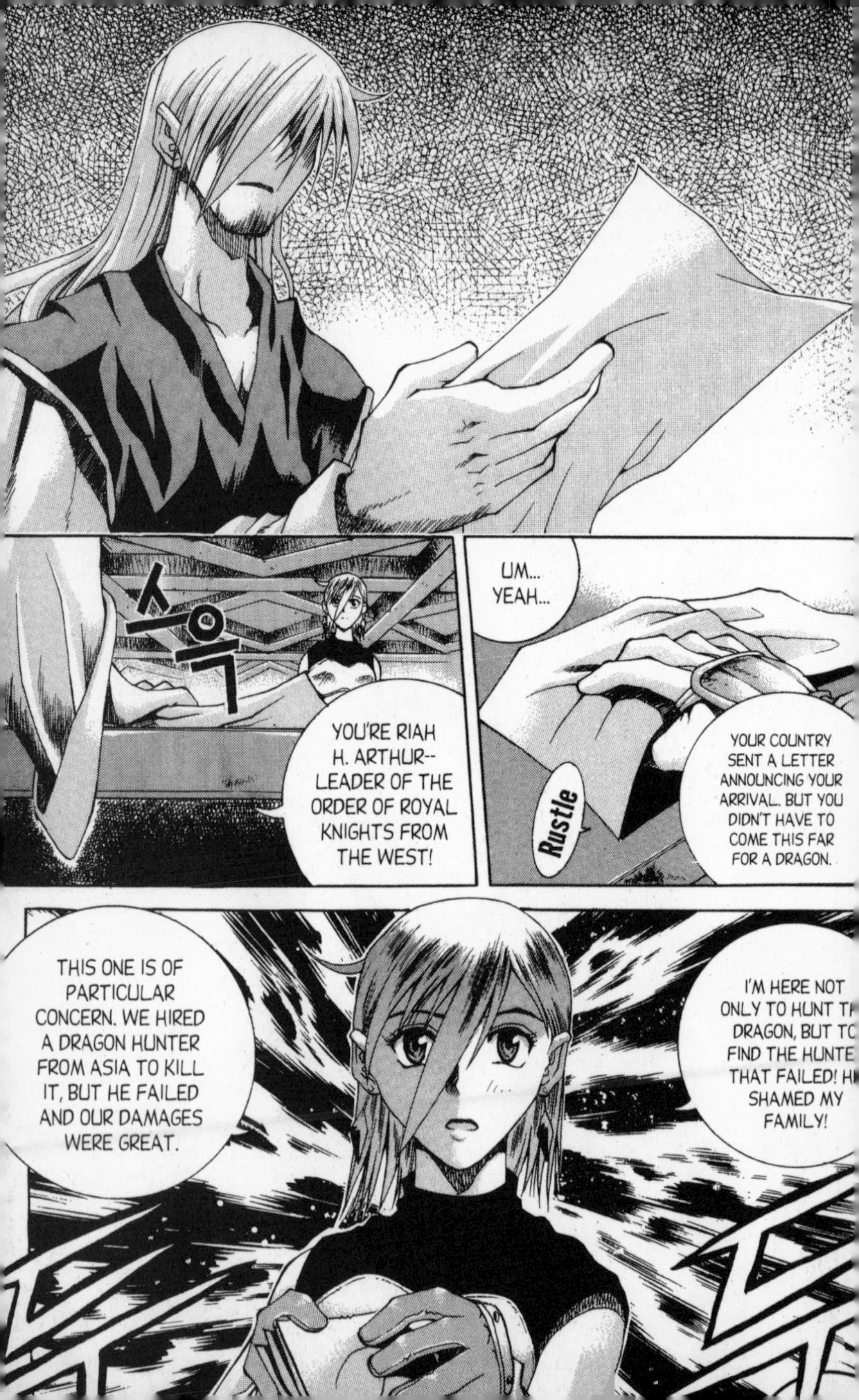

YOU'RE RIAH H. ARTHUR-- LEADER OF THE ORDER OF ROYAL KNIGHTS FROM THE WEST!
UM... YEAH...
Rustle
YOUR COUNTRY SENT A LETTER ANNOUNCING YOUR ARRIVAL. BUT YOU DIDN'T HAVE TO COME THIS FAR FOR A DRAGON.
THIS ONE IS OF PARTICULAR CONCERN. WE HIRED A DRAGON HUNTER FROM ASIA TO KILL IT, BUT HE FAILED AND OUR DAMAGES WERE GREAT.
I'M HERE NOT ONLY TO HUNT TH DRAGON, BUT TO FIND THE HUNTE THAT FAILED! H SHAMED MY FAMILY!

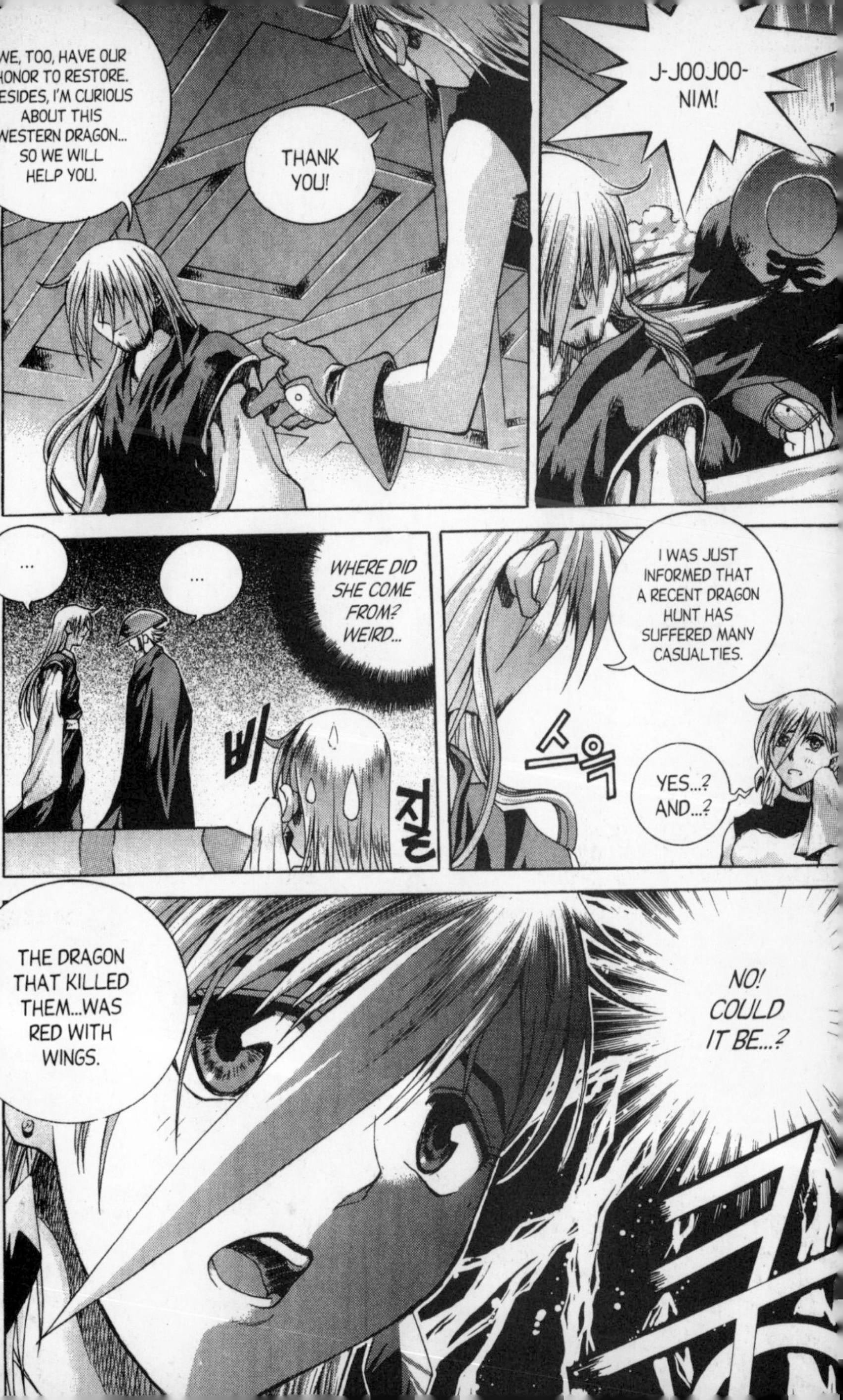
WE, TOO, HAVE OUR HONOR TO RESTORE. BESIDES, I'M CURIOUS ABOUT THIS WESTERN DRAGON... SO WE WILL HELP YOU.
THANK YOU!
J-JOOJOO-NIM!
...
...
WHERE DID SHE COME FROM? WEIRD...
삐질
I WAS JUST INFORMED THAT A RECENT DRAGON HUNT HAS SUFFERED MANY CASUALTIES.
스윽
YES...? AND...?
THE DRAGON THAT KILLED THEM...WAS RED WITH WINGS.
NO! COULD IT BE...?

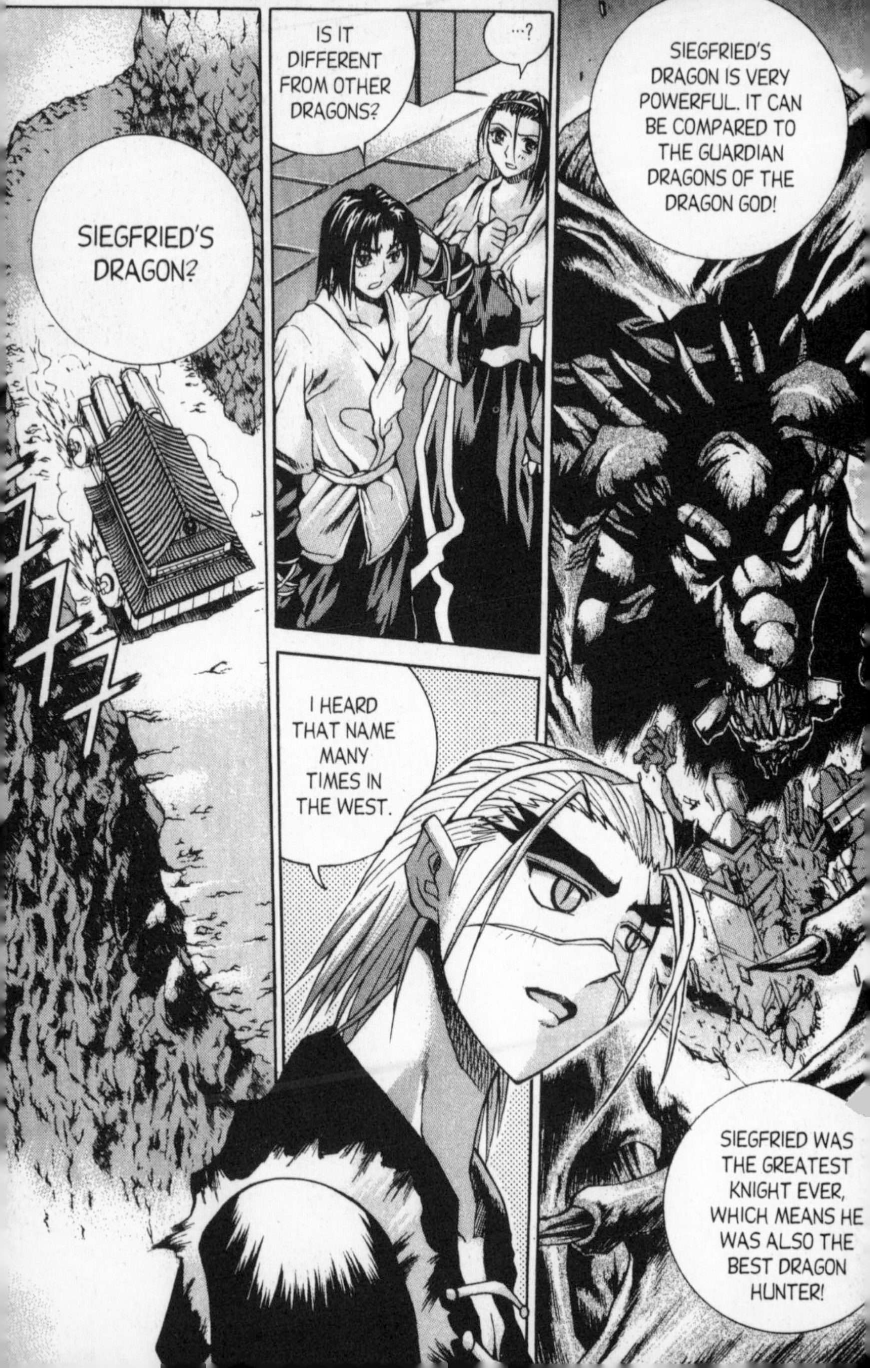
SIEGFRIED'S DRAGON?
IS IT DIFFERENT FROM OTHER DRAGONS?
...?
I HEARD THAT NAME MANY TIMES IN THE WEST.
SIEGFRIED'S DRAGON IS VERY POWERFUL. IT CAN BE COMPARED TO THE GUARDIAN DRAGONS OF THE DRAGON GOD!
SIEGFRIED WAS THE GREATEST KNIGHT EVER, WHICH MEANS HE WAS ALSO THE BEST DRAGON HUNTER!

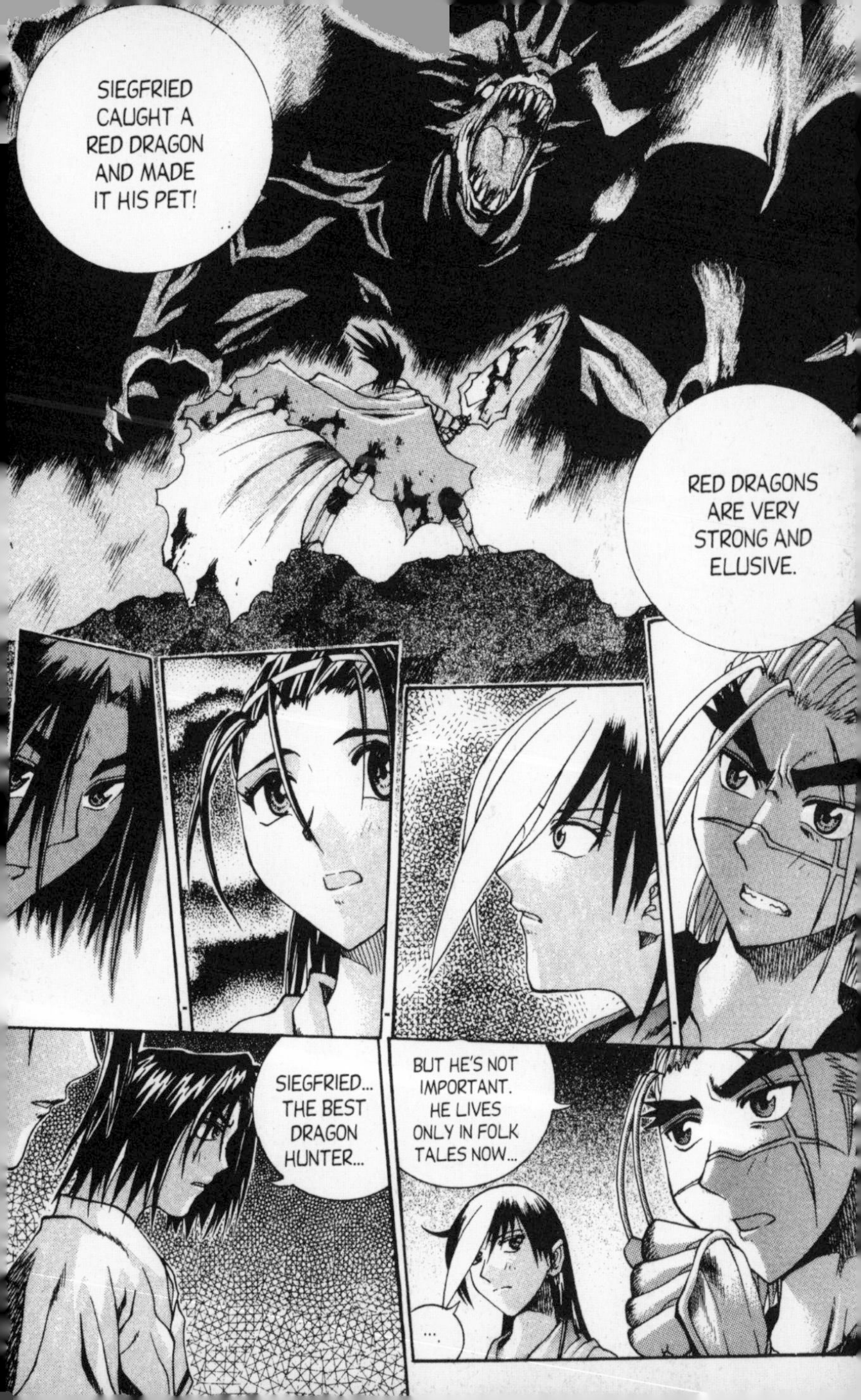
SIEGFRIED CAUGHT A RED DRAGON AND MADE IT HIS PET!
RED DRAGONS ARE VERY STRONG AND ELUSIVE.
SIEGFRIED... THE BEST DRAGON HUNTER...
BUT HE'S NOT IMPORTANT. HE LIVES ONLY IN FOLK TALES NOW...
...

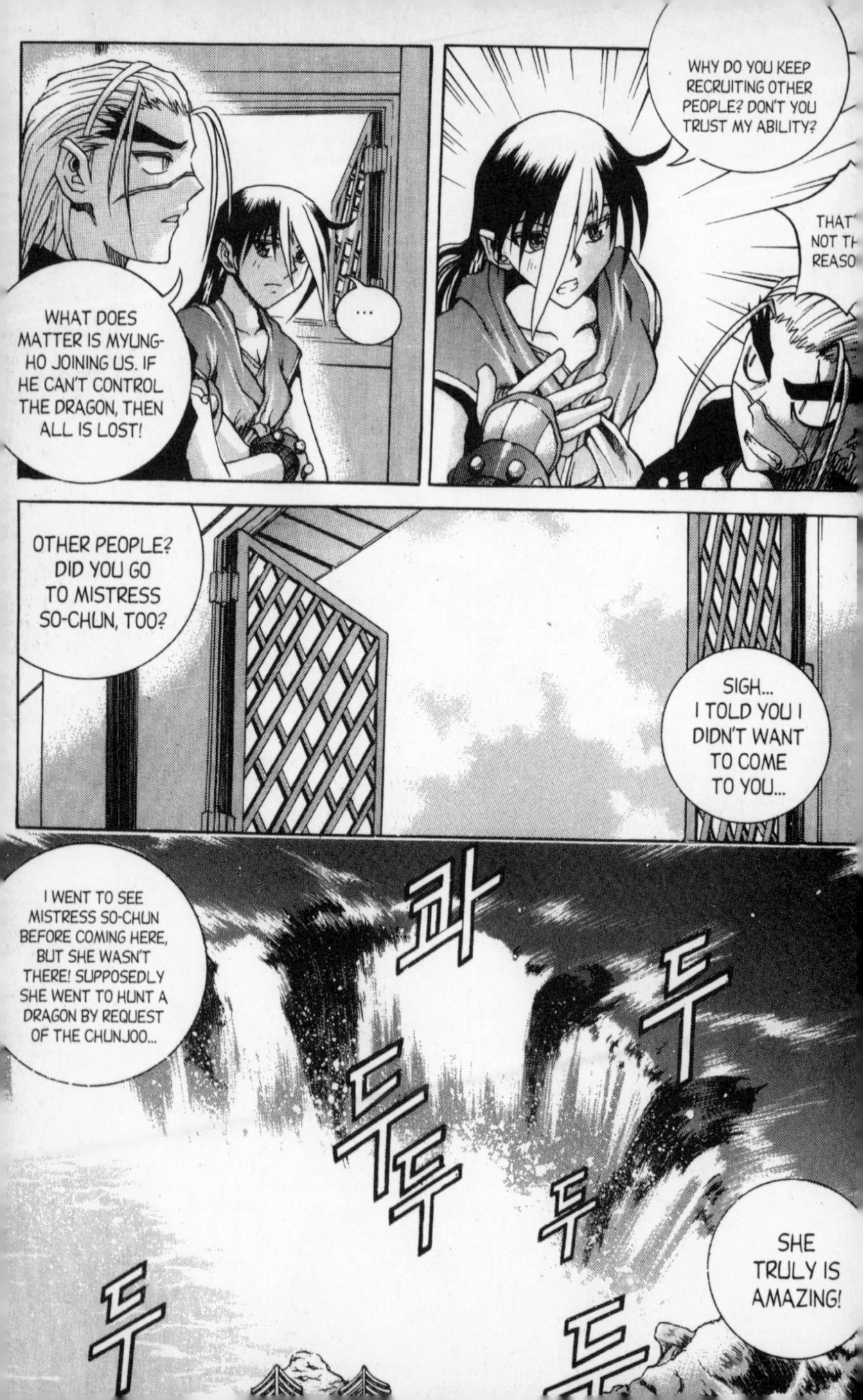

WHAT DOES MATTER IS MYUNG-HO JOINING US. IF HE CAN'T CONTROL THE DRAGON, THEN ALL IS LOST!
...
WHY DO YOU KEEP RECRUITING OTHER PEOPLE? DON'T YOU TRUST MY ABILITY?
THAT' NOT TH REASO
OTHER PEOPLE? DID YOU GO TO MISTRESS SO-CHUN, TOO?
SIGH... I TOLD YOU I DIDN'T WANT TO COME TO YOU...
I WENT TO SEE MISTRESS SO-CHUN BEFORE COMING HERE, BUT SHE WASN'T THERE! SUPPOSEDLY SHE WENT TO HUNT A DRAGON BY REQUEST OF THE CHUNJOO...
콰
SHE TRULY IS AMAZING!

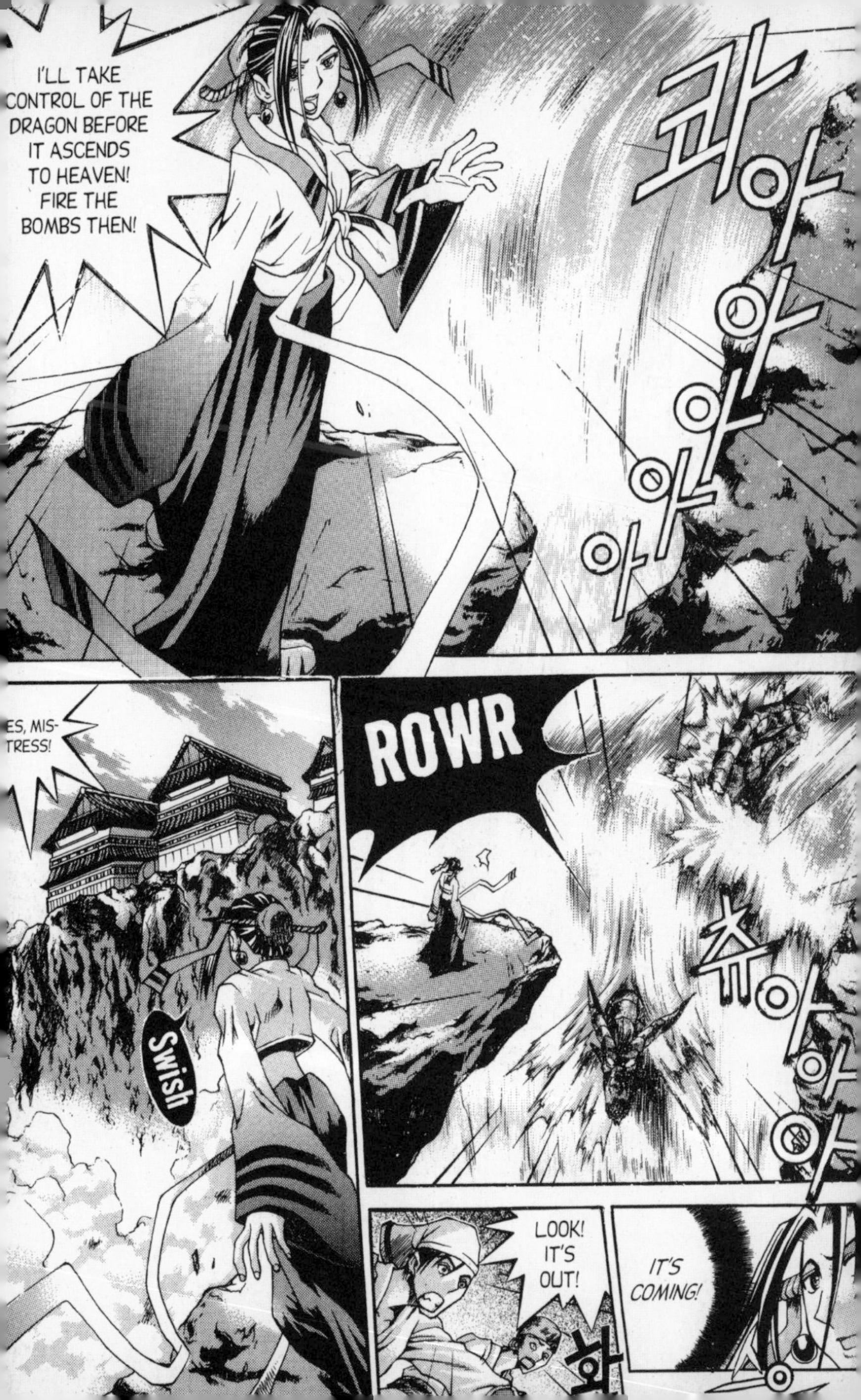
I'LL TAKE CONTROL OF THE DRAGON BEFORE IT ASCENDS TO HEAVEN! FIRE THE BOMBS THEN!
콰아아아아아
ES, MIS-TRESS!
Swish
ROWR
슈아아아
LOOK! IT'S OUT!
IT'S COMING!

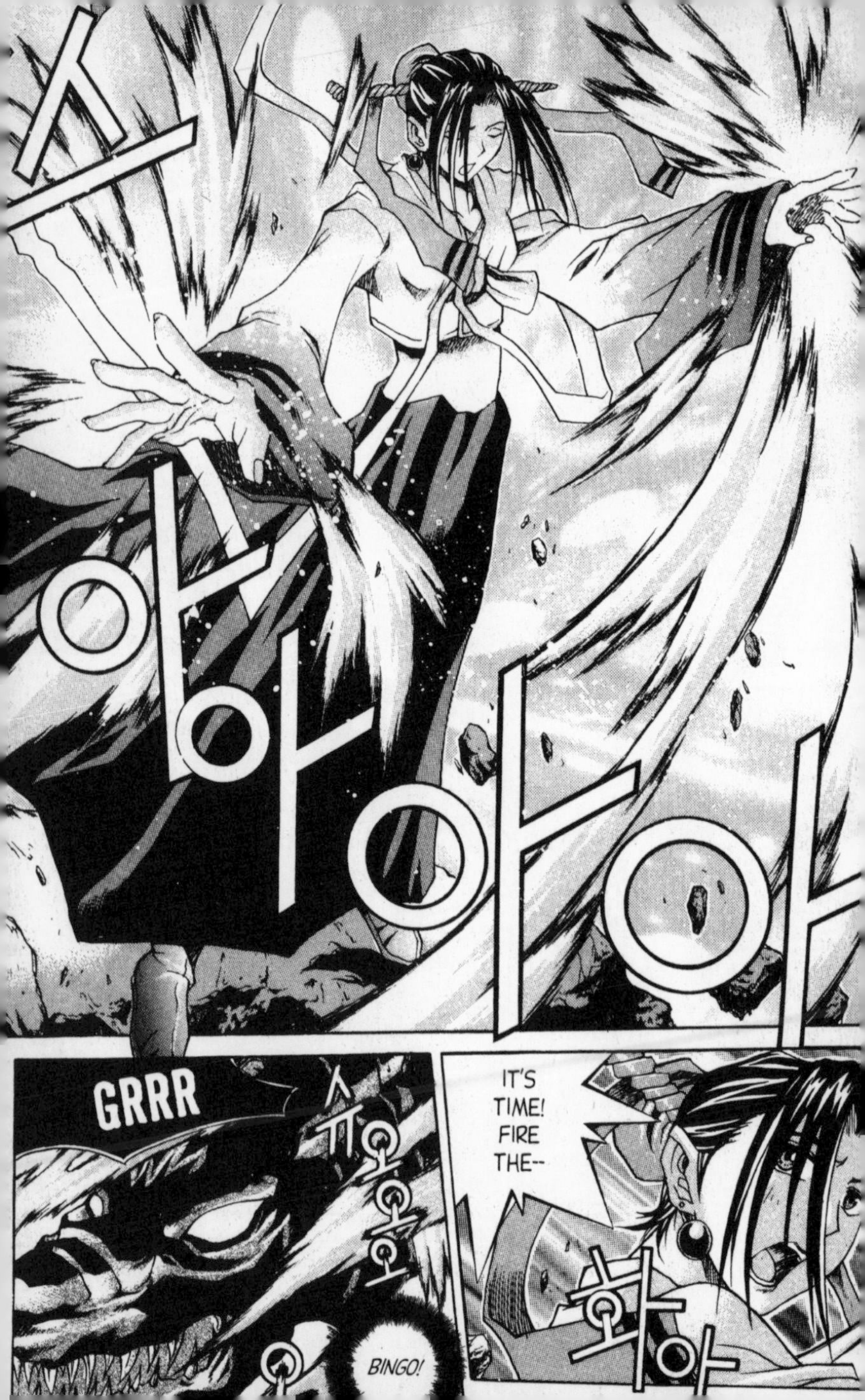
GRRR
BINGO!
IT'S TIME! FIRE THE--

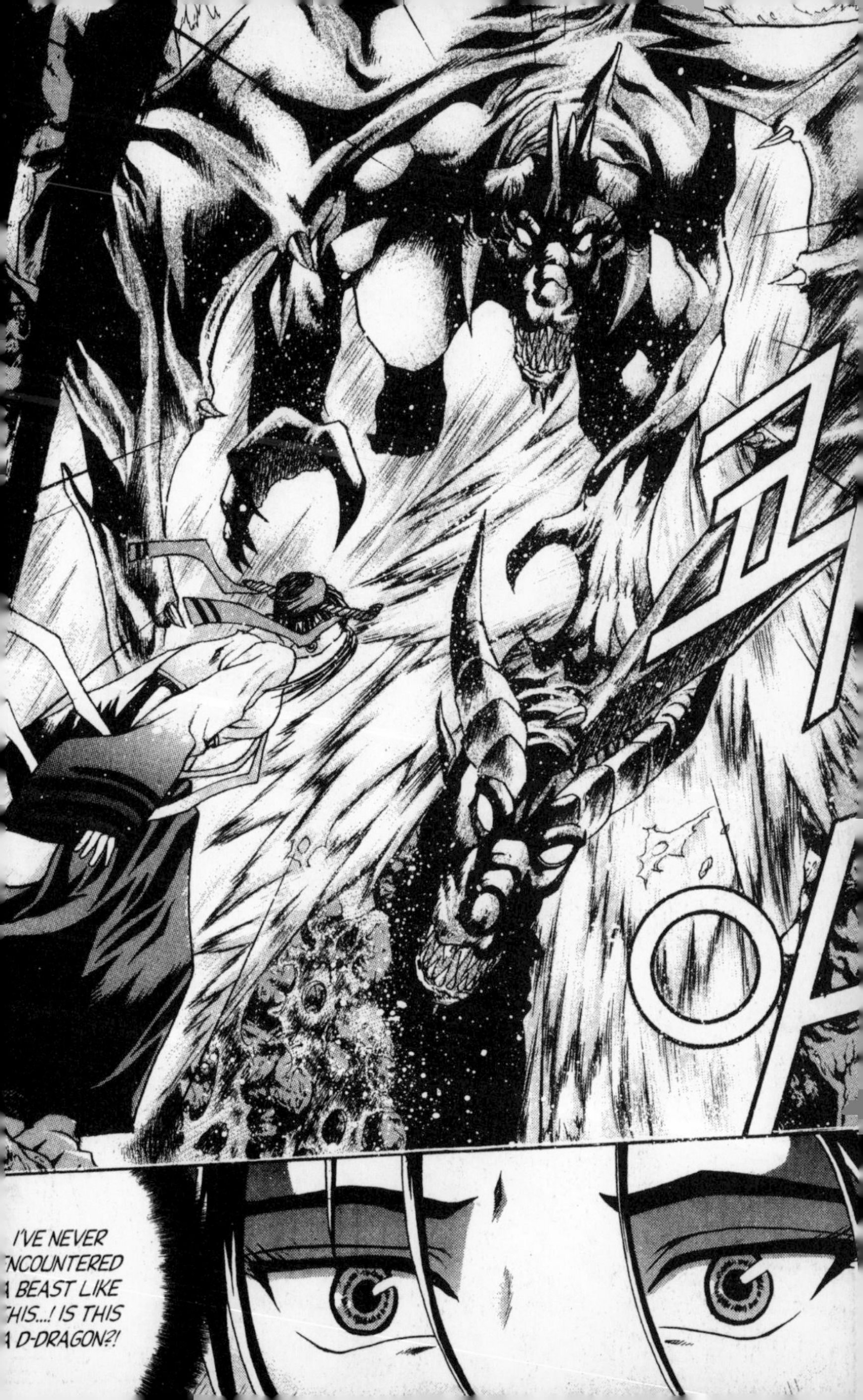
I'VE NEVER
ENCOUNTERED
A BEAST LIKE
THIS...! IS THIS
A D-DRAGON?!

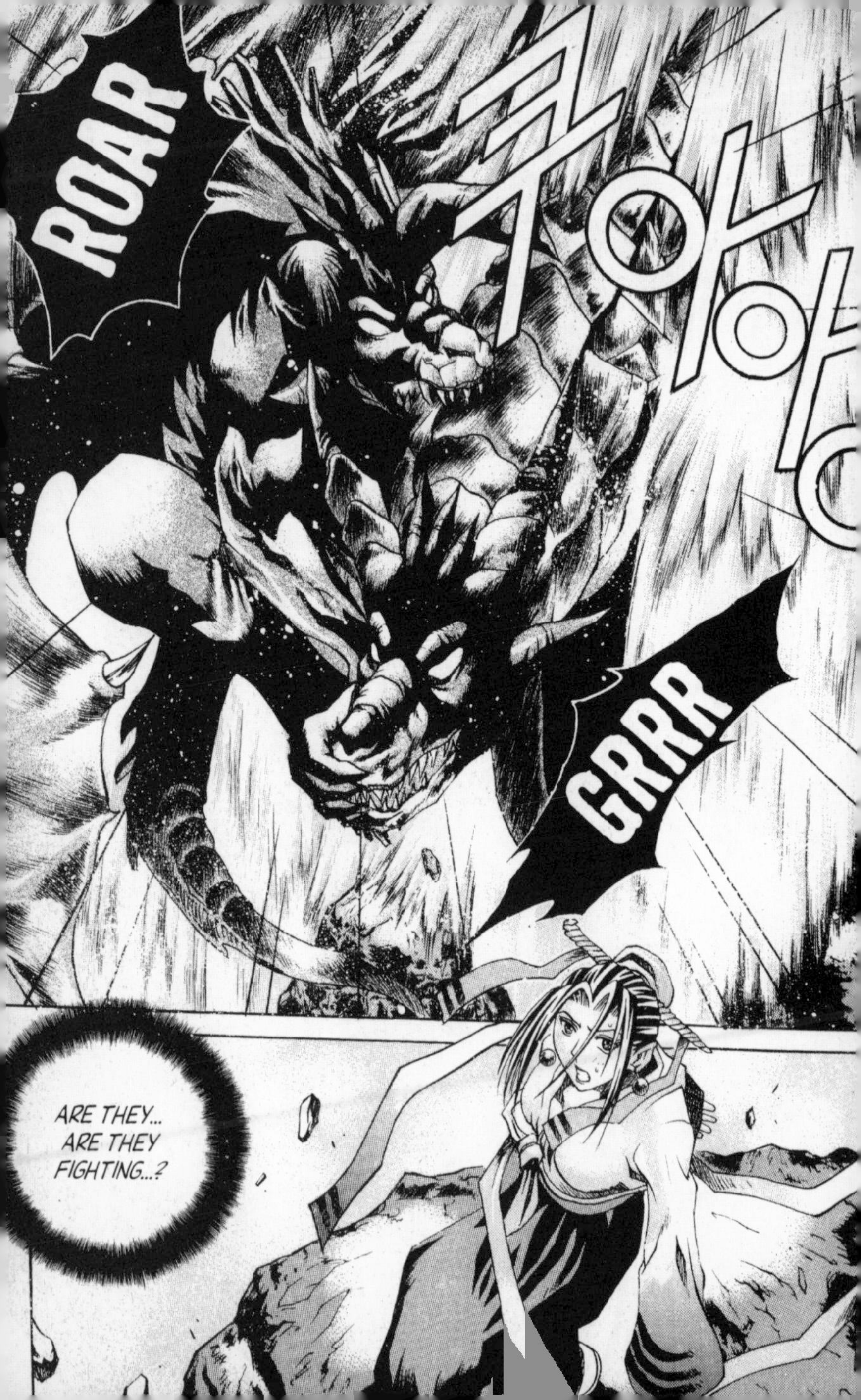
ROAR
GRRR
ARE THEY... ARE THEY FIGHTING...?

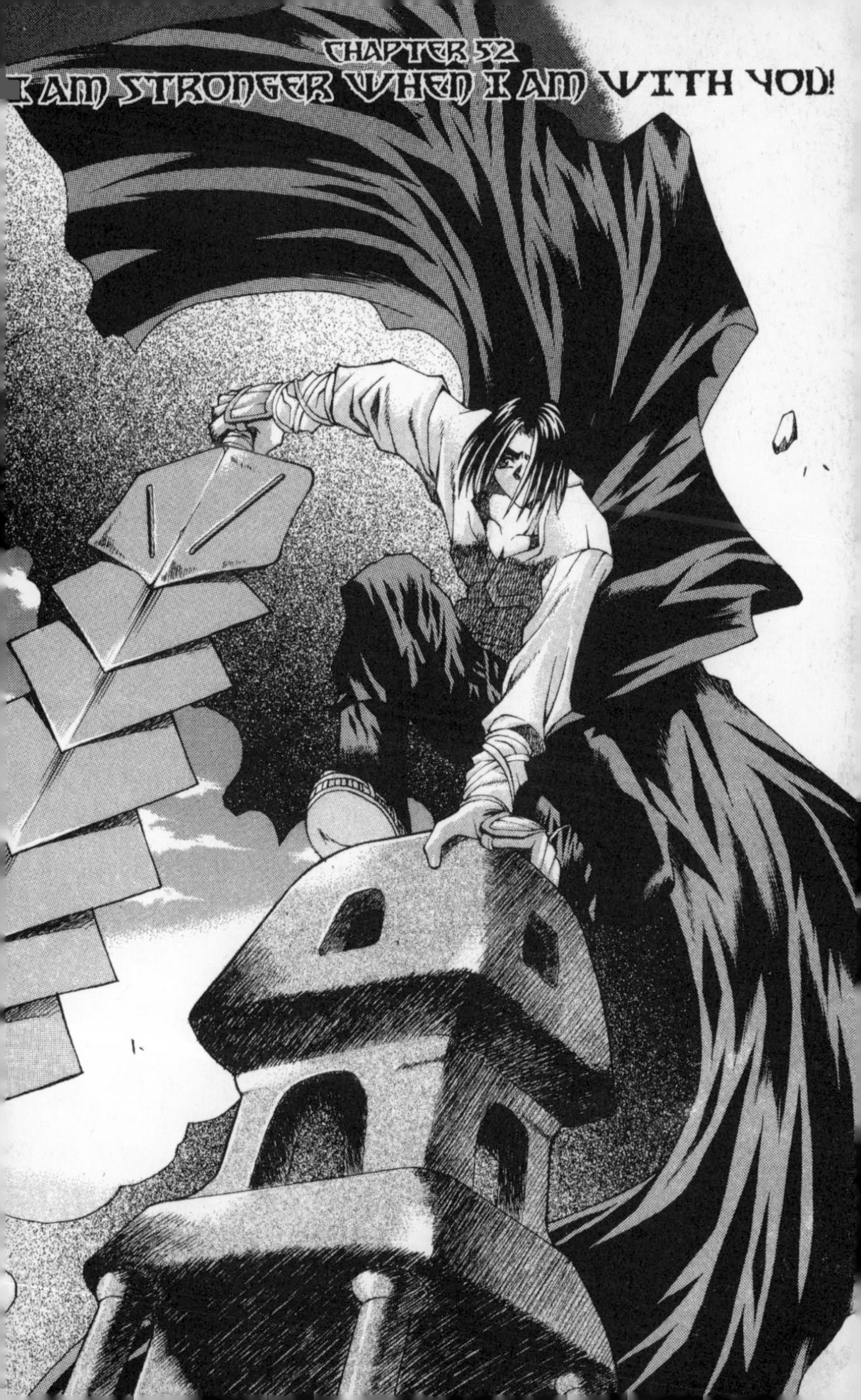
CHAPTER 52
I AM STRONGER WHEN I AM WITH YOU!

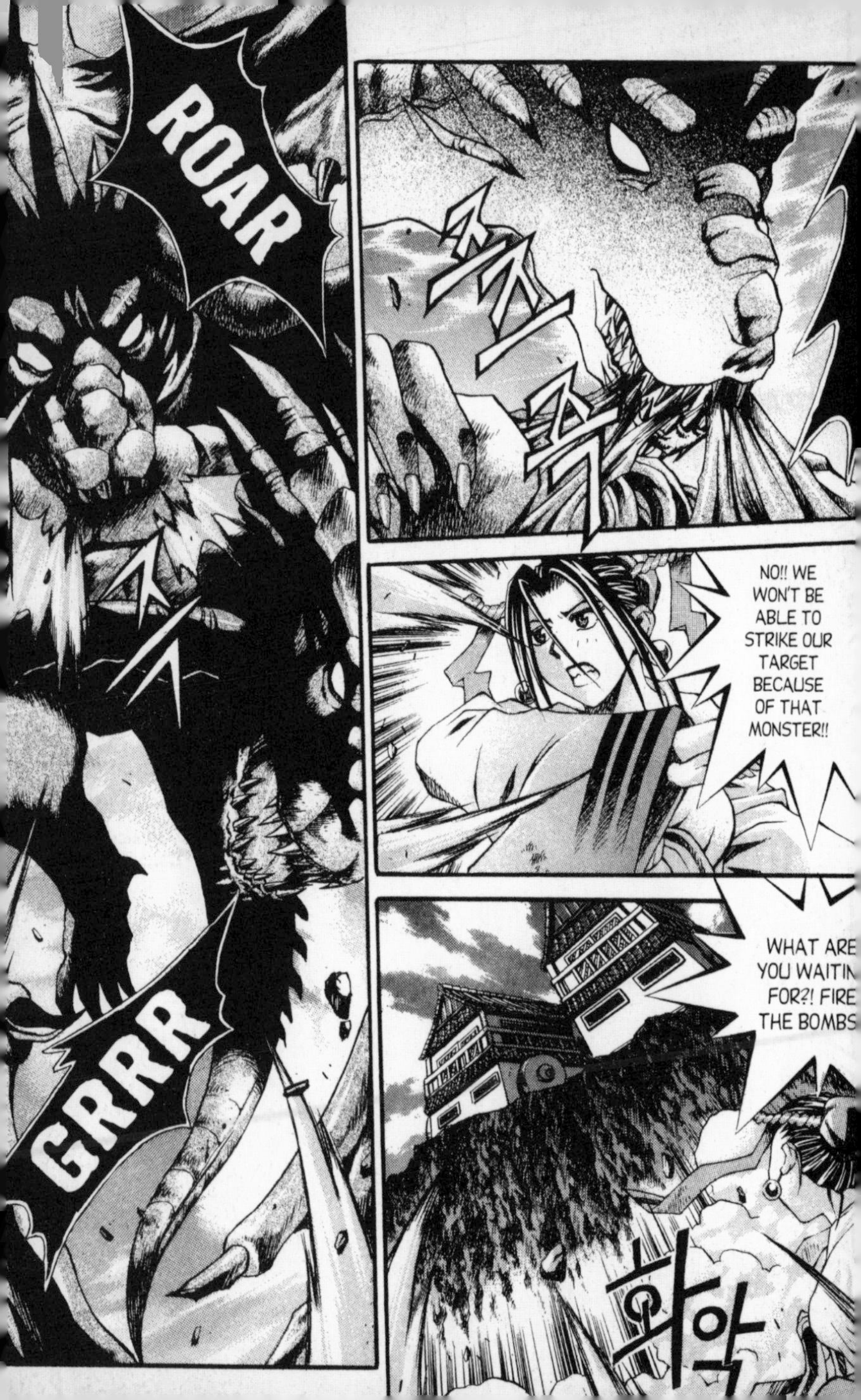
ROAR
GRRR
NO!! WE WON'T BE ABLE TO STRIKE OUR TARGET BECAUSE OF THAT MONSTER!!
WHAT ARE YOU WAITIN FOR?! FIRE THE BOMBS

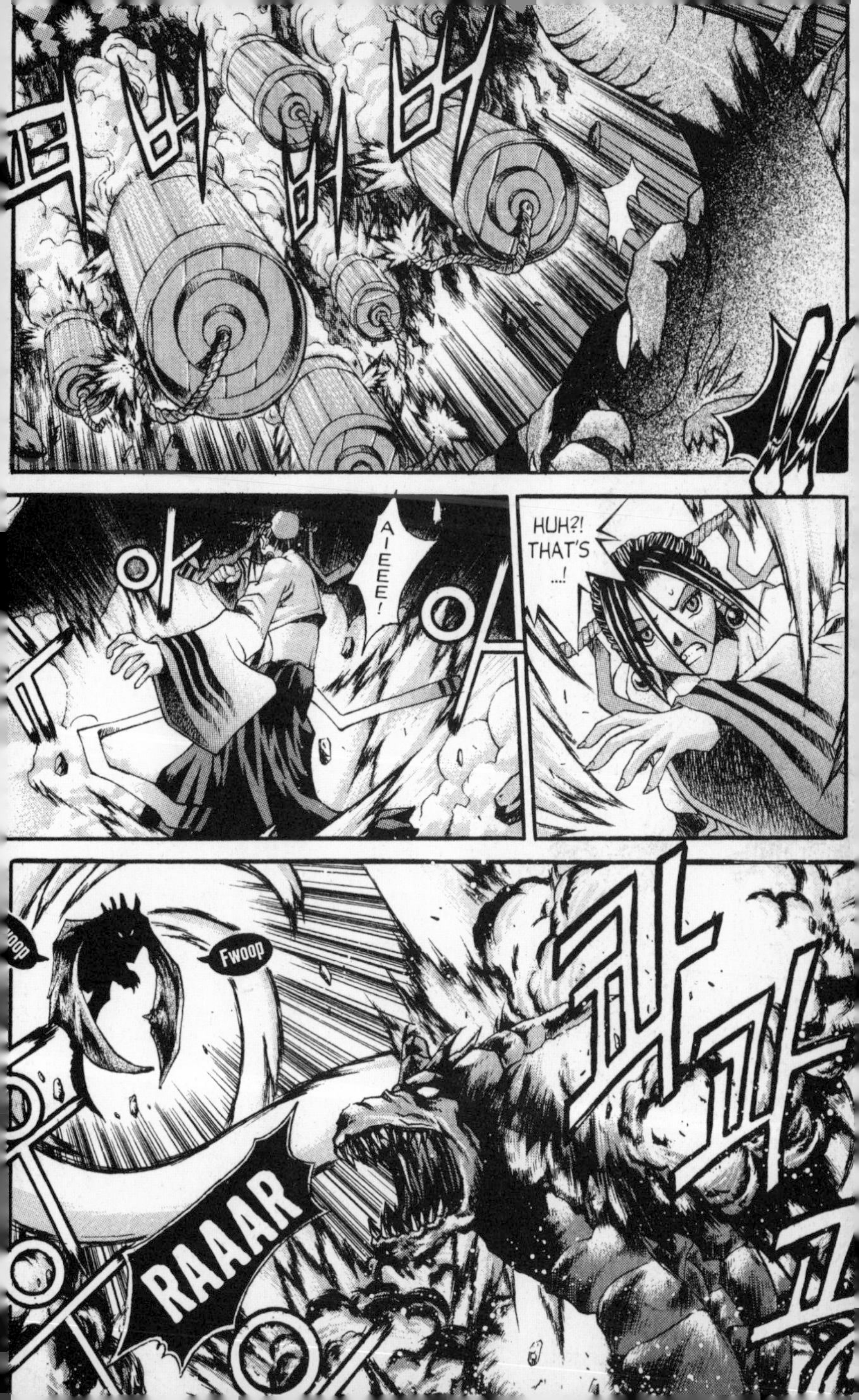
AIEEEE!
HUH?! THAT'S ...!
Fwoop
RAAAR

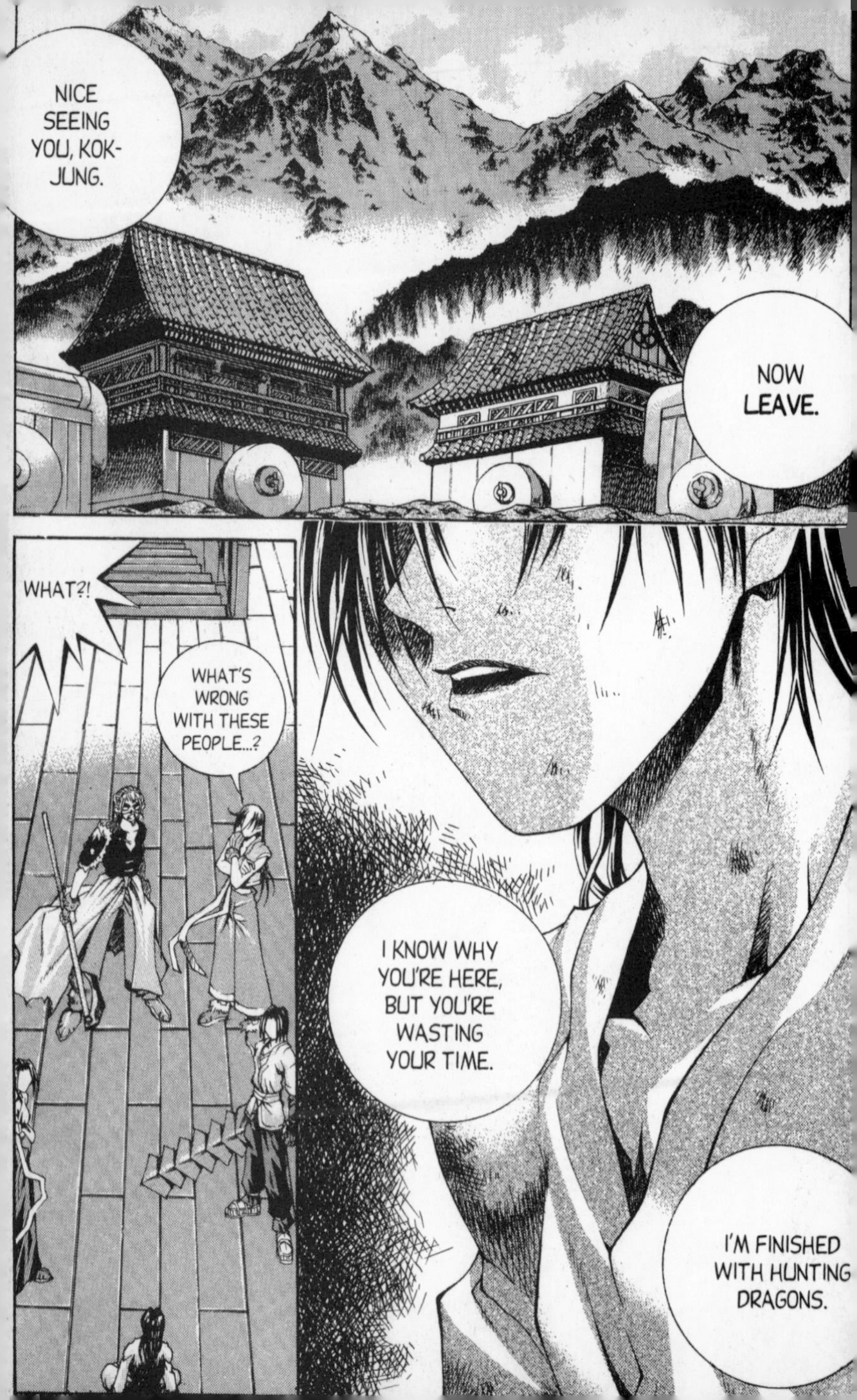
NICE SEEING YOU, KOK-JUNG.
NOW LEAVE.
WHAT?!
WHAT'S WRONG WITH THESE PEOPLE...?
I KNOW WHY YOU'RE HERE, BUT YOU'RE WASTING YOUR TIME.
I'M FINISHED WITH HUNTING DRAGONS.

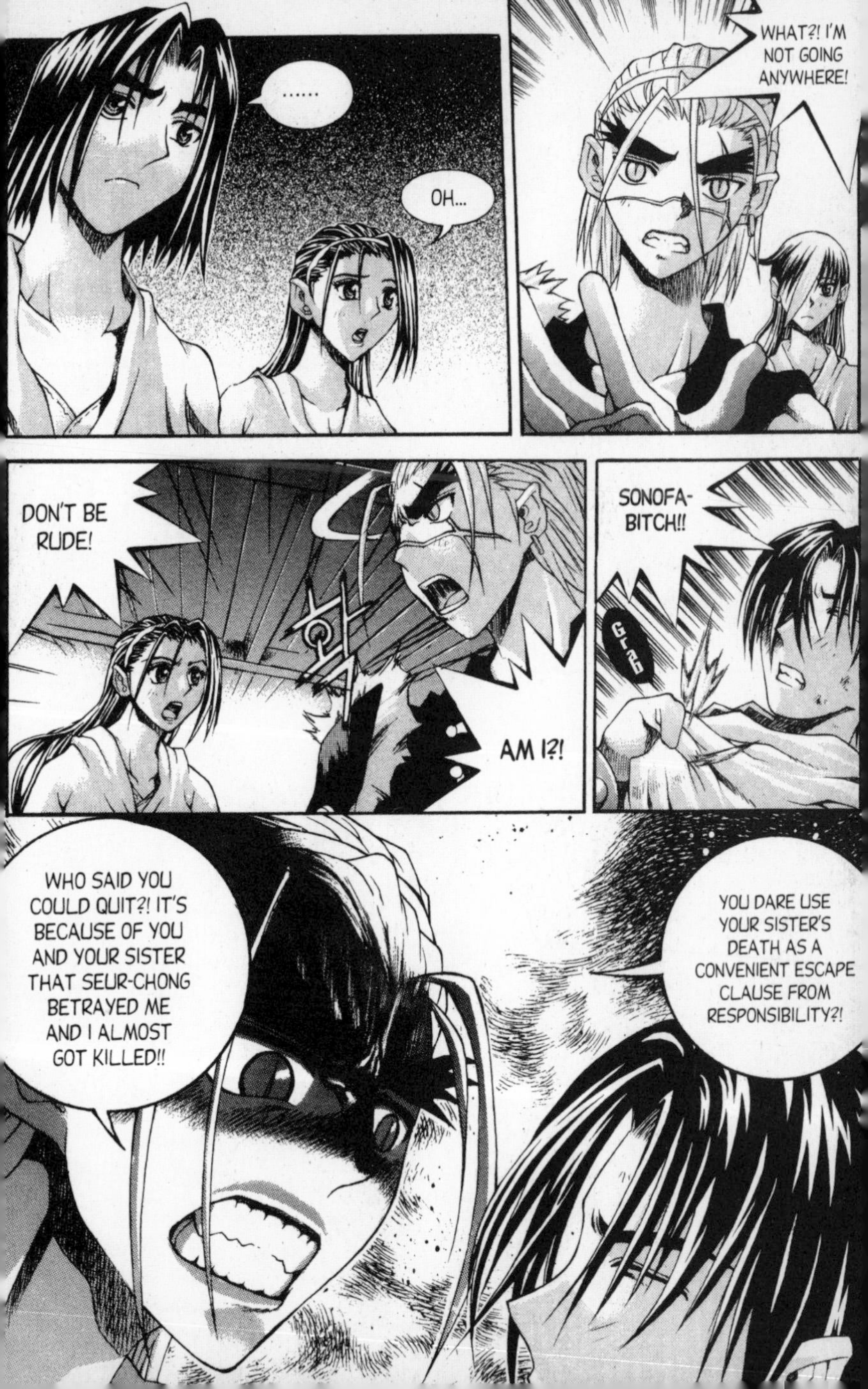
......
OH...
WHAT?! I'M NOT GOING ANYWHERE!
DON'T BE RUDE!
AM I?!
SONOFA-BITCH!!
Grab
WHO SAID YOU COULD QUIT?! IT'S BECAUSE OF YOU AND YOUR SISTER THAT SEUR-CHONG BETRAYED ME AND I ALMOST GOT KILLED!!
YOU DARE USE YOUR SISTER'S DEATH AS A CONVENIENT ESCAPE CLAUSE FROM RESPONSIBILITY?!

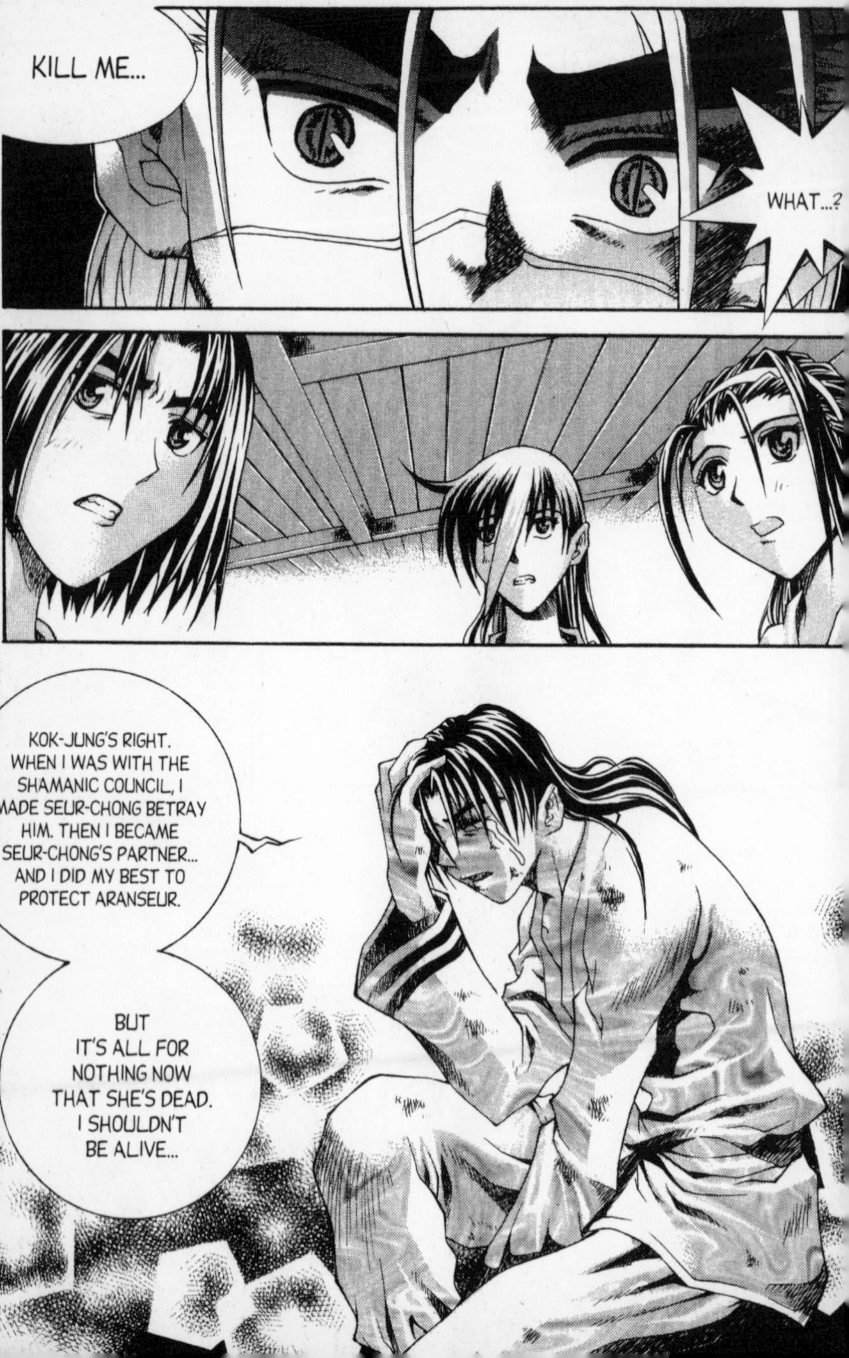
KILL ME...
WHAT...?
KOK-JUNG'S RIGHT. WHEN I WAS WITH THE SHAMANIC COUNCIL, I MADE SEUR-CHONG BETRAY HIM. THEN I BECAME SEUR-CHONG'S PARTNER... AND I DID MY BEST TO PROTECT ARANSEUR.
BUT IT'S ALL FOR NOTHING NOW THAT SHE'S DEAD. I SHOULDN'T BE ALIVE...

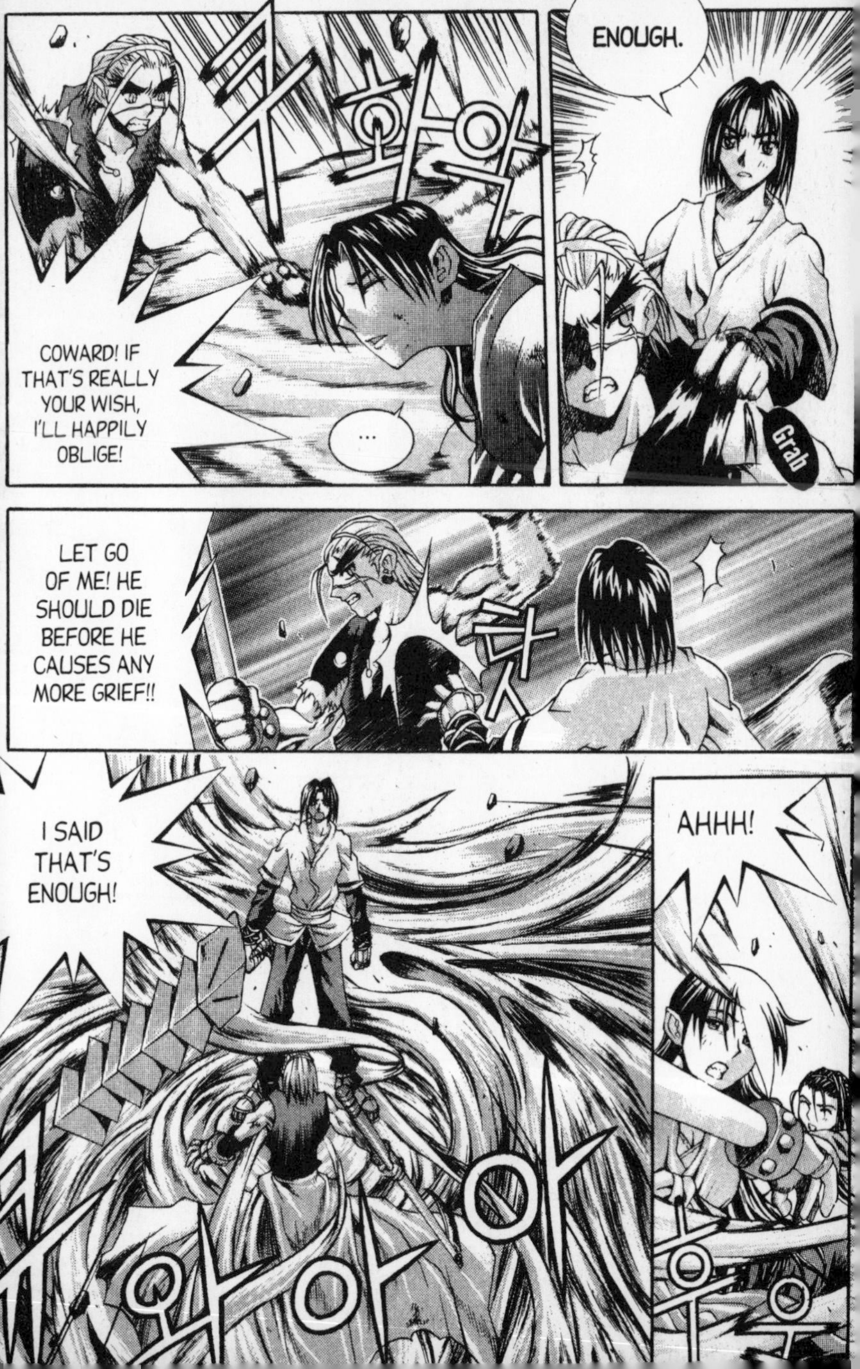
COWARD! IF THAT'S REALLY YOUR WISH, I'LL HAPPILY OBLIGE!
...
ENOUGH.
Grab
LET GO OF ME! HE SHOULD DIE BEFORE HE CAUSES ANY MORE GRIEF!!
I SAID THAT'S ENOUGH!
AHHH!

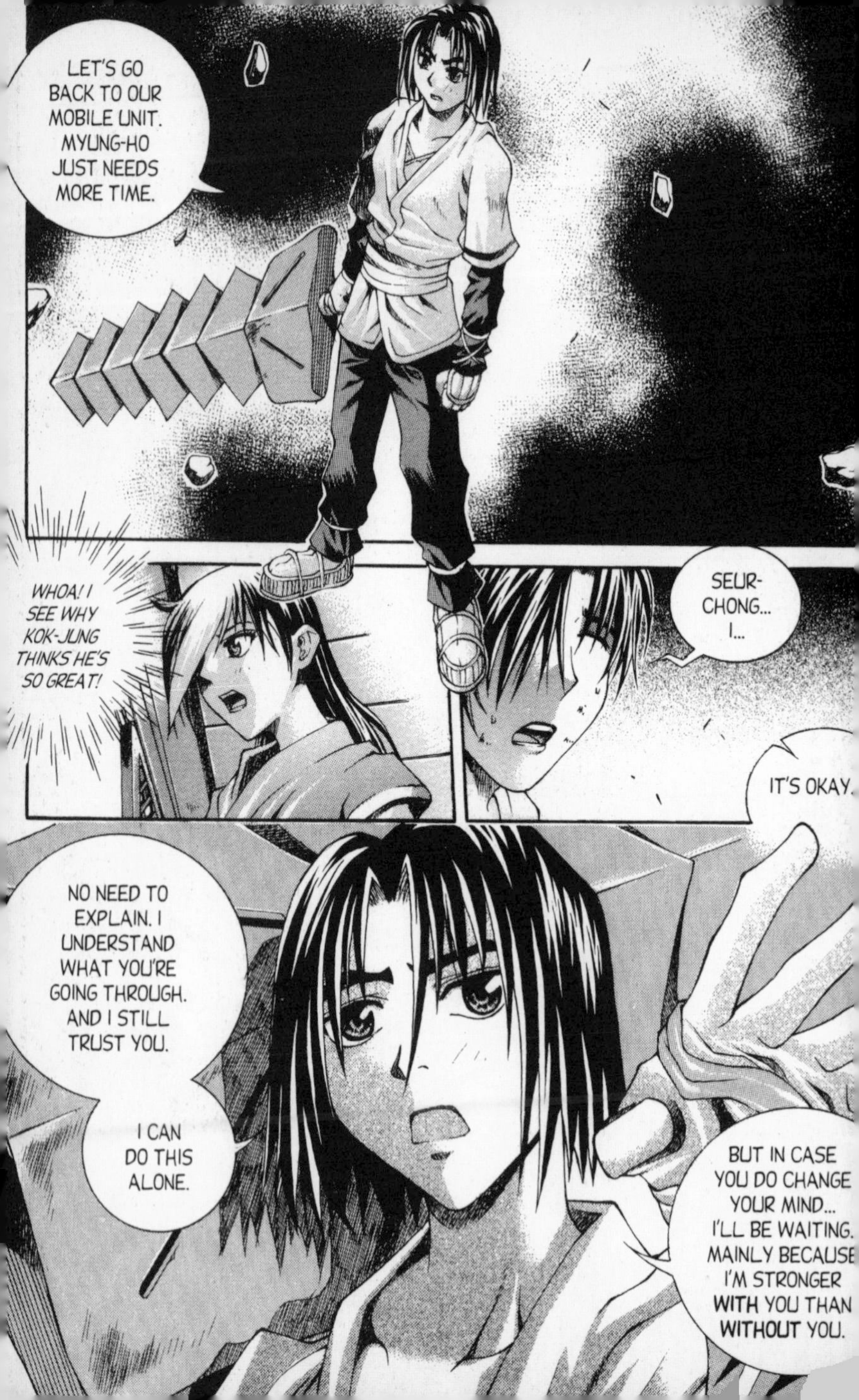
LET'S GO BACK TO OUR MOBILE UNIT. MYUNG-HO JUST NEEDS MORE TIME.
WHOA! I SEE WHY KOK-JUNG THINKS HE'S SO GREAT!
SEUR-CHONG... I...
IT'S OKAY.
NO NEED TO EXPLAIN. I UNDERSTAND WHAT YOU'RE GOING THROUGH. AND I STILL TRUST YOU.
I CAN DO THIS ALONE.
BUT IN CASE YOU DO CHANGE YOUR MIND... I'LL BE WAITING. MAINLY BECAUSE I'M STRONGER WITH YOU THAN WITHOUT YOU.

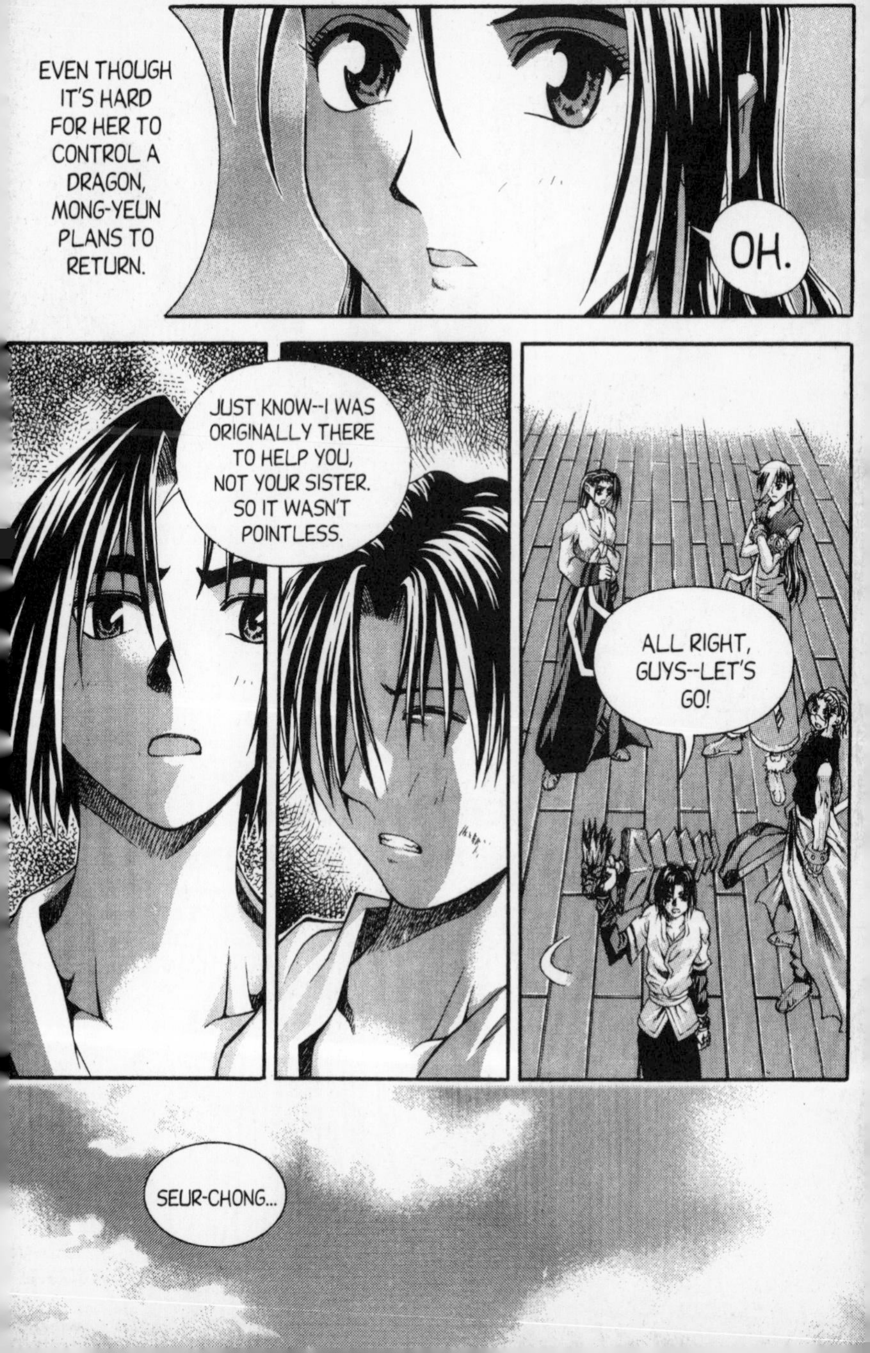
EVEN THOUGH IT'S HARD FOR HER TO CONTROL A DRAGON, MONG-YEUN PLANS TO RETURN.
OH.
JUST KNOW--I WAS ORIGINALLY THERE TO HELP YOU, NOT YOUR SISTER. SO IT WASN'T POINTLESS.
ALL RIGHT, GUYS--LET'S GO!
SEUR-CHONG...

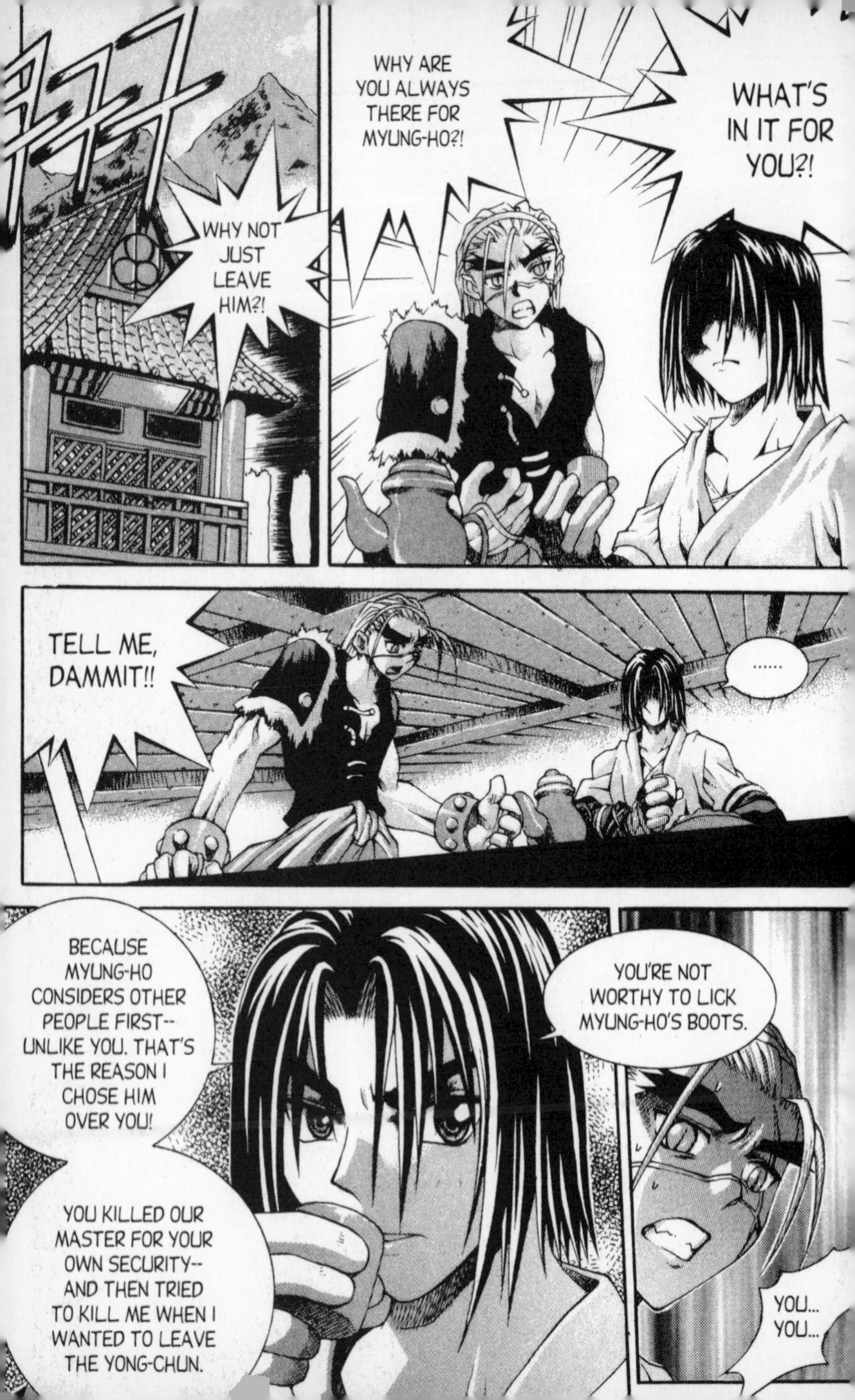
WHY NOT JUST LEAVE HIM?!
WHY ARE YOU ALWAYS THERE FOR MYUNG-HO?!
WHAT'S IN IT FOR YOU?!
TELL ME, DAMMIT!!
......
BECAUSE MYUNG-HO CONSIDERS OTHER PEOPLE FIRST-- UNLIKE YOU. THAT'S THE REASON I CHOSE HIM OVER YOU!
YOU KILLED OUR MASTER FOR YOUR OWN SECURITY-- AND THEN TRIED TO KILL ME WHEN I WANTED TO LEAVE THE YONG-CHUN.
YOU'RE NOT WORTHY TO LICK MYUNG-HO'S BOOTS.
YOU... YOU...

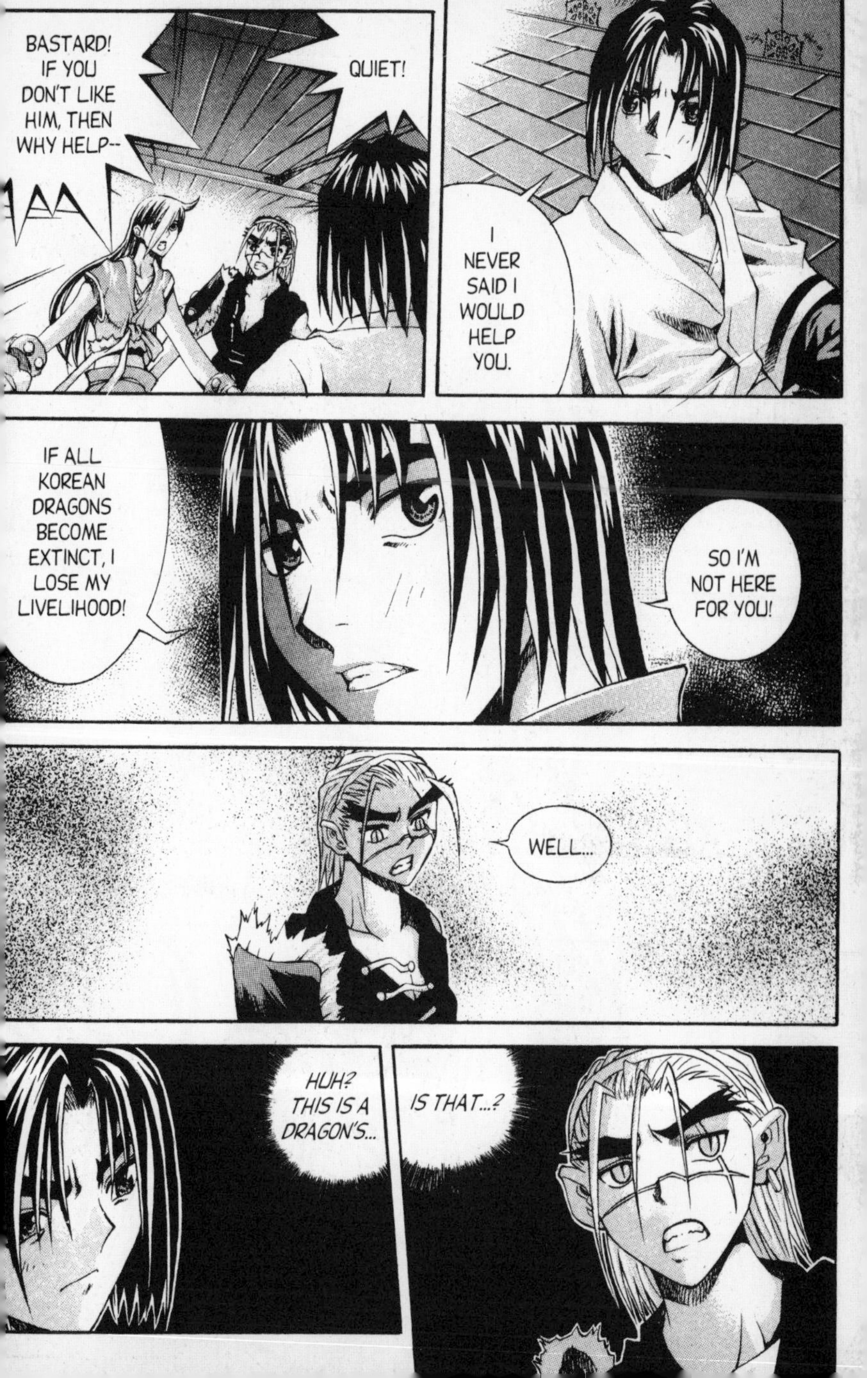
BASTARD! IF YOU DON'T LIKE HIM, THEN WHY HELP--
QUIET!
I NEVER SAID I WOULD HELP YOU.
IF ALL KOREAN DRAGONS BECOME EXTINCT, I LOSE MY LIVELIHOOD!
SO I'M NOT HERE FOR YOU!
WELL...
HUH? THIS IS A DRAGON'S...
IS THAT...?

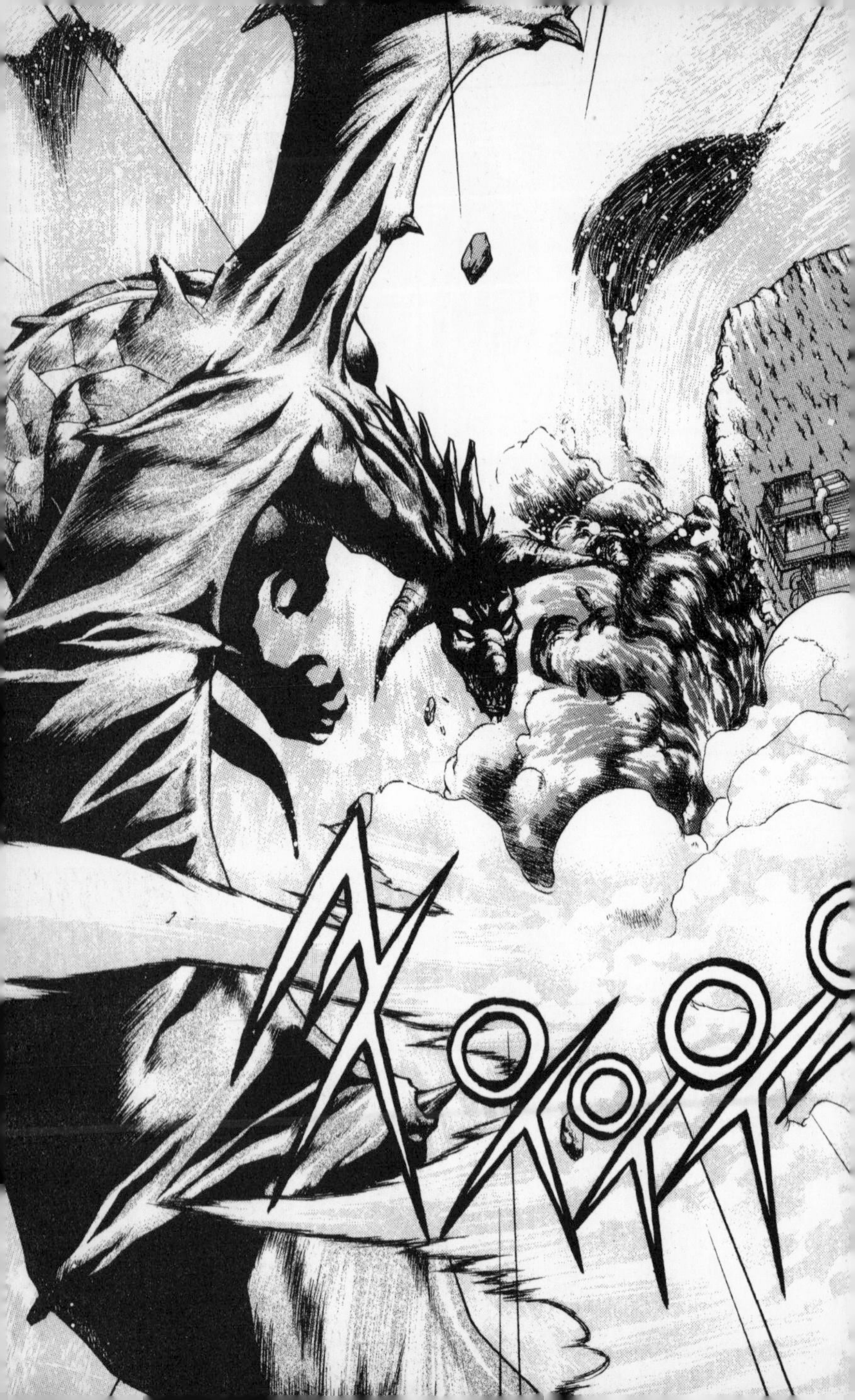

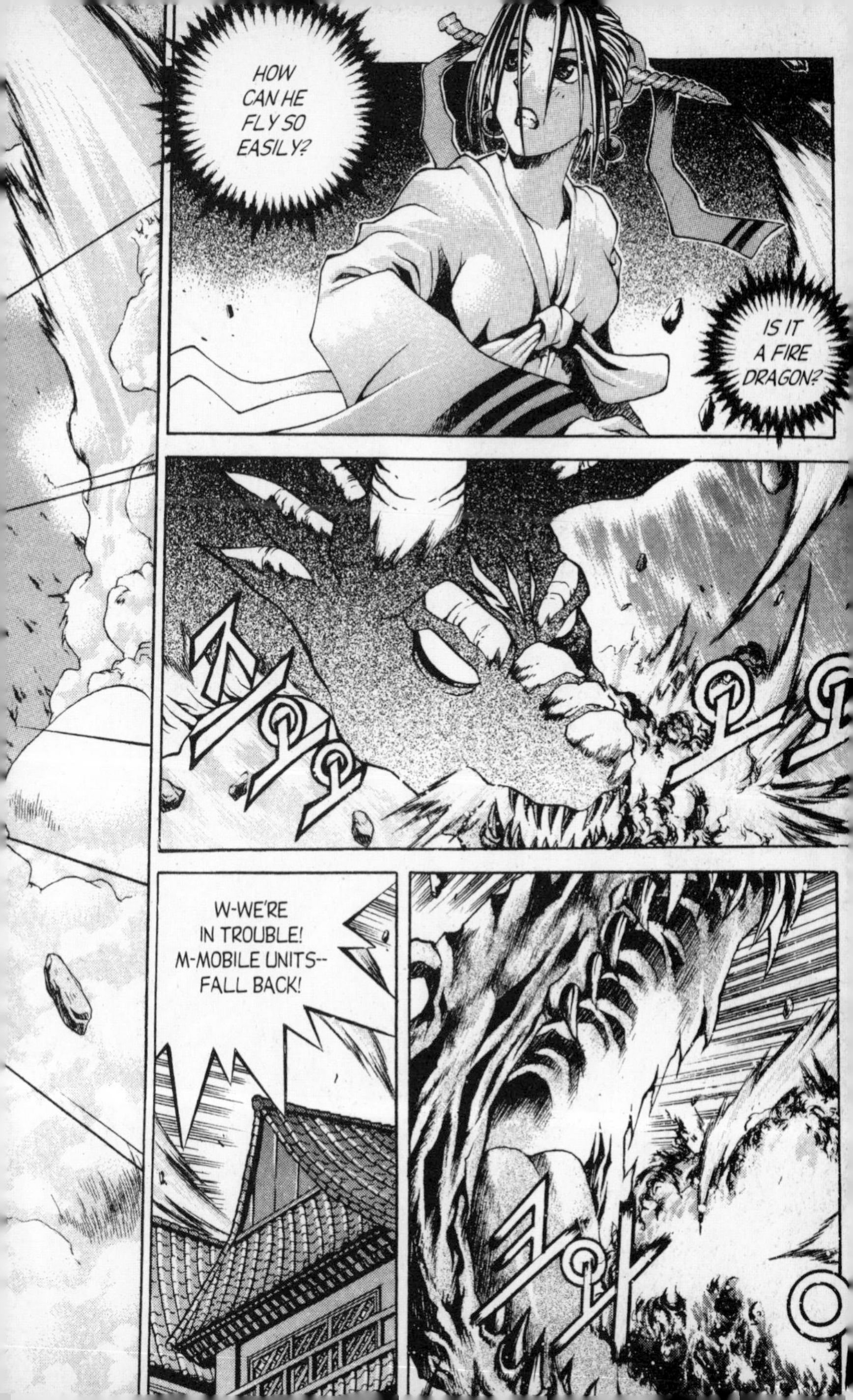
HOW CAN HE FLY SO EASILY?
IS IT A FIRE DRAGON?
W-WE'RE IN TROUBLE! M-MOBILE UNITS-- FALL BACK!

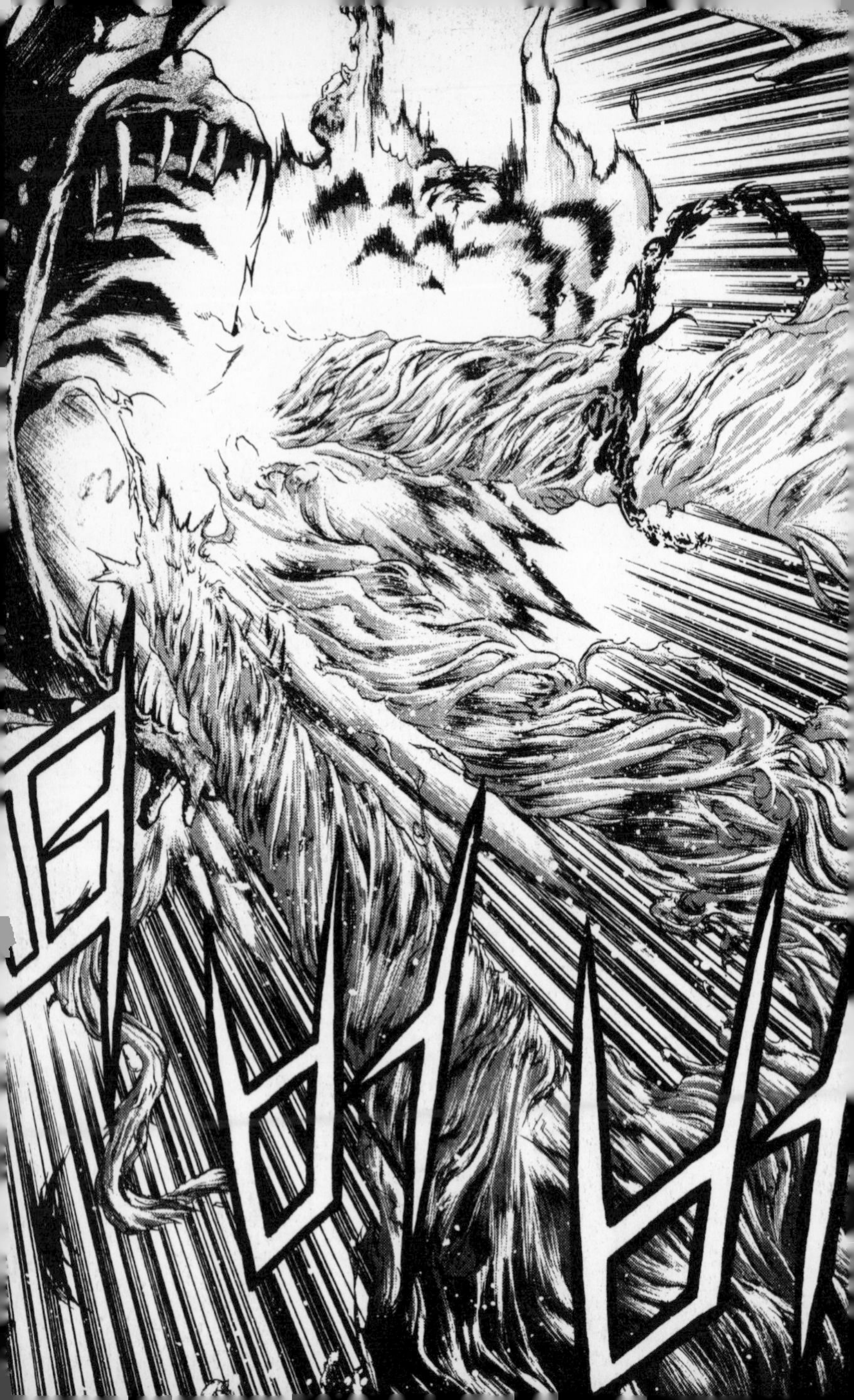

CHAPTER 53
RIAH H. ARTHUR (PART 1)

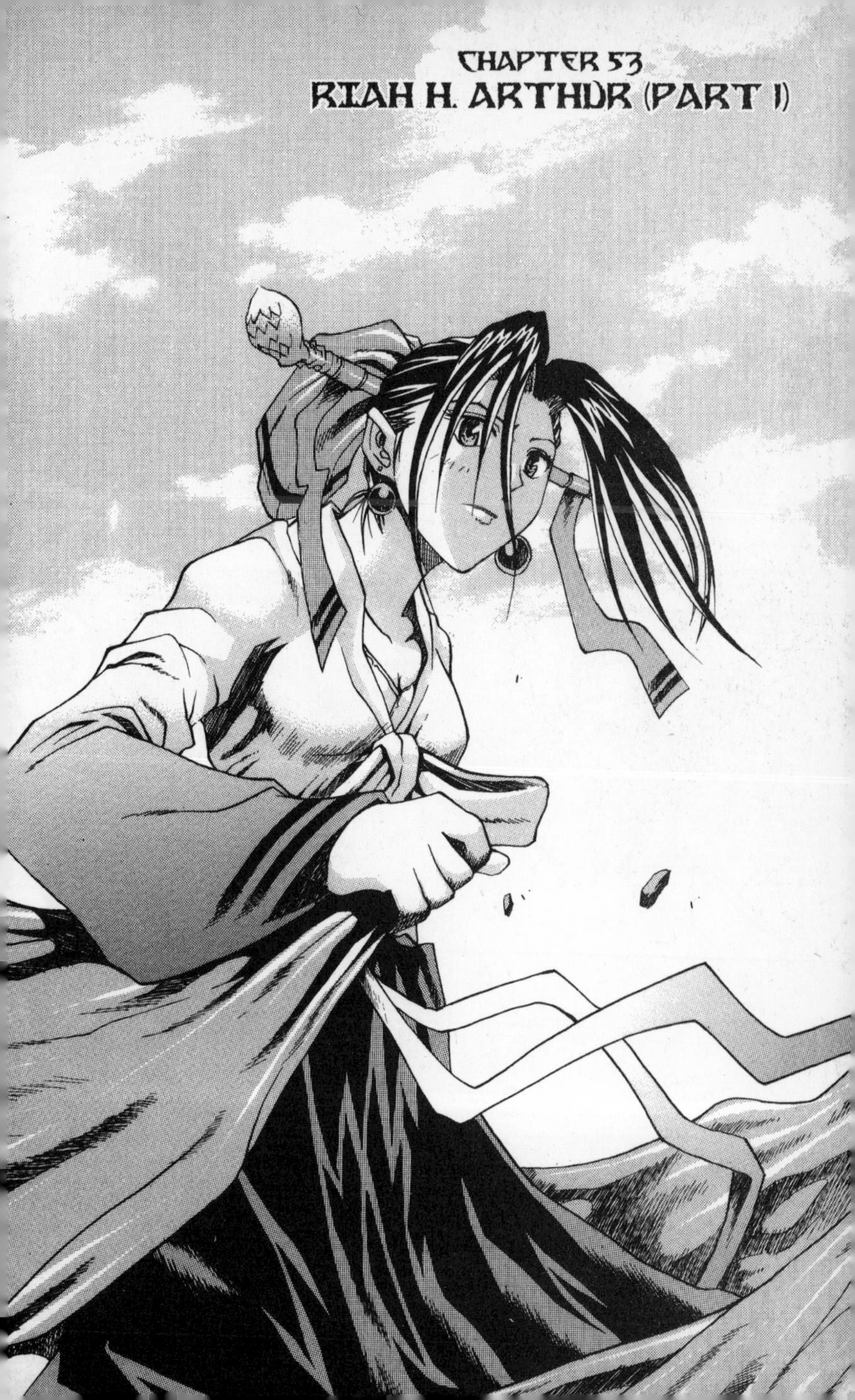

Rargh

OH NO! I'M
TOAST!

I DON'T
WANNA
DIE--!!

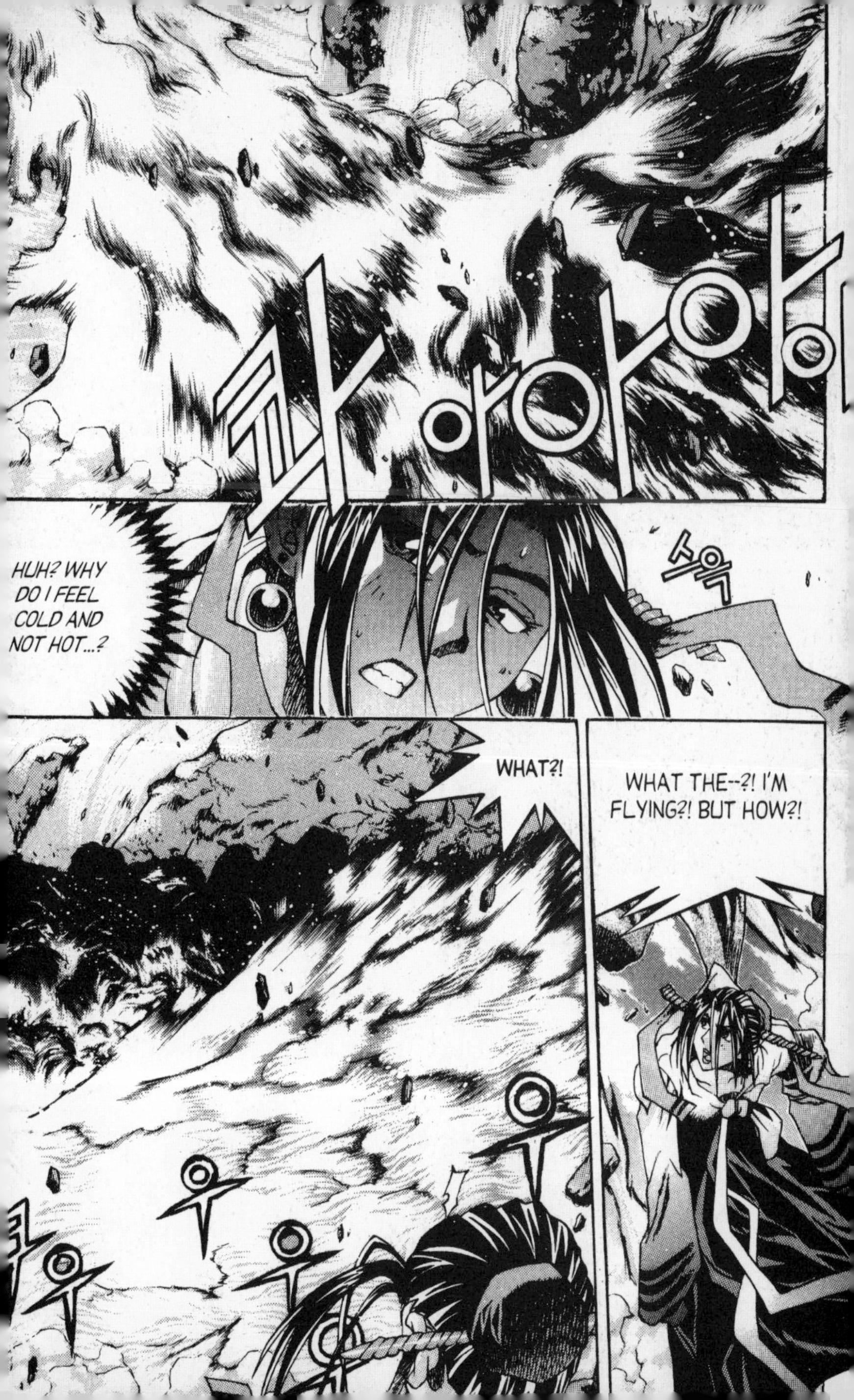
HUH? WHY DO I FEEL COLD AND NOT HOT...?
WHAT?!
WHAT THE--?! I'M FLYING?! BUT HOW?!

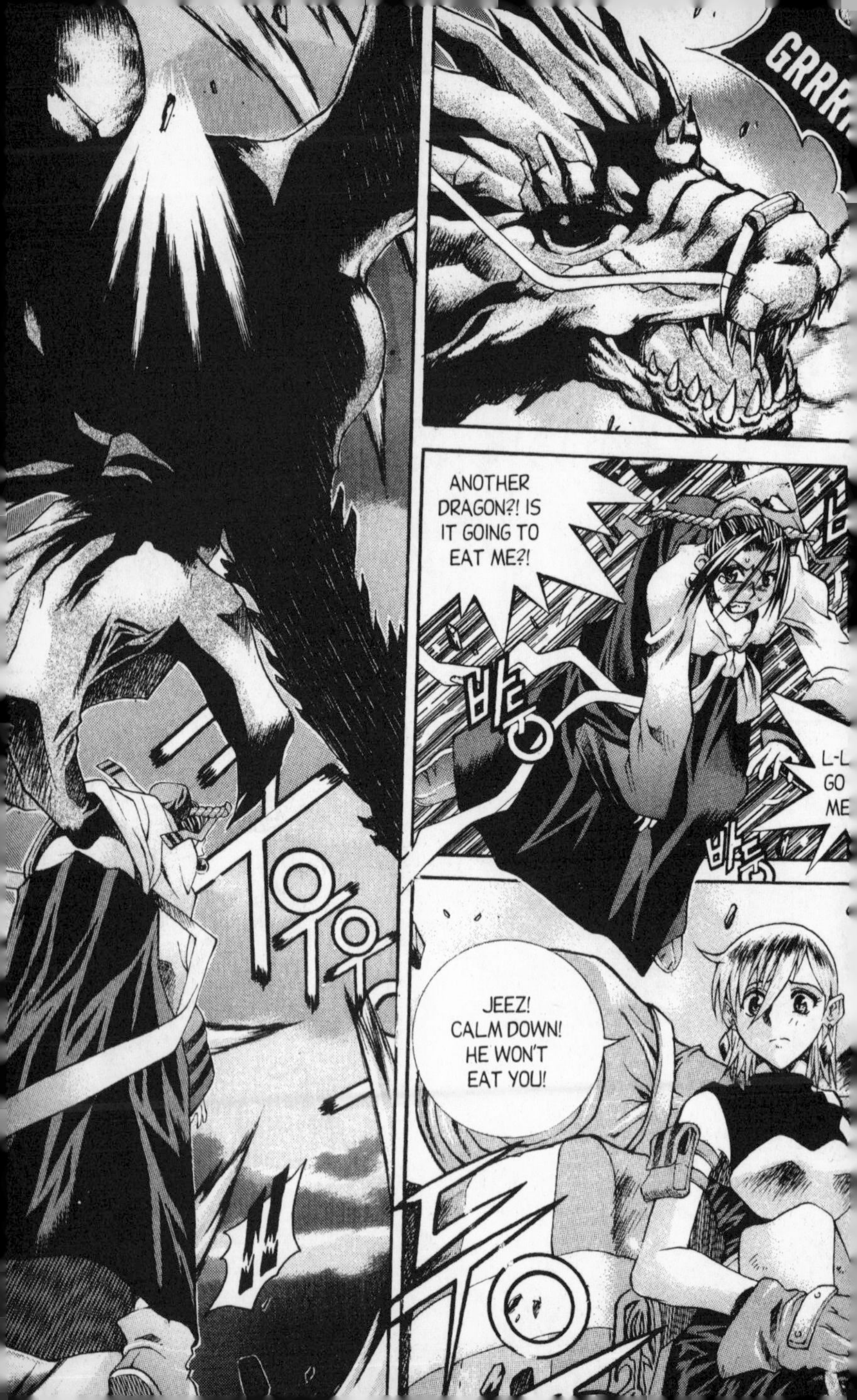
GRRR
ANOTHER DRAGON?! IS IT GOING TO EAT ME?!
바둥
L-L
GO
ME
바둥
JEEZ! CALM DOWN! HE WON'T EAT YOU!

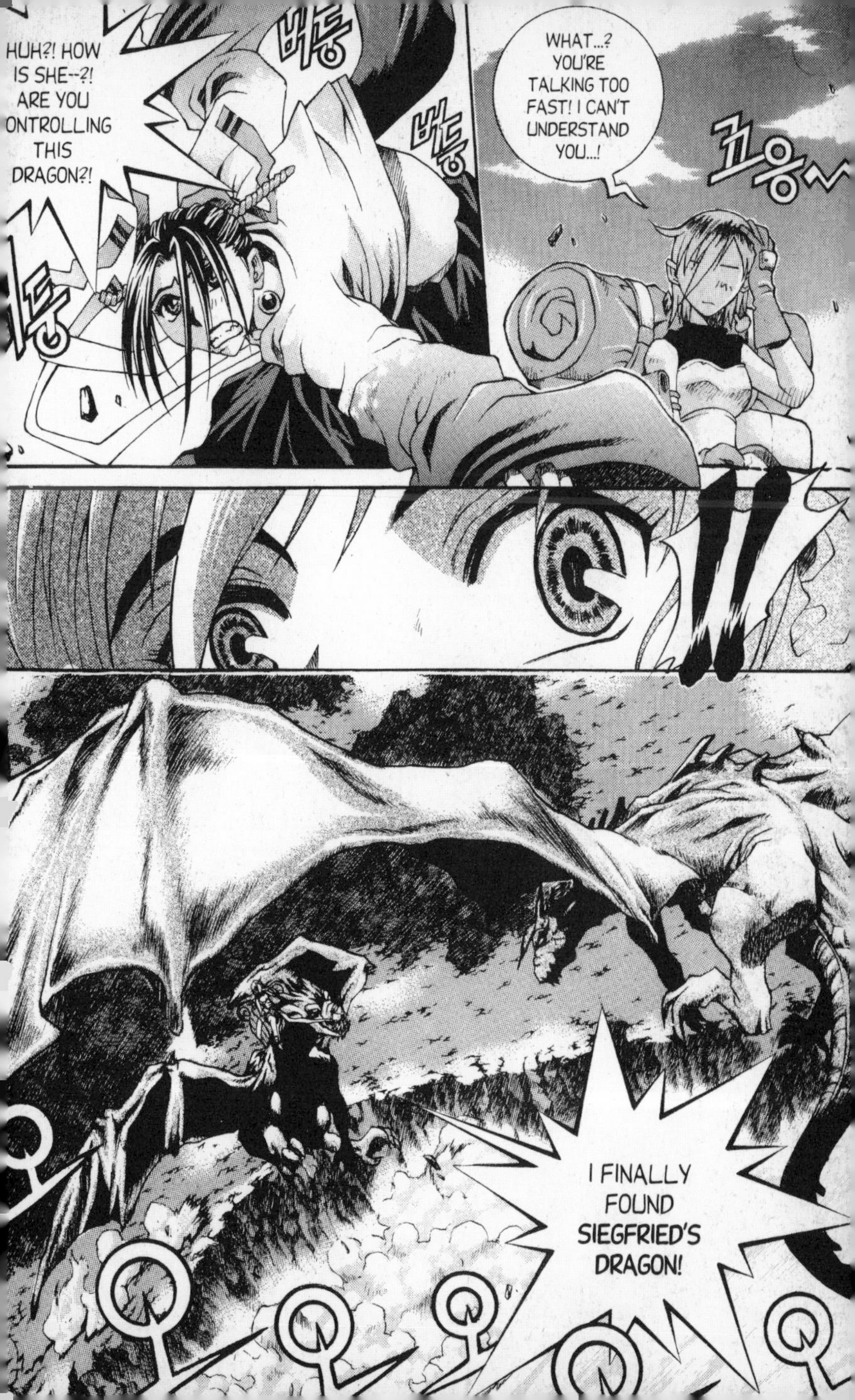
HUH?! HOW IS SHE--?! ARE YOU ONTROLLING THIS DRAGON?!
WHAT...? YOU'RE TALKING TOO FAST! I CAN'T UNDERSTAND YOU...!
I FINALLY FOUND SIEGFRIED'S DRAGON!

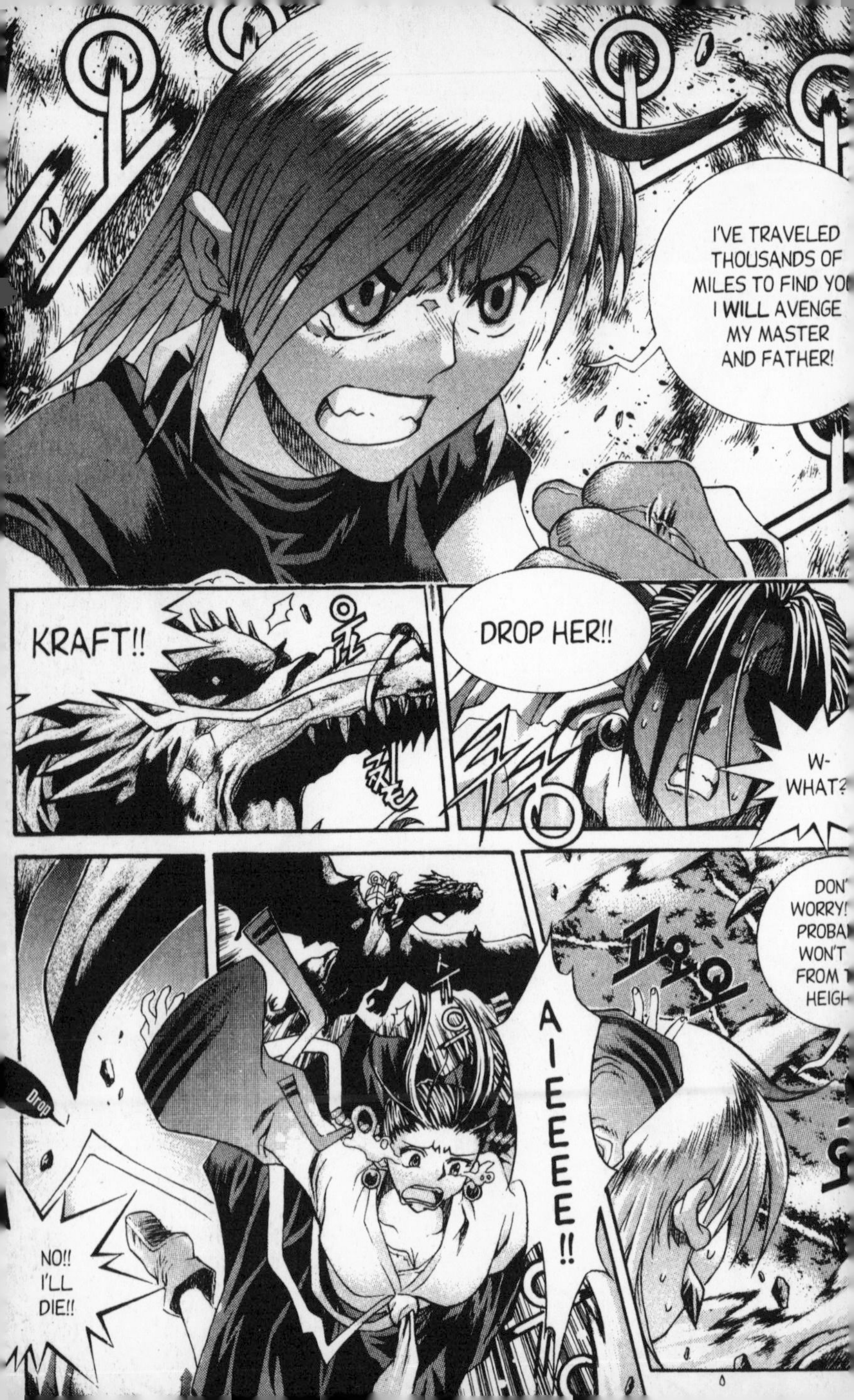
I'VE TRAVELED THOUSANDS OF MILES TO FIND YO I WILL AVENGE MY MASTER AND FATHER!
KRAFT!!
DROP HER!!
W- WHAT?
Drop
NO!! I'LL DIE!!
AIEEEE!!
DON' WORRY! PROBA WON'T FROM T HEIGH

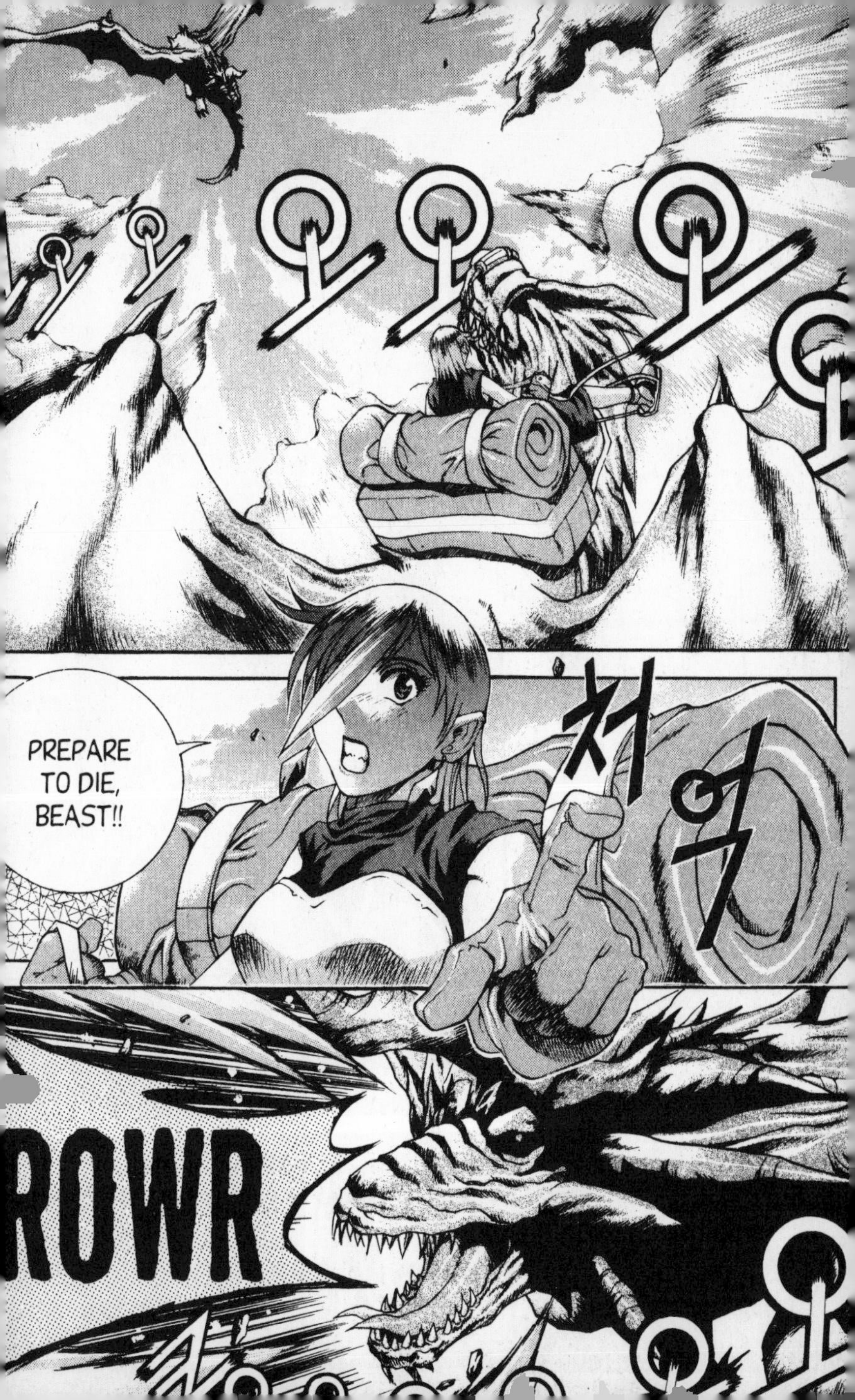
PREPARE TO DIE, BEAST!!
ROWR

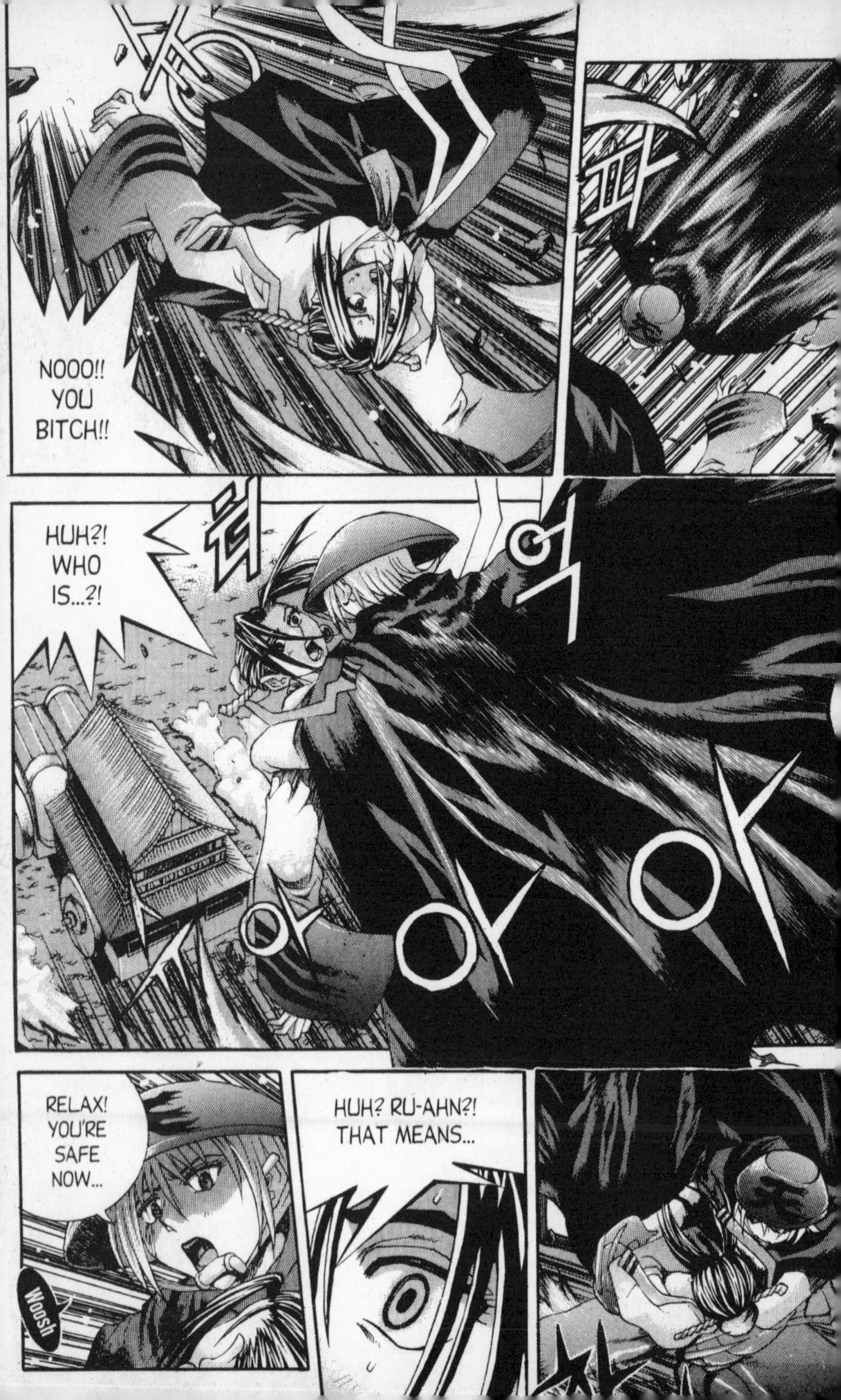
NOOO!! YOU BITCH!!
HUH?! WHO IS...?!
RELAX! YOU'RE SAFE NOW...
Woosh
HUH? RU-AHN?! THAT MEANS...

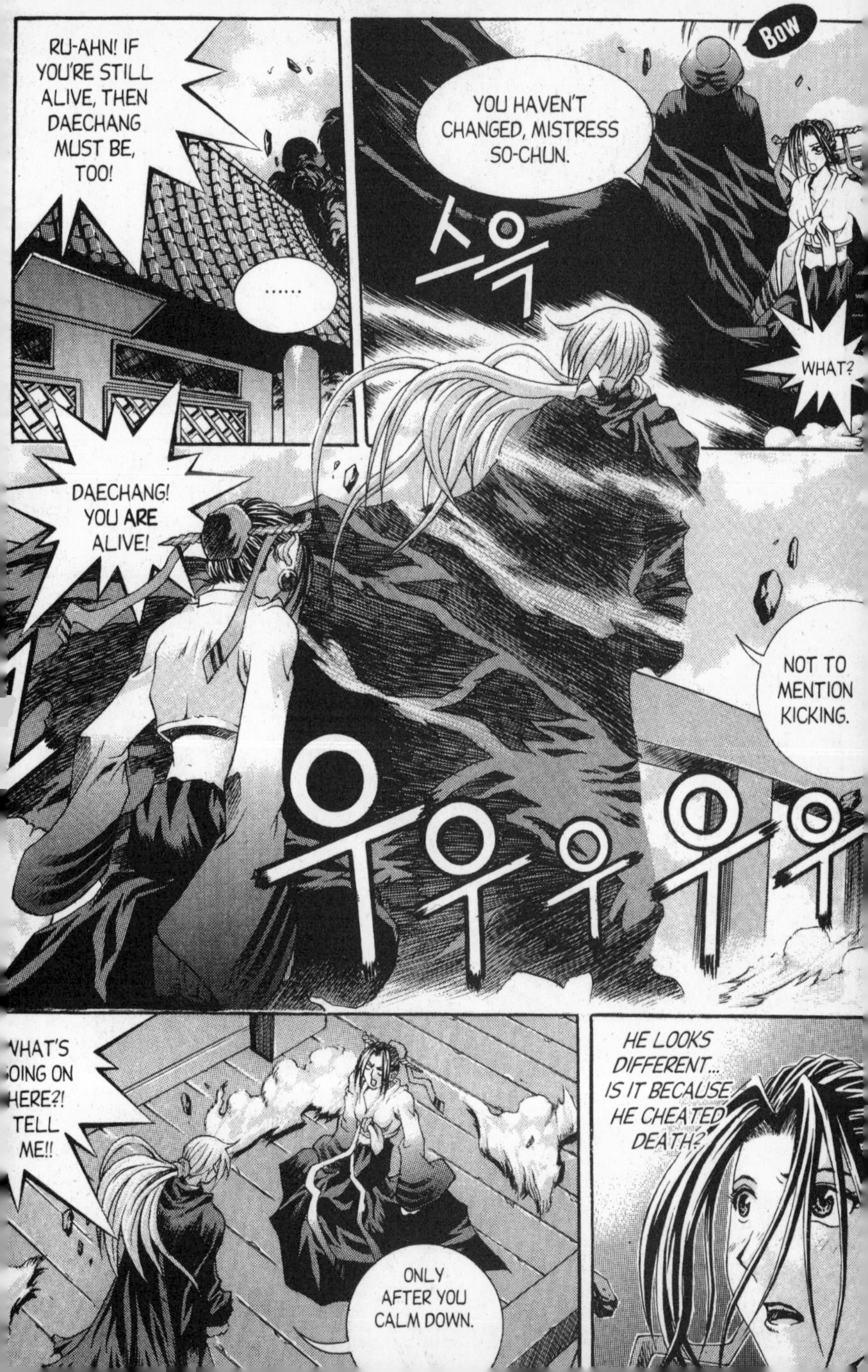
RU-AHN! IF YOU'RE STILL ALIVE, THEN DAECHANG MUST BE, TOO!
......
YOU HAVEN'T CHANGED, MISTRESS SO-CHUN.
Bow
WHAT?
DAECHANG! YOU ARE ALIVE!
NOT TO MENTION KICKING.
우우우우우
WHAT'S GOING ON HERE?! TELL ME!!
ONLY AFTER YOU CALM DOWN.
HE LOOKS DIFFERENT... IS IT BECAUSE HE CHEATED DEATH?

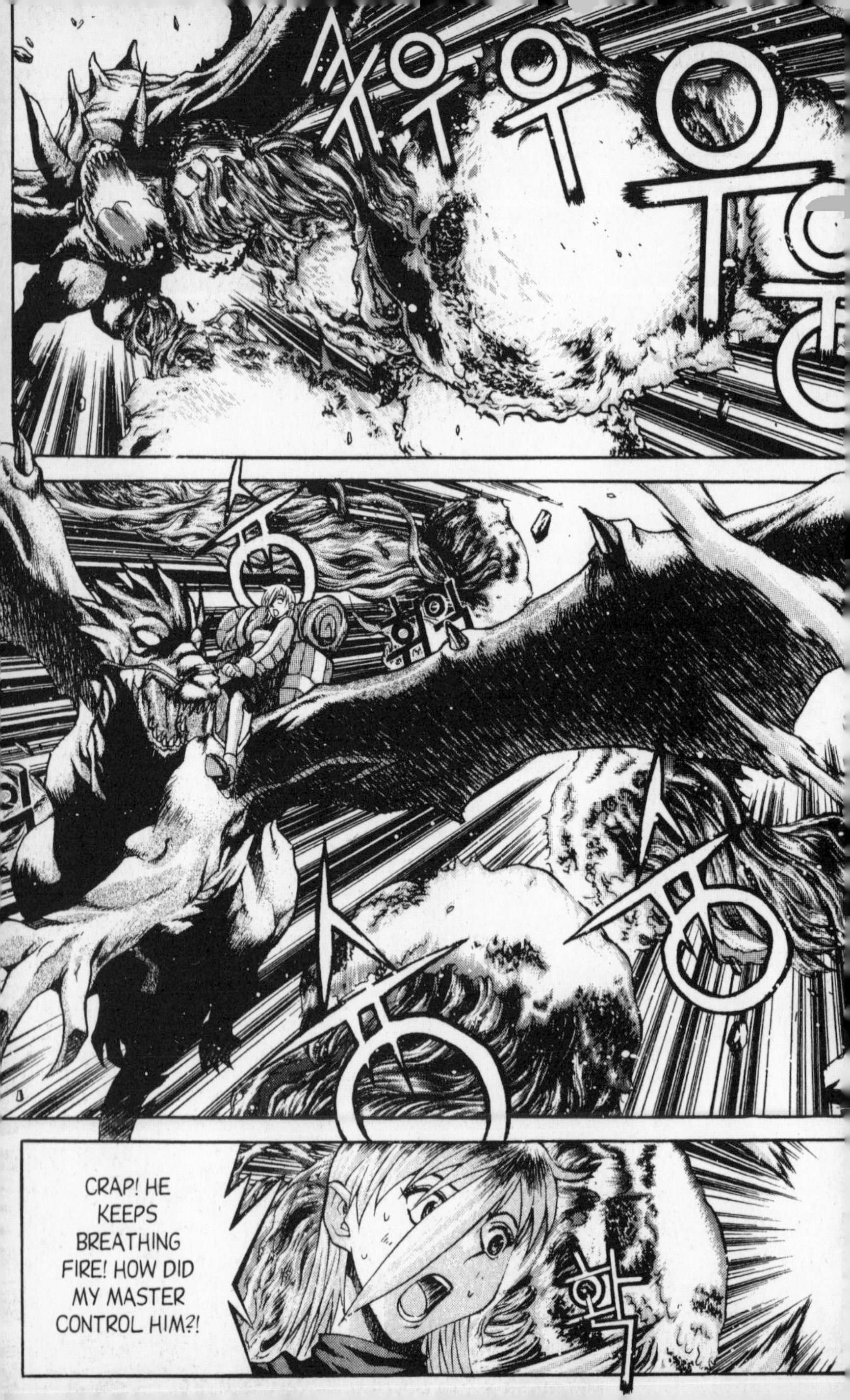
CRAP! HE KEEPS BREATHING FIRE! HOW DID MY MASTER CONTROL HIM?!

ROWR

AHHH!!

WE CAN'T COUNTER-ATTACK BECAUSE KRAFT IS TOO YOUNG TO BREATHE FIRE! WE CAN'T GET CLOSE...!

Grind

KRAFT! WE HAVE TO DIVE TOWARDS HIM!

IT'S THE ONLY WAY WE CAN DEFEAT HIM!!

RARGH

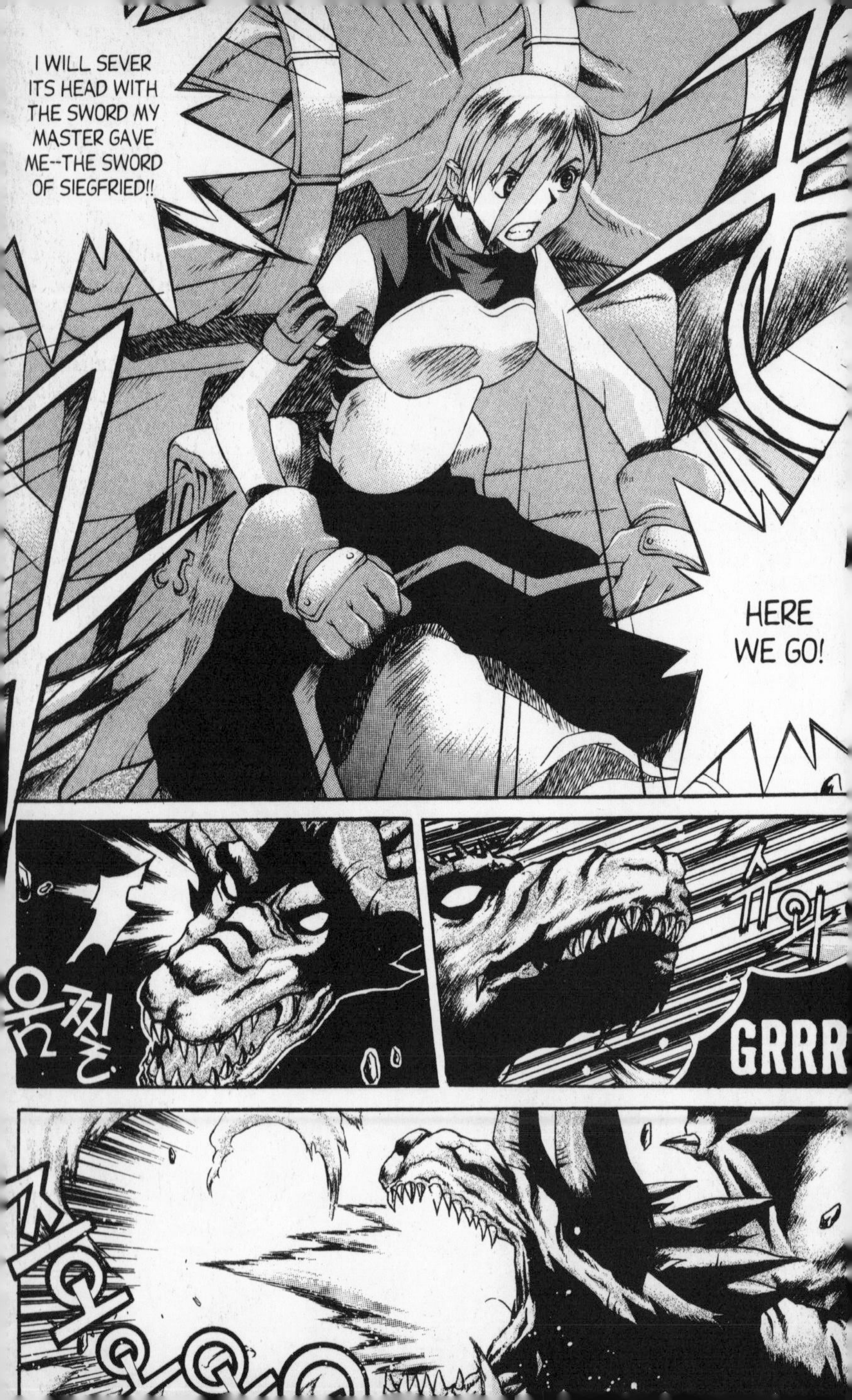
I WILL SEVER ITS HEAD WITH THE SWORD MY MASTER GAVE ME--THE SWORD OF SIEGFRIED!!
HERE WE GO!
GRRR

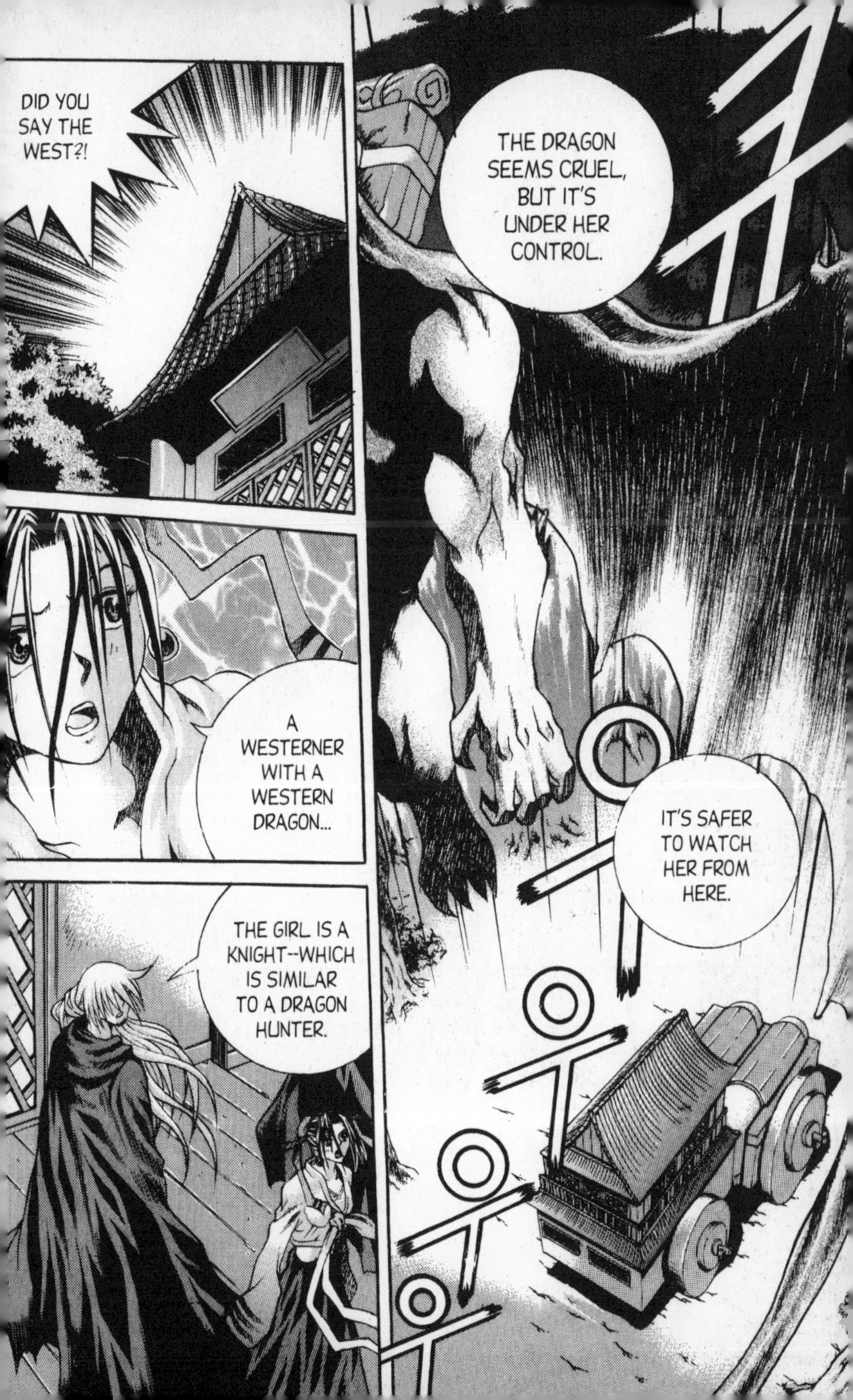
DID YOU SAY THE WEST?!
A WESTERNER WITH A WESTERN DRAGON...
THE GIRL IS A KNIGHT--WHICH IS SIMILAR TO A DRAGON HUNTER.
THE DRAGON SEEMS CRUEL, BUT IT'S UNDER HER CONTROL.
IT'S SAFER TO WATCH HER FROM HERE.

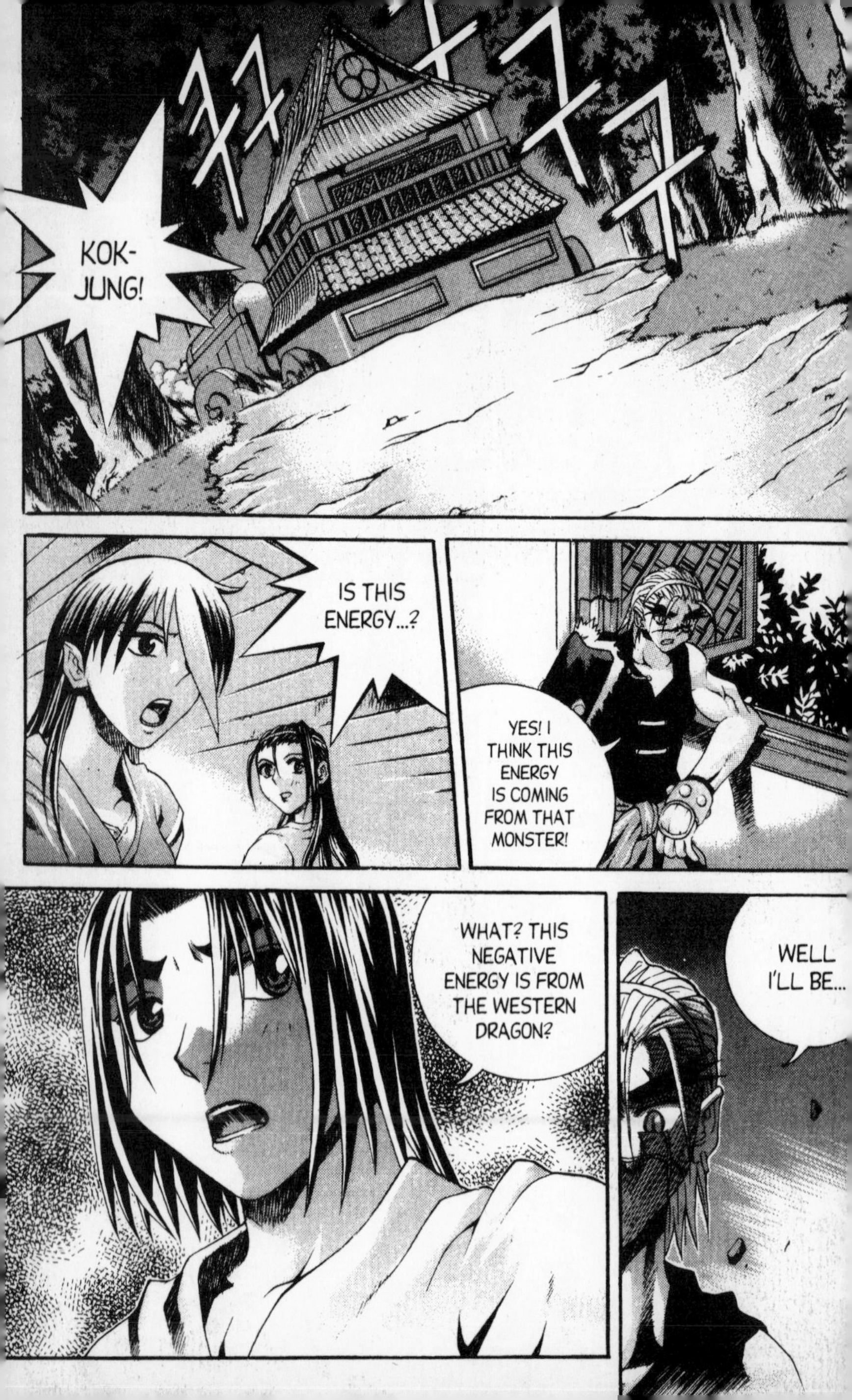
KOK-JUNG!
IS THIS ENERGY...?
YES! I THINK THIS ENERGY IS COMING FROM THAT MONSTER!
WHAT? THIS NEGATIVE ENERGY IS FROM THE WESTERN DRAGON?
WELL I'LL BE...

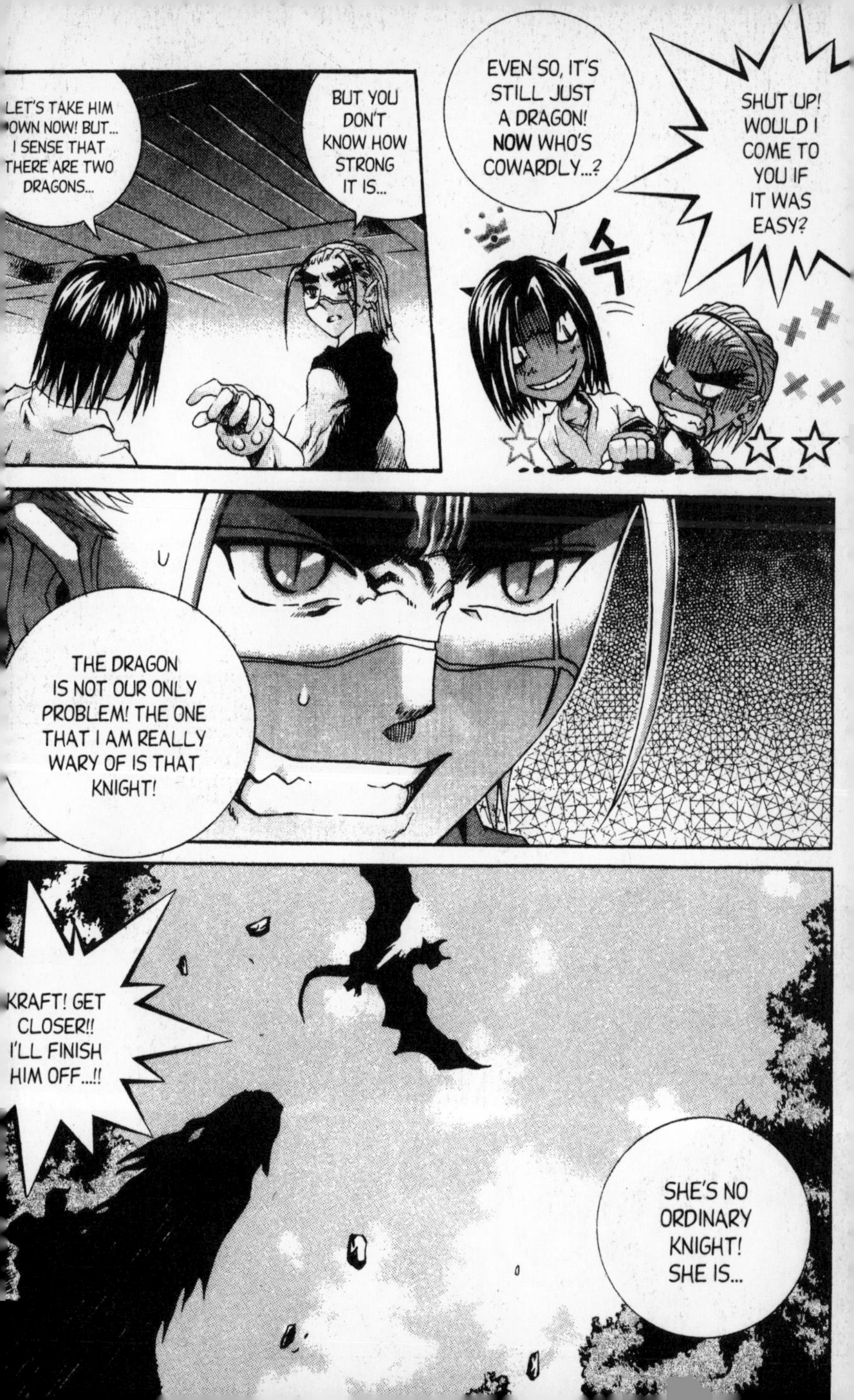
LET'S TAKE HIM DOWN NOW! BUT... I SENSE THAT THERE ARE TWO DRAGONS...
BUT YOU DON'T KNOW HOW STRONG IT IS...
EVEN SO, IT'S STILL JUST A DRAGON! **NOW** WHO'S COWARDLY...?
SHUT UP! WOULD I COME TO YOU IF IT WAS EASY?
THE DRAGON IS NOT OUR ONLY PROBLEM! THE ONE THAT I AM REALLY WARY OF IS THAT KNIGHT!
KRAFT! GET CLOSER!! I'LL FINISH HIM OFF...!!
SHE'S NO ORDINARY KNIGHT! SHE IS...

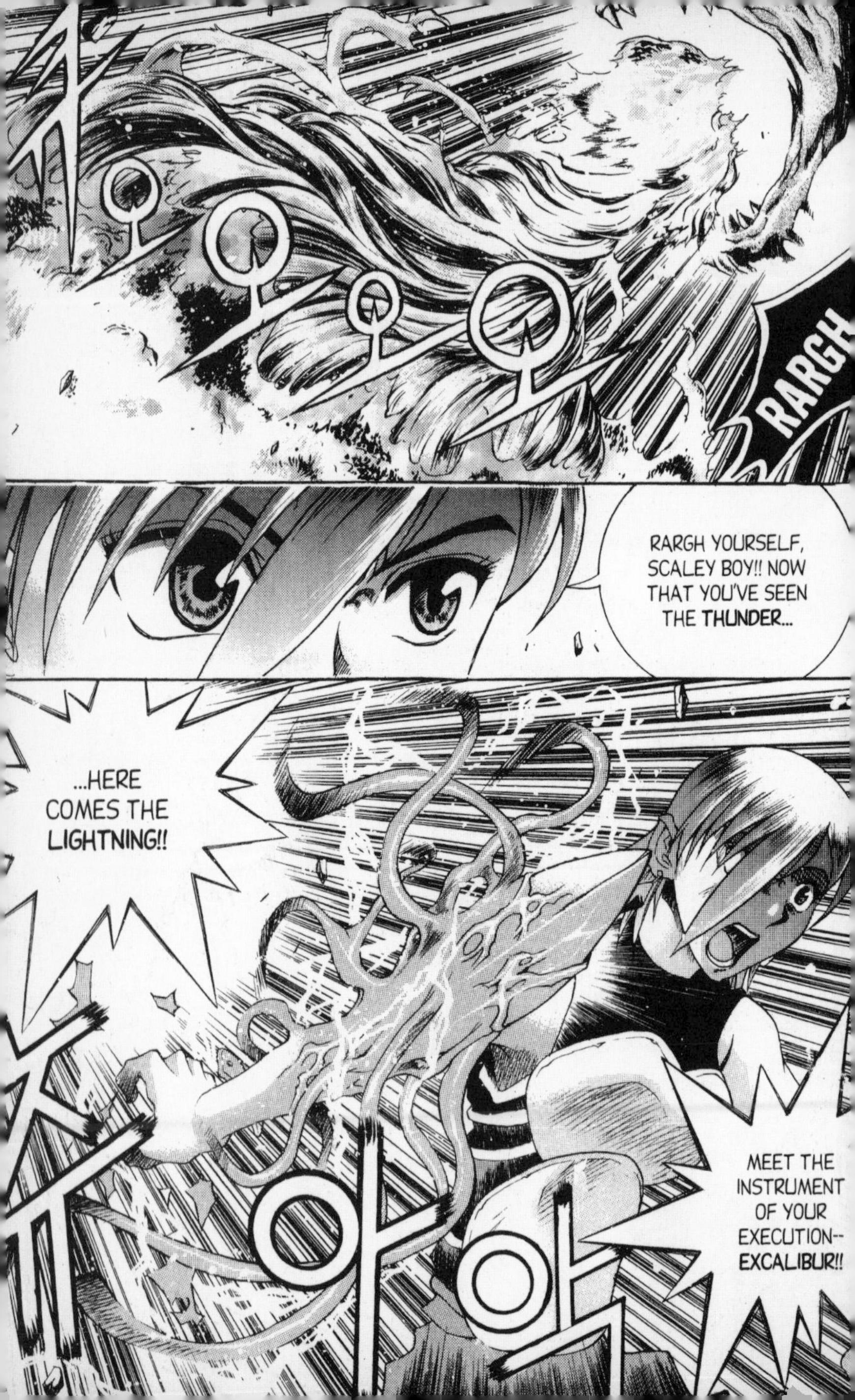
RARGH
RARGH YOURSELF, SCALEY BOY!! NOW THAT YOU'VE SEEN THE **THUNDER**...
...HERE COMES THE **LIGHTNING!!**
MEET THE INSTRUMENT OF YOUR EXECUTION-- **EXCALIBUR!!**

CHAPTER 53
RIAH H. ARTHUR (PART 2)

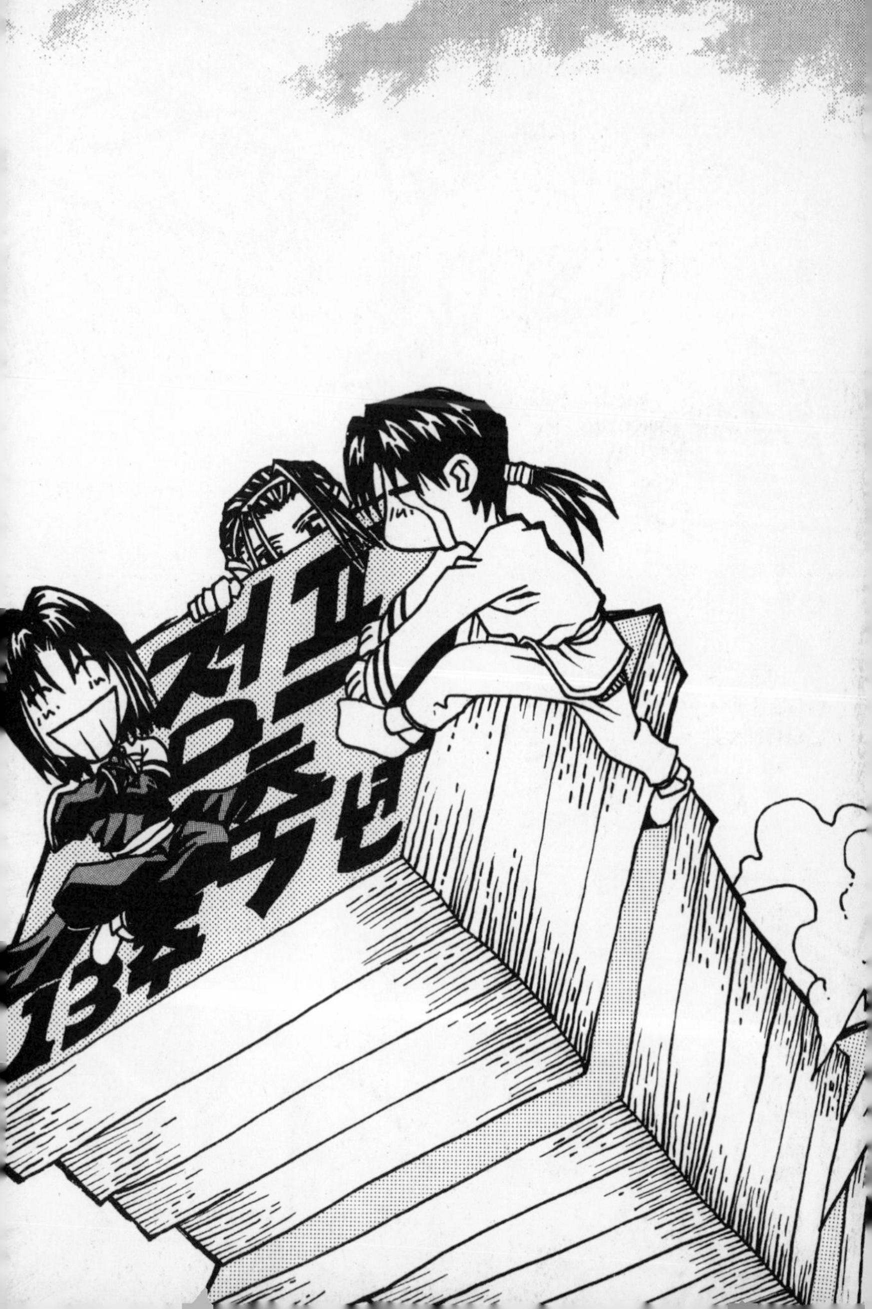

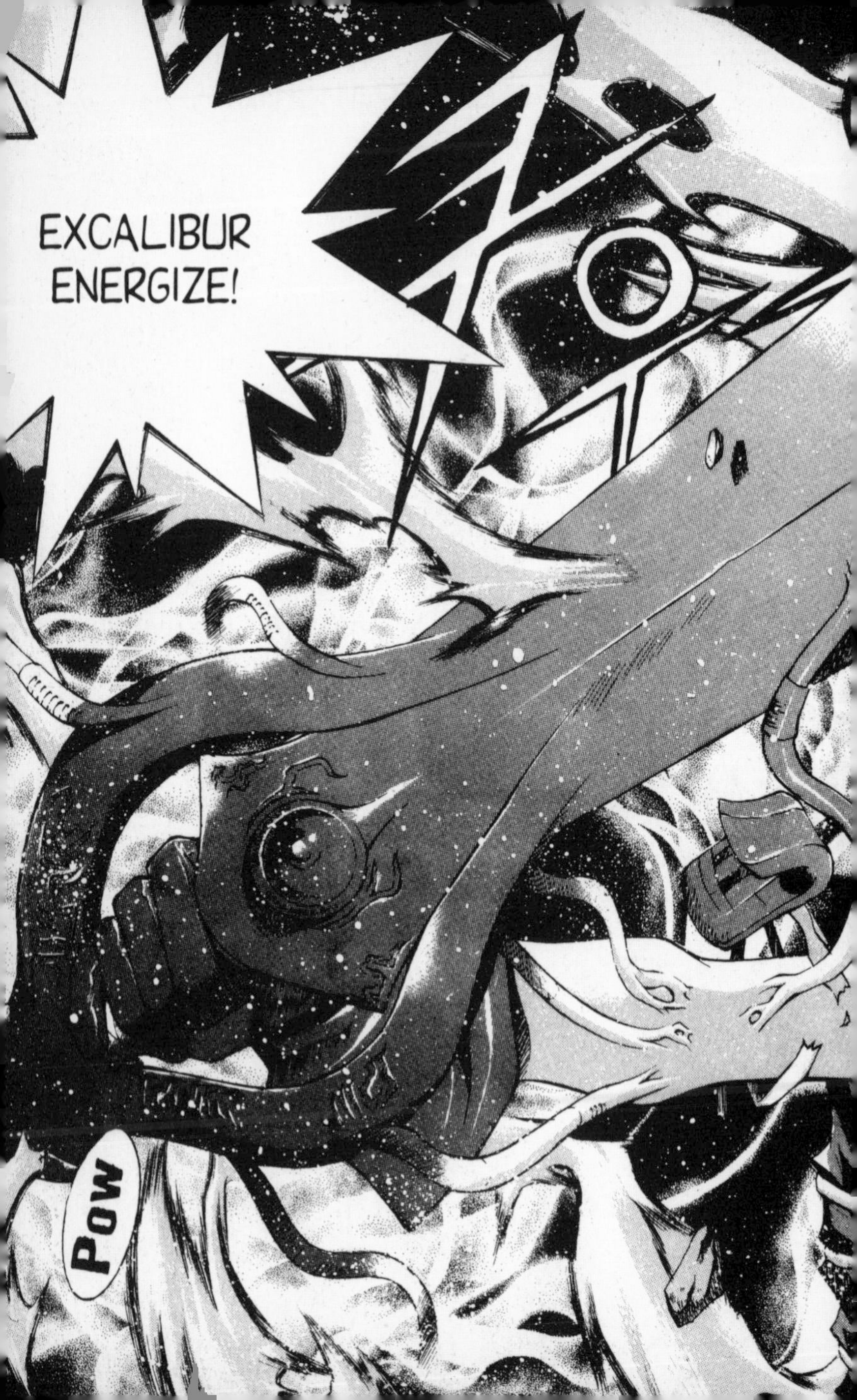
EXCALIBUR ENERGIZE!
POW

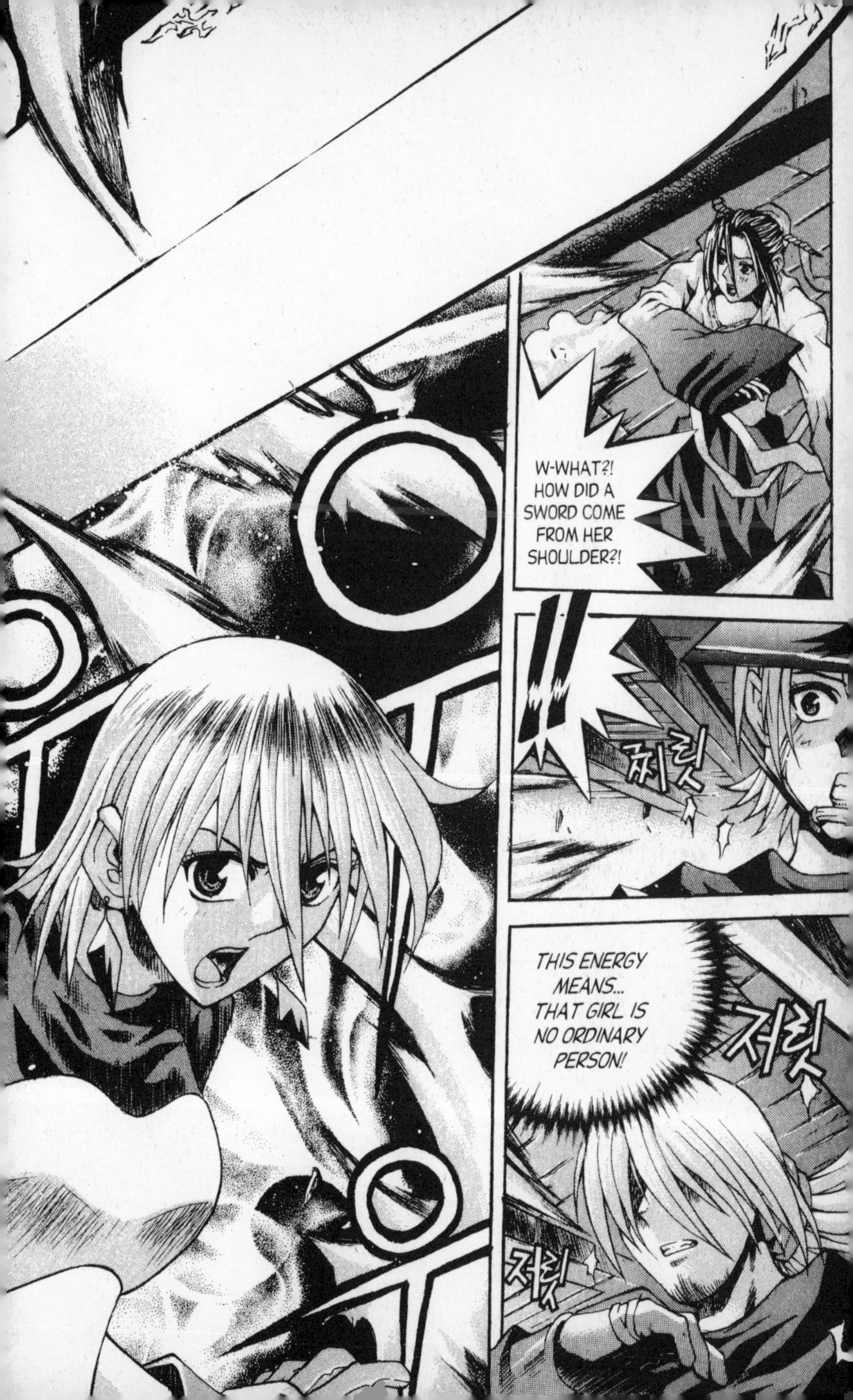
W-WHAT?! HOW DID A SWORD COME FROM HER SHOULDER?!
!!
짜릿
THIS ENERGY MEANS... THAT GIRL IS NO ORDINARY PERSON!
지릿
지릿

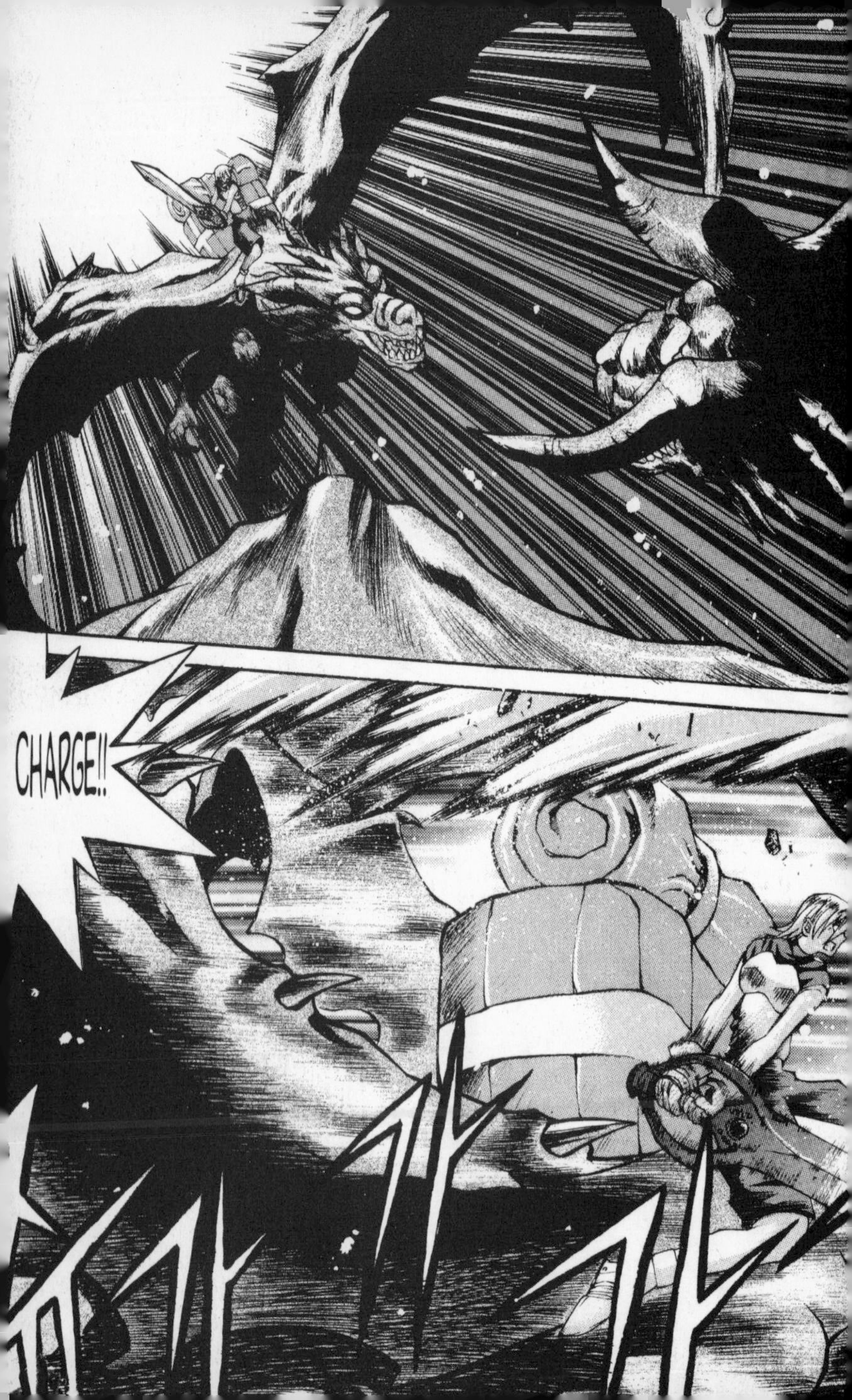
CHARGE!!

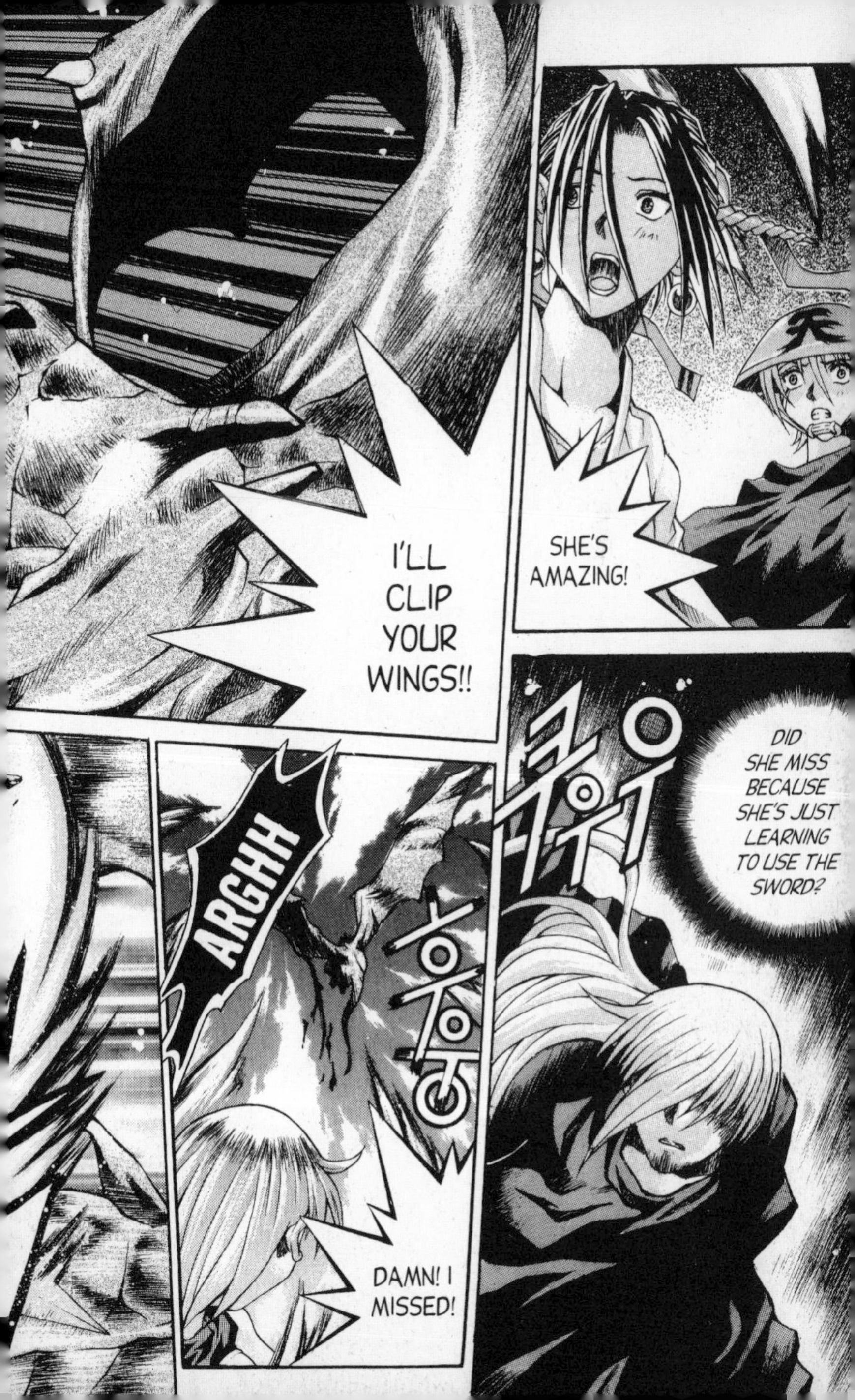
I'LL CLIP YOUR WINGS!!
SHE'S AMAZING!
ARGHH
DAMN! I MISSED!
DID SHE MISS BECAUSE SHE'S JUST LEARNING TO USE THE SWORD?

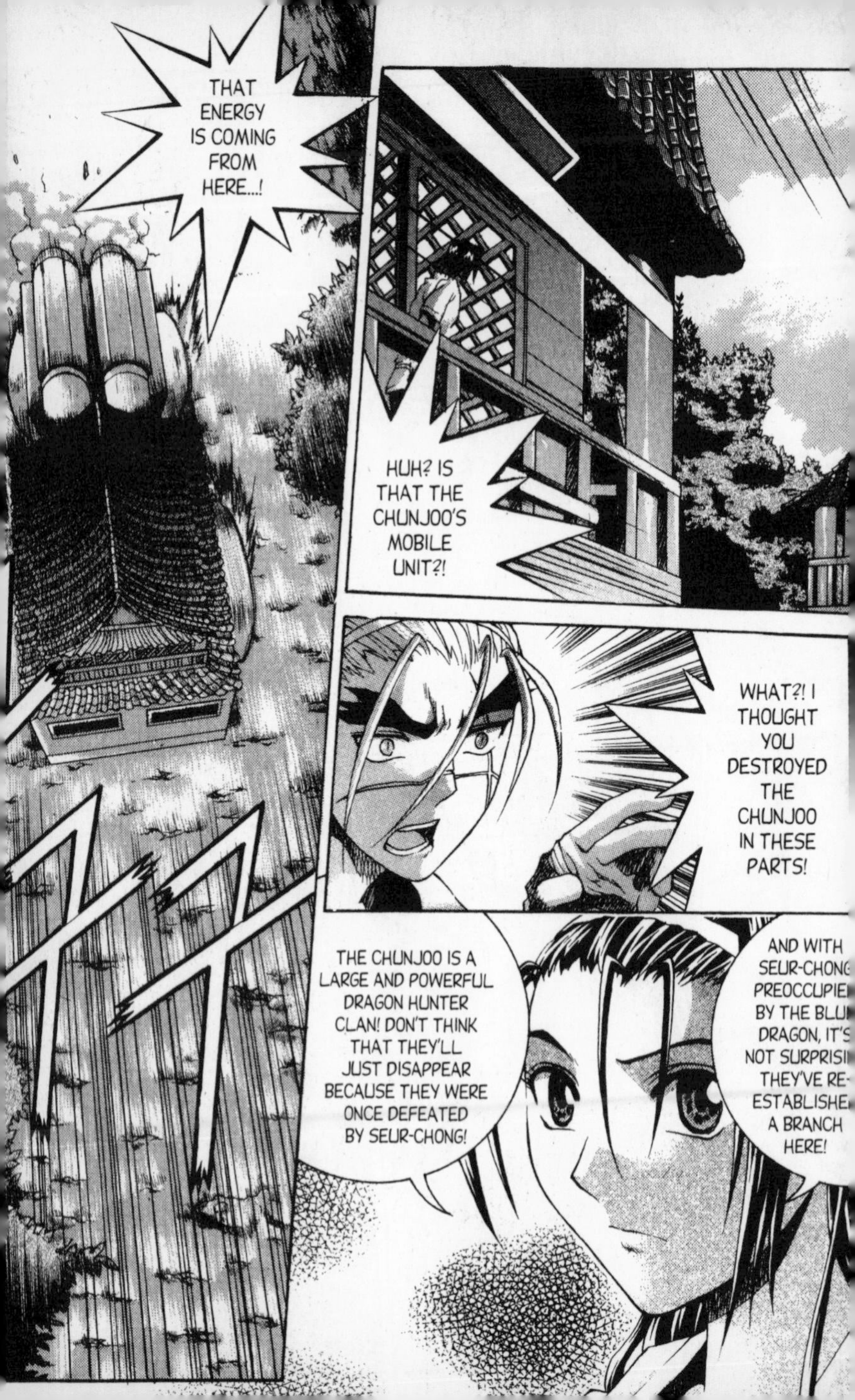
THAT ENERGY IS COMING FROM HERE...!
HUH? IS THAT THE CHUNJOO'S MOBILE UNIT?!
WHAT?! I THOUGHT YOU DESTROYED THE CHUNJOO IN THESE PARTS!
THE CHUNJOO IS A LARGE AND POWERFUL DRAGON HUNTER CLAN! DON'T THINK THAT THEY'LL JUST DISAPPEAR BECAUSE THEY WERE ONCE DEFEATED BY SEUR-CHONG!
AND WITH SEUR-CHONG PREOCCUPIE BY THE BLU DRAGON, IT'S NOT SURPRISI THEY'VE RE-ESTABLISHE A BRANCH HERE!

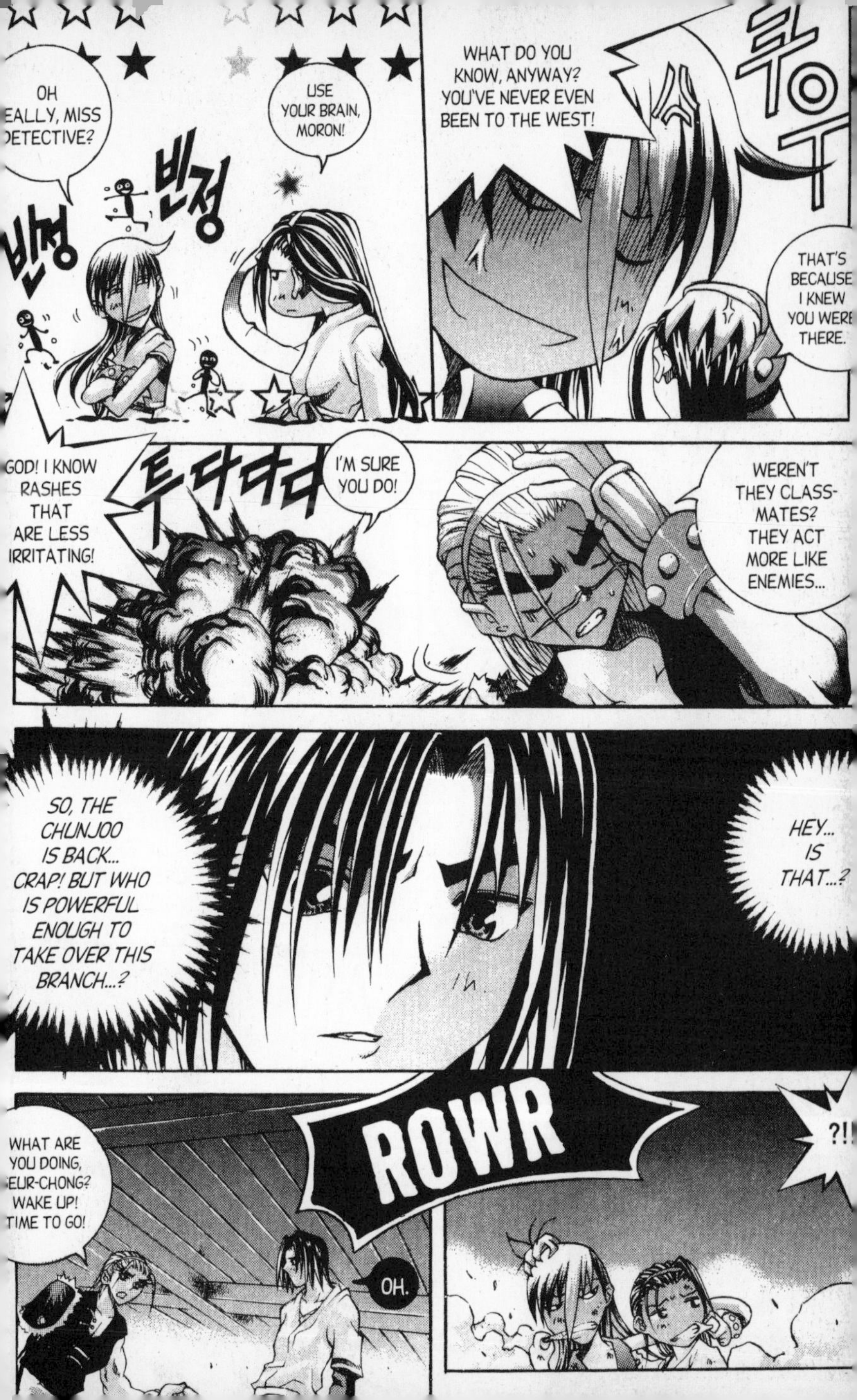
OH EALLY, MISS ETECTIVE?
빈정
빈정
USE YOUR BRAIN, MORON!
WHAT DO YOU KNOW, ANYWAY? YOU'VE NEVER EVEN BEEN TO THE WEST!
THAT'S BECAUSE I KNEW YOU WERE THERE.
GOD! I KNOW RASHES THAT ARE LESS RRITATING!
투다다다
I'M SURE YOU DO!
WEREN'T THEY CLASS-MATES? THEY ACT MORE LIKE ENEMIES...
SO, THE CHUNJOO IS BACK... CRAP! BUT WHO IS POWERFUL ENOUGH TO TAKE OVER THIS BRANCH...?
HEY... IS THAT...?
WHAT ARE YOU DOING, EUR-CHONG? WAKE UP! TIME TO GO!
ROWR
OH.
?!

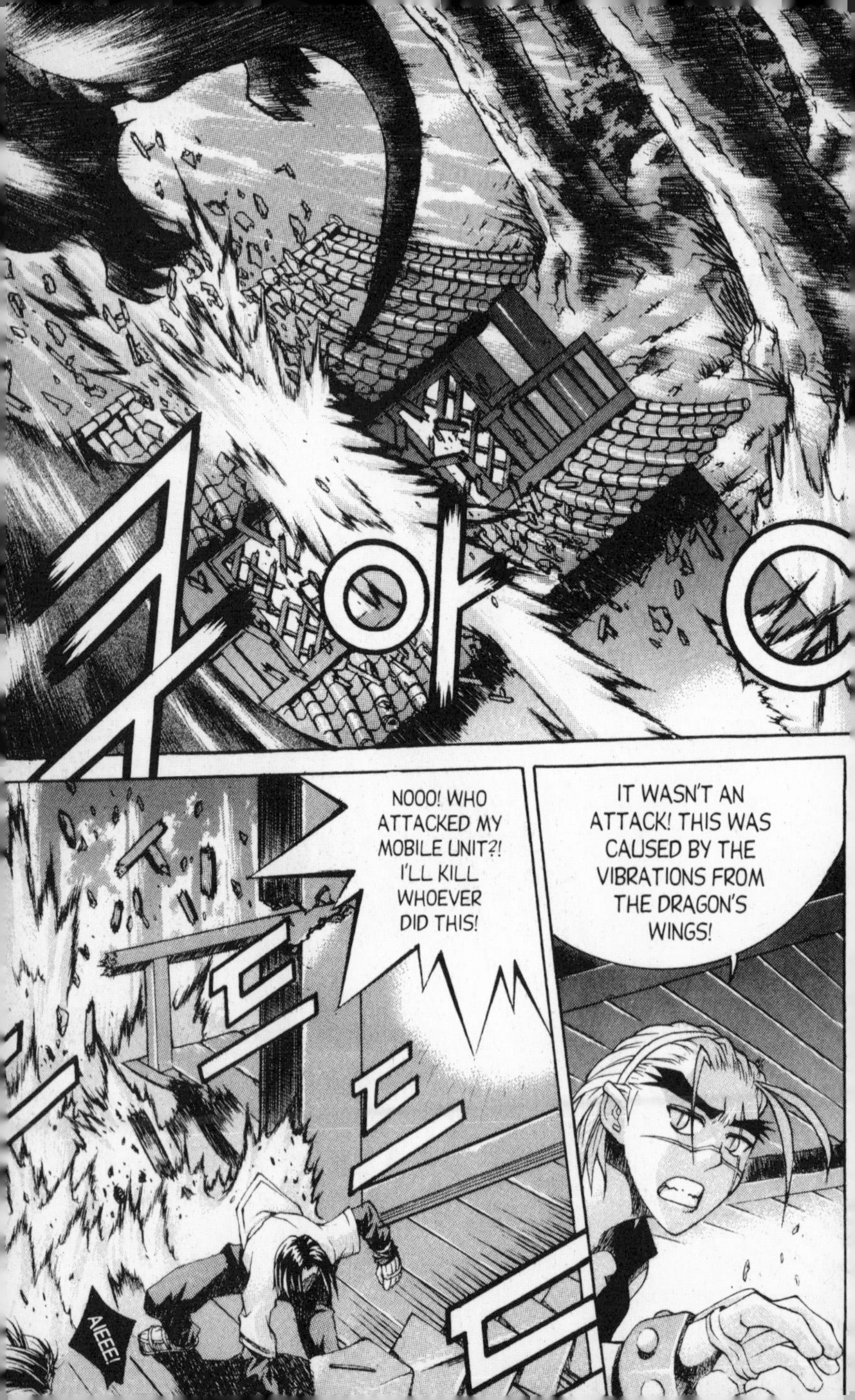
NOOO! WHO ATTACKED MY MOBILE UNIT?! I'LL KILL WHOEVER DID THIS!
IT WASN'T AN ATTACK! THIS WAS CAUSED BY THE VIBRATIONS FROM THE DRAGON'S WINGS!
AIEEE!

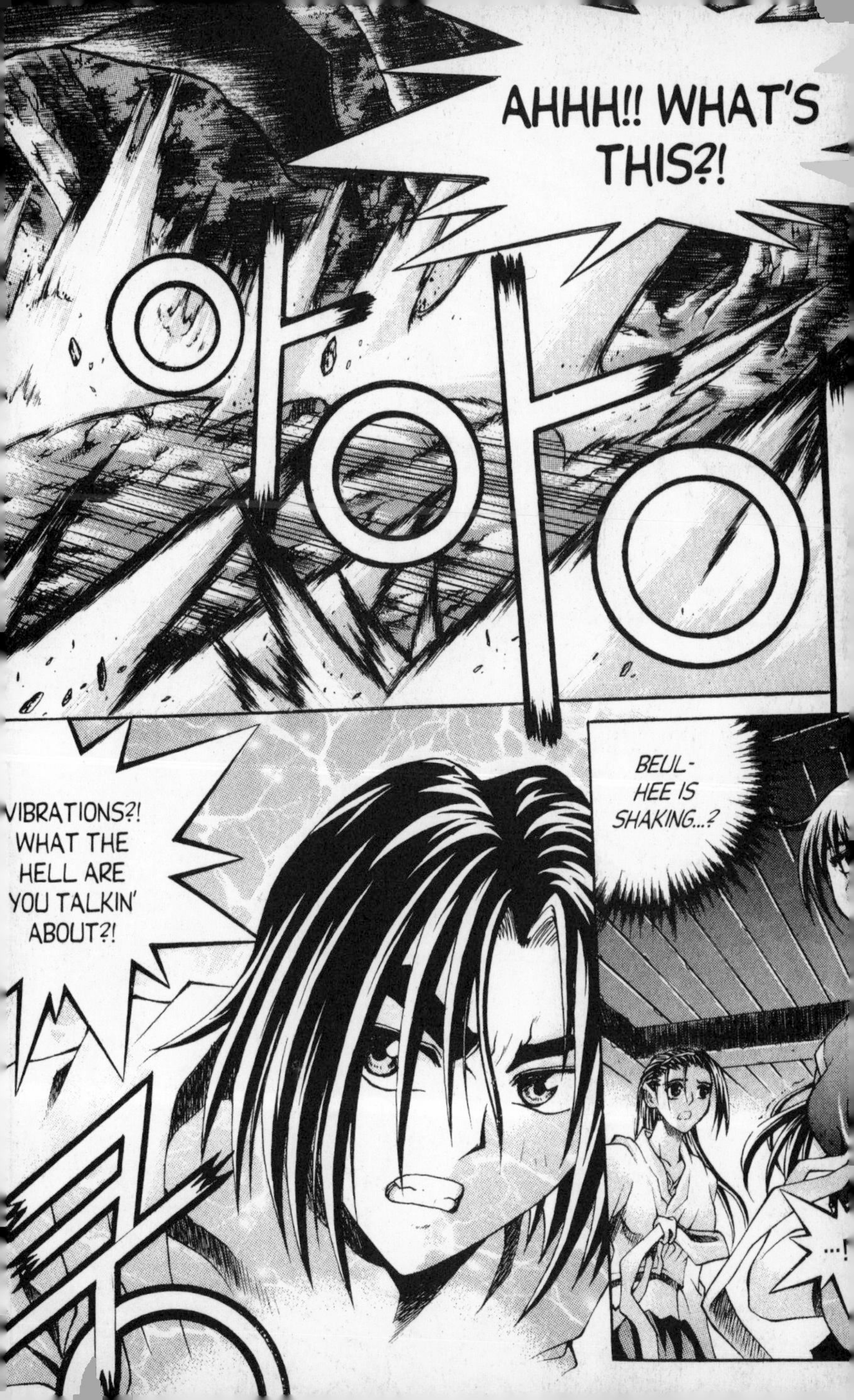
AHHH!! WHAT'S THIS?!
VIBRATIONS?! WHAT THE HELL ARE YOU TALKIN' ABOUT?!
BEUL-HEE IS SHAKING...?
...!

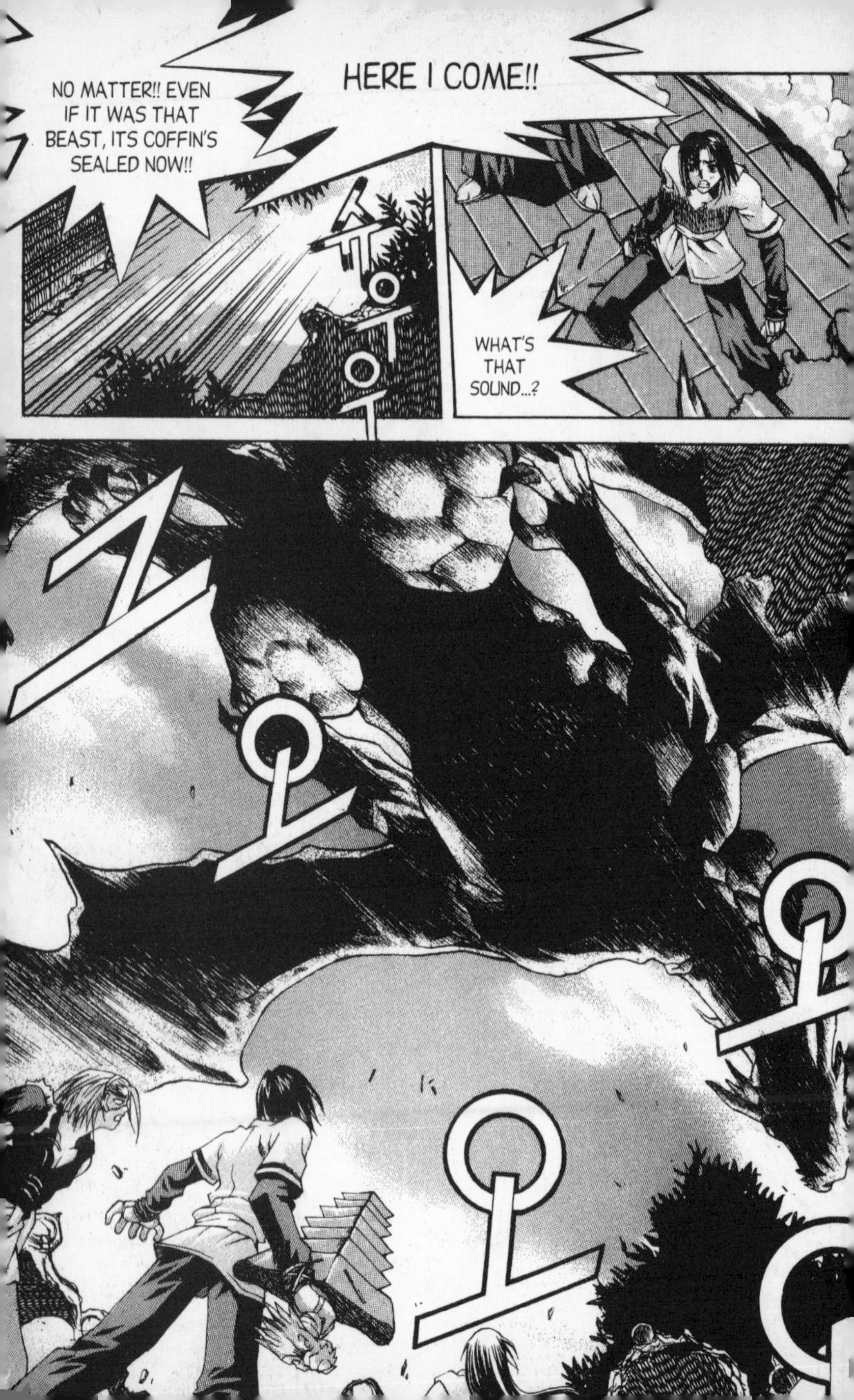
NO MATTER!! EVEN IF IT WAS THAT BEAST, ITS COFFIN'S SEALED NOW!!
HERE I COME!!
WHAT'S THAT SOUND...?

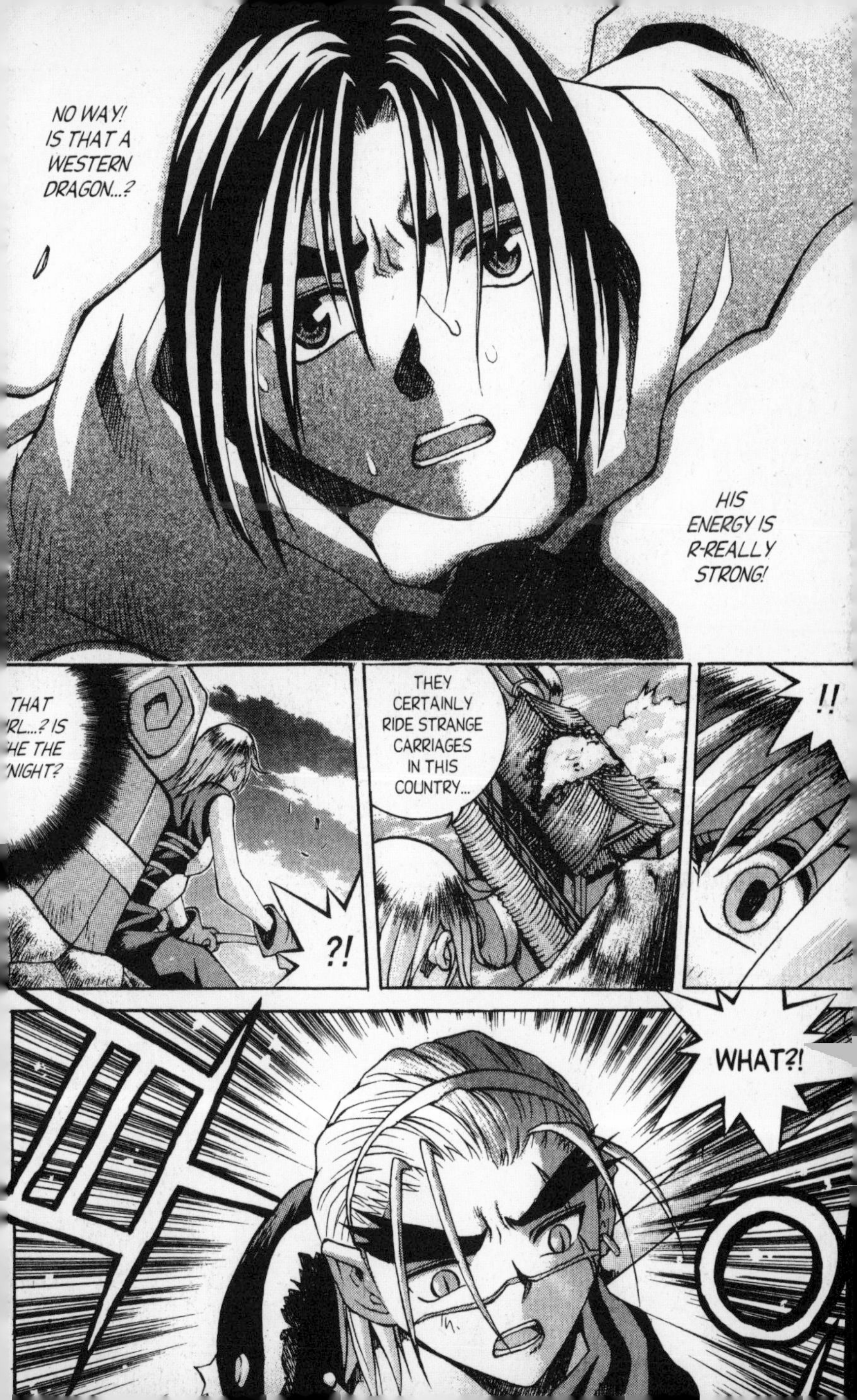
NO WAY! IS THAT A WESTERN DRAGON...?
HIS ENERGY IS R-REALLY STRONG!
THAT RL...? IS HE THE NIGHT?
?!
THEY CERTAINLY RIDE STRANGE CARRIAGES IN THIS COUNTRY...
!!
WHAT?!

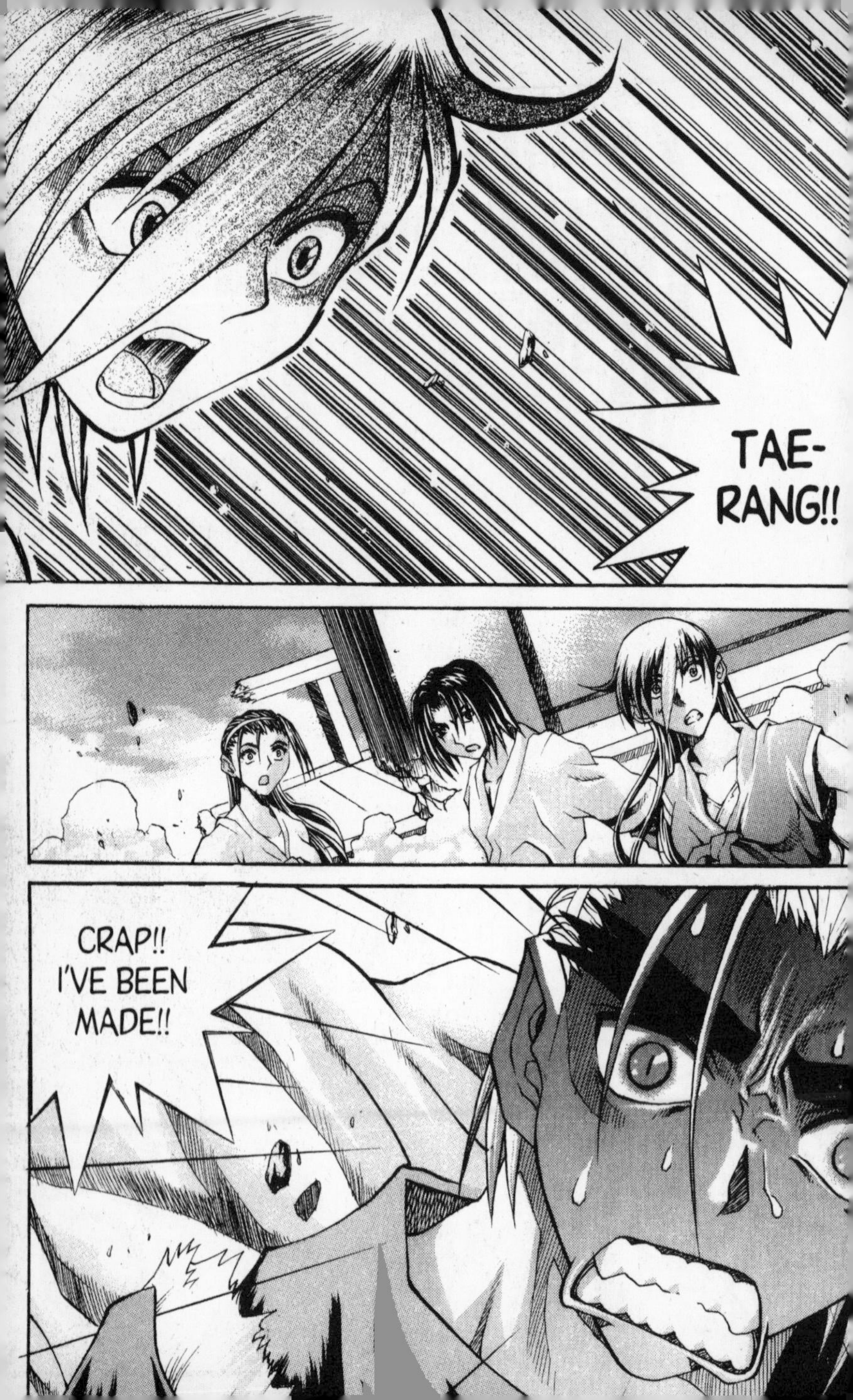
TAE-
RANG!!
CRAP!!
I'VE BEEN
MADE!!

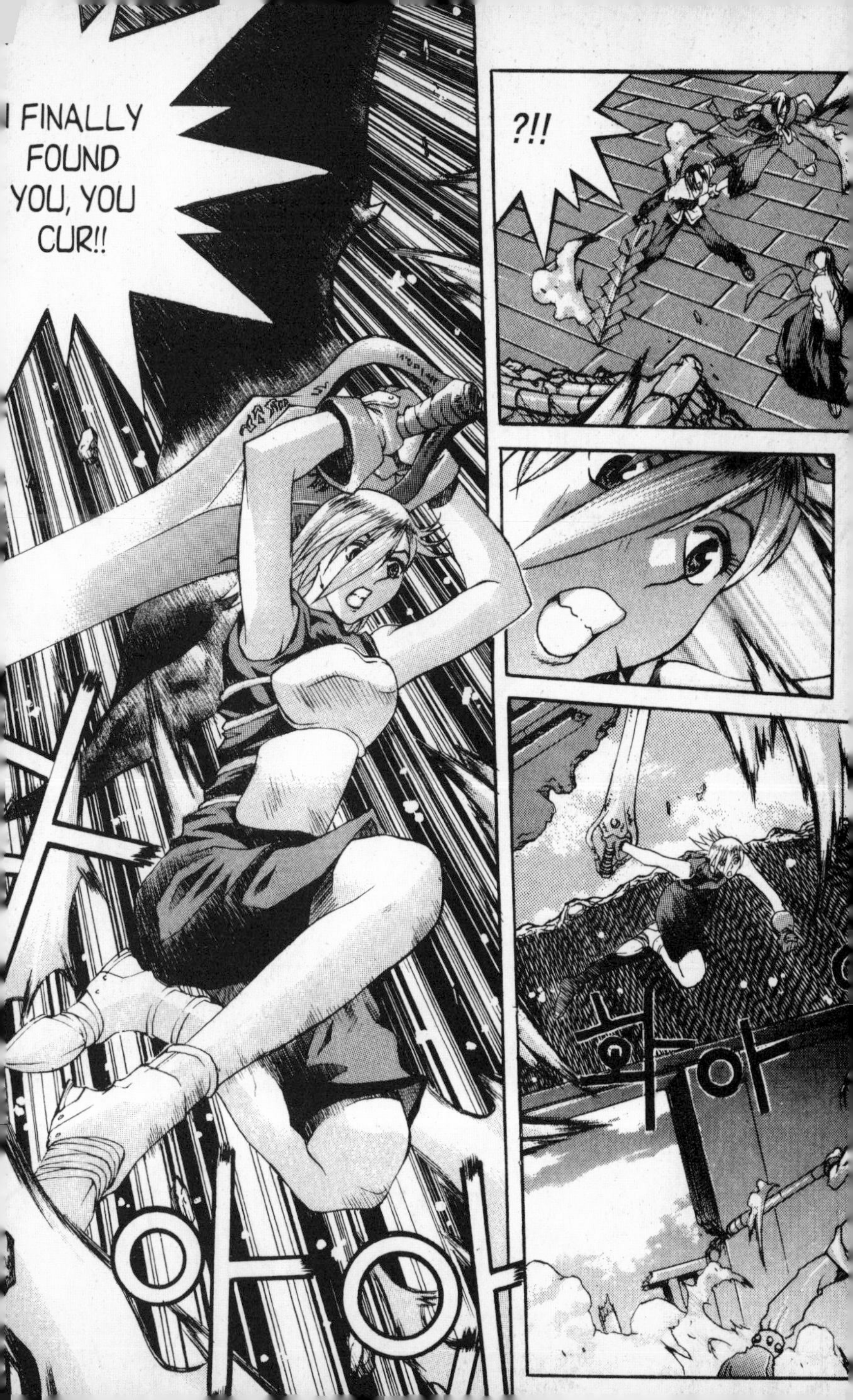
I FINALLY FOUND YOU, YOU CUR!!
?!!

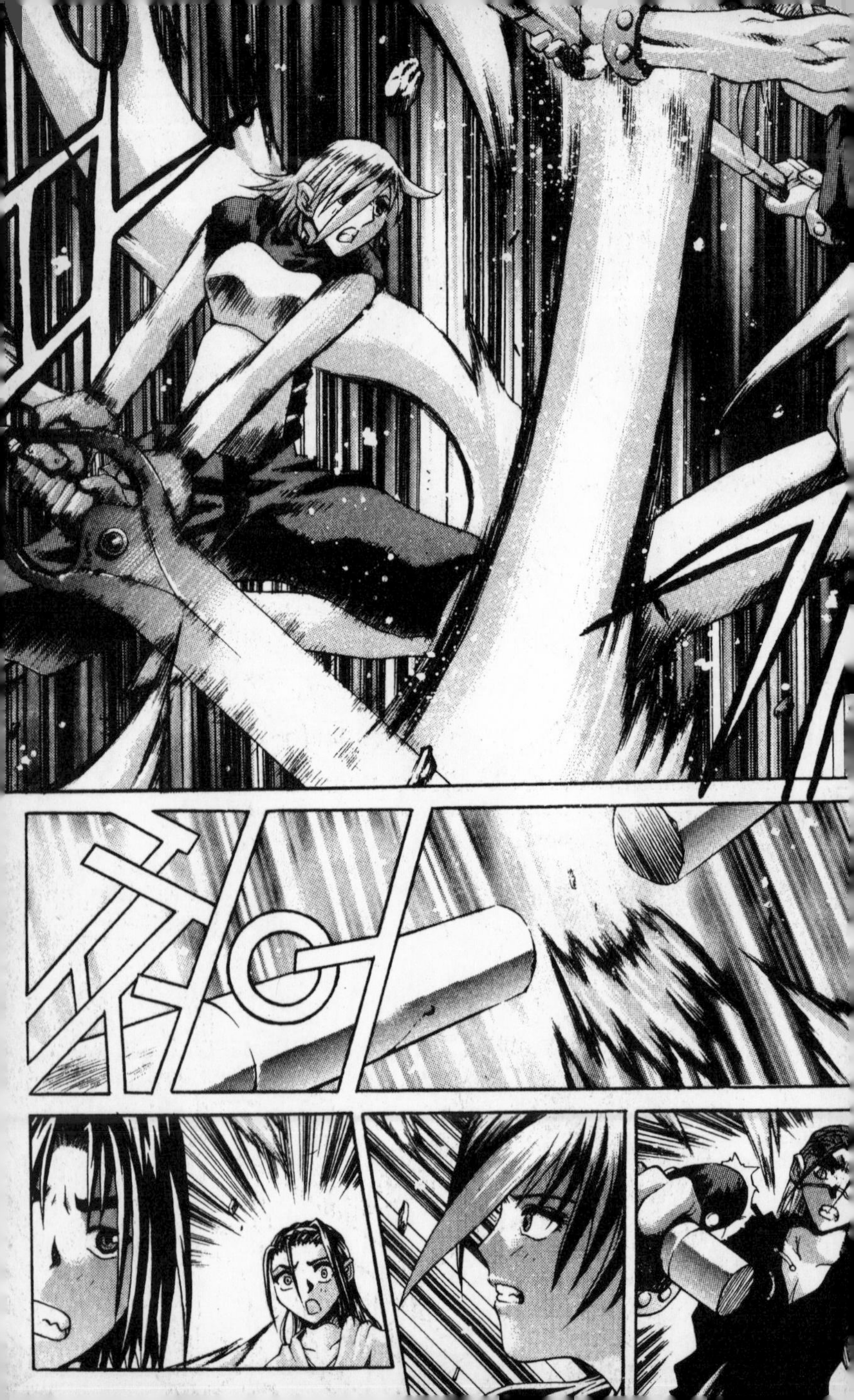

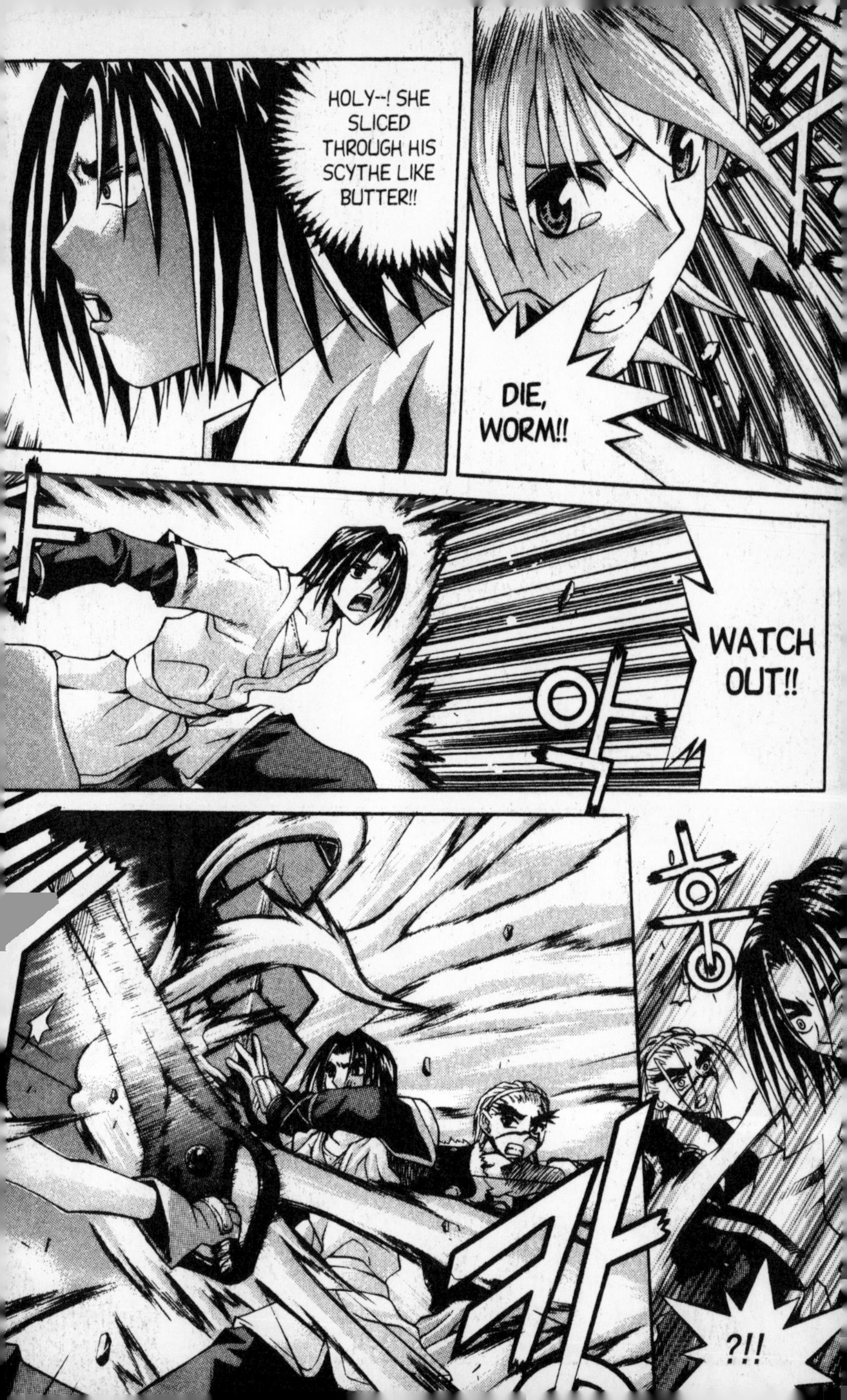
HOLY--! SHE SLICED THROUGH HIS SCYTHE LIKE BUTTER!!
DIE, WORM!!
WATCH OUT!!
?!!

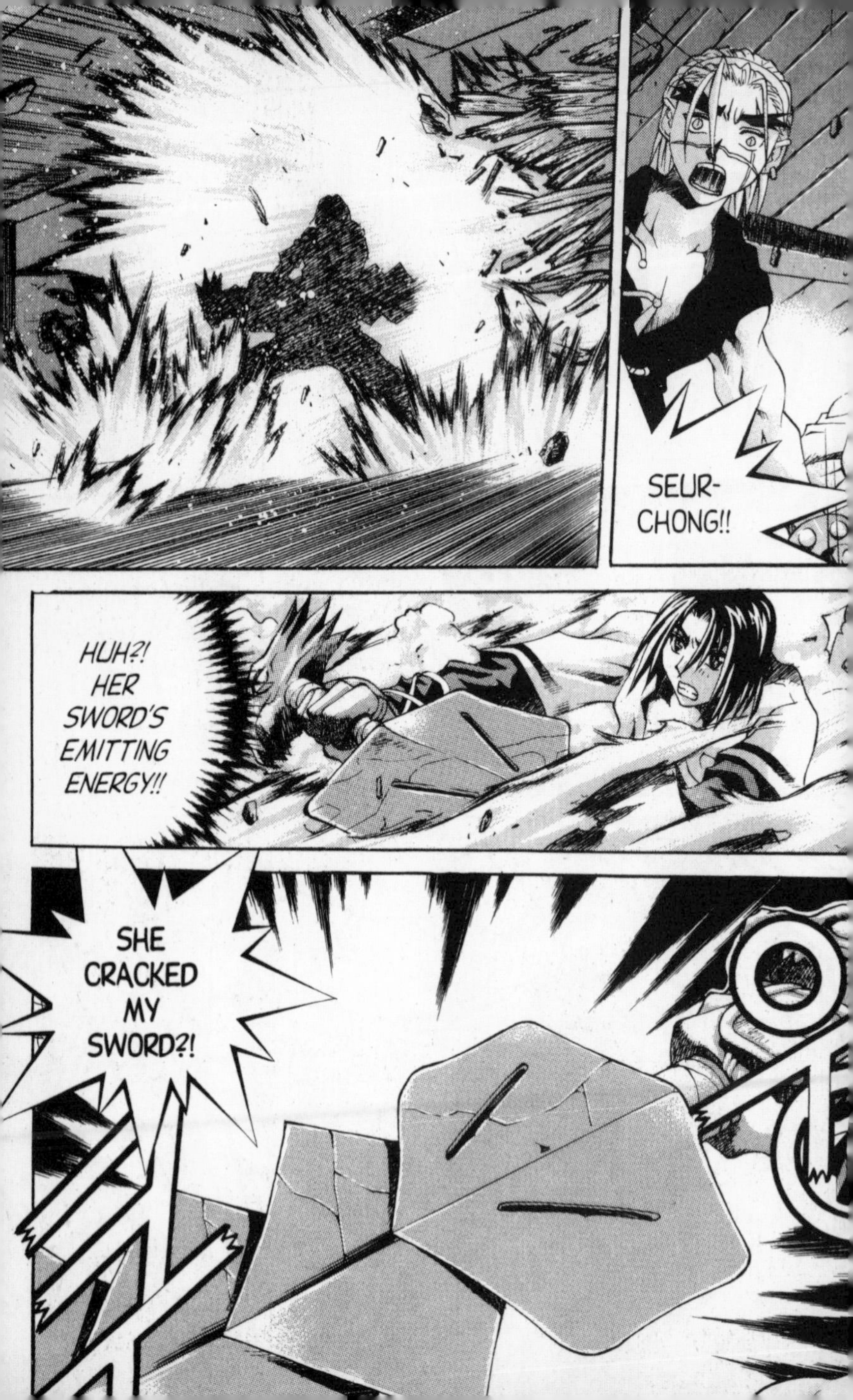
SEUR-CHONG!!
HUH?! HER SWORD'S EMITTING ENERGY!!
SHE CRACKED MY SWORD?!

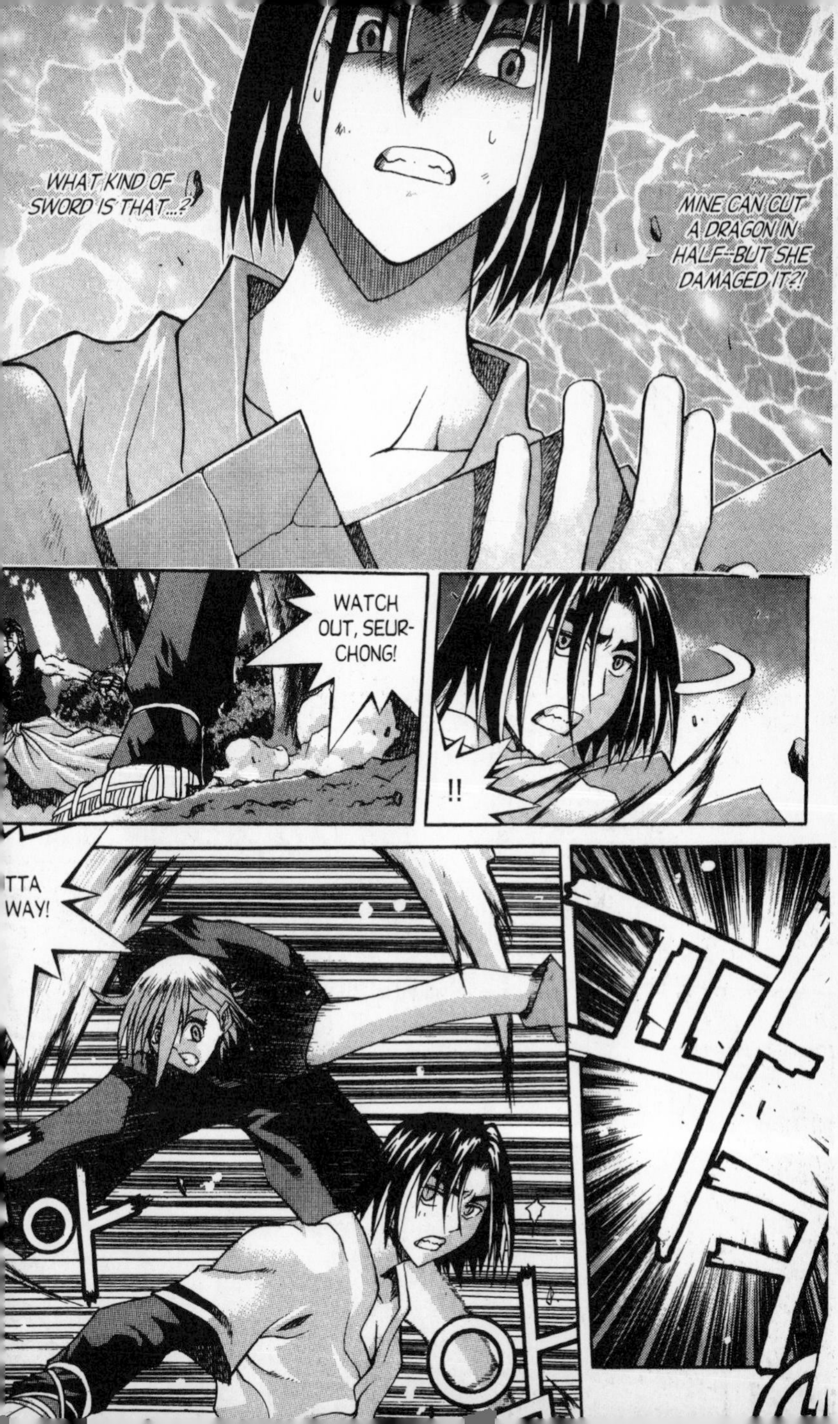
WHAT KIND OF SWORD IS THAT...?
MINE CAN CUT A DRAGON IN HALF--BUT SHE DAMAGED IT?!
WATCH OUT, SEUR-CHONG!
!!
TTA WAY!

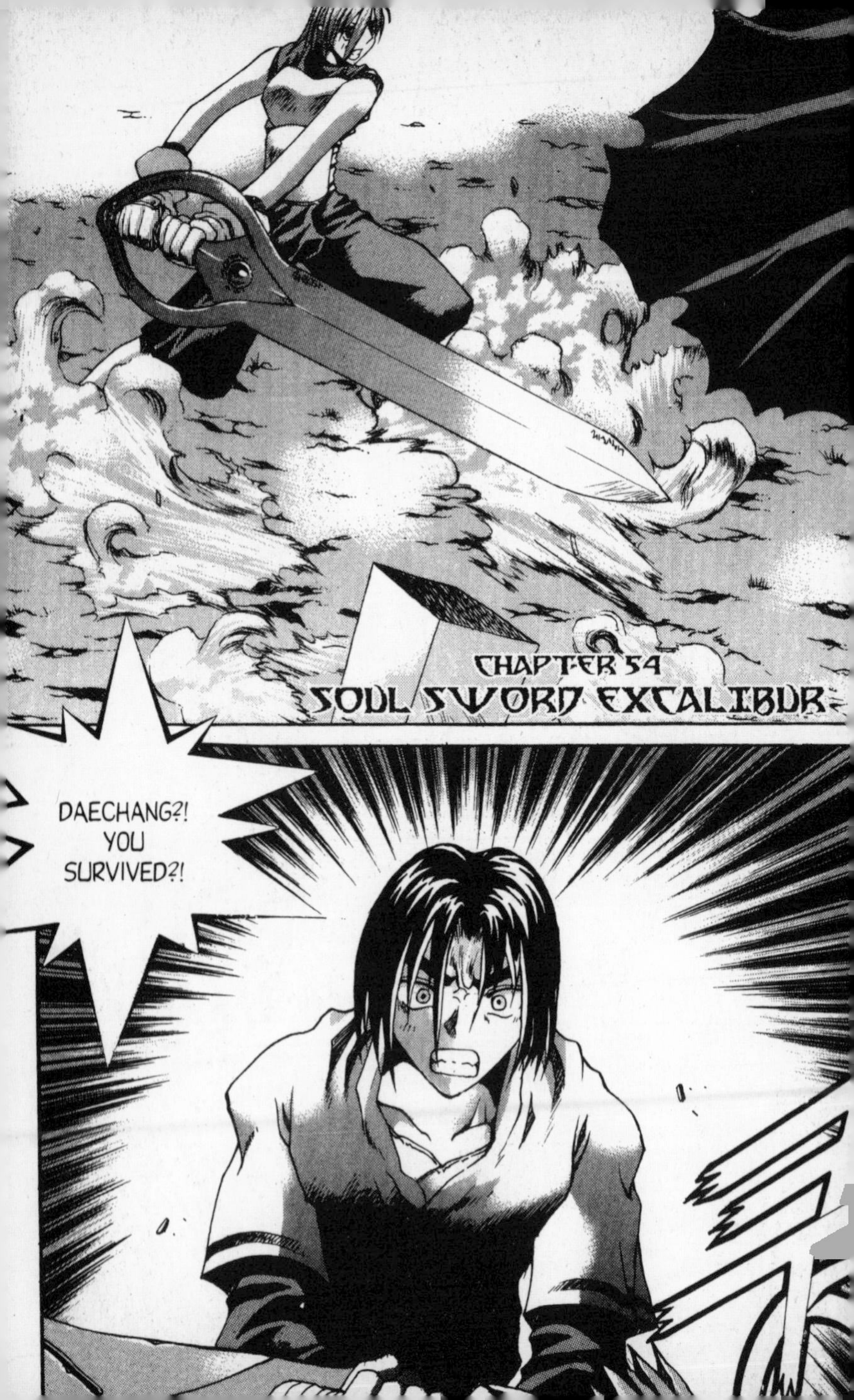
CHAPTER 54
SOUL SWORD EXCALIBUR
DAECHANG?! YOU SURVIVED?!

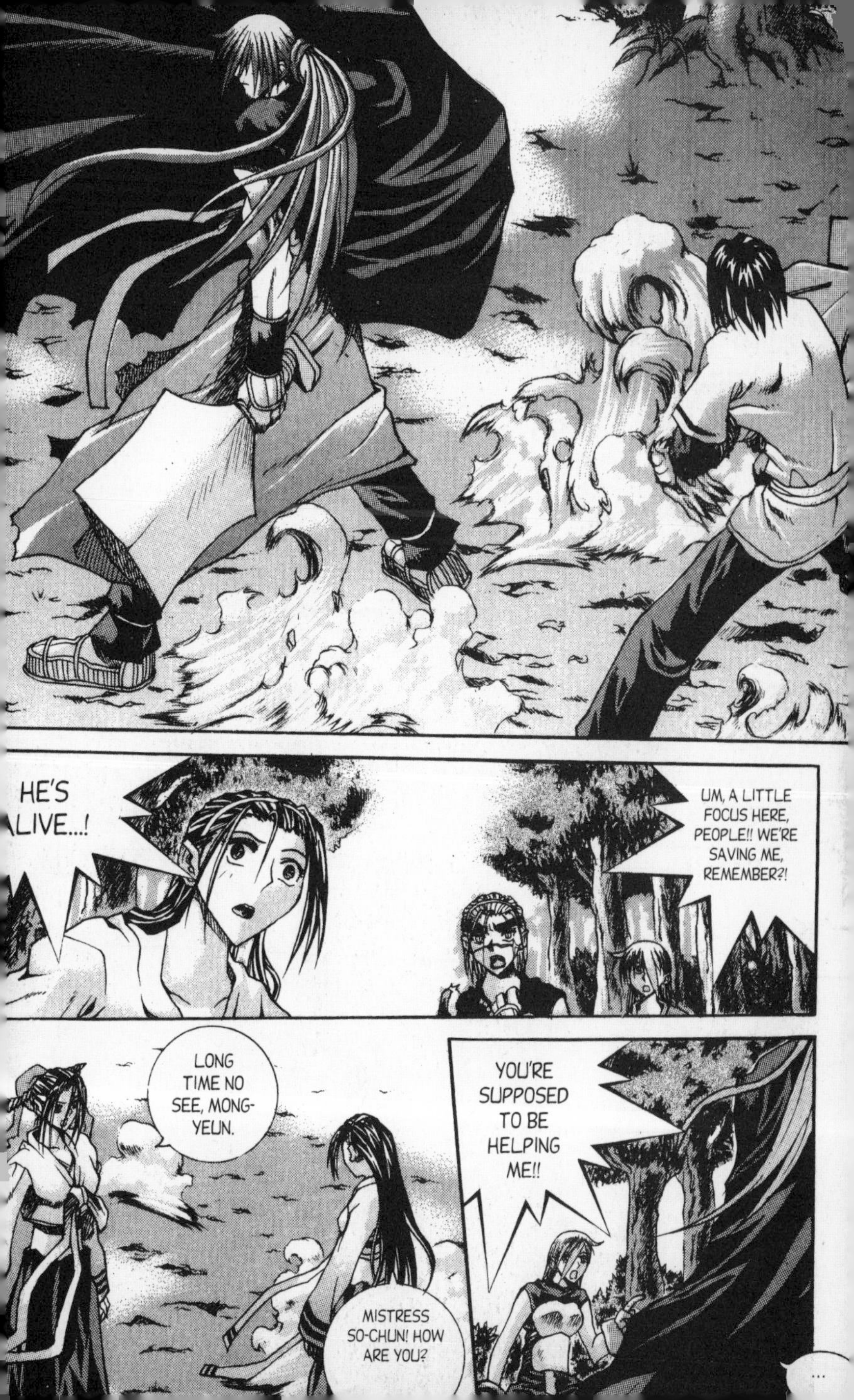
HE'S ALIVE...!
UM, A LITTLE FOCUS HERE, PEOPLE!! WE'RE SAVING ME, REMEMBER?!
LONG TIME NO SEE, MONG-YEUN.
MISTRESS SO-CHUN! HOW ARE YOU?
YOU'RE SUPPOSED TO BE HELPING ME!!
...

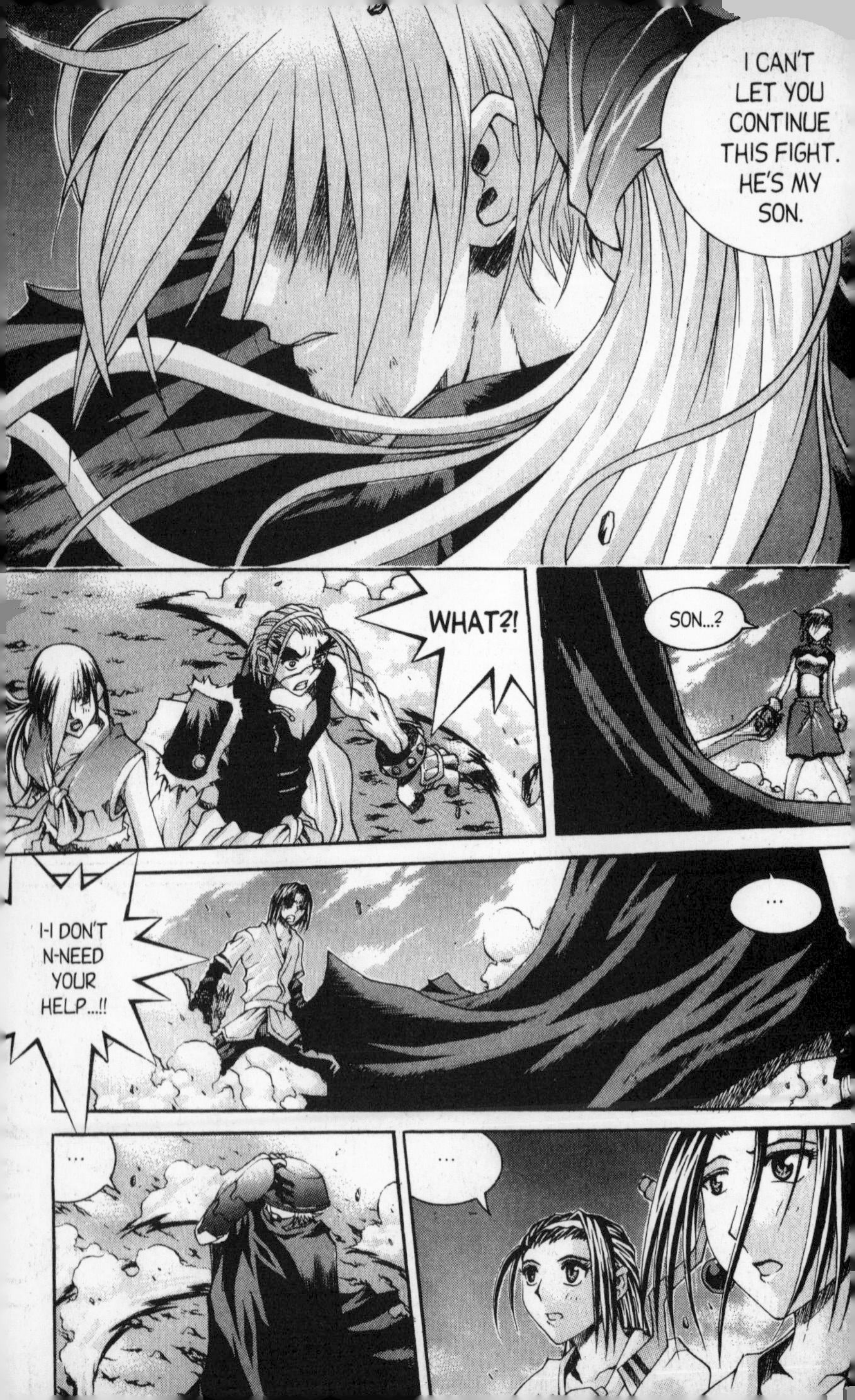
I CAN'T LET YOU CONTINUE THIS FIGHT. HE'S MY SON.
WHAT?!
SON...?
I-I DON'T N-NEED YOUR HELP...!!
...
...
...

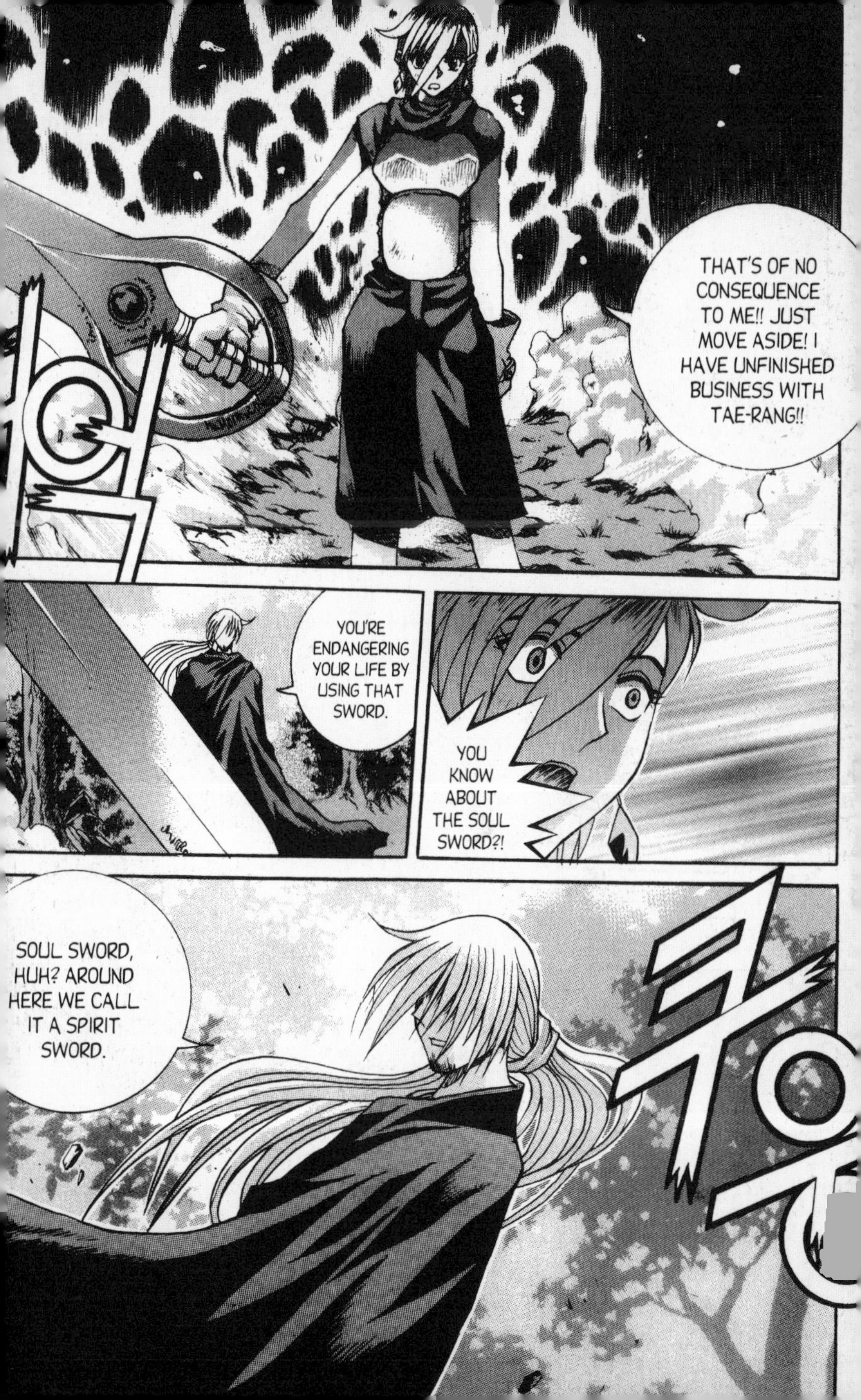
THAT'S OF NO CONSEQUENCE TO ME!! JUST MOVE ASIDE! I HAVE UNFINISHED BUSINESS WITH TAE-RANG!!
YOU'RE ENDANGERING YOUR LIFE BY USING THAT SWORD.
YOU KNOW ABOUT THE SOUL SWORD?!
SOUL SWORD, HUH? AROUND HERE WE CALL IT A SPIRIT SWORD.

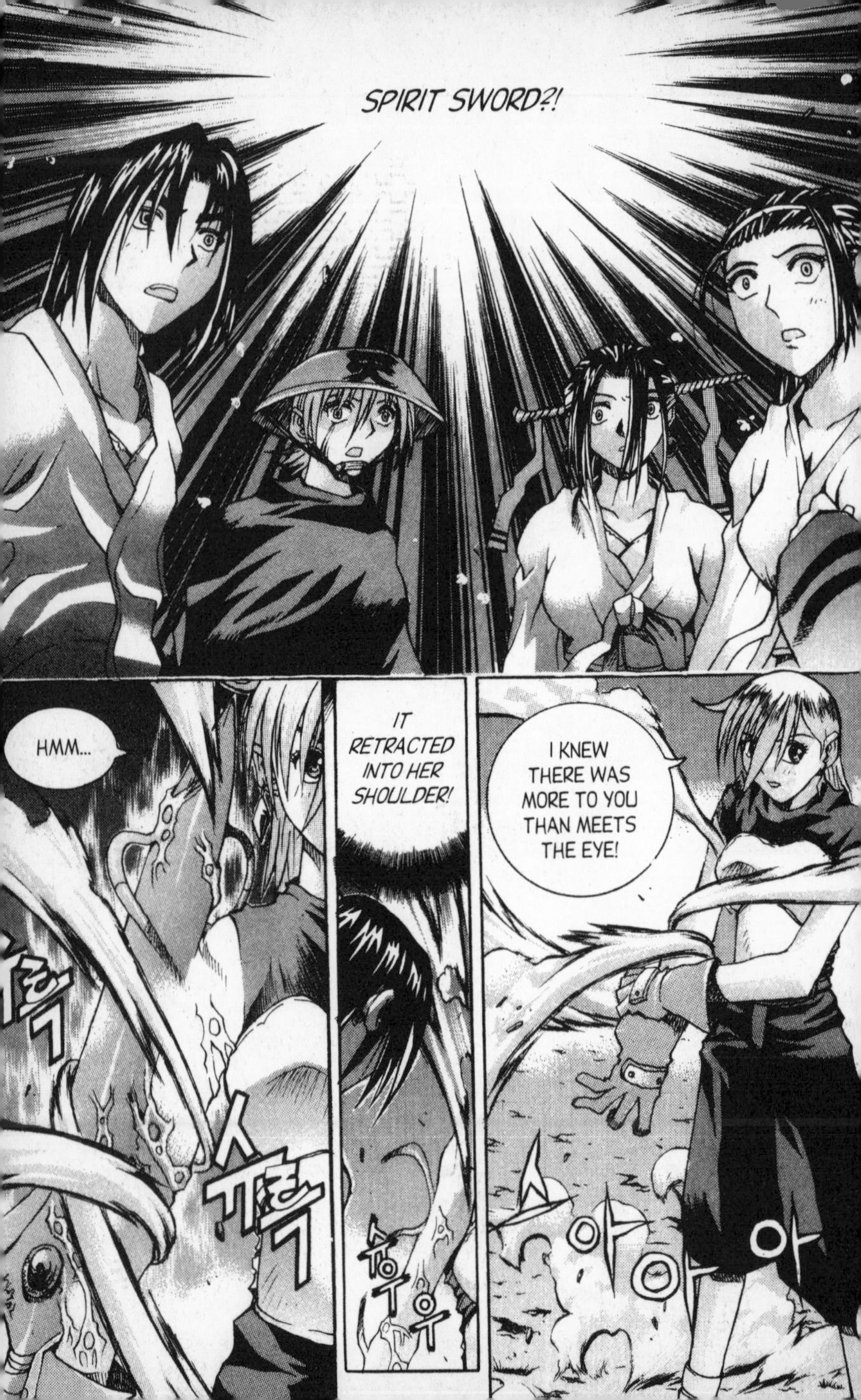
SPIRIT SWORD?!
HMM...
IT RETRACTED INTO HER SHOULDER!
I KNEW THERE WAS MORE TO YOU THAN MEETS THE EYE!

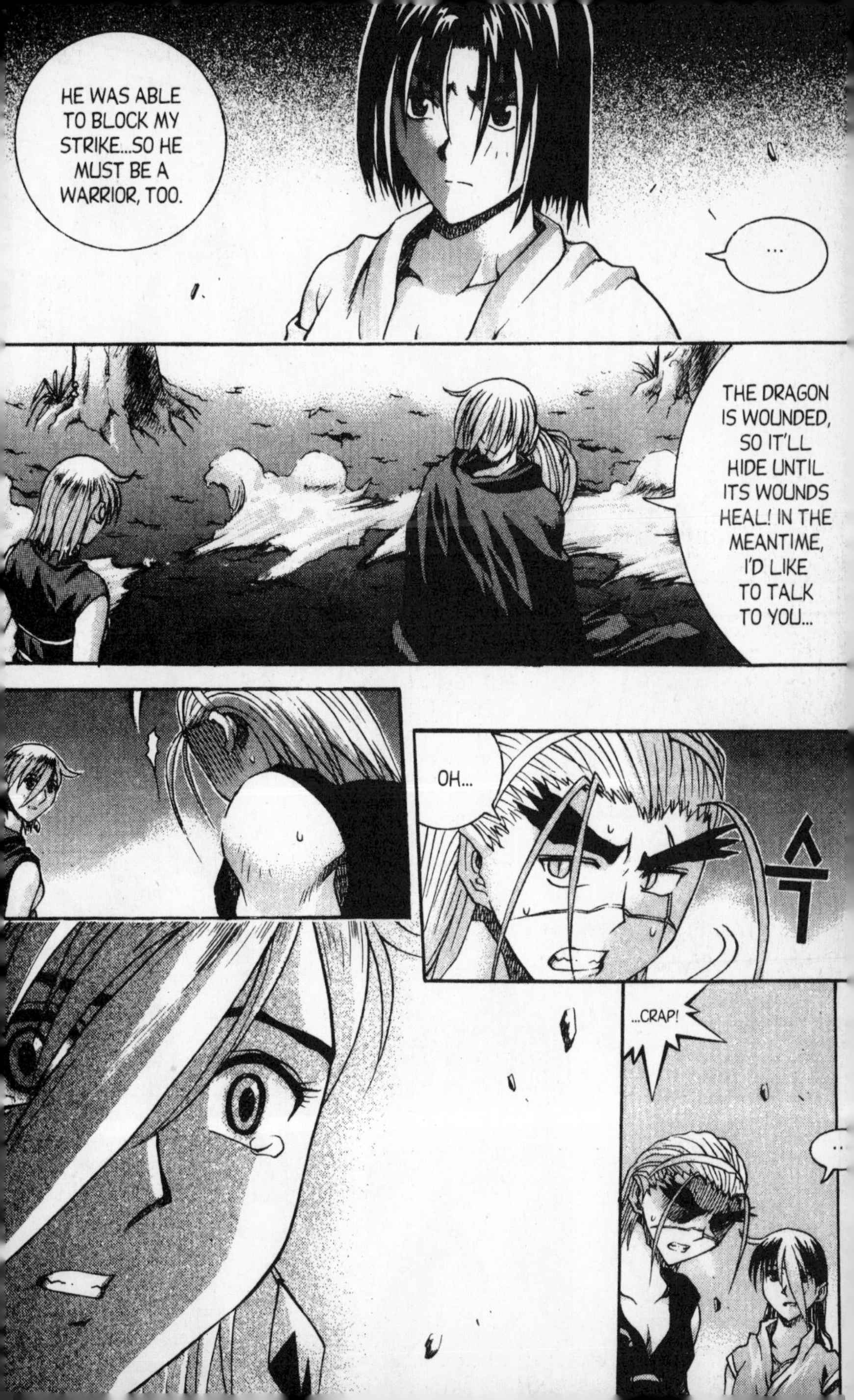
HE WAS ABLE TO BLOCK MY STRIKE...SO HE MUST BE A WARRIOR, TOO.
...
THE DRAGON IS WOUNDED, SO IT'LL HIDE UNTIL ITS WOUNDS HEAL! IN THE MEANTIME, I'D LIKE TO TALK TO YOU...
OH...
...CRAP!
...

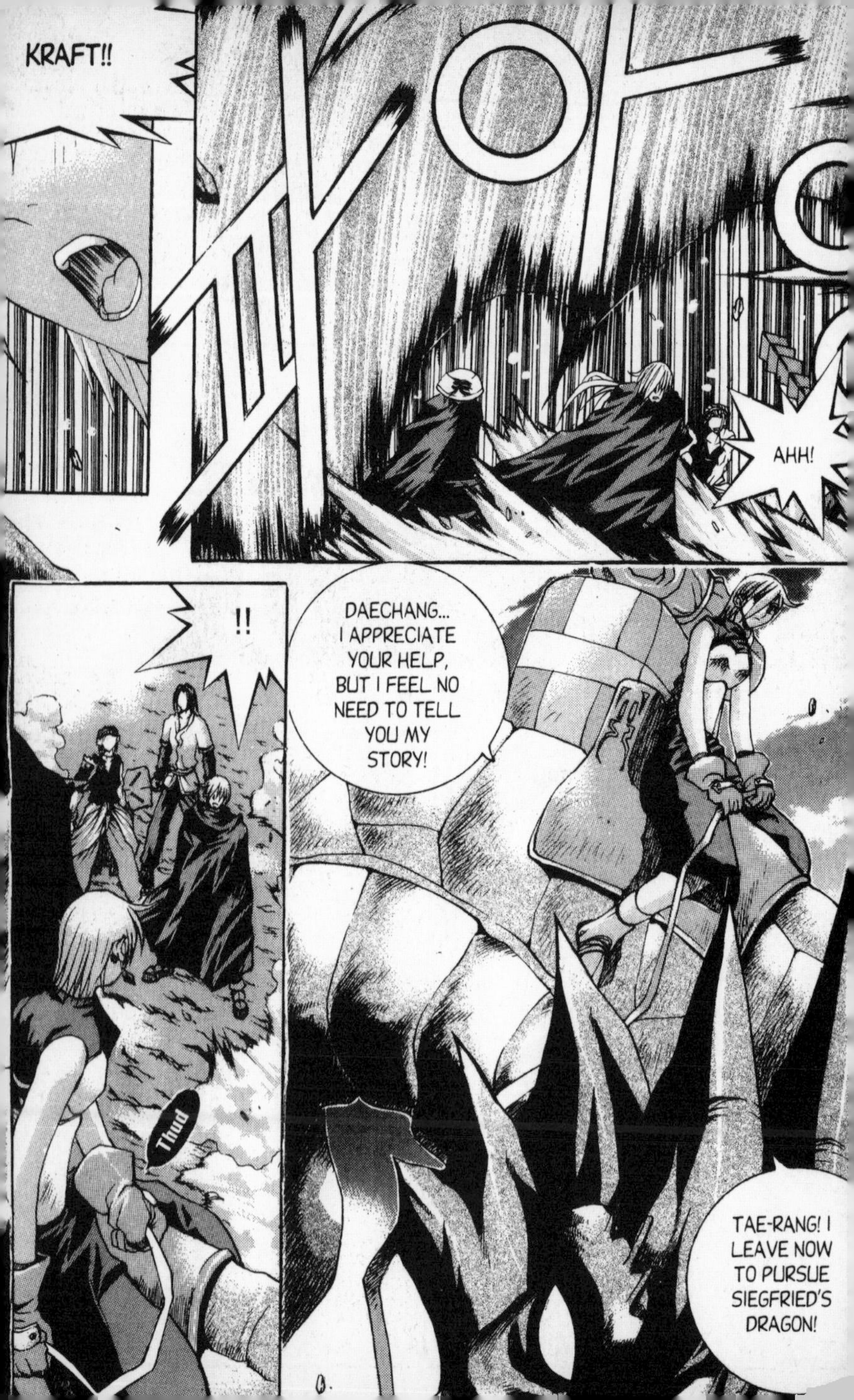
KRAFT!!
AHH!
!!
Thud
DAECHANG... I APPRECIATE YOUR HELP, BUT I FEEL NO NEED TO TELL YOU MY STORY!
TAE-RANG! I LEAVE NOW TO PURSUE SIEGFRIED'S DRAGON!

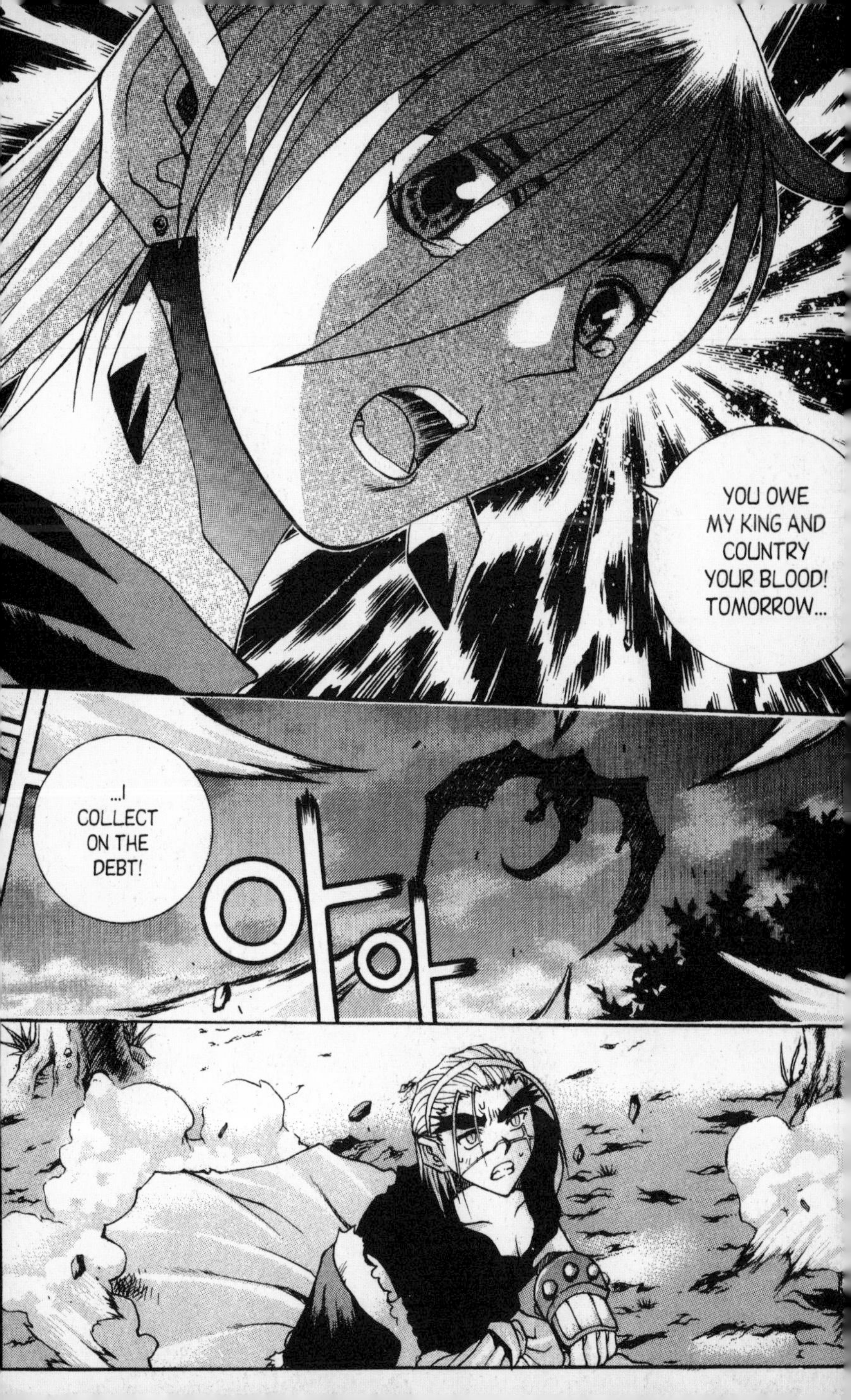
YOU OWE MY KING AND COUNTRY YOUR BLOOD! TOMORROW...
...I COLLECT ON THE DEBT!

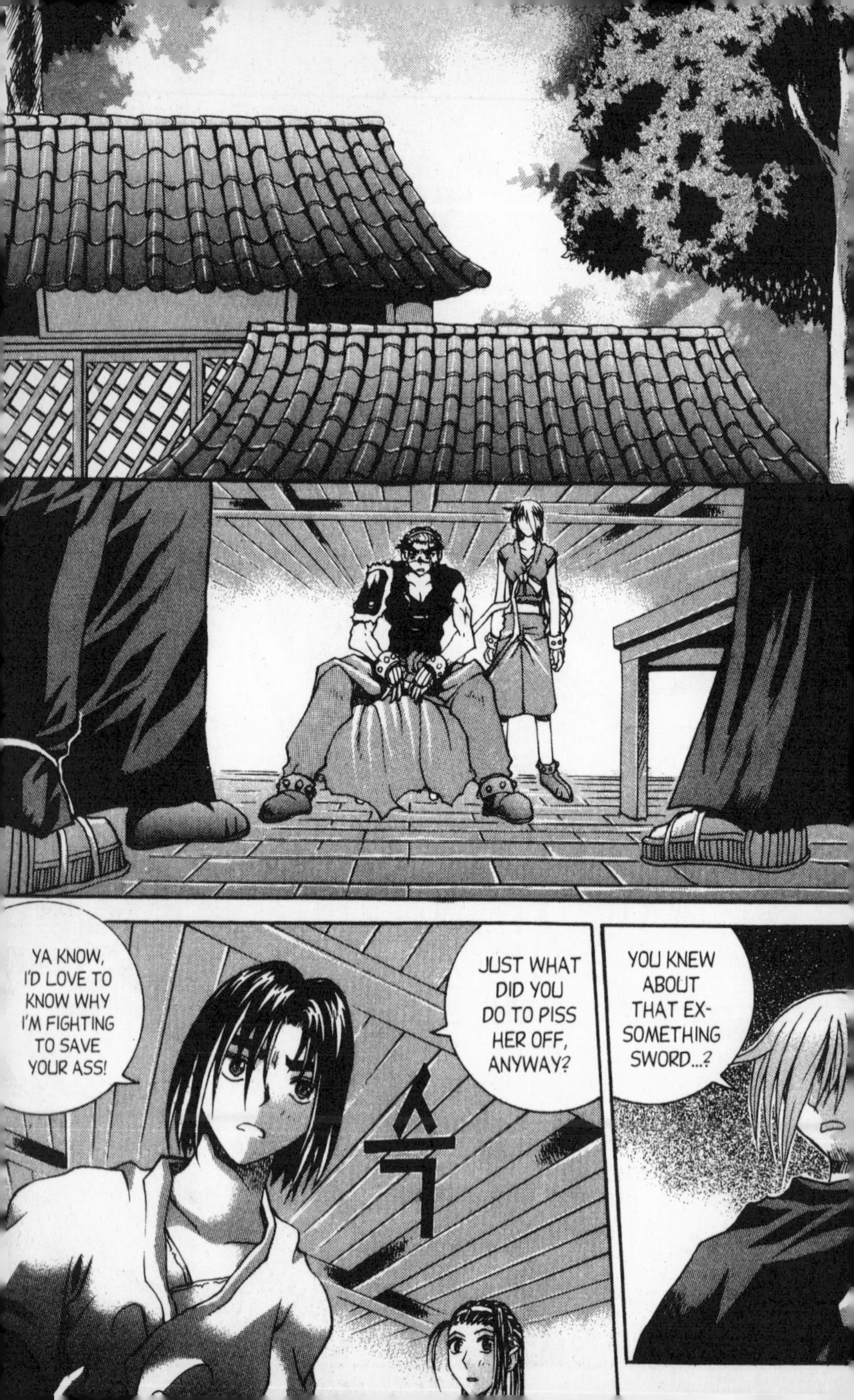
YA KNOW, I'D LOVE TO KNOW WHY I'M FIGHTING TO SAVE YOUR ASS!
JUST WHAT DID YOU DO TO PISS HER OFF, ANYWAY?
YOU KNEW ABOUT THAT EX-SOMETHING SWORD...?

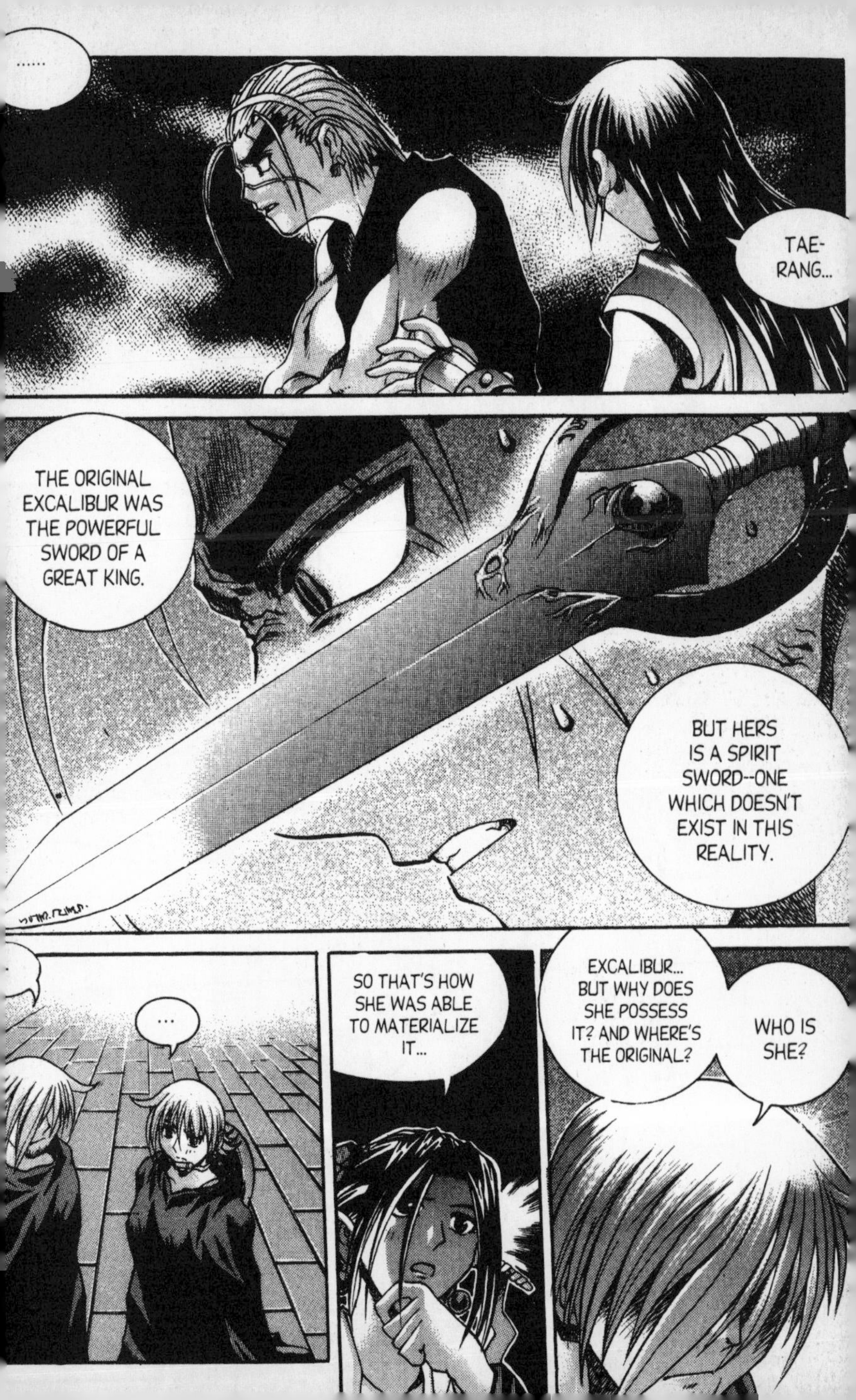
......
TAE-RANG...
THE ORIGINAL EXCALIBUR WAS THE POWERFUL SWORD OF A GREAT KING.
BUT HERS IS A SPIRIT SWORD--ONE WHICH DOESN'T EXIST IN THIS REALITY.
...
SO THAT'S HOW SHE WAS ABLE TO MATERIALIZE IT...
EXCALIBUR... BUT WHY DOES SHE POSSESS IT? AND WHERE'S THE ORIGINAL?
WHO IS SHE?

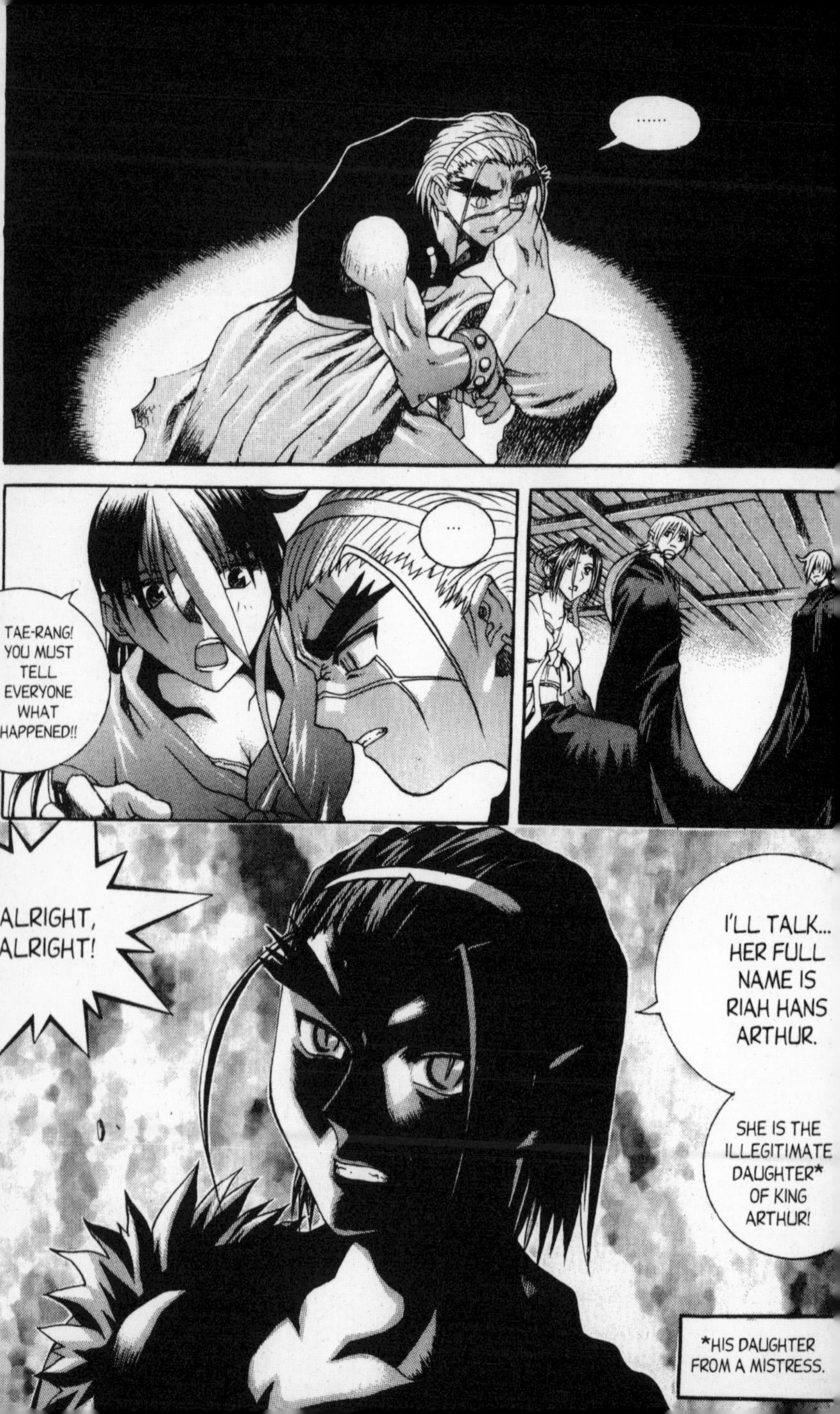
......
TAE-RANG! YOU MUST TELL EVERYONE WHAT HAPPENED!!
...
ALRIGHT, ALRIGHT!
I'LL TALK... HER FULL NAME IS RIAH HANS ARTHUR.
SHE IS THE ILLEGITIMATE DAUGHTER* OF KING ARTHUR!
*HIS DAUGHTER FROM A MISTRESS.

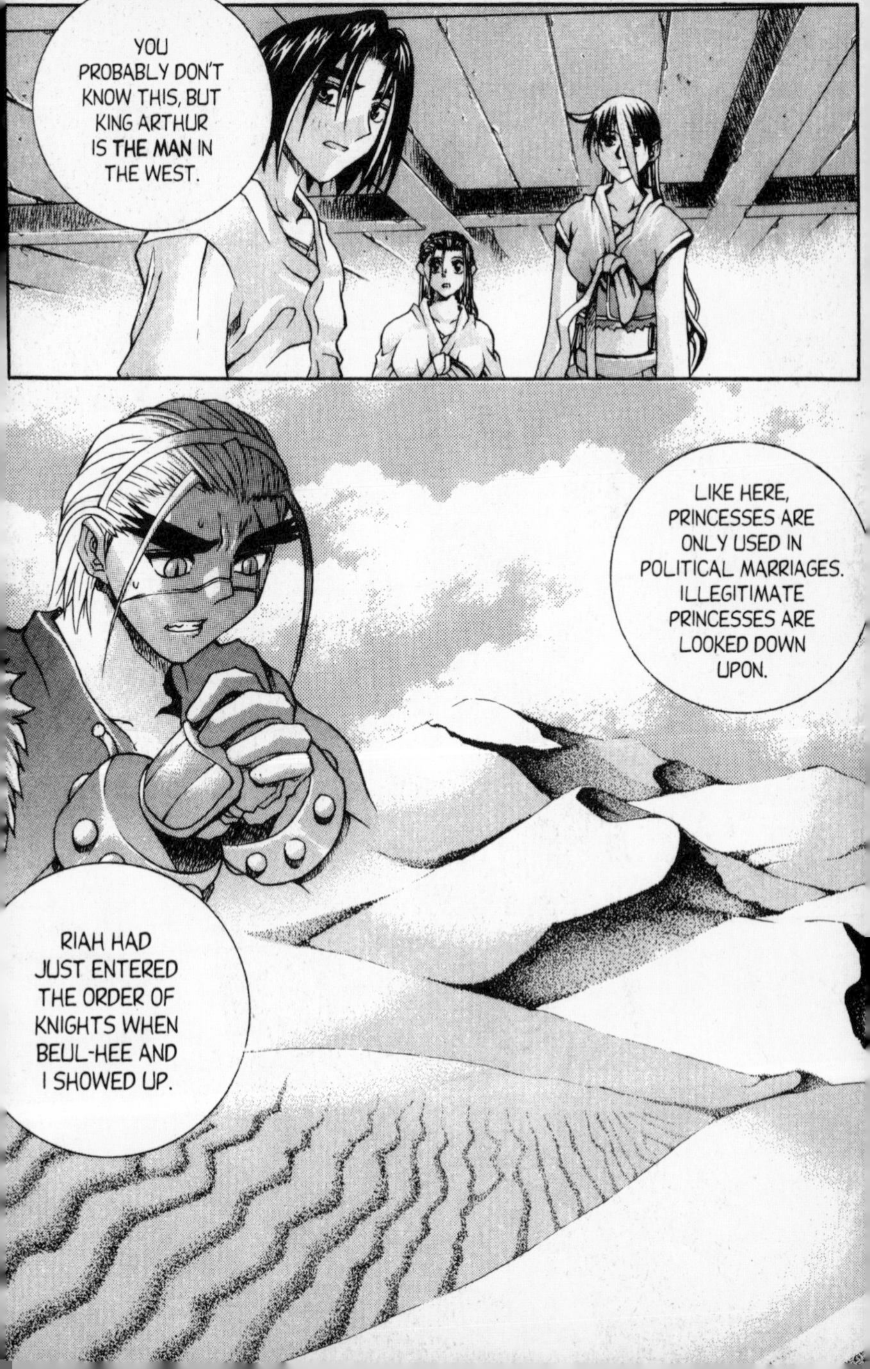
YOU PROBABLY DON'T KNOW THIS, BUT KING ARTHUR IS THE MAN IN THE WEST.
LIKE HERE, PRINCESSES ARE ONLY USED IN POLITICAL MARRIAGES. ILLEGITIMATE PRINCESSES ARE LOOKED DOWN UPON.
RIAH HAD JUST ENTERED THE ORDER OF KNIGHTS WHEN BEUL-HEE AND I SHOWED UP.

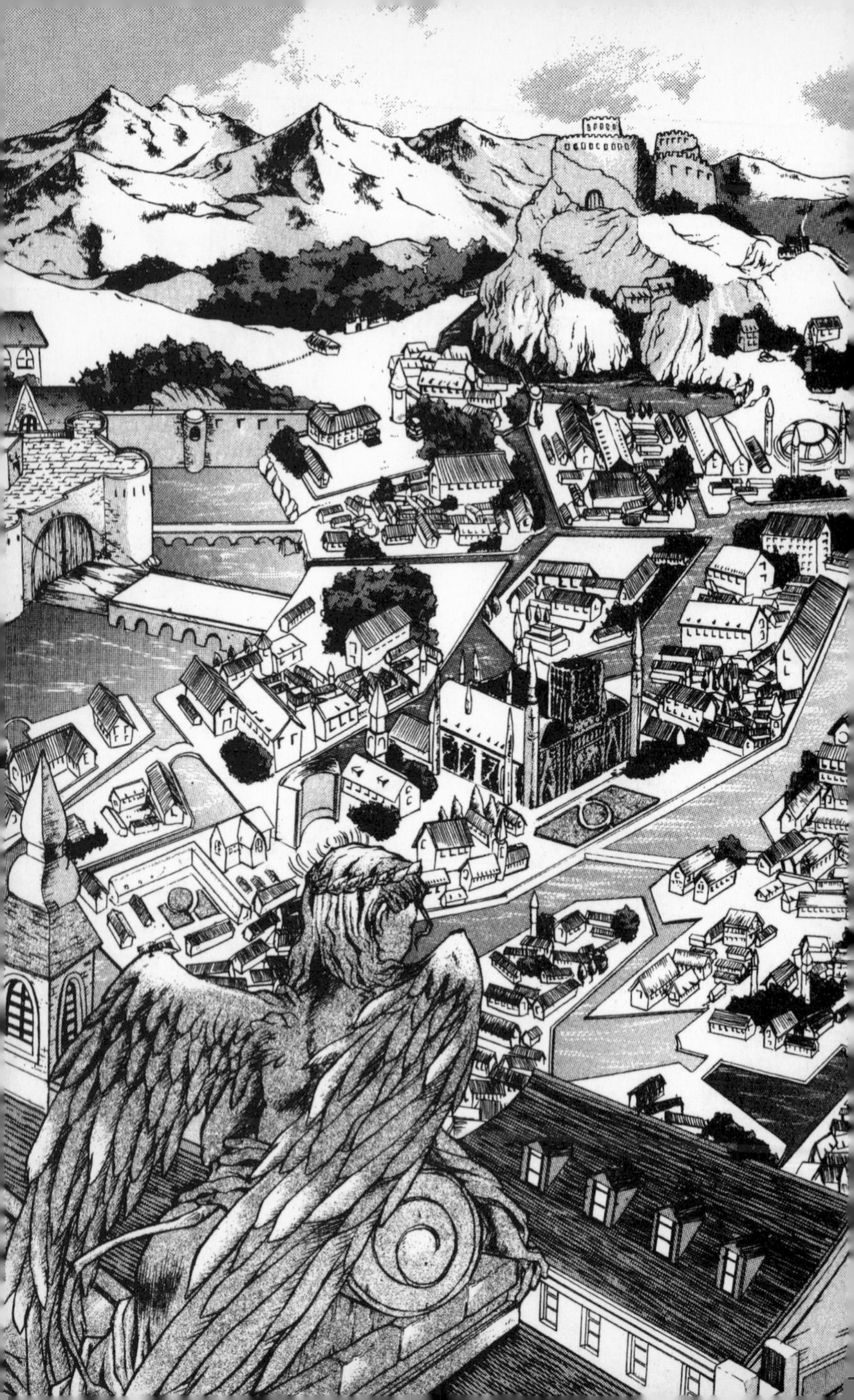

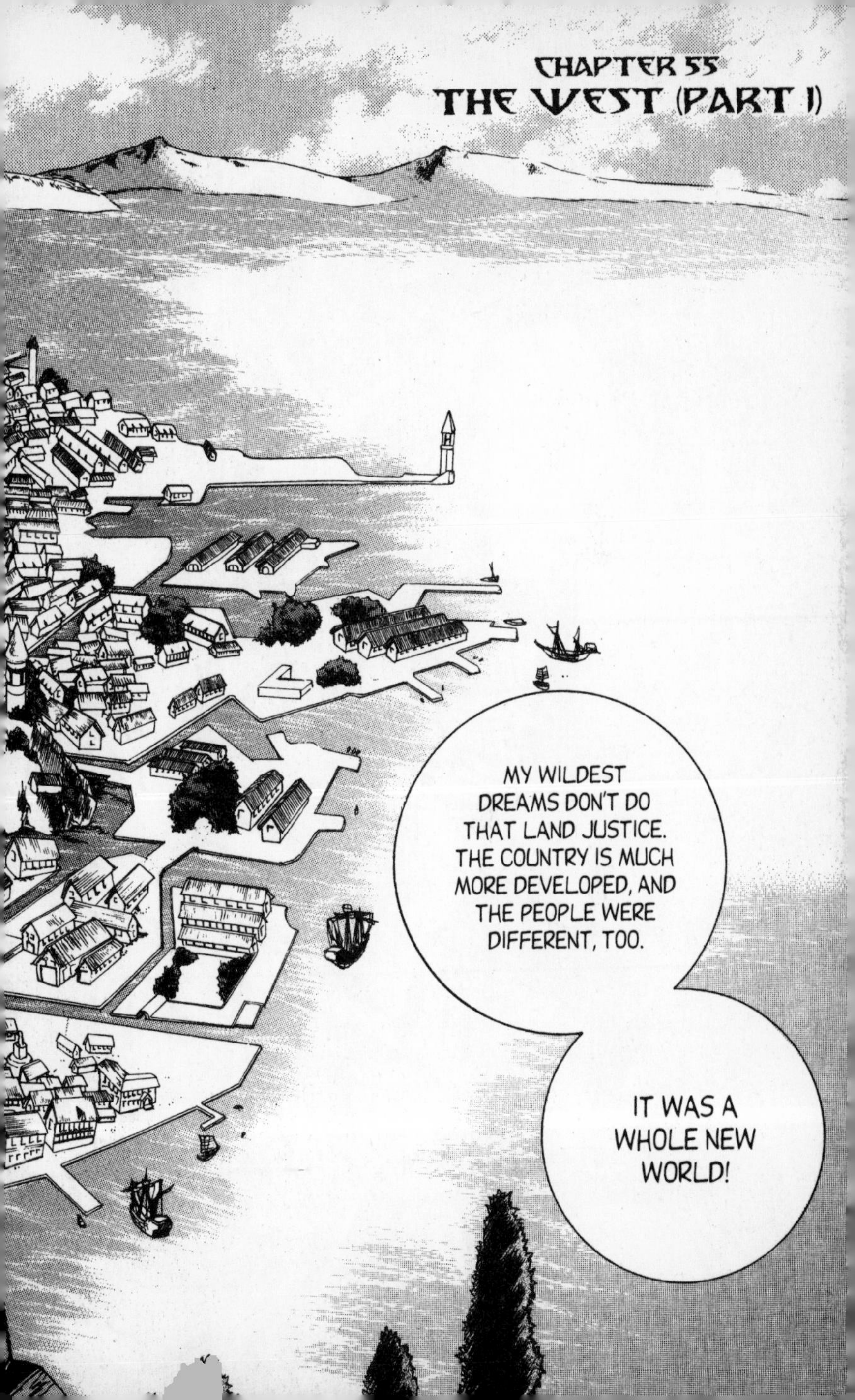
CHAPTER 55
THE WEST (PART 1)
MY WILDEST DREAMS DON'T DO THAT LAND JUSTICE. THE COUNTRY IS MUCH MORE DEVELOPED, AND THE PEOPLE WERE DIFFERENT, TOO.
IT WAS A WHOLE NEW WORLD!

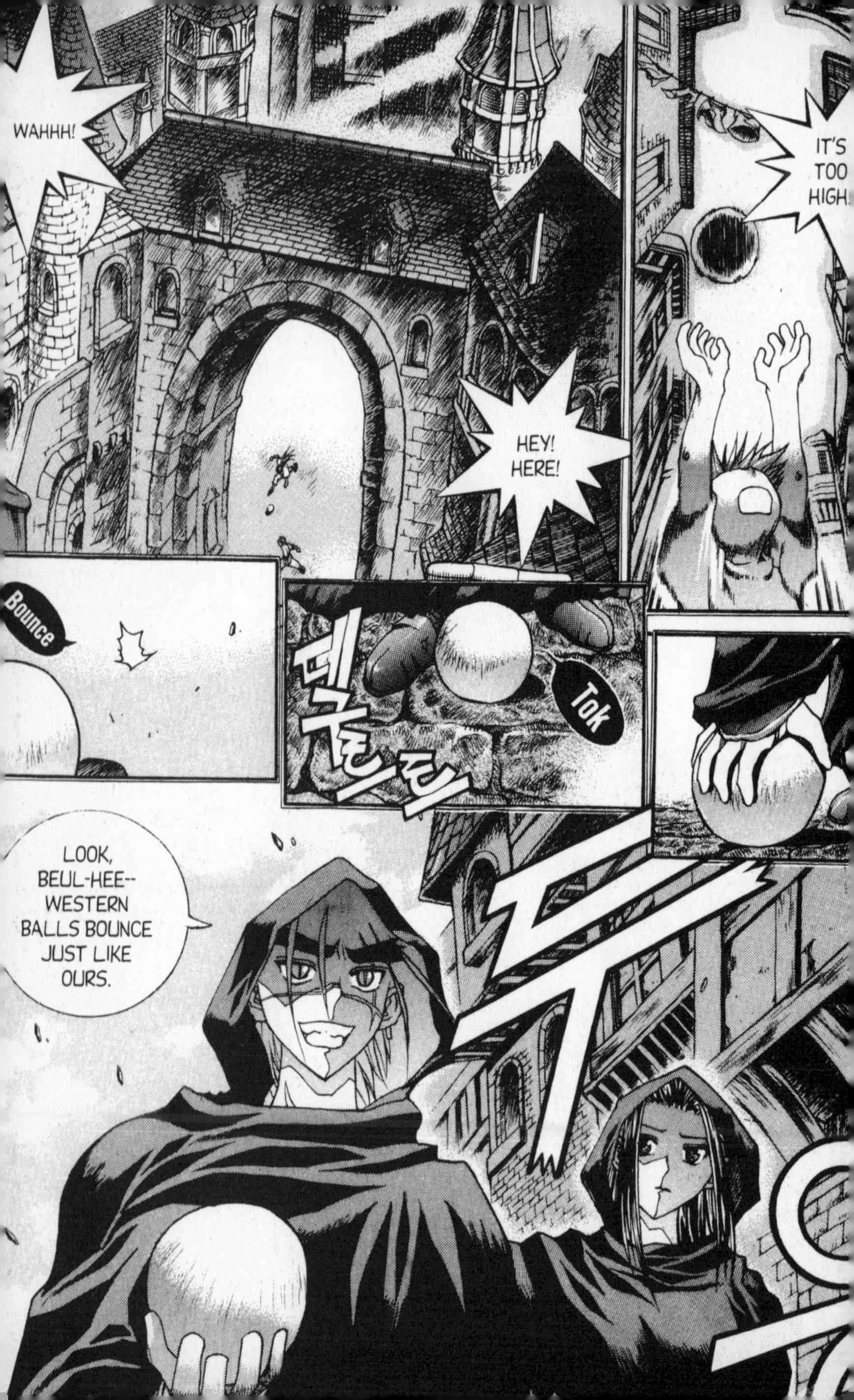
WAHHH!
IT'S TOO HIGH!
HEY! HERE!
Bounce
Tok
LOOK, BEUL-HEE-- WESTERN BALLS BOUNCE JUST LIKE OURS.

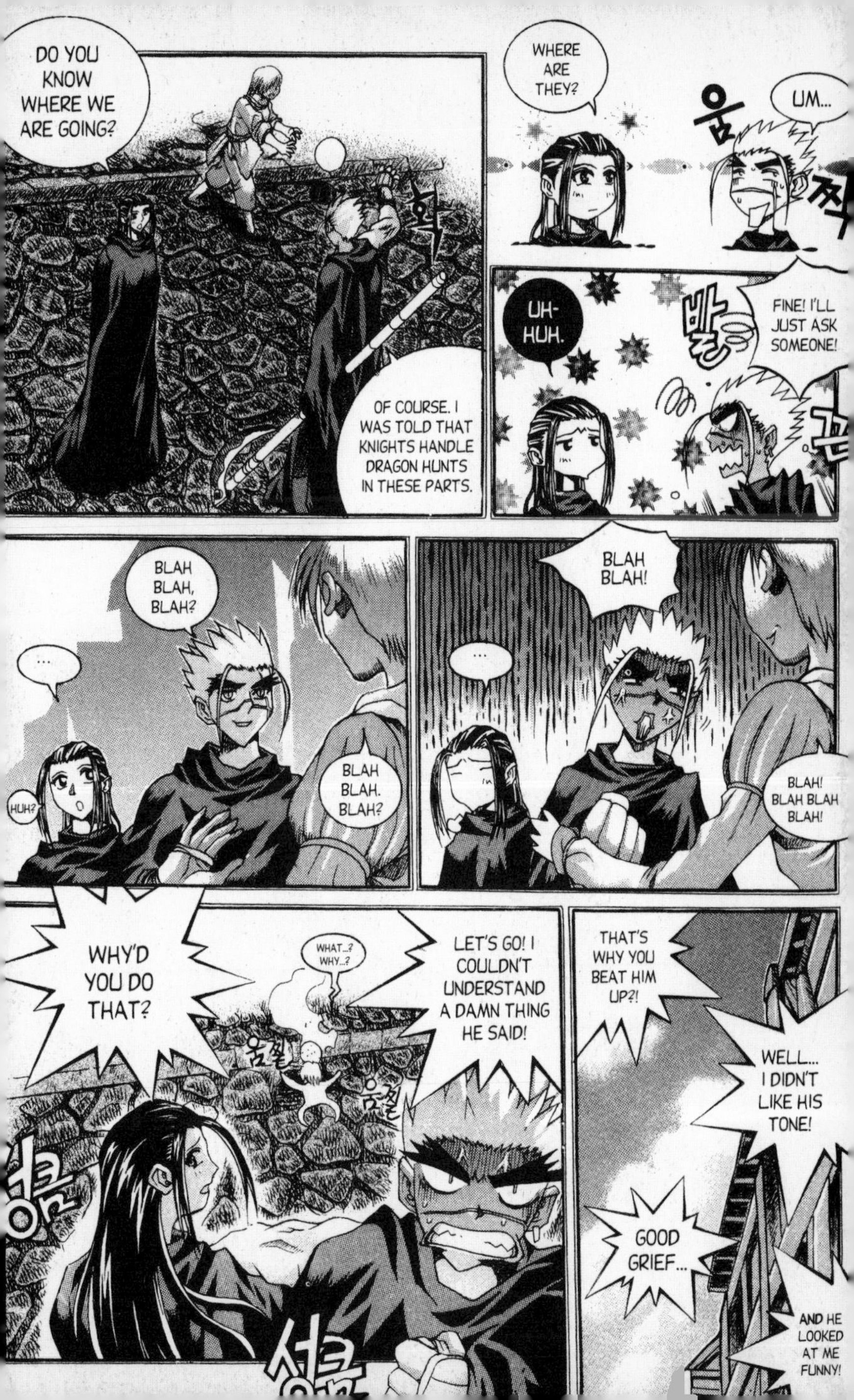

DO YOU KNOW WHERE WE ARE GOING?
OF COURSE. I WAS TOLD THAT KNIGHTS HANDLE DRAGON HUNTS IN THESE PARTS.
WHERE ARE THEY?
UM...
UH-HUH.
FINE! I'LL JUST ASK SOMEONE!
BLAH BLAH, BLAH?
...
HUH?
BLAH BLAH. BLAH?
BLAH BLAH!
...
BLAH! BLAH BLAH BLAH!
WHY'D YOU DO THAT?
WHAT...? WHY...?
LET'S GO! I COULDN'T UNDERSTAND A DAMN THING HE SAID!
THAT'S WHY YOU BEAT HIM UP?!
WELL... I DIDN'T LIKE HIS TONE!
GOOD GRIEF...
AND HE LOOKED AT ME FUNNY!

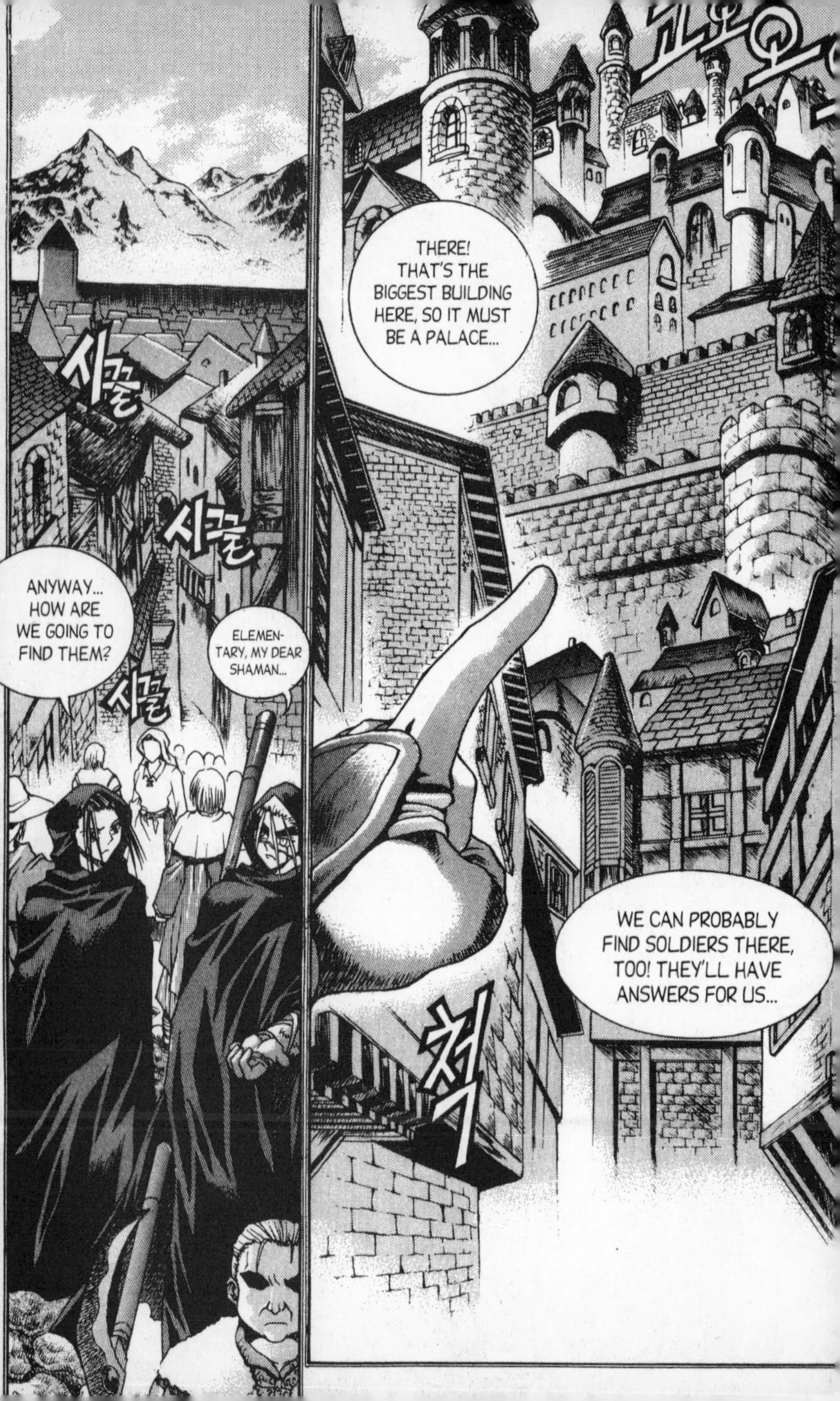
ANYWAY... HOW ARE WE GOING TO FIND THEM?
ELEMENTARY, MY DEAR SHAMAN...
THERE! THAT'S THE BIGGEST BUILDING HERE, SO IT MUST BE A PALACE...
WE CAN PROBABLY FIND SOLDIERS THERE, TOO! THEY'LL HAVE ANSWERS FOR US...

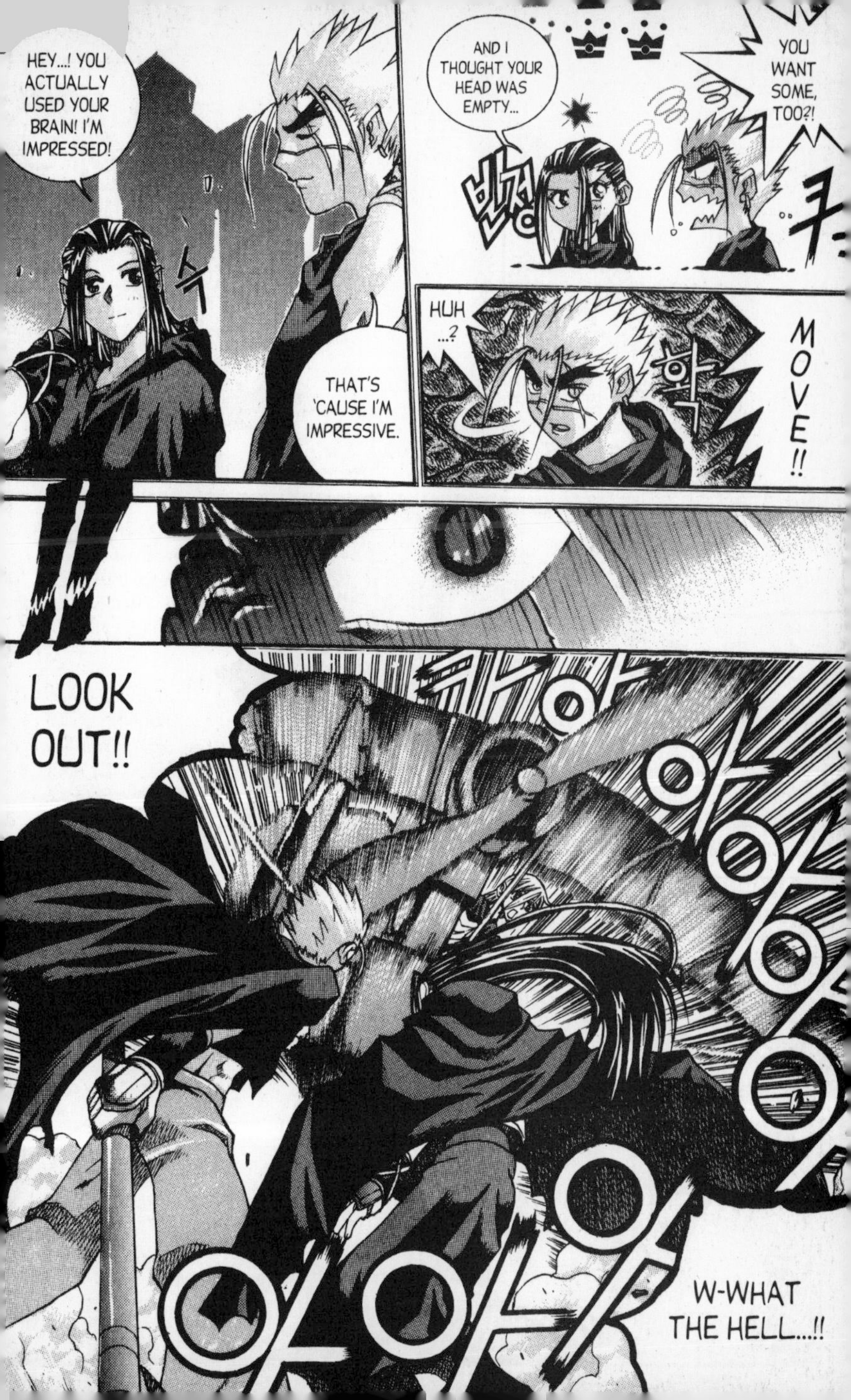
HEY...! YOU ACTUALLY USED YOUR BRAIN! I'M IMPRESSED!
THAT'S 'CAUSE I'M IMPRESSIVE.
AND I THOUGHT YOUR HEAD WAS EMPTY...
YOU WANT SOME, TOO?!
HUH ...?
MOVE!!
LOOK OUT!!
W-WHAT THE HELL...!!

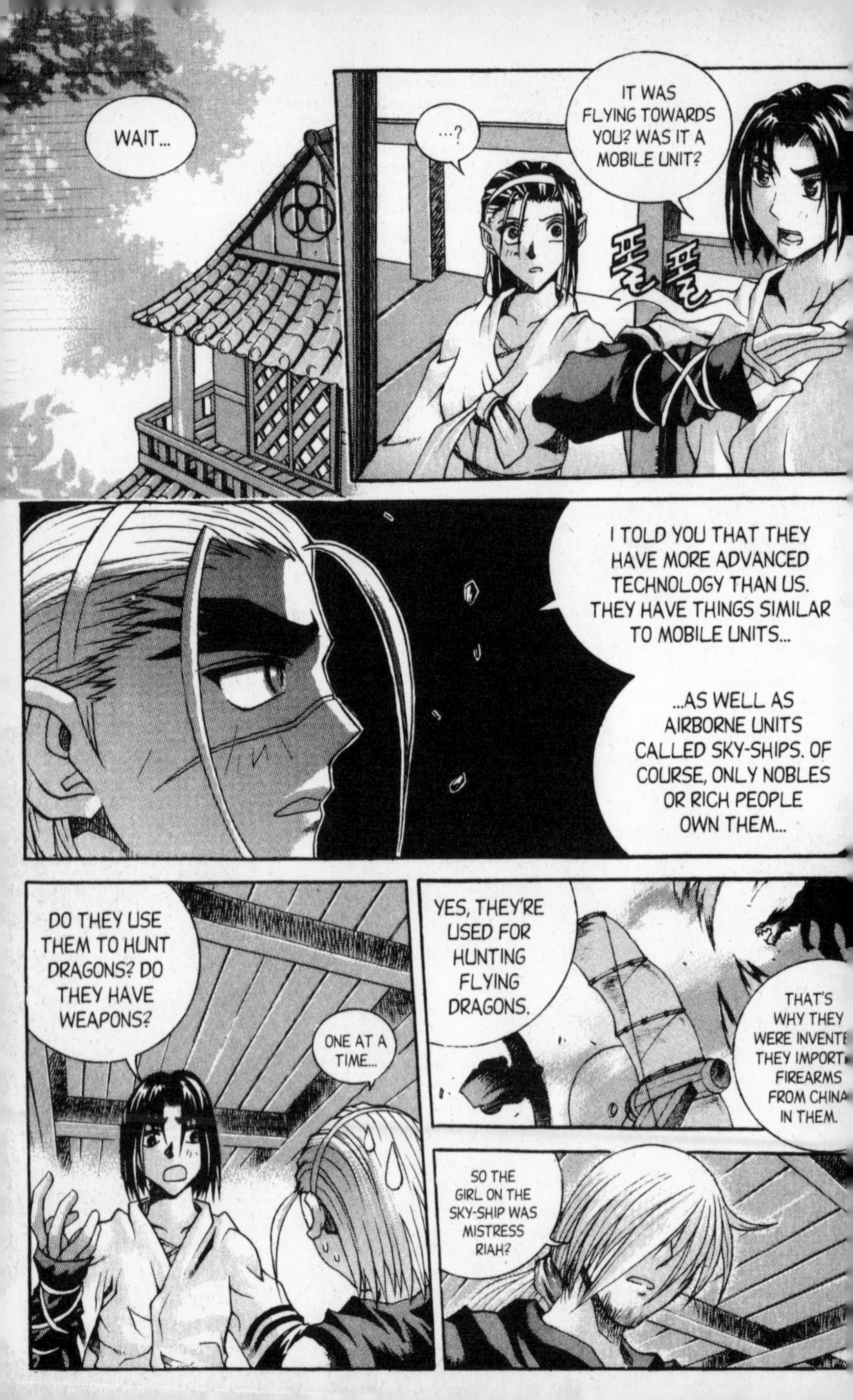
WAIT...
...?
IT WAS FLYING TOWARDS YOU? WAS IT A MOBILE UNIT?
I TOLD YOU THAT THEY HAVE MORE ADVANCED TECHNOLOGY THAN US. THEY HAVE THINGS SIMILAR TO MOBILE UNITS...
...AS WELL AS AIRBORNE UNITS CALLED SKY-SHIPS. OF COURSE, ONLY NOBLES OR RICH PEOPLE OWN THEM...
DO THEY USE THEM TO HUNT DRAGONS? DO THEY HAVE WEAPONS?
ONE AT A TIME...
YES, THEY'RE USED FOR HUNTING FLYING DRAGONS.
THAT'S WHY THEY WERE INVENTE THEY IMPORT FIREARMS FROM CHINA IN THEM.
SO THE GIRL ON THE SKY-SHIP WAS MISTRESS RIAH?

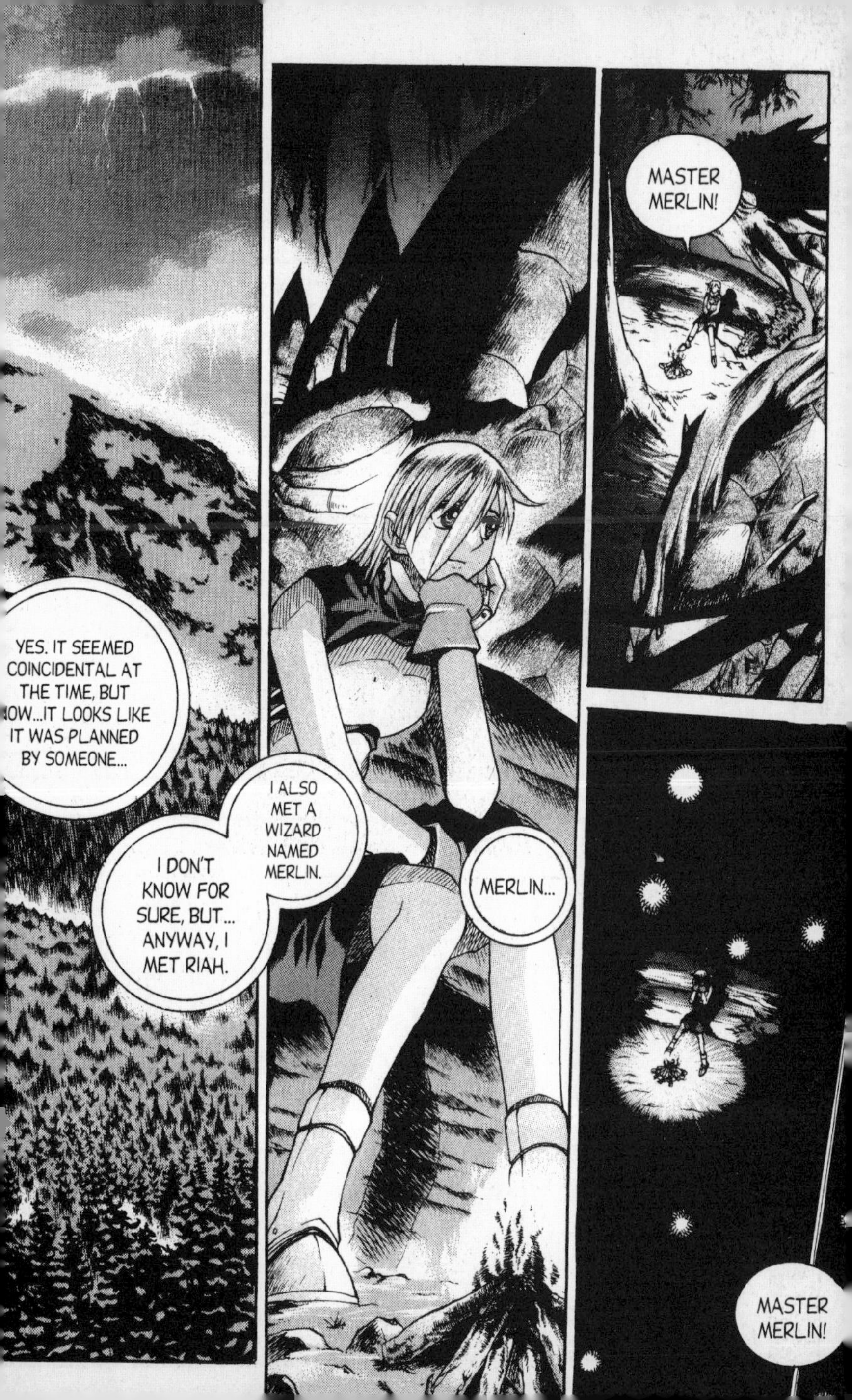
YES. IT SEEMED COINCIDENTAL AT THE TIME, BUT OW...IT LOOKS LIKE IT WAS PLANNED BY SOMEONE...
I DON'T KNOW FOR SURE, BUT... ANYWAY, I MET RIAH.
I ALSO MET A WIZARD NAMED MERLIN.
MERLIN...
MASTER MERLIN!
MASTER MERLIN!

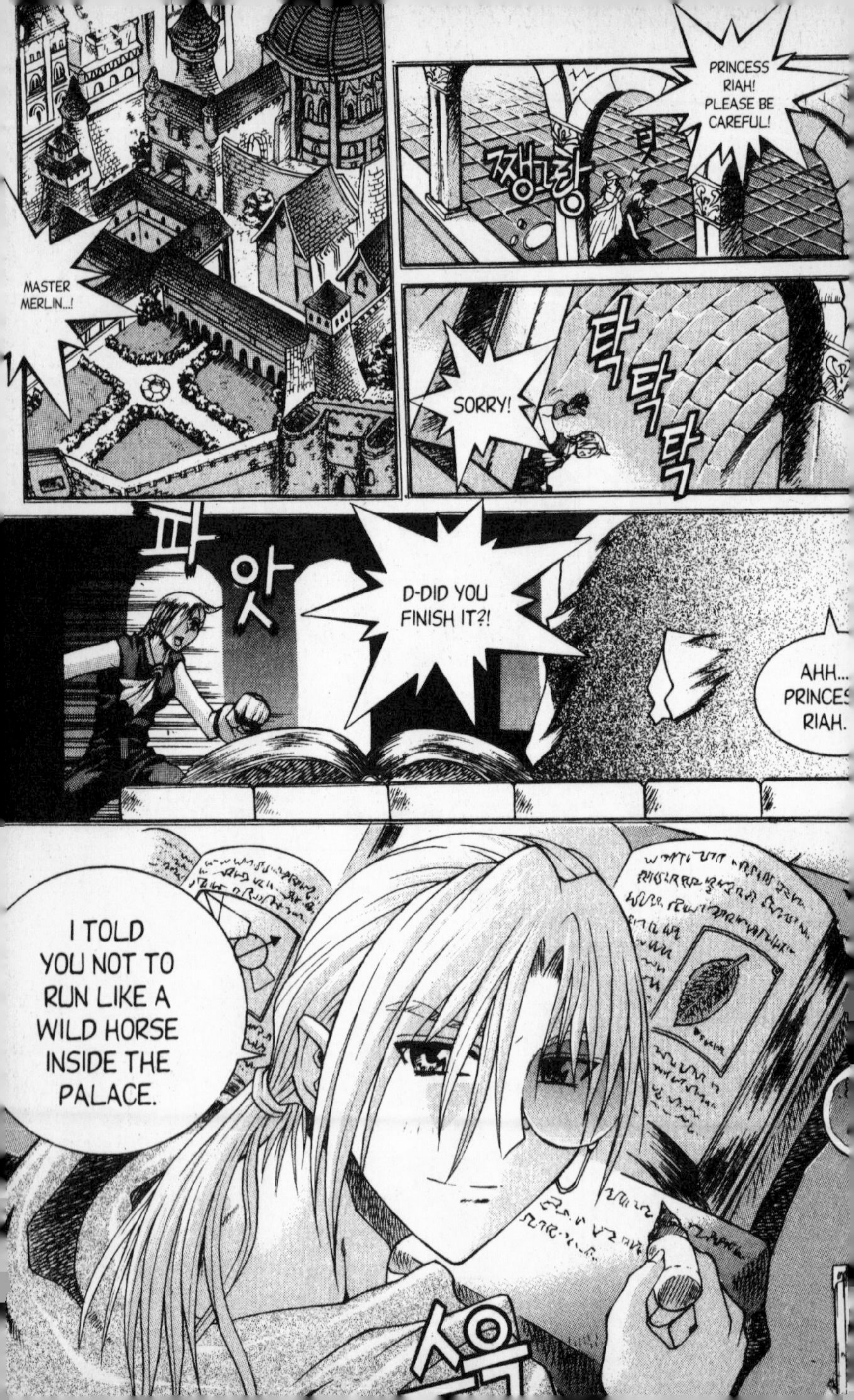
MASTER MERLIN...!
쨍그랑
PRINCESS RIAH! PLEASE BE CAREFUL!
SORRY!
탁탁탁
파앗
D-DID YOU FINISH IT?!
AHH... PRINCES RIAH.
I TOLD YOU NOT TO RUN LIKE A WILD HORSE INSIDE THE PALACE.

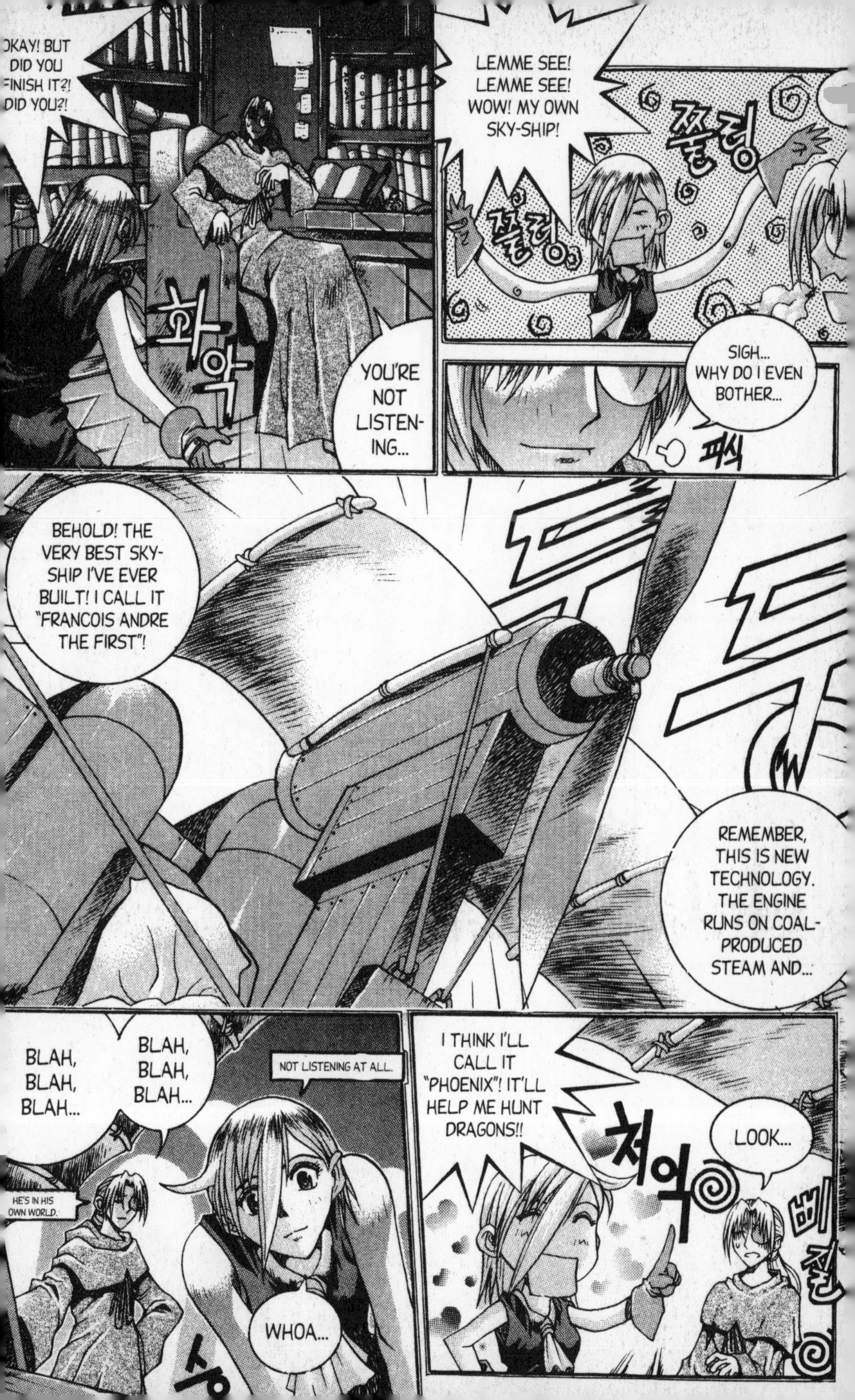

OKAY! BUT DID YOU FINISH IT?! DID YOU?!
화악
YOU'RE NOT LISTENING...
LEMME SEE! LEMME SEE! WOW! MY OWN SKY-SHIP!
쭐렁
쭐렁
SIGH... WHY DO I EVEN BOTHER...
피식
BEHOLD! THE VERY BEST SKY-SHIP I'VE EVER BUILT! I CALL IT "FRANCOIS ANDRE THE FIRST"!
REMEMBER, THIS IS NEW TECHNOLOGY. THE ENGINE RUNS ON COAL-PRODUCED STEAM AND...
BLAH, BLAH, BLAH...
BLAH, BLAH, BLAH...
NOT LISTENING AT ALL.
HE'S IN HIS OWN WORLD.
WHOA...
I THINK I'LL CALL IT "PHOENIX"! IT'LL HELP ME HUNT DRAGONS!!
처억
LOOK...

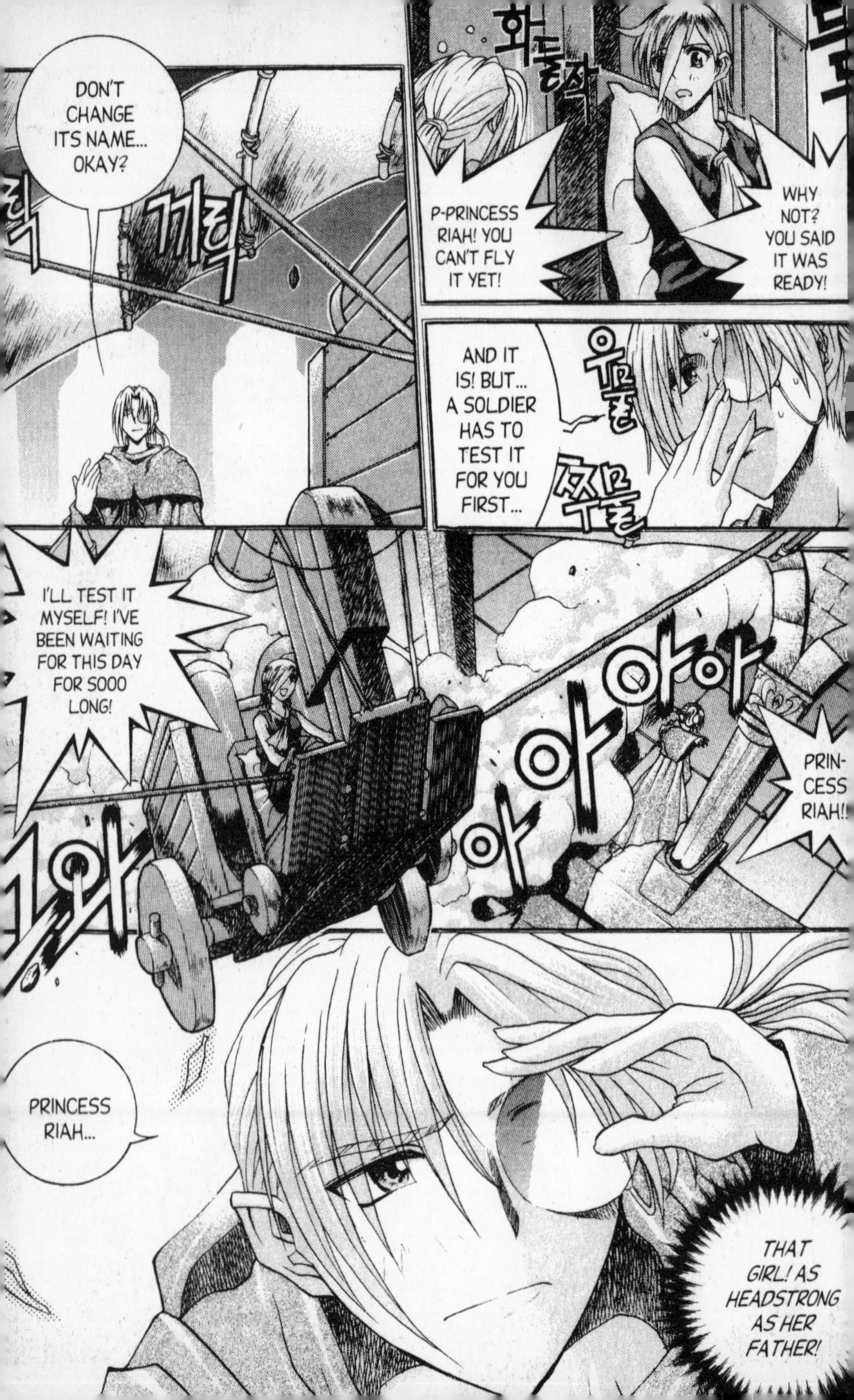

DON'T CHANGE ITS NAME... OKAY?
끼릭
화들짝
P-PRINCESS RIAH! YOU CAN'T FLY IT YET!
WHY NOT? YOU SAID IT WAS READY!
AND IT IS! BUT... A SOLDIER HAS TO TEST IT FOR YOU FIRST...
I'LL TEST IT MYSELF! I'VE BEEN WAITING FOR THIS DAY FOR SOOO LONG!
PRIN-CESS RIAH!!
PRINCESS RIAH...
THAT GIRL! AS HEADSTRONG AS HER FATHER!

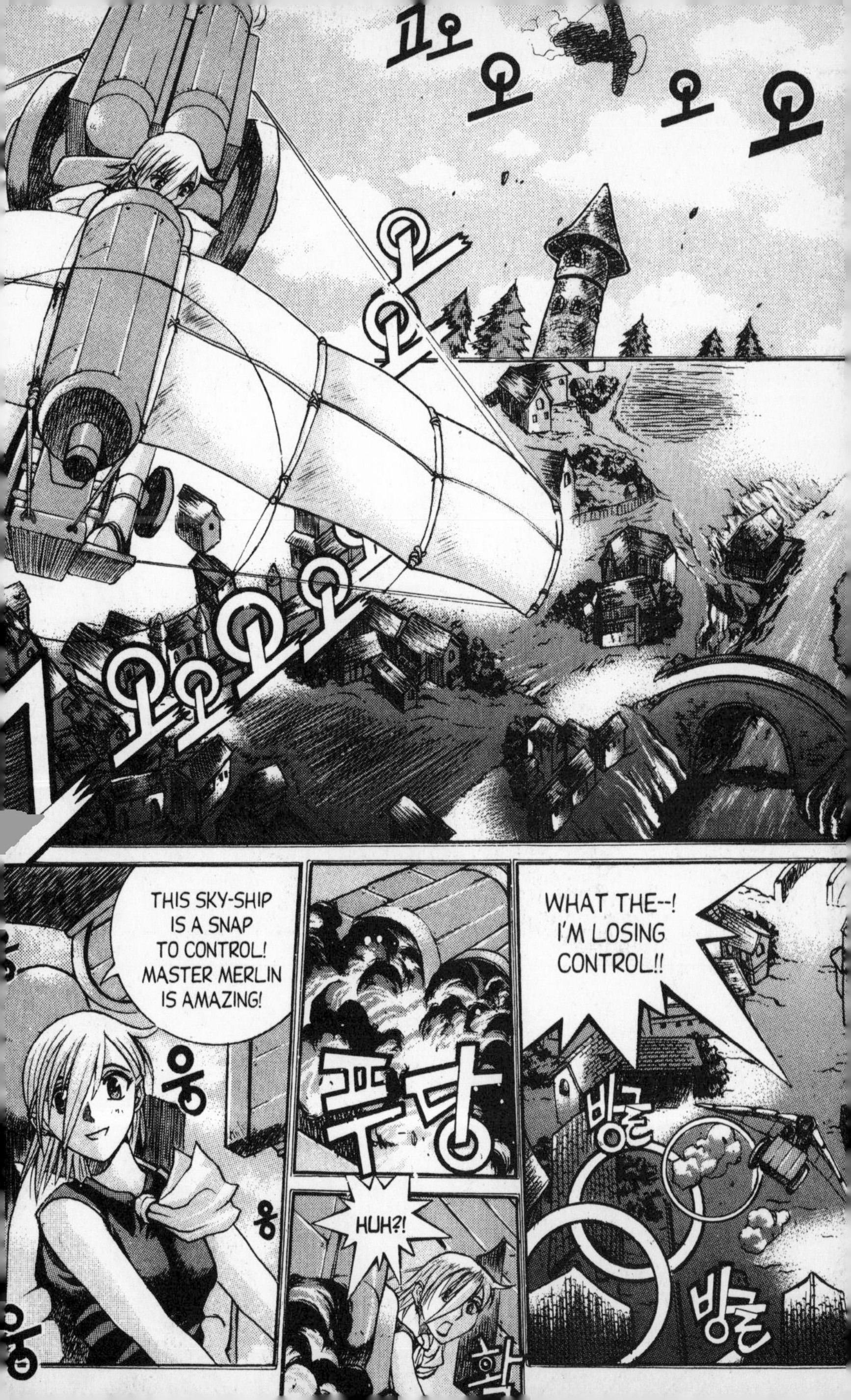

THIS SKY-SHIP IS A SNAP TO CONTROL! MASTER MERLIN IS AMAZING!
웅
웅
웅
HUH?!
WHAT THE--! I'M LOSING CONTROL!!

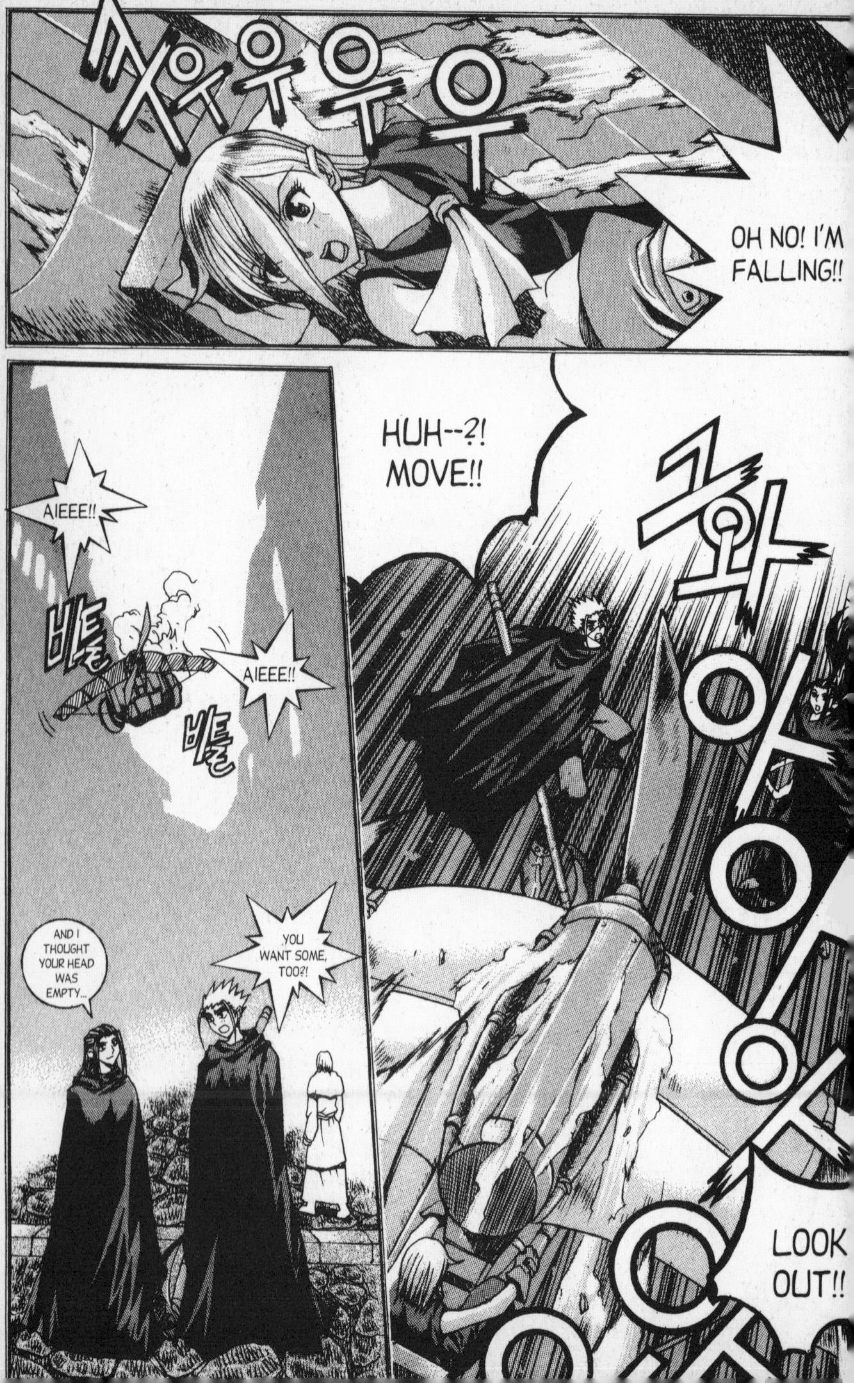
OH NO! I'M FALLING!!
AIEEE!!
비틀
AIEEE!!
비틀
AND I THOUGHT YOUR HEAD WAS EMPTY...
YOU WANT SOME, TOO?!
HUH--?! MOVE!!
LOOK OUT!!

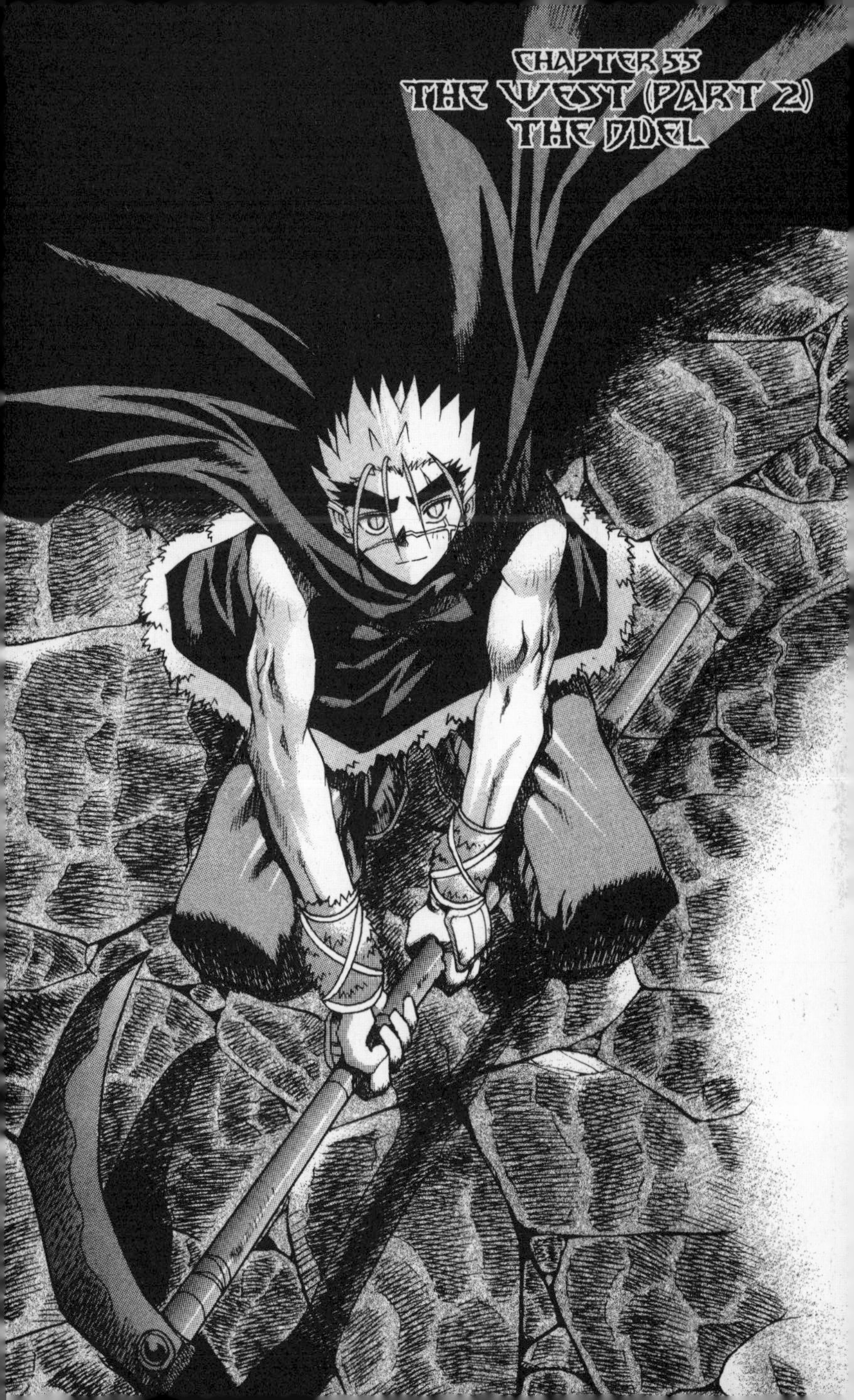
CHAPTER 55
THE WEST (PART 2)
THE DUEL

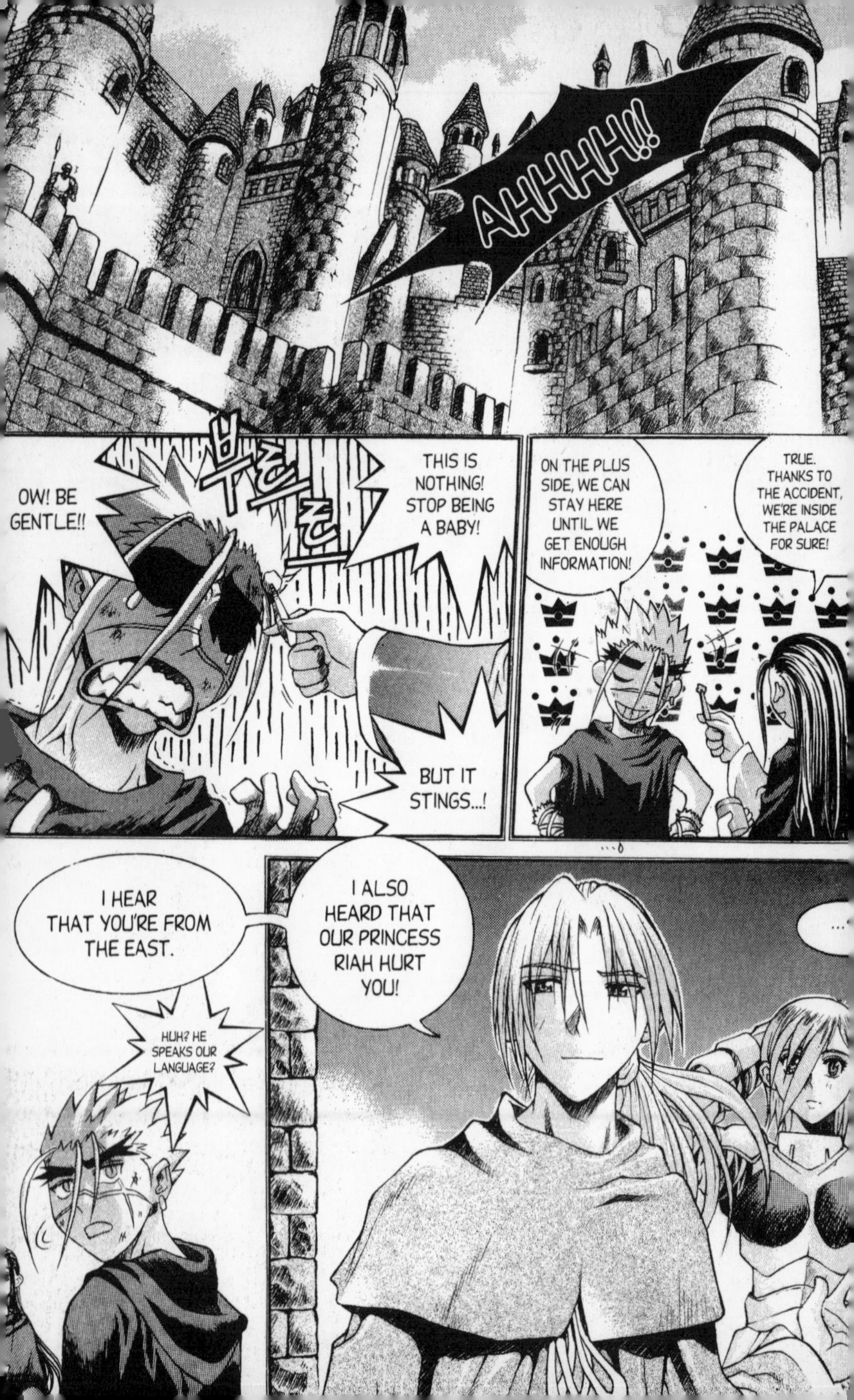
AHHHH!!
OW! BE GENTLE!!
THIS IS NOTHING! STOP BEING A BABY!
BUT IT STINGS...!
ON THE PLUS SIDE, WE CAN STAY HERE UNTIL WE GET ENOUGH INFORMATION!
TRUE. THANKS TO THE ACCIDENT, WE'RE INSIDE THE PALACE FOR SURE!
I HEAR THAT YOU'RE FROM THE EAST.
HUH? HE SPEAKS OUR LANGUAGE?
I ALSO HEARD THAT OUR PRINCESS RIAH HURT YOU!
...

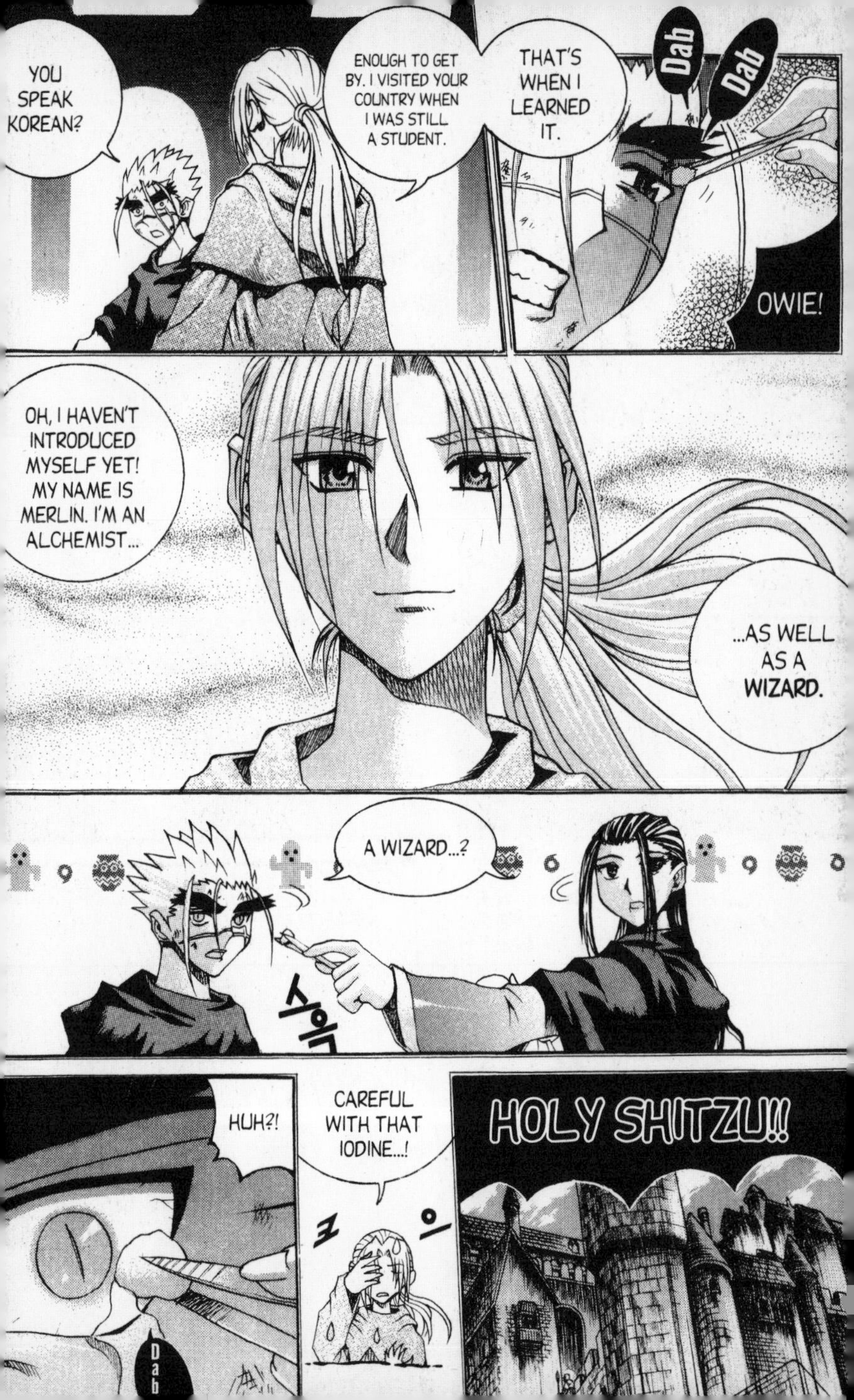
YOU SPEAK KOREAN?
ENOUGH TO GET BY. I VISITED YOUR COUNTRY WHEN I WAS STILL A STUDENT.
THAT'S WHEN I LEARNED IT.
Dab
Dab
OWIE!
OH, I HAVEN'T INTRODUCED MYSELF YET! MY NAME IS MERLIN. I'M AN ALCHEMIST...
...AS WELL AS A WIZARD.
A WIZARD...?
HUH?!
Dab
CAREFUL WITH THAT IODINE...!
HOLY SHITZU!!

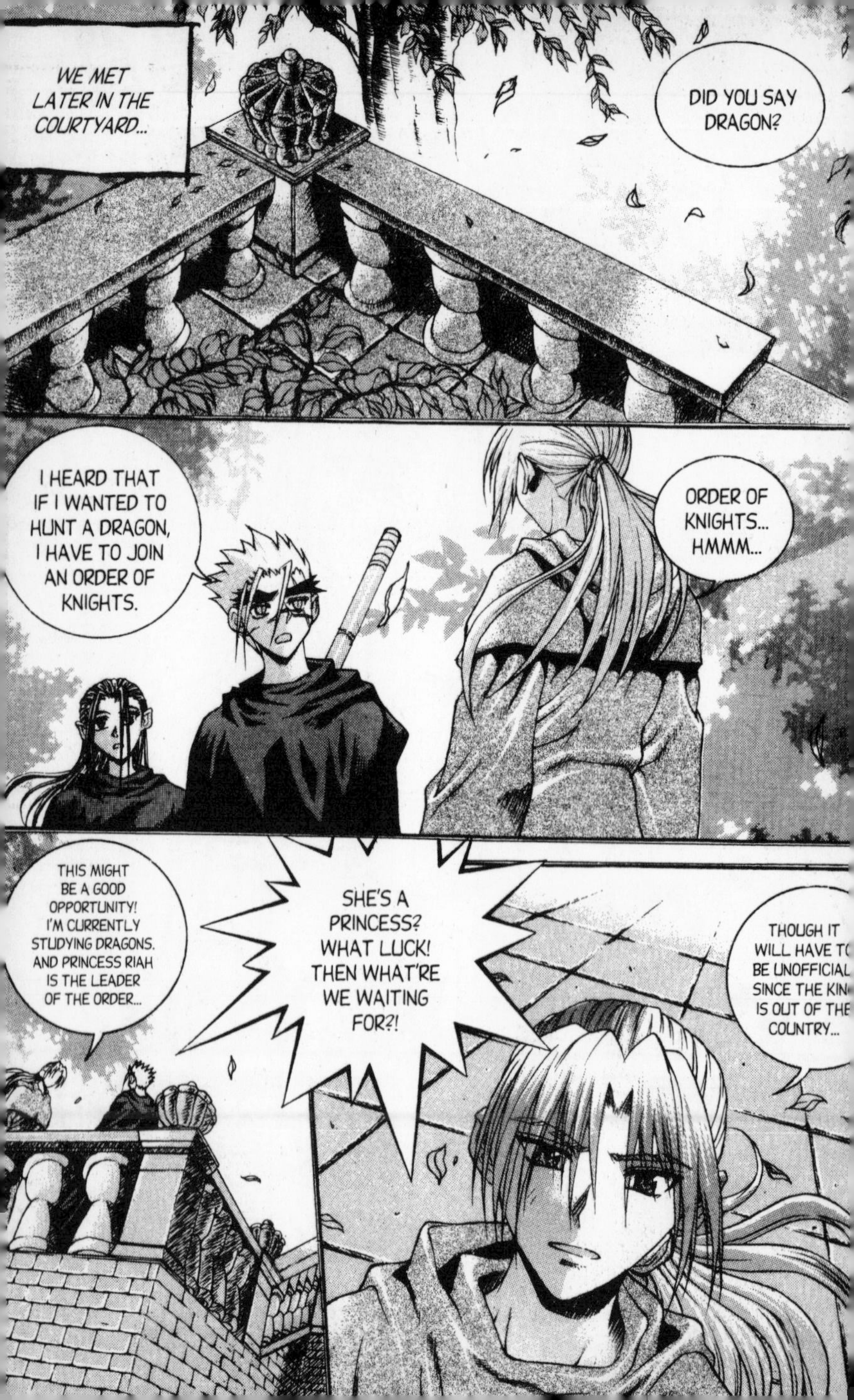
WE MET LATER IN THE COURTYARD...
DID YOU SAY DRAGON?
I HEARD THAT IF I WANTED TO HUNT A DRAGON, I HAVE TO JOIN AN ORDER OF KNIGHTS.
ORDER OF KNIGHTS... HMMM...
THIS MIGHT BE A GOOD OPPORTUNITY! I'M CURRENTLY STUDYING DRAGONS. AND PRINCESS RIAH IS THE LEADER OF THE ORDER...
SHE'S A PRINCESS? WHAT LUCK! THEN WHAT'RE WE WAITING FOR?!
THOUGH IT WILL HAVE TO BE UNOFFICIAL SINCE THE KING IS OUT OF THE COUNTRY...

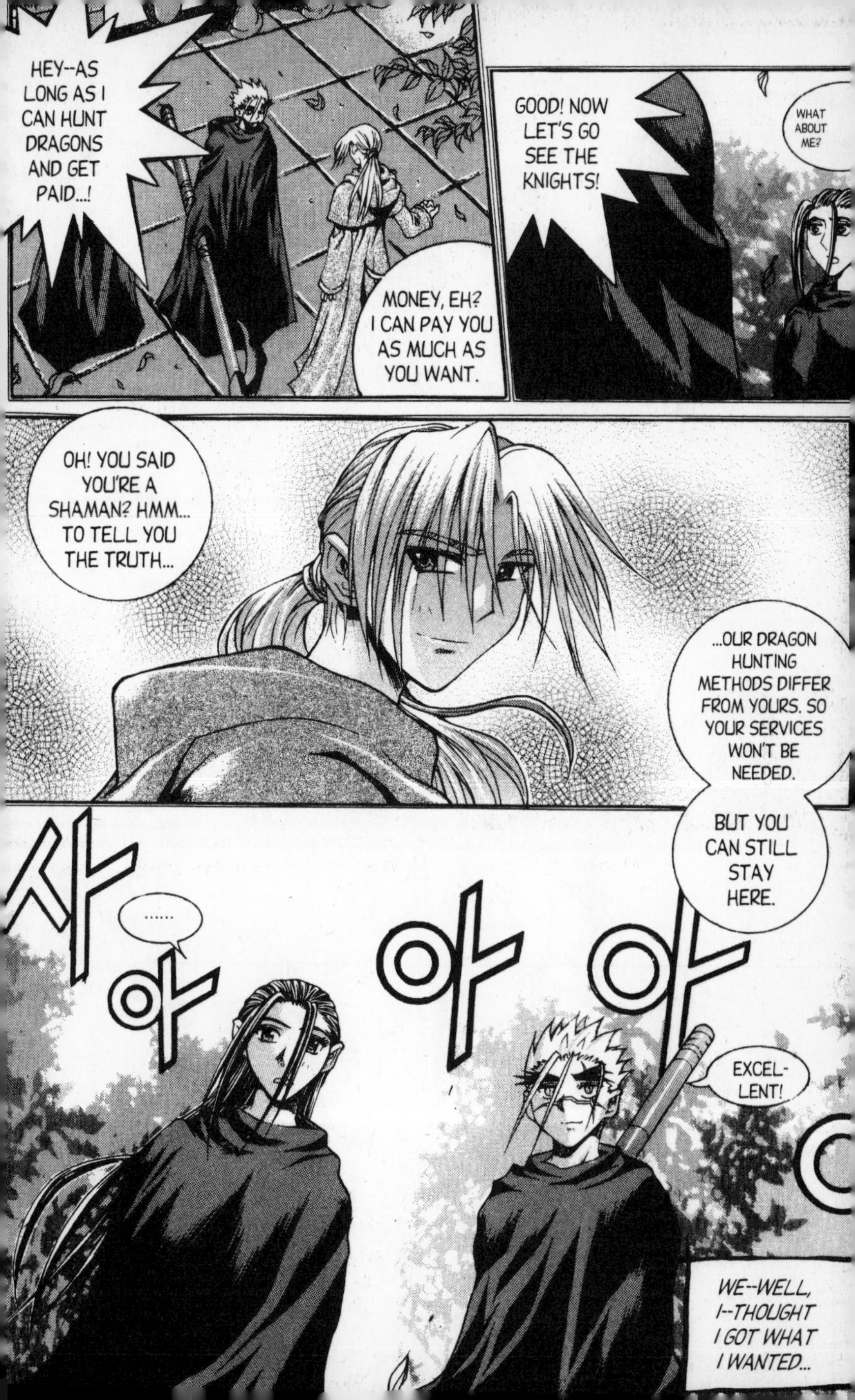
HEY--AS LONG AS I CAN HUNT DRAGONS AND GET PAID...!
MONEY, EH? I CAN PAY YOU AS MUCH AS YOU WANT.
GOOD! NOW LET'S GO SEE THE KNIGHTS!
WHAT ABOUT ME?
OH! YOU SAID YOU'RE A SHAMAN? HMM... TO TELL YOU THE TRUTH...
...OUR DRAGON HUNTING METHODS DIFFER FROM YOURS. SO YOUR SERVICES WON'T BE NEEDED.
BUT YOU CAN STILL STAY HERE.
사아아아
......
EXCEL-LENT!
WE--WELL, I--THOUGHT I GOT WHAT I WANTED...

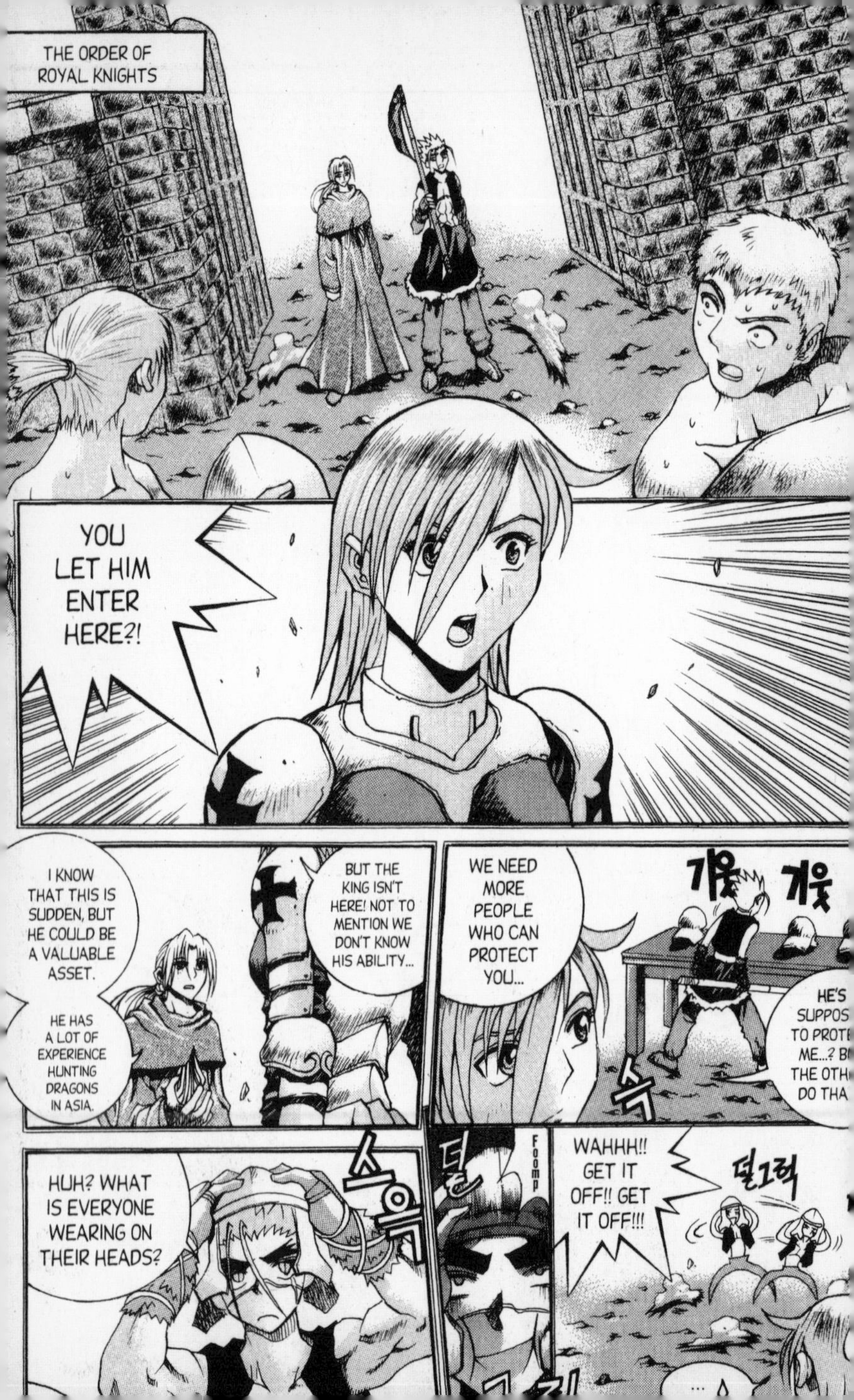
THE ORDER OF ROYAL KNIGHTS
YOU LET HIM ENTER HERE?!
I KNOW THAT THIS IS SUDDEN, BUT HE COULD BE A VALUABLE ASSET.
HE HAS A LOT OF EXPERIENCE HUNTING DRAGONS IN ASIA.
BUT THE KING ISN'T HERE! NOT TO MENTION WE DON'T KNOW HIS ABILITY...
WE NEED MORE PEOPLE WHO CAN PROTECT YOU...
기웃 기웃
슥
HE'S SUPPOS TO PROTE ME...? B THE OTH DO THA
HUH? WHAT IS EVERYONE WEARING ON THEIR HEADS?
스윽
Foomp
WAHHH!! GET IT OFF!! GET IT OFF!!!
덜그럭
...

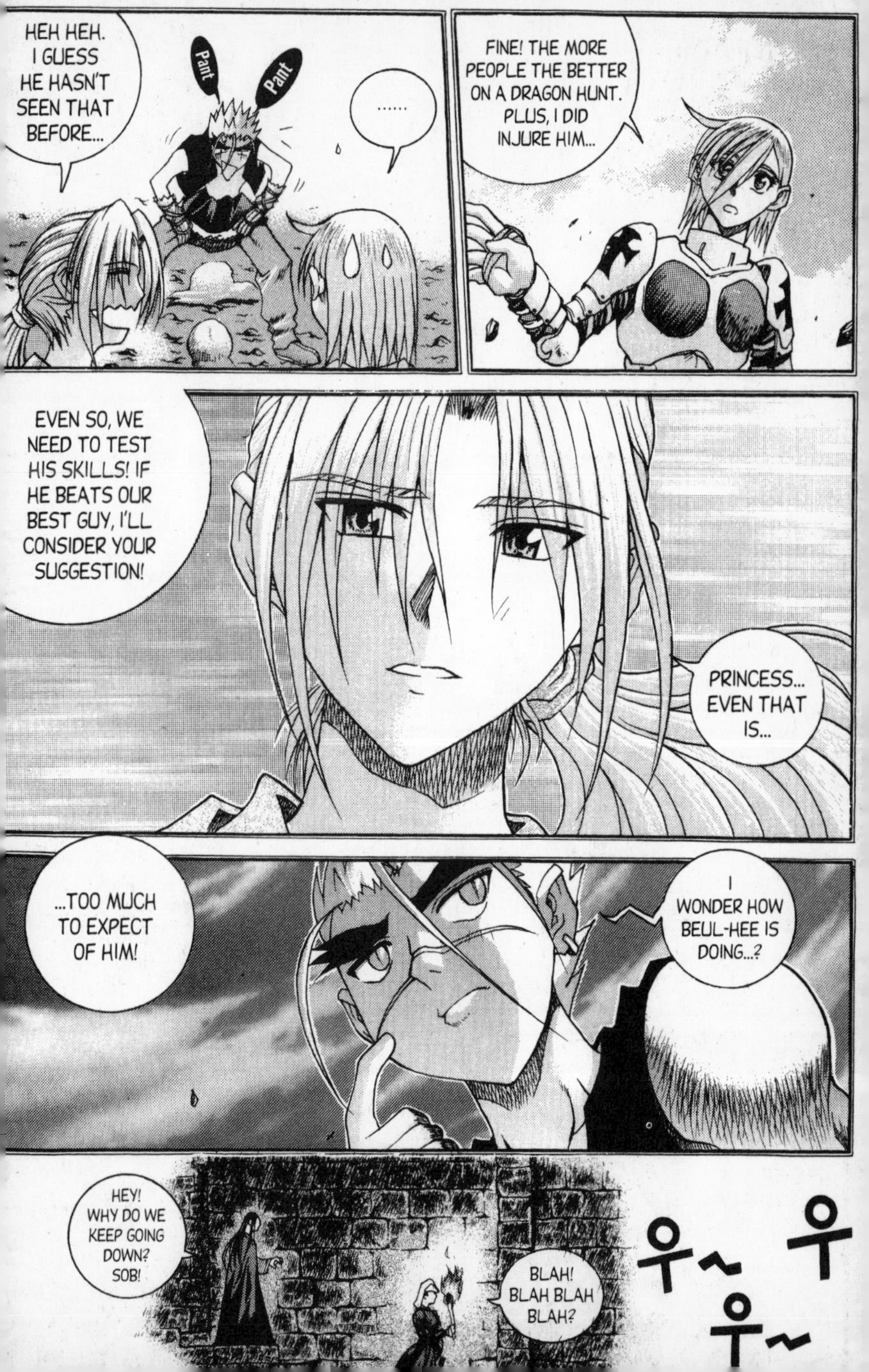
HEH HEH. I GUESS HE HASN'T SEEN THAT BEFORE...
Pant
Pant
......
FINE! THE MORE PEOPLE THE BETTER ON A DRAGON HUNT. PLUS, I DID INJURE HIM...
EVEN SO, WE NEED TO TEST HIS SKILLS! IF HE BEATS OUR BEST GUY, I'LL CONSIDER YOUR SUGGESTION!
PRINCESS... EVEN THAT IS...
...TOO MUCH TO EXPECT OF HIM!
I WONDER HOW BEUL-HEE IS DOING...?
HEY! WHY DO WE KEEP GOING DOWN? SOB!
BLAH! BLAH BLAH BLAH?
우~ 우 우~

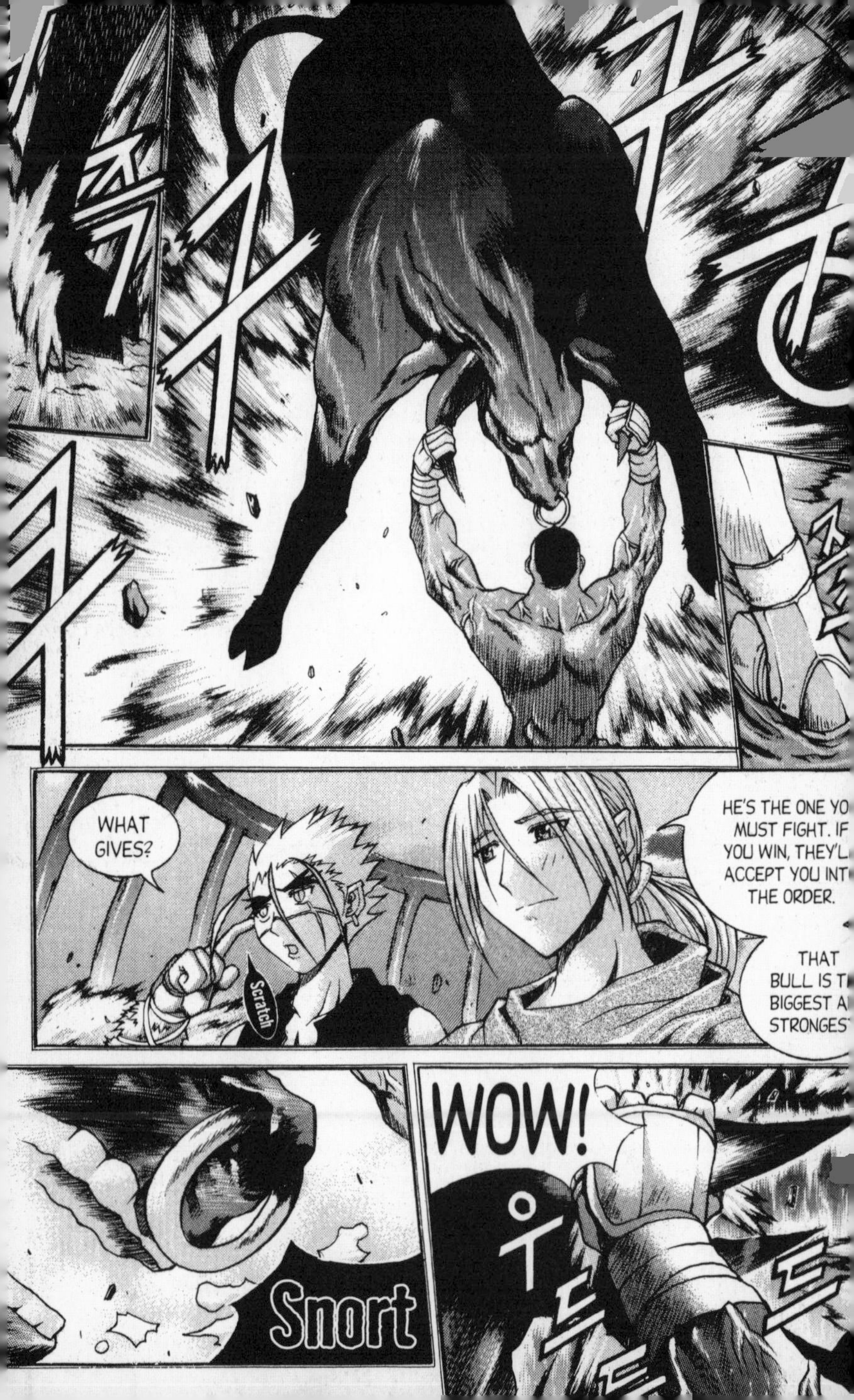
WHAT GIVES?
Scratch
HE'S THE ONE YO MUST FIGHT. IF YOU WIN, THEY'L ACCEPT YOU INT THE ORDER.
THAT BULL IS T BIGGEST A STRONGES
Snort
WOW!

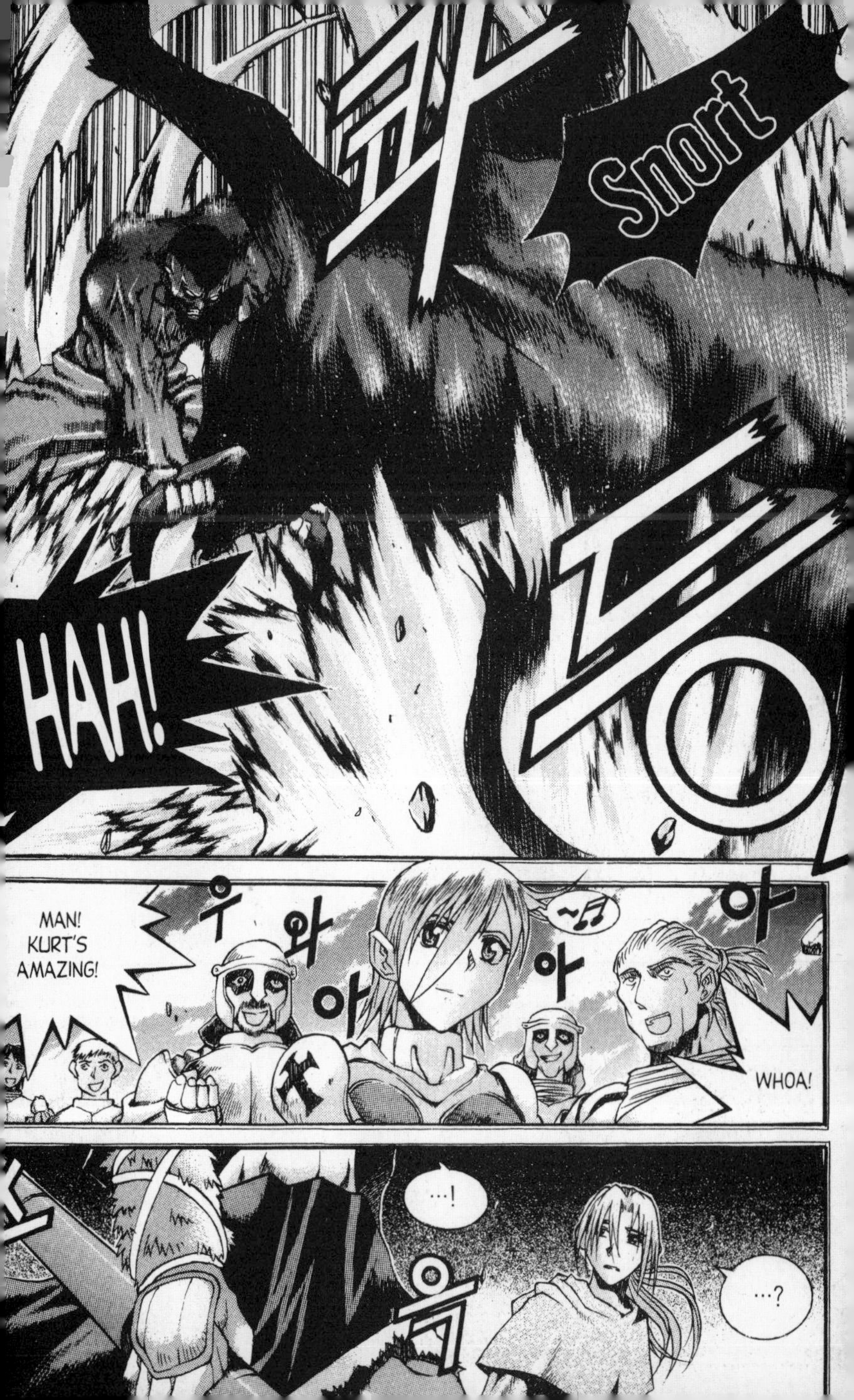
Snort
HAH!
MAN! KURT'S AMAZING!
우와아아아
WHOA!
...!
...?

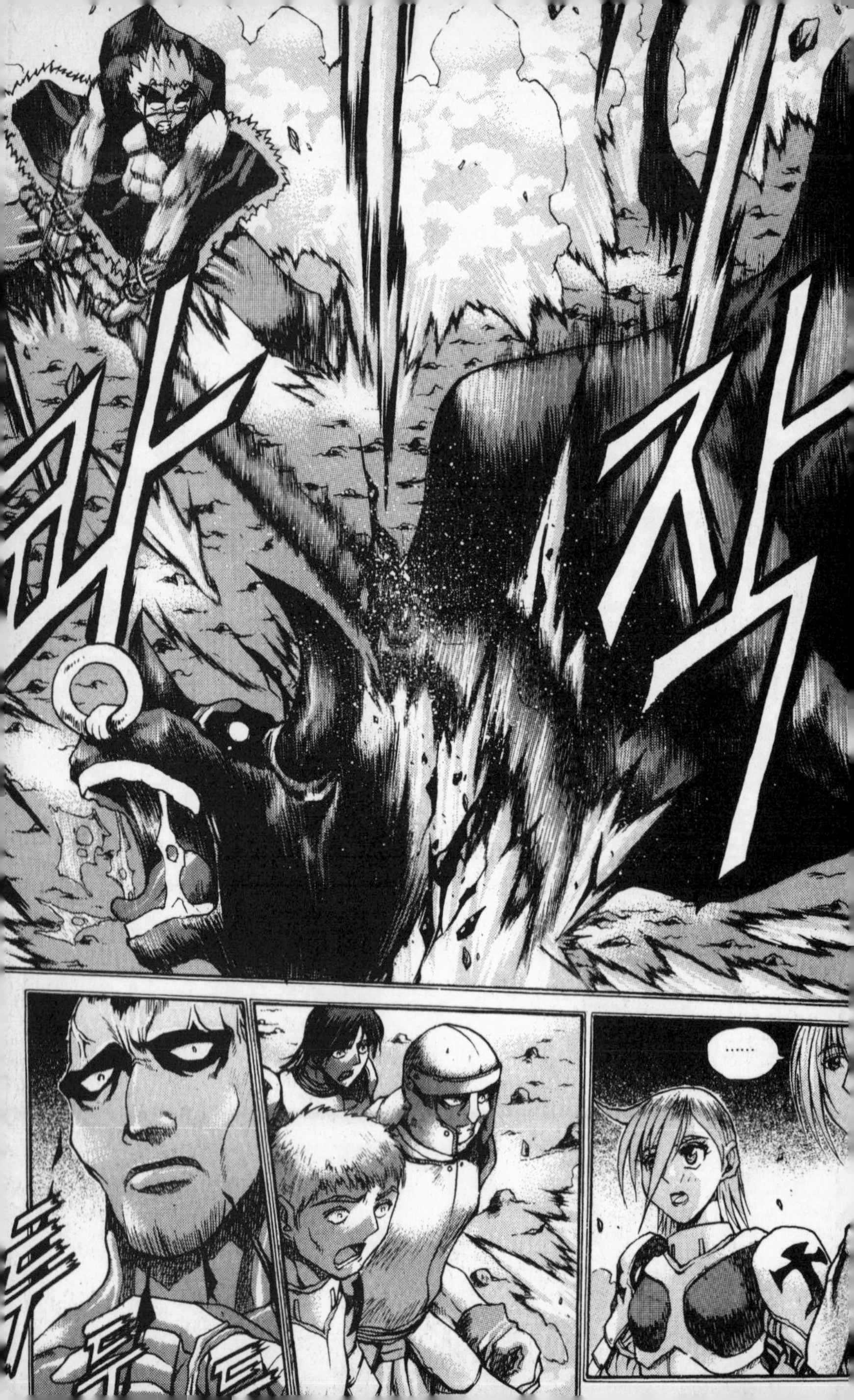
......

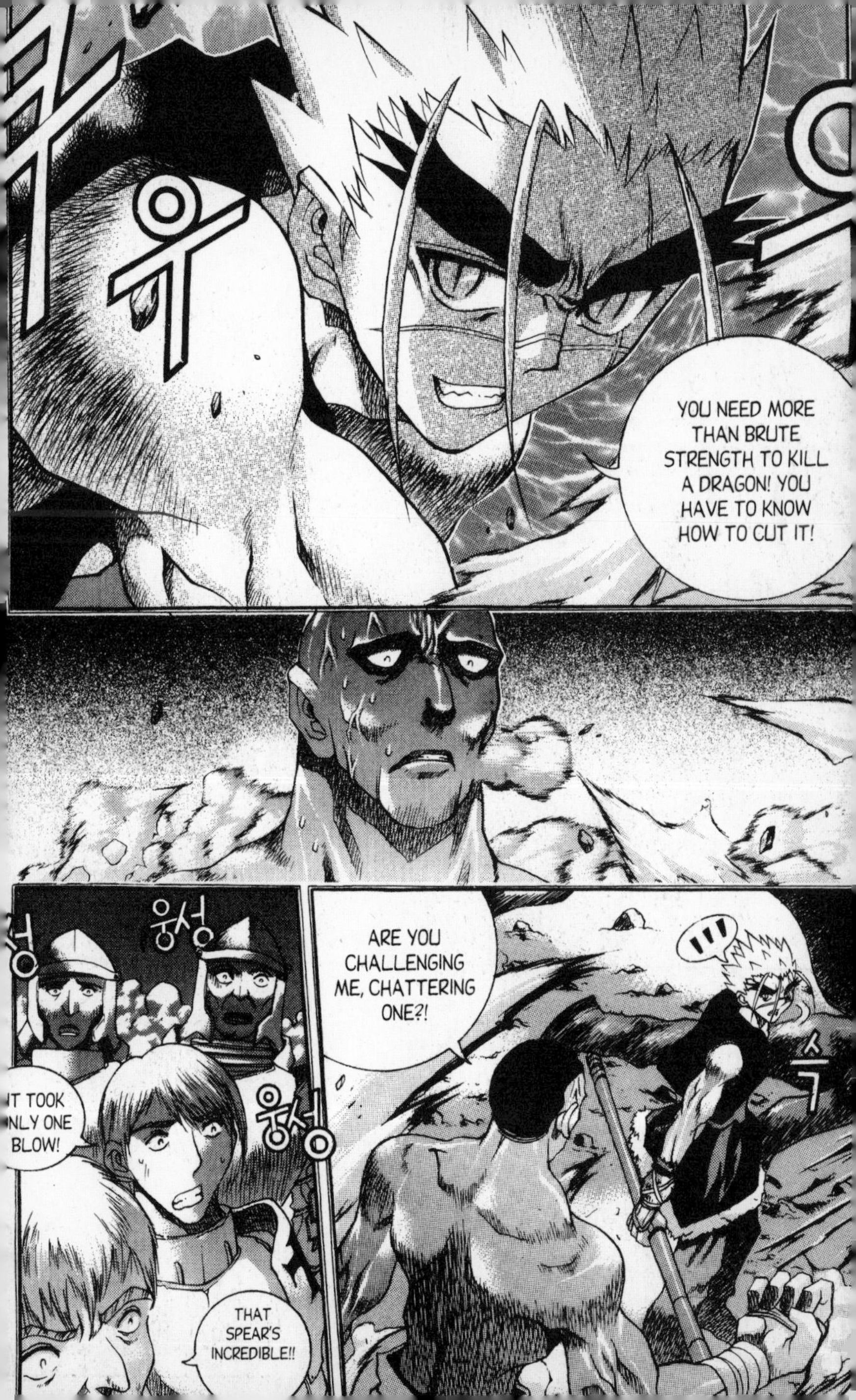
YOU NEED MORE THAN BRUTE STRENGTH TO KILL A DRAGON! YOU HAVE TO KNOW HOW TO CUT IT!
웅성
웅성
IT TOOK NLY ONE BLOW!
THAT SPEAR'S INCREDIBLE!!
ARE YOU CHALLENGING ME, CHATTERING ONE?!
!!!

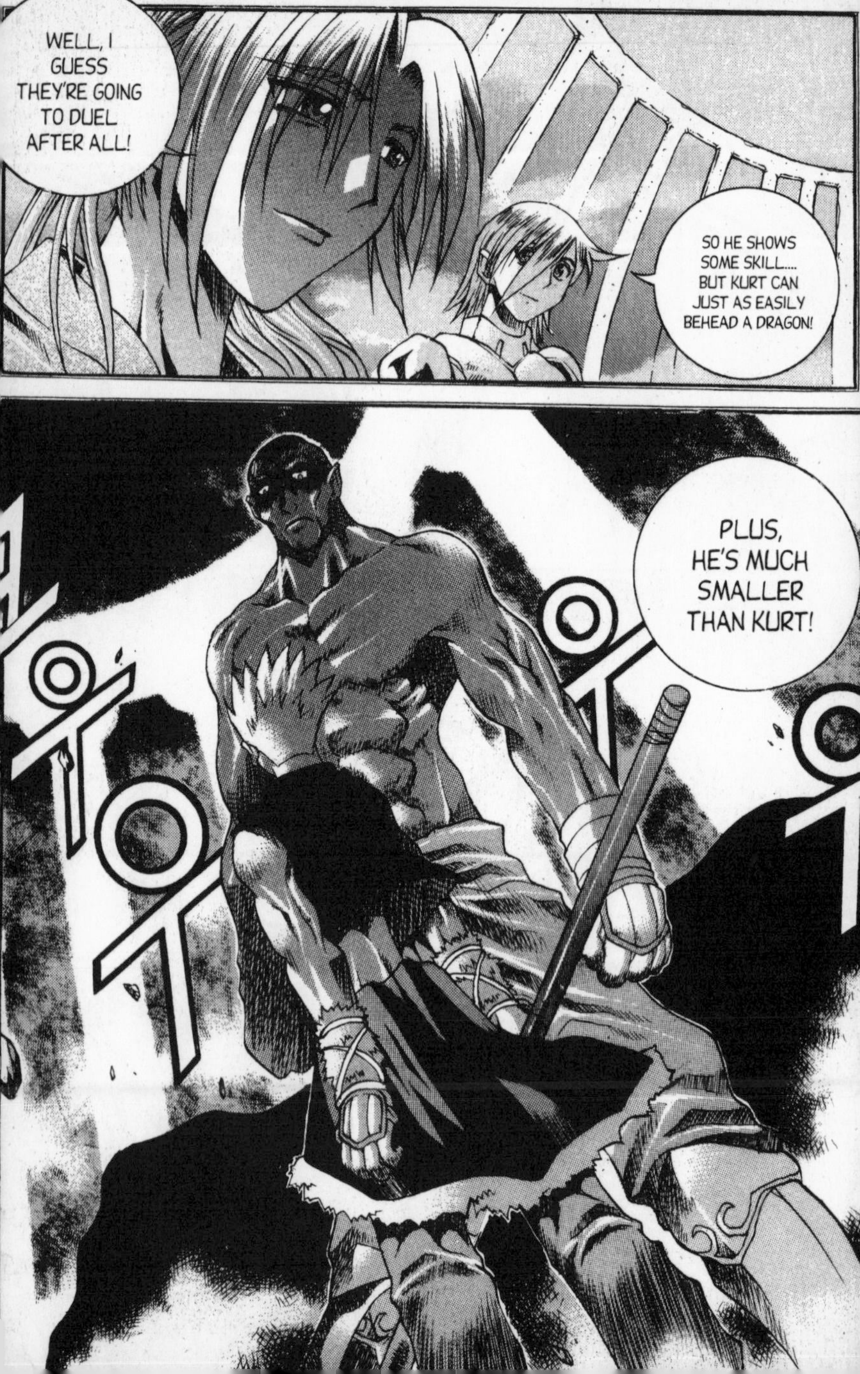
WELL, I GUESS THEY'RE GOING TO DUEL AFTER ALL!
SO HE SHOWS SOME SKILL.... BUT KURT CAN JUST AS EASILY BEHEAD A DRAGON!
PLUS, HE'S MUCH SMALLER THAN KURT!

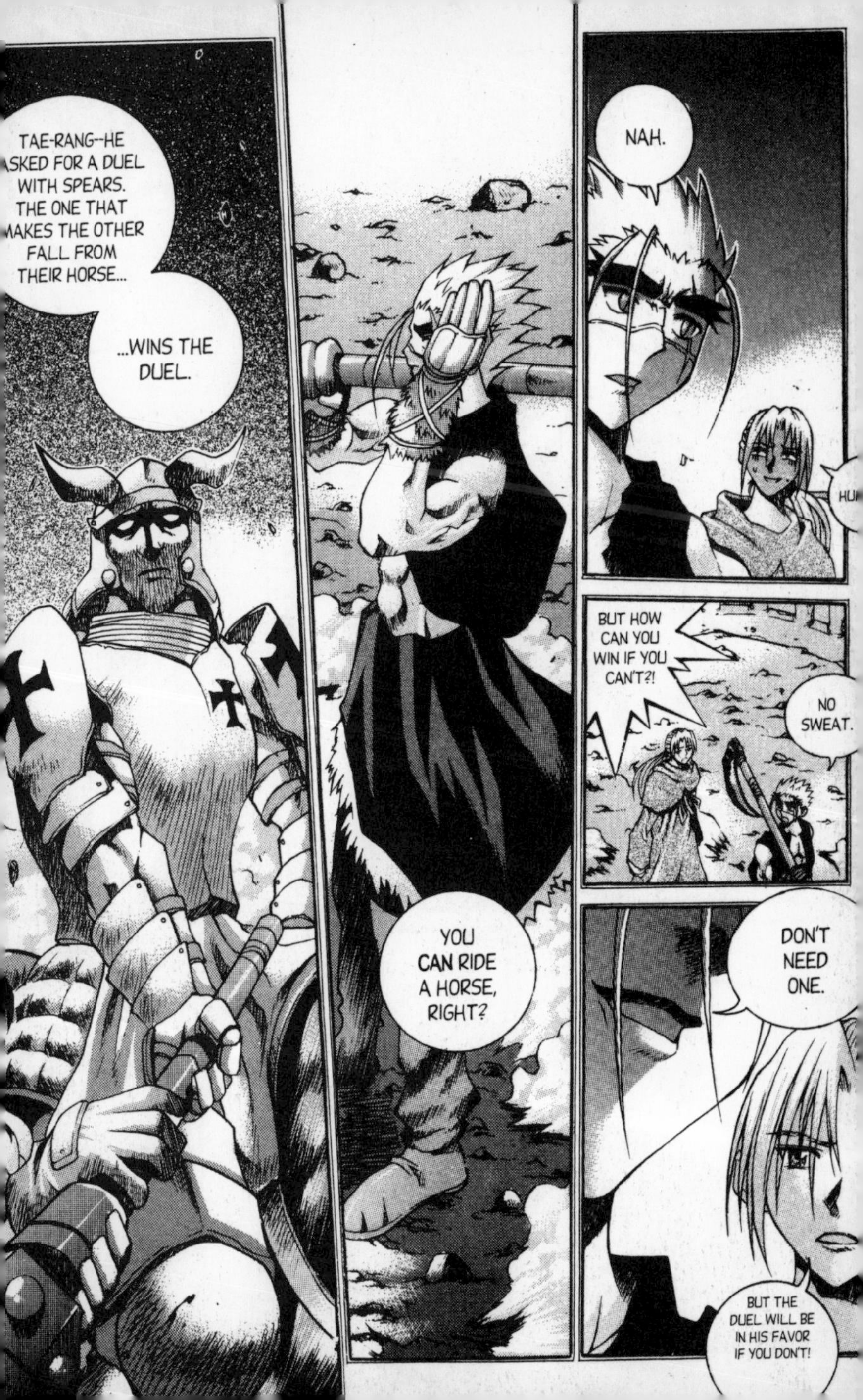
TAE-RANG--HE ASKED FOR A DUEL WITH SPEARS. THE ONE THAT MAKES THE OTHER FALL FROM THEIR HORSE...
...WINS THE DUEL.
YOU CAN RIDE A HORSE, RIGHT?
NAH.
HU
BUT HOW CAN YOU WIN IF YOU CAN'T?!
NO SWEAT.
DON'T NEED ONE.
BUT THE DUEL WILL BE IN HIS FAVOR IF YOU DON'T!

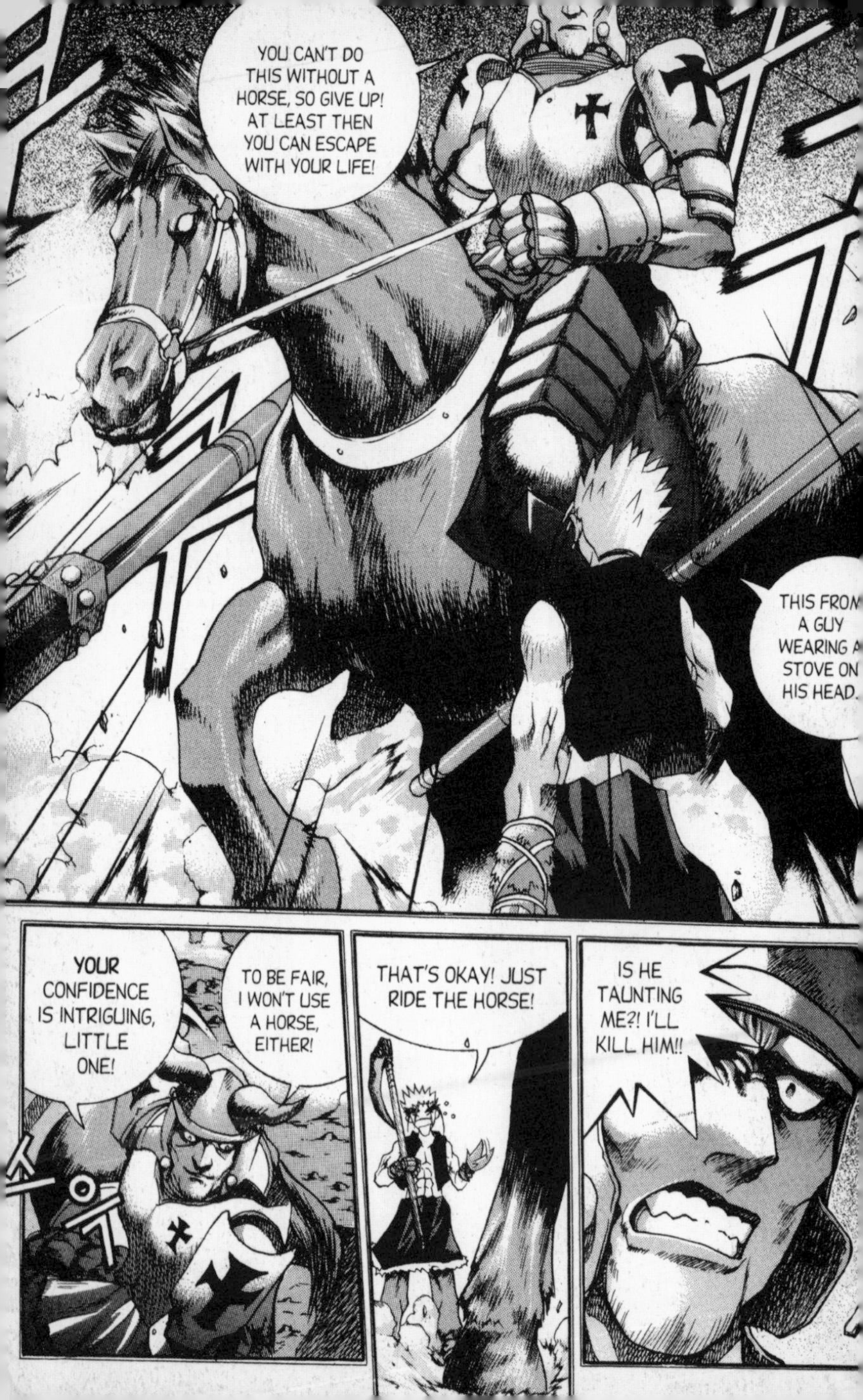
YOU CAN'T DO THIS WITHOUT A HORSE, SO GIVE UP! AT LEAST THEN YOU CAN ESCAPE WITH YOUR LIFE!
THIS FROM A GUY WEARING A STOVE ON HIS HEAD.
YOUR CONFIDENCE IS INTRIGUING, LITTLE ONE!
TO BE FAIR, I WON'T USE A HORSE, EITHER!
THAT'S OKAY! JUST RIDE THE HORSE!
IS HE TAUNTING ME?! I'LL KILL HIM!!

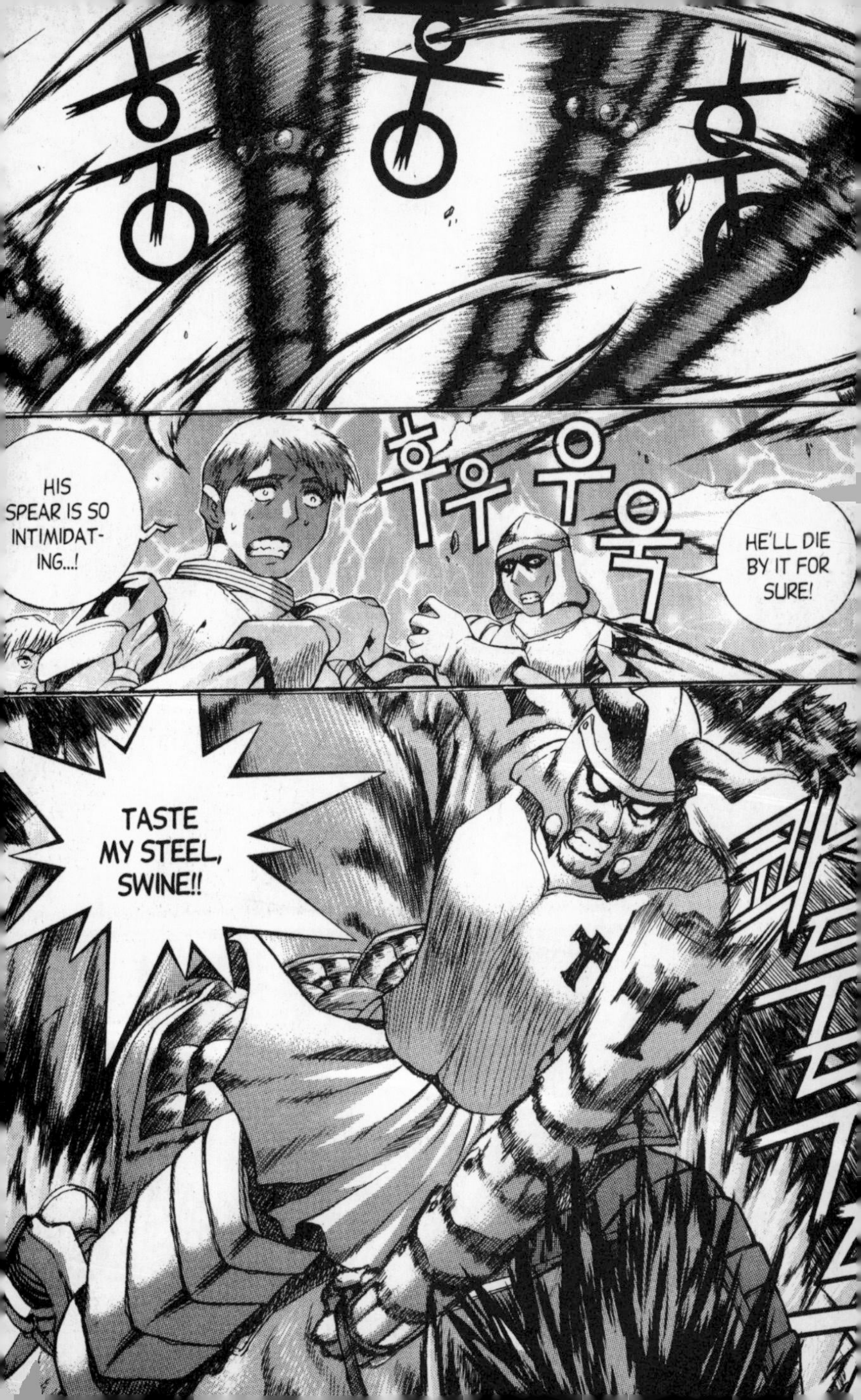

훙 훙 훙
HIS SPEAR IS SO INTIMIDATING...!
후우우웅
HE'LL DIE BY IT FOR SURE!
TASTE MY STEEL, SWINE!!

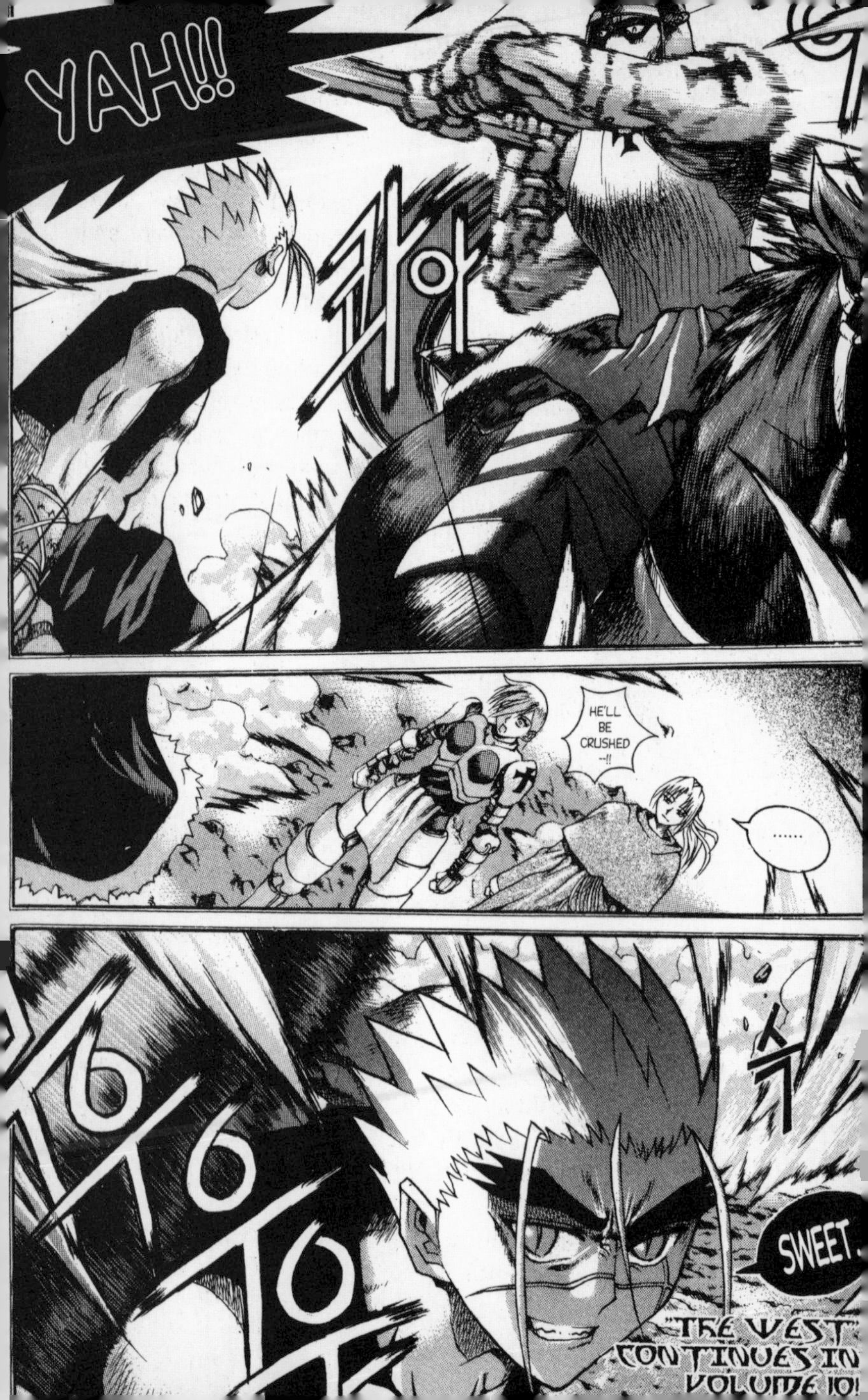
YAH!!
HE'LL BE CRUSHED--!!
......
SWEET.
"THE WEST" CONTINUES IN VOLUME 10!

The Studio Redstone Story (Chapter 9)

Hey, gang! Hong Seock here! Well, volume 9 came out faster than previous volumes. Even so, it still took three months, though. Ha!

It's spring over here now...but it's still the same old, same old. But I'm crazy about digital cameras these days, and not into much else. It's hard to stop using these cameras once you get a taste of how fun they are. I take pictures of this and that, and love the fact that you don't need film--that you can see the pictures right away, and can erase or edit pictures easily. I really love it! People say that you have to take many pictures to improve your photography skills, so I'm snapping away, baby! But I only take pictures at home, so all the pictures are the same. Ho hum...

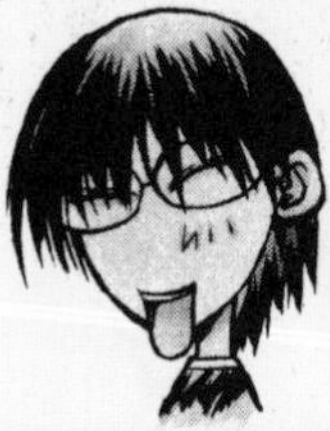

Hong Seock Seo

I wanted to go somewhere beautiful to take pictures, but I was too busy working on the comic. But I would love to go somewhere nice with my digital camera soon.

My camera is the Fuji Fine Fix 6900. Its color quality is excellent. It's especially good in dark places. It's only 3,000,000 pixels, so I'd like to upgrade to 5,000,000 pixels someday. However, the color quality is too good to sell or buy another one. I should just buy another camera and keep this one. But I don't know if my wife would let me do that...

Well, it's only camera talk in this volume because I'm kind of obsessive about things and have no other hobby right now. I sometimes wonder why I have such an expensive hobby. But even though it's expensive, a digital camera is fun! Ha ha ha!

Anyway, I hope you continue enjoying Dragon Hunter! I'll see you in volume 10!

April 2002

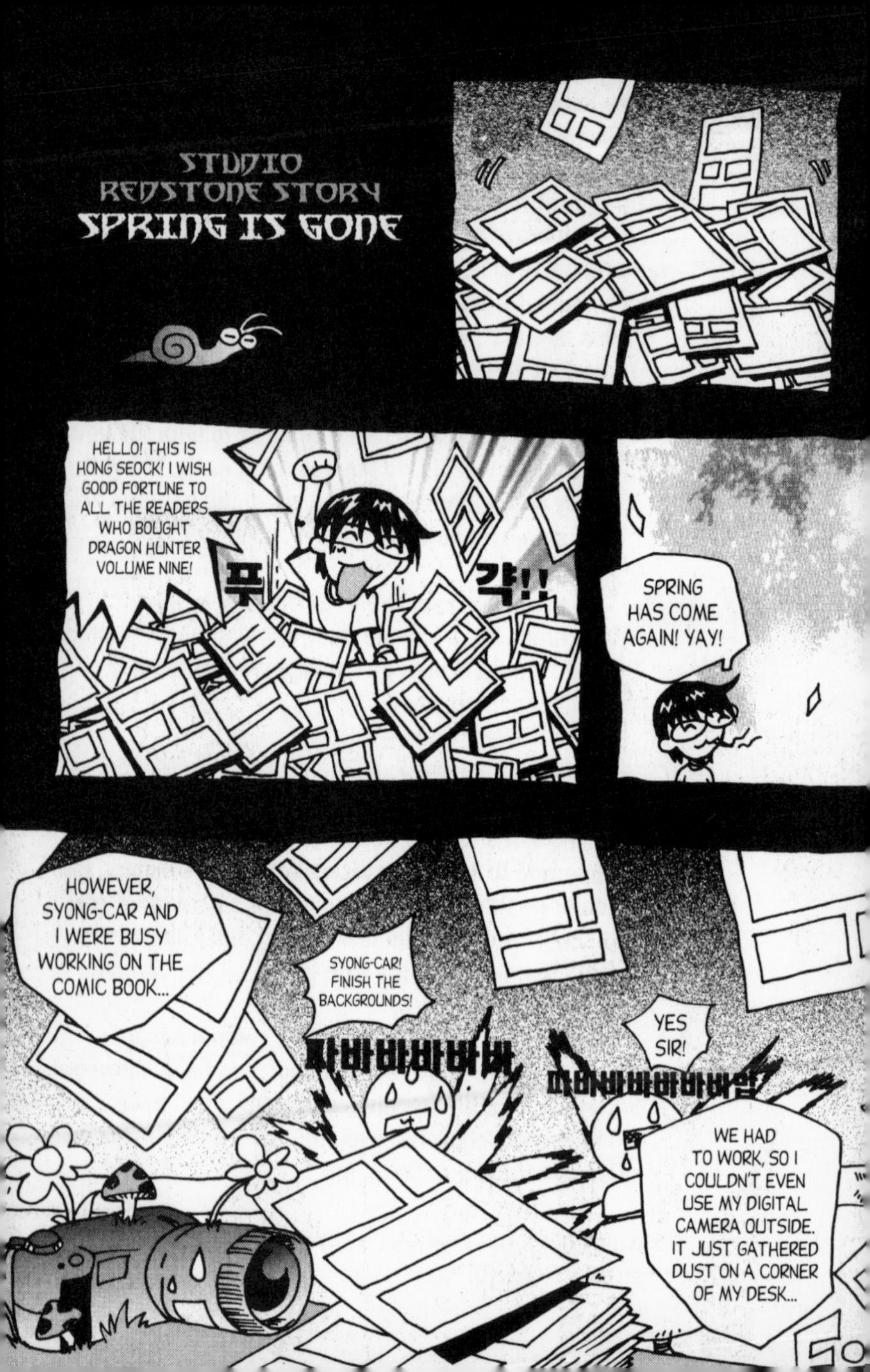
STUDIO REDSTONE STORY
SPRING IS GONE
HELLO! THIS IS HONG SEOCK! I WISH GOOD FORTUNE TO ALL THE READERS WHO BOUGHT DRAGON HUNTER VOLUME NINE!
푸각!!
SPRING HAS COME AGAIN! YAY!
HOWEVER, SYONG-CAR AND I WERE BUSY WORKING ON THE COMIC BOOK...
SYONG-CAR! FINISH THE BACKGROUNDS!
파바바바바바
YES SIR!
파바바바바바바밥
WE HAD TO WORK, SO I COULDN'T EVEN USE MY DIGITAL CAMERA OUTSIDE. IT JUST GATHERED DUST ON A CORNER OF MY DESK...

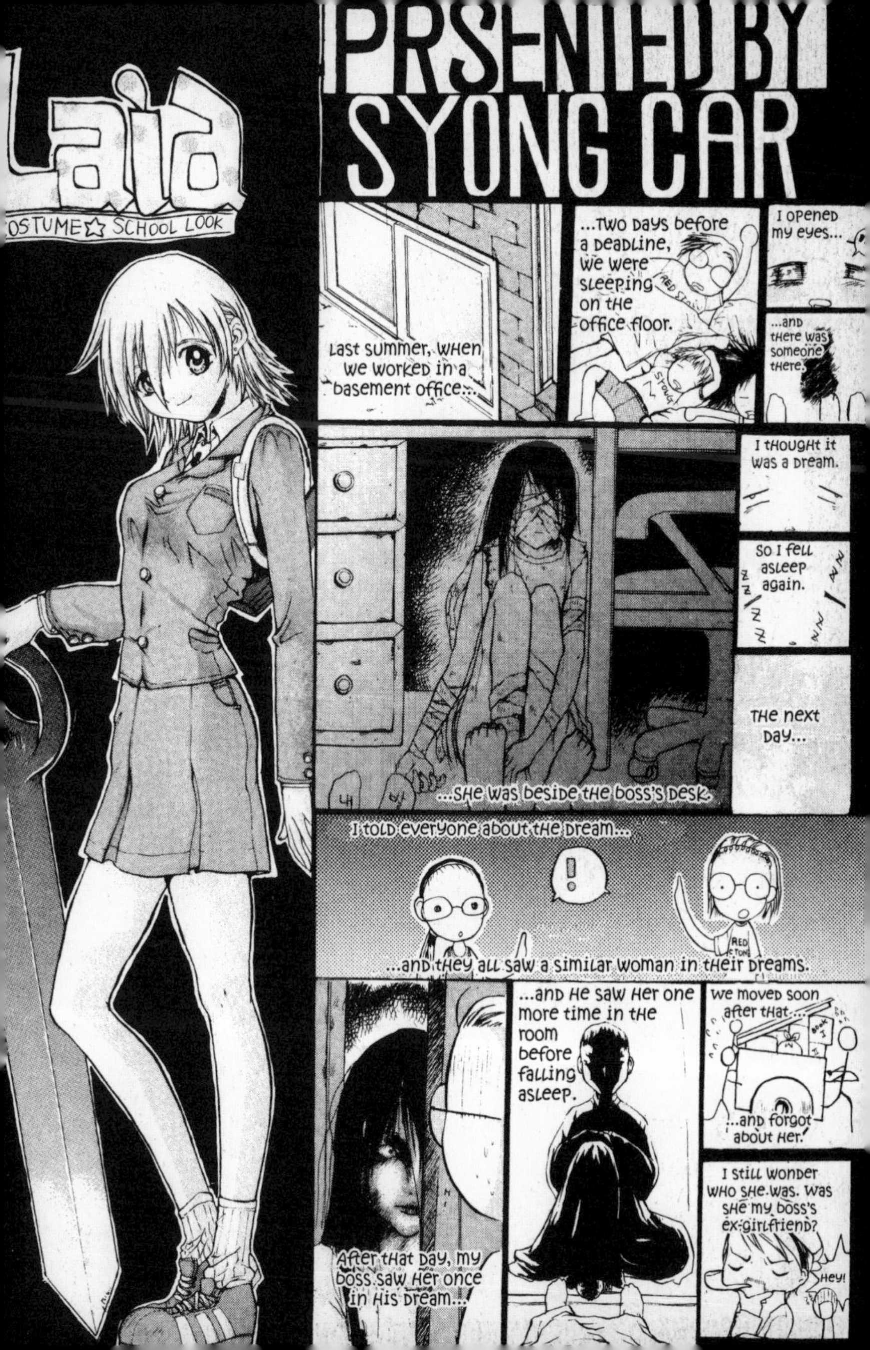

Laita
OSTUME☆ SCHOOL LOOK
PRSENIED BY SYONG CAR
Last summer, when we worked in a basement office...
...Two days before a deadline, we were sleeping on the office floor.
I opened my eyes...
...and there was someone there.
...she was beside the boss's desk.
I thought it was a dream.
So I fell asleep again.
The next day...
I told everyone about the dream...
!
...and they all saw a similar woman in their dreams.
After that day, my boss saw her once in his dream...
...and he saw her one more time in the room before falling asleep.
We moved soon after that...
...and forgot about her.
I still wonder who she was. Was she my boss's ex-girlfriend?
Hey!

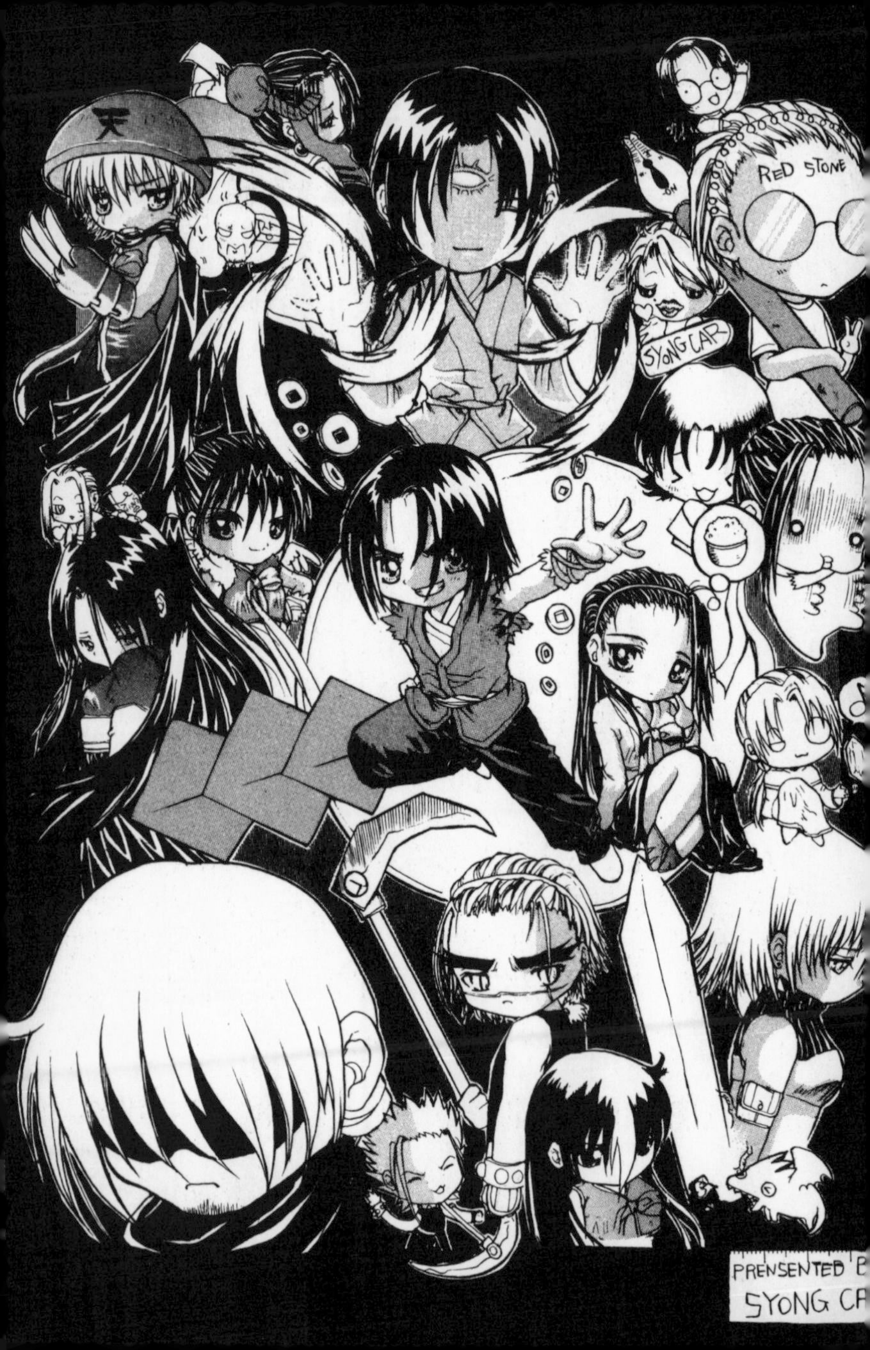
天
RED STONE
SYONG CAR
PRENSENTED
SYONG

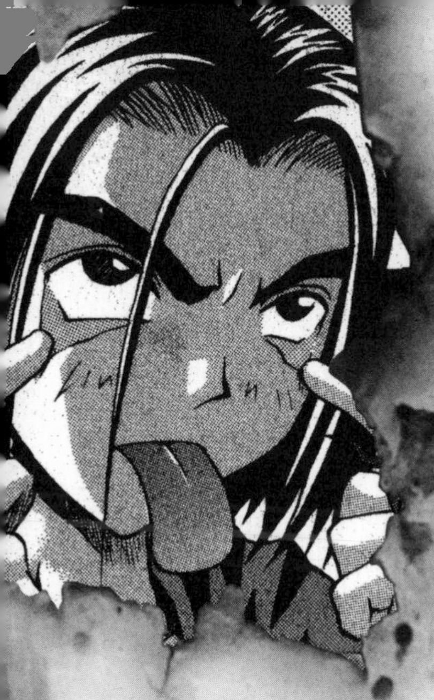

DRAGON HUNTER

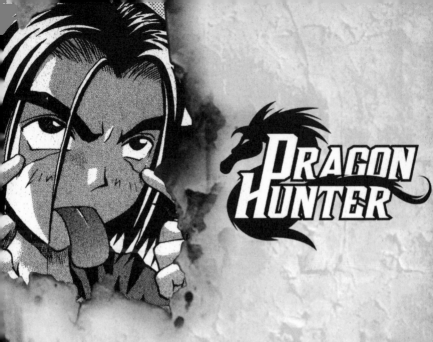

IN THE NEXT VOLUME OF
DRAGON HUNTER

• • • • • • •

TAE–RANG CONTINUES HIS TALE OF HIGH ADVENTURE AND INTRIGUE IN KING ARTHUR'S CAMELOT, AND SHEDS FURTHER LIGHT ON HIS RELATIONSHIP WITH RIAH. HE WILL ALSO REVEAL THE IDENTITY OF THE EVIL MASTERMIND THAT SET ALL THESE EVENTS IN MOTION...

WHAT DOES THIS VILLAIN HAVE IN STORE FOR TAE–RANG?

FIND OUT IN DRAGON HUNTER VOLUME 10!

ALSO AVAILABLE FROM 🎮 TOKYOPOP®

MANGA

.HACK//LEGEND OF THE TWILIGHT
@LARGE
ABENOBASHI: MAGICAL SHOPPING ARCADE
A.I. LOVE YOU
AI YORI AOSHI
ALICHINO
ANGELIC LAYER
ARM OF KANNON
BABY BIRTH
BATTLE ROYALE
BATTLE VIXENS
BOYS BE...
BRAIN POWERED
BRIGADOON
B'TX
CANDIDATE FOR GODDESS, THE
CARDCAPTOR SAKURA
CARDCAPTOR SAKURA - MASTER OF THE CLOW
CHOBITS
CHRONICLES OF THE CURSED SWORD
CLAMP SCHOOL DETECTIVES
CLOVER
COMIC PARTY
CONFIDENTIAL CONFESSIONS
CORRECTOR YUI
COWBOY BEBOP
COWBOY BEBOP: SHOOTING STAR
CRAZY LOVE STORY
CRESCENT MOON
CROSS
CULDCEPT
CYBORG 009
D•N•ANGEL
DEARS
DEMON DIARY
DEMON ORORON, THE
DEUS VITAE
DIGIMON
DIGIMON TAMERS
DIGIMON ZERO TWO
DOLL
DRAGON HUNTER
DRAGON KNIGHTS
DRAGON VOICE
DREAM SAGA
DUKLYON: CLAMP SCHOOL DEFENDERS
EERIE QUEERIE!
ERICA SAKURAZAWA: COLLECTED WORKS
ET CETERA
ETERNITY
EVIL'S RETURN
FAERIES' LANDING
FAKE
FLCL
FLOWER OF THE DEEP SLEEP, THE
FORBIDDEN DANCE
FRUITS BASKET

G GUNDAM
GATEKEEPERS
GETBACKERS
GIRL GOT GAME
GRAVITATION
GTO
GUNDAM SEED ASTRAY
GUNDAM WING
GUNDAM WING: BATTLEFIELD OF PACIFISTS
GUNDAM WING: ENDLESS WALTZ
GUNDAM WING: THE LAST OUTPOST (G-UNIT)
HANDS OFF!
HAPPY MANIA
HARLEM BEAT
HYPER RUNE
I.N.V.U.
IMMORTAL RAIN
INITIAL D
INSTANT TEEN: JUST ADD NUTS
ISLAND
JING: KING OF BANDITS
JING: KING OF BANDITS - TWILIGHT TALES
JULINE
KARE KANO
KILL ME, KISS ME
KINDAICHI CASE FILES, THE
KING OF HELL
KODOCHA: SANA'S STAGE
LAMENT OF THE LAMB
LEGAL DRUG
LEGEND OF CHUN HYANG, THE
LES BIJOUX
LOVE HINA
LOVE OR MONEY
LUPIN III
LUPIN III: WORLD'S MOST WANTED
MAGIC KNIGHT RAYEARTH I
MAGIC KNIGHT RAYEARTH II
MAHOROMATIC: AUTOMATIC MAIDEN
MAN OF MANY FACES
MARMALADE BOY
MARS
MARS: HORSE WITH NO NAME
MINK
MIRACLE GIRLS
MIYUKI-CHAN IN WONDERLAND
MODEL
MOURYOU KIDEN: LEGEND OF THE NYMPHS
NECK AND NECK
ONE
ONE I LOVE, THE
PARADISE KISS
PARASYTE
PASSION FRUIT
PEACH GIRL
PEACH GIRL: CHANGE OF HEART
PET SHOP OF HORRORS
PITA-TEN
PLANET LADDER

08.20.04

ALSO AVAILABLE FROM TOKYOPOP®

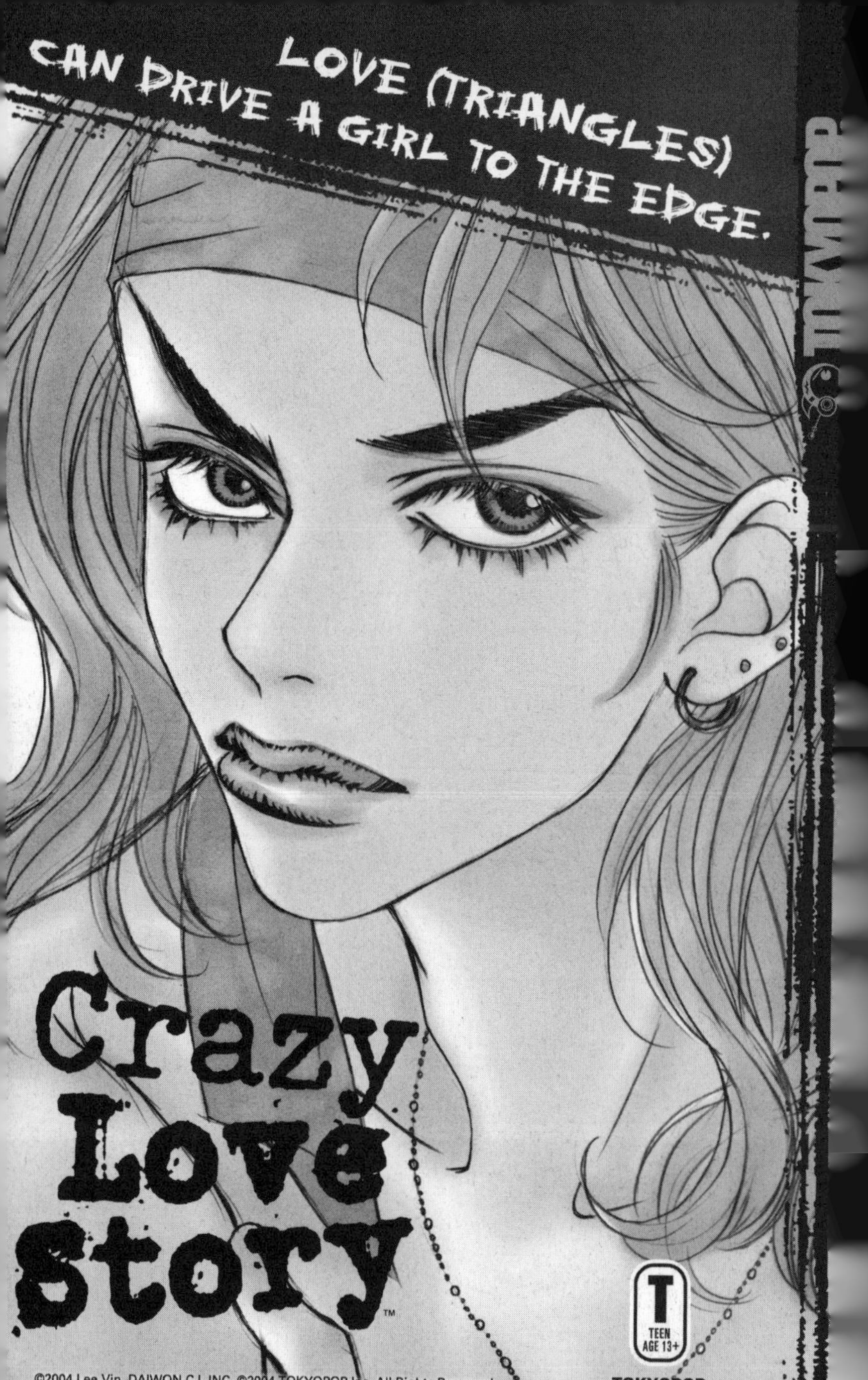
LOVE (TRIANGLES)
CAN DRIVE A GIRL TO THE EDGE.
TOKYOPOP
Crazy Love Story™
T
TEEN
AGE 13+

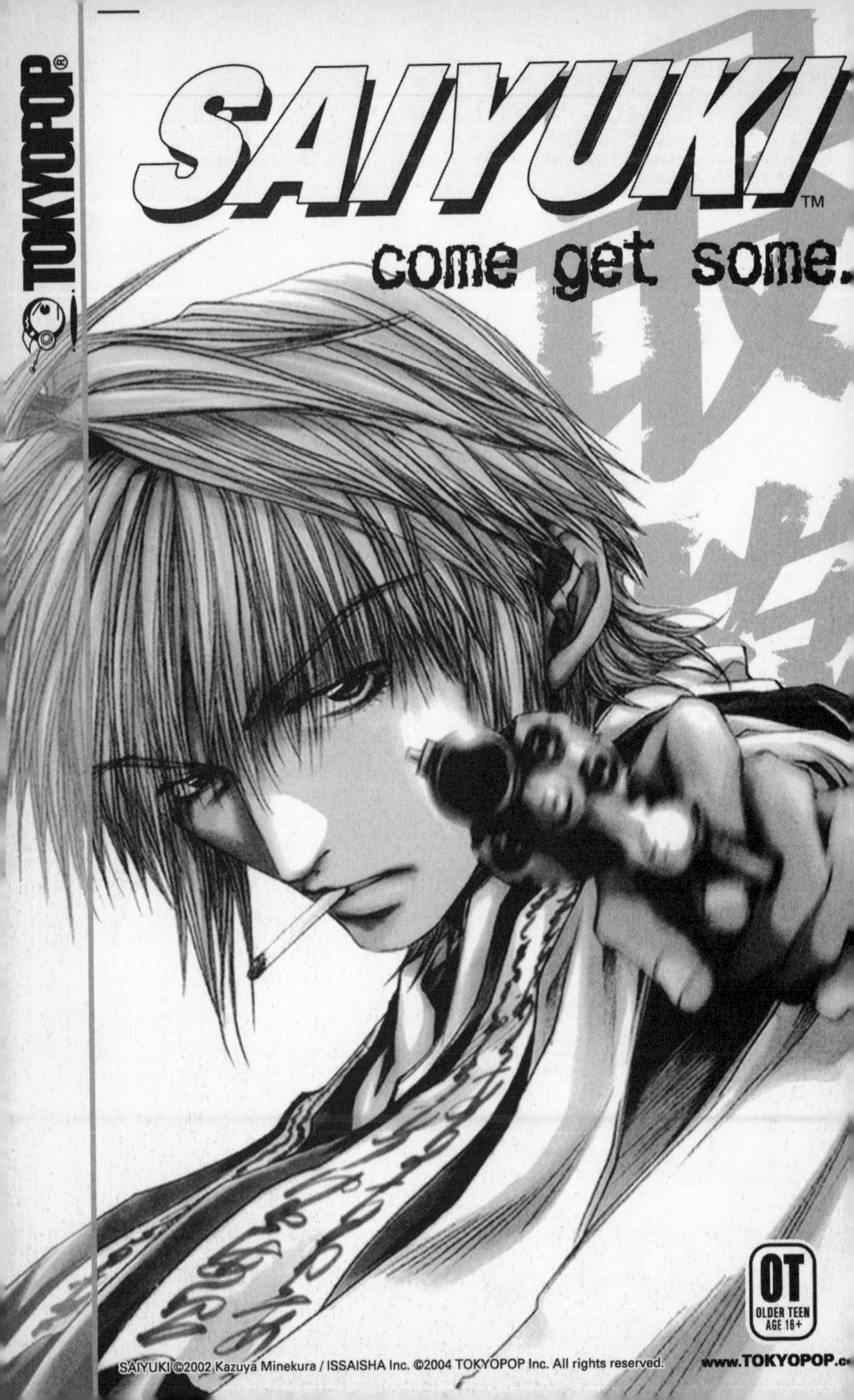
TOKYOPOP®
SAIYUKI™
come get some.
OT
OLDER TEEN
AGE 16+
SAIYUKI ©2002 Kazuya Minekura / ISSAISHA Inc. ©2004 TOKYOPOP Inc. All rights reserved.
www.TOKYOPOP.co

Threads of Time